Canadian Marxists and the Search for a Third Way

In this study of the theory and practice of four Canadian socialists whose names are known but whose lives, thoughts, feelings, and political beliefs are not, Peter Campbell explores the ideas and actions of four individuals – Ernest Winch, Bill Pritchard, Arthur Mould, and Bob Russell – who made major contributions to the history of the Canadian left. Campbell traces their childhoods in late Victorian England and Scotland, explores their early political and religious influences, details their involvement in the labour and socialist movements of Canada, and assesses their legacy to the Canadian working class.

These four Canadian socialists belonged to a much larger group Campbell calls "Marxists of the third way." These Marxists fought long and hard for a classless society, but did so as socialists who were very much shaped by the influence of religion, respect for the constitutionality of the British parliamentary system, and the desire to maintain honesty, fair dealing, and democratic politics in the trade union and socialist movements. They opposed both the reformism of social democracy and the emphasis placed on armed struggle by the Communist Party. Marxism of the third way was not, Campbell argues, just a middle course between the two tendencies but rather a comprehensive, alternative Marxist politics.

In telling the story of these four Canadians, Campbell demonstrates that histories of the Canadian left need to pay more attention to the role of ideas in shaping the lives and actions of Canadian workers. Marxists of the third way, and other Canadian socialists, deserve more recognition as theorists than has previously been acknowledged. Recognizing this requires that Marxism be seen as a dynamic system of thought passed from leaders to followers and back again, not a static prop used to support party ideologues. Marxists of the third way were guided not by a Marxist vision of economic determinism, dogmatism, and authoritarianism but by a vision of the education and empowerment of the workers themselves.

PETER CAMPBELL is a research assistant at the Disraeli Project, Queen's University.

Canadian Marxists and the Search for a Third Way

PETER CAMPBELL

McGill-Queen's University Press
Montreal & Kingston · London · Ithaca

ISBN 0-7735-1848-7

Legal deposit fourth quarter 1999
Bibliothèque nationale du Québec

Printed in Canada on acid-free paper

This book has been published with the help of a grant from the Humanities and Social Sciences Federation of Canada, using funds provided by the Social Sciences and Humanities Research Council of Canada.

McGill-Queen's University Press acknowledges the financial support of the Government of Canada through the Book Publishing Industry Development Program (BPIDP) for its activities. We also acknowledge the support of the Canada Council for the Arts for our publishing program.

Canada

Canadian Cataloguing in Publication Data

Campbell, J. Peter, 1952–
Canadian Marxists and the search for a third way
Includes bibliographical references and index.
ISBN 0-7735-1848-7
1. Winch, Ernest Edward, 1879–1957. 2. Pritchard, W.A., b.1888. 3. Mould, Arthur, 1879–1961. 4. Russell, Robert Boyd, 1888–1964. 5. Labor movement – Canada – History. 6. Socialists – Canada – Biography. 7. Labor leaders – Canada – Biography. I. Title.
FC3218.1.C34 2000 331'.092'271 C99-901055-7
F1060.9.C34 2000

This book was typeset by Typo Litho Composition Inc. in 10/12 Sabon.

for Richard

Contents

Acknowledgments ix

Introduction 3

1 Ernest Edward Winch: The Administrator of Class Struggle 31

2 William Arthur Pritchard: The Marxist as Worker Intellectual 73

3 Arthur Mould: The Conscience of Class Conflict 124

4 Robert Boyd Russell: The Search for a Third Way 168

Conclusion 220

Notes 231

Bibliography 275

Index 289

Acknowledgments

In the spirit of opposition I begin where others end. My wife, Anna, and my children, Sarah and Aidan, have put up with me for more years than I care to remember, and helped me through many late nights of self-doubt. They have made me a better scholar, father, and friend.

I owe a great debt of gratitude to the entire staff of the Queen's history office, especially to Ruth Bryson and Margaret Nash. Both retired during the transformation of my thesis into this book; maybe they were trying to tell me something. I also wish to thank the archivists and staff at the Burnaby Village Heritage Museum, the Metro Toronto Reference Library, the Provincial Archives of Manitoba, the Public Archives of Ontario, the National Archives of Canada, Queen's University Archives, Simon Fraser University Archives, the Thomas Fisher Rare Book Library, the University of British Columbia, the United Church Archives in Toronto, the University of Western Ontario, and York University. A very special thanks goes to George Brandak at UBC for his help, humour, and that free lunch at the Faculty Club. Thanks as well to Gregory Kealey, Linda Kealey, Bettina Bradbury, Gerald Friesen, Bruce Magnuson, Jim McKenzie, Rick Stow, Peter Newell, Adam Buick, Jesse Mihlik, Helen Rawson, Larry Tickner, Archie Green, Don Watson, Ross McCormack, Joan Sangster, the late George Rawlyk, Allen Seager, Nancy Forestell, Norman Penner, the late Al Bernhardt, and Daniel Goldstick. To William Rab I can only say that I hope I did justice to Bill. Many thanks go out to Don Akenson and the staff at McGill-Queen's Press for their encouragement and support. The two Joans – Harcourt and McGilvray – have been especially helpful, patient, and persevering.

A special thanks to Maureen Garvie for her thorough and insightful copy editing and the much improved book that has resulted from it.

The research on which this book is based was made possible by the funding support of Queen's University and the Social Sciences and Humanities Research Council of Canada.

These are not good days for Canadian labour historians, but it has been my great fortune to share friendship and debate with three of the best. I have gone back again and again to the work of Jim Naylor, who has seen things in my work I did not even know were there. One of the central arguments of this book I owe to him, and for his suggestions, honesty, and encouragement I will always be grateful. During the writing of this book I have shared with Ian McKay a love and respect for Canadian Marxian socialists that may not be trendy but is nonetheless very meaningful and real. Ian's own work on Colin McKay has been both guide and inspiration, and it is a privilege to share with him the task of bringing respect where once was derision, understanding where once was prejudice. Bryan Palmer has been my most insightful critic, unfailing in his ability to point out the very weaknesses in my work that I have tried most desperately to pretend were not there. He has sensed my defensive tone, pointed out the overstated argument, and responded to my criticisms of his tradition with respect for and understanding of my own politics.

Canadian Marxists and the Search for a Third Way

I still quote Eugene Debs (1855–1926), late of Terre Haute, Indiana, five times the Socialist Party's candidate for President, in every speech:

"While there is a lower class I am in it, while there is a criminal element I am of it, while there is a soul in prison I am not free."

In recent years, I've found it prudent to say before quoting Debs that he is to be taken *seriously.* Otherwise many in the audience will start to laugh. They are being nice, not mean, knowing I like to be funny. But it is also a sign of these times that such a moving echo of the Sermon on the Mount can be perceived as outdated, wholly discredited horsecrap.

Which it is not.

Kurt Vonnegut, *Timequake*

Introduction

Once upon a time there were Marxists on the street corners, and crowds at Vancouver's Empress Theatre on a Sunday night eager to hear the socialist message. Once upon a time they came in their hundreds to experience the fire of E.T. Kingsley, the passion of Sophie Mushkat, and the oratorical splendour of H.M. Fitzgerald. Once upon a time socialist and non-socialist alike sat for hours as Bill Pritchard assailed the hypocrisy of the bourgeoisie, Winnipeg's Fred Dixon espoused the wonders of the single tax, and Charlie Lestor exposed the evil inner workings of the price system. Once upon a time capitalism's days were numbered, and thousands of workers could explain why. This was Canada.

Those voices are silent now: there are many who do not care that this is so and some who very much like it that way. Some lost causes are popular – the lost cause these people fought for is not. Disparagement of their voices has come easily, on the left as well as on the right. Little attention has been paid to what they had to say: if Canadian writers and thinkers as a whole have had considerable difficulty earning the respect they deserve, the difficulty has been much greater for Canadian Marxists. It is argued they were derivative, dogmatic, pedestrian, and lacking in originality.[1] Canadian Marxists were people on the margins, confined to the mining towns of British Columbia, Alberta, and Nova Scotia, the bush camps of British Columbia and northern Ontario, and working-class areas of Winnipeg, Toronto, Montreal, and Calgary.

This book is about taking issue with these contentions. It seeks, in a partisan but I hope even-handed and revealing manner, to convince the reader that Canadian Marxists of the early decades of the twentieth century comprised one of the most important groups of thinkers and activists in Canadian history.[2] It attempts, as much as possible, to see the world through their eyes. It seeks to avoid the moral and political judgments of a world grown disillusioned with socialist alternatives to the capitalist system; it takes us back to a world of not so long ago when socialism seemed the hope, not the bane, of humanity. Within the broad category of Canadian socialists committed to the creation of a socialist society was a group of Marxists who maintained a commitment through many setbacks and challenges to a simple yet powerful idea. These were the Marxists who adhered to the heart and soul of Karl Marx's historical materialism, his belief that the emancipation of the working class must be the work of the working class itself. I have called these individuals "Marxists of the third way."

The description requires explanation, because these socialists might more accurately be called Marxists of the first way. Their guiding philosophy is to be found in the provisional rules of the International Workingmen's Association, founded in London, England, in September 1864, to the effect that "the emancipation of the working classes must be conquered by the working classes themselves; that the struggle for the emancipation of the working classes means not a struggle for class privileges and monopolies, but for equal rights and duties, and the abolition of all class rule."[3] At the time it must have seemed a straightforward, even self-evident proposition. Karl Marx, Friedrich Engels, and other members of the association cannot have imagined just how difficult it would be for their followers, including Canada's Marxists of the third way, to put the theory into practice. It did not take long for the idea of working-class self-emancipation to find itself interpreted in radically different ways, indeed serving as the theoretical underpinning of very different socialist tendencies.

In order to understand the designation of the third way, it is necessary to look at the history of Marxist thought and the development of Marxist-based organizations following the demise of the First International (1864–76), during the period of the Second International (1889–1914), and the Third or Communist International organized in 1919. The major Marxist tendency of the Second International period was the development of a mass-based parliamentary socialism, whose leading spokespersons tended to identify working-class self-emancipation with the workers voting themselves into power by electing representatives to bourgeois-dominated legislatures. The largest socialist party in Europe was in Germany, where the Social Democratic Party had not only survived but flourished under Otto von Bismarck's anti-socialist laws in the years 1878–90. The continued growth of the party, and increasing electoral success, produced a dominant leadership group which dedicated itself to not antagonizing the military and business leaders of Germany, sought to avoid mass action, and believed that the triumph of socialism in Germany was inevitable. The growth of the party became an end in itself for many German Social Democrats, and revolutionaries such as Rosa Luxemburg criticized party leaders for their "organizational fetishism." Most party leaders were characterized by what Roger Fletcher calls political "immobilism," the belief that "nothing precipitate must be done to provoke the bourgeoisie into repressive action against the cherished party organisations."[4] In effect, on the eve of the First World War, the idea of working-class self-emancipation had been almost entirely subsumed under the necessity of always acting for the good of the party as defined by the leadership, including supporting Germany's entry into the war. Opponents of political immobilism and Germany's involvement in the war, notably Rosa Luxemburg and Karl Liebknecht, found themselves very much isolated as constant defenders of the idea of working-class self-emancipation.

In the North American context the counterpart of the German Social Democratic Party was the Socialist Party of America (SPA), whose best-known leaders were Eugene Debs and Victor Berger. More eclectic than the German Social Democratic Party, the SPA nevertheless shared the German party's focus on electoral activity and the mainstream leadership's resistance to rank and file activism that might damage the party's growth. As Mark Pittenger points out, the leading theorists and propagandists of the party were advocates of a socialist evolutionism derived from Darwin's theory of natural selection, a belief that the growth of capitalist monopolies and government involvement in the economy were preparing the way for the inevitable triumph of socialist collectivism over capitalist individualism and competition. Gaylord Wilshire, editor of *Wilshire's Magazine*, and a leading SPA spokesperson, believed that the existence of the trusts was "an unambiguous sign of socialism's imminent arrival." Wilshire, in effect, identified socialism with government ownership of the trusts. Morris Hillquit, another prominent party leader, came to believe that the "existence of the trusts showed that the United States was ready for socialism," and Victor Berger, the leading right-wing member of the party, also espoused socialist evolutionism, the idea that capitalism was evolving inevitably into socialism.[5]

The strongest countervailing trend to socialist evolutionism in Europe was syndicalism, a largely French product which found its greatest influence outside the country in Spain and Latin America. While syndicalism has always been devilishly difficult to classify, and has repeatedly been mistakenly associated with the advocacy of "sabotage" and violence, historians do tend to agree that it was a movement committed to direct action in the economic sphere, the most important form of which was the general strike. Syndicalism, at least formally, was a theory of economic transformation of capitalist society that rejected involvement in electoral politics. As Peter Stearns points out, syndicalists tended to espouse a vague notion "that the future society would be organized without a central political structure, on the basis of local economic units directed by producers themselves."[6] The capitalist state, according to the syndicalists, would be entirely eradicated by the revolutionary transformation brought on by the general strike, although they were rarely more explicit about how this would actually happen than the socialist evolutionists were about how monopolies were to be socialized.

In the North American context the syndicalist tendency was represented by the Industrial Workers of the World (IWW), organized in Chicago in 1905. Influenced by European syndicalist thought, the IWW was formally opposed to involvement in electoral politics, although leading members, including Eugene Debs, were for a time supporters of both the IWW and the Socialist Party.[7] An advocate of direct action, primarily in the form of the general strike, the IWW was no more explicit about how the state was to be eradicated than were the French syndicalists. In a sense, therefore, the IWW could be as evolutionary in its thinking as were the socialist evolutionists who placed their faith in electoral politics. Although the Wobblies were completely and sincerely committed to the idea of worker self-emancipation, they often invoked the idea of the general strike as if it were an evolutionary certainty. At times the idea of a socialist society being brought about by the general strike took on the same kind of mythical or metaphysical quality for Wobblies that the belief in socialism developing out of the trustification of American capitalism took on for the formally Marxist socialist evolutionists in the Socialist Party.

Most historians tend to forget or downplay the fact that the basic ideas of the Industrial Workers of the World were more Marxist than anarchist or syndicalist. It is rarely recognized, even by labour historians, that the IWW's slogan, "forming the structure of the new society within the shell of the old," is taken from *The Communist Manifesto*.[8] It is not surprising, therefore, that many supporters of the IWW were Marxists of the third way who fervently believed in worker self-emancipation, and therefore had a great deal in common with socialists in parties formally antagonistic to the Wobblies. This commitment to worker self-emancipation transcended party affiliation: three of Canada's most important Marxists of the third way – J.A. McDonald, John "Jack" Leheney, and Fred Thompson – were members of both the Industrial Workers of the World and the Socialist Party of Canada (SPC).[9] As SPC members they were part of an organization that placed more emphasis on electoral politics than on direct action, and whose leadership was generally quite critical of the IWW. The contradiction was more apparent than real: both the IWW and SPC were dedicated to the idea of worker self-emancipation, and both organizations believed that the workers themselves would construct a socialist society out of the materials at hand once capitalism was overthrown. Members of both organizations were also influenced by socialist evolutionism, but the Marxists of the third way among them, following the arguments of influential critics of determinism and fatalism like Louis Boudin, did not believe that socialism was inevitable or could be accomplished by taking over the trusts.[10] Nor did they tend to believe, with the anarchists and anarchist-influenced syndicalists, that revolutionaries could dispense with the party or other central organizing bodies in the creation of a classless society.

The commitment to worker self-emancipation continued to be torn between competing Marxist tendencies following the Russian Revolution of 1917 and the formation of the Third International in 1919. With the formation of the Workers' (Communist) Party of Canada in 1922, Marxists of the third way found themselves caught between the Scylla of the Independent Labour Party (ILP)/Co-operative Commonwealth Federation (CCF)'s commitment to labourism and social democracy through parliamentary gradualism and the Charybdis of the Communist Party's advocacy of a revolution of arms organized and led by the vanguard party. Throughout the course of the 1920s and '30s it became increasingly difficult for Marxists of the third way to maintain their commitment to worker self-emancipation, as the choice increasingly became one of parliamentary gradualism versus revolutionary activism. There was little room in the CCF by the late 1930s for working-class intellectuals, as the generating of ideas was entrusted to university-based intellectuals like Frank Scott, Frank Underhill, Leonard Marsh, and other members of the League for Social Reconstruction (LSR).[11] The Communist break with Marxism of the third way was made explicit in the theses of the Third International, which argued that workers should be educated after, not before, the revolution. Martin Robin has argued that by the early 1920s "the days of the armchair socialists had passed," and "practice was ready to succeed theory."[12] Interestingly, the differences between the parliamentary gradualists and the revolutionaries of the deed notwithstanding, a characteristic they shared was the marginalization of worker intellectuals and the idea of worker self-emancipation. It was an international trend: Stuart MacIntyre has pointed out that in Britain the worker intellectuals who had been nurtured in the heydey of the commitment to worker self-emancipation were increasingly marginalized in both the Labour Party and the Communist Party in the 1920s and 1930s.[13]

The discarding of the worker intellectual corresponded with a tendency to be contemptuous of the rank and file workers, especially if their ideas did not coincide with those of the leadership. Their ideological differences notwithstanding, socialist evolutionists and revolutionaries of the deed shared a common trait – dependence on elites. The leadership cadre of the German Social Democratic Party, individuals such as Friedrich Ebert, Philipp Scheidemann, and Gustav Noske, took very seriously their role of protecting the party from the radicals who appealed to the rank and file workers to engage in strikes and street actions. In Britain the Fabians saw people like themselves – the experts – as integral to the realization of socialism, and were often openly contemptuous of the workers, whom they believed could not be trusted with so important a job.[14] It is often forgotten, however, that anarchists and syndicalists could be as elitist, or even more so, than the social democratic leaders. Mikhail Bakunin, the most important anarchist leader of his generation, sought to blame the conspiratorial actions of Karl Marx for the breakup of the First International. Yet as Richard Hunt points out, following the revolutions of 1848 Bakunin himself became convinced "of the need for a secret cadre organization through which the prospective leaders of the revolution, under his own benign guidance, could invisibly coordinate the work of the masses."[15] In spite of efforts by Bakunin's followers and sympathizers to deny or downplay the significance of the International Brotherhood, the secret organization Bakunin led during the period of the First International, its existence seems beyond question.[16] Nor does one have to believe that Lenin was a dictator or the Bolshevik Party a conspiratorial force to recognize that Lenin's call for iron party discipline and his dismissal of internal party democracy as a "useless toy" owed more to advocates of the revolutionary elite than they did to Marx.[17]

The purpose of this study is not to deny that Marxists of the third way were capable of and at times exhibited autocratic behaviour. They could be intolerant of legitimate dissent and minority opinions, and considered themselves indispensable bulwarks between the working class and the influence of the capitalist class. There will always be historians and other observers who see them as little different from the party leaders and labour bureaucrats they so forthrightly condemned. But they were different, because they believed, following Marx and Engels, that "leadership could be provided without creating a professional class of leaders."[18] They were individuals more interested in exerting influence than wielding power, and as a result ideas and education were very important to them. Marxists of the third way realized that without taking this position on leaders in the socialist movement, any commitment to worker self-emancipation and the creation of a classless society must ultimately prove a snare and a delusion.

In order to appreciate the contributions of these Marxists of the third way, it is necessary for them to emerge from the negative portrayals of Canadian Marxists as a whole. The most common assessment of the Marxian socialists of the pre-1919 years is that their supposed immersion in Marxist theory caused them to be sectarian, dogmatic, and other-worldly.[19] These dismissals have been made on the basis of very limited empirical investigation of the thoughts, beliefs, ideas, and actions of the leading Marxian socialists.[20] Very little analysis of individual lives and careers has been done, and the actual theoretical contributions of leading Marxian socialists have rarely been acknowledged.[21] Assessments of the theoretical contributions of Marxian socialists in Canada have concentrated on their failure to develop a comprehensive analysis of the Canadian economy and the Canadian political system.[22] In the process, however, their important analysis of the relationship between worker self-emancipation and the leadership question has been overlooked.

A further problem has been the tendency of authors to collapse Marxism into particular political trajectories. Ross Johnson argues that the "Marxist phase" of the B.C. left ended with the collapse of the Socialist Party of Canada in 1925.[23] Phyllis Clarke in her 1977 doctoral thesis argues that the Marxist tradition began with the creation of the Communist Party of Canada in the early 1920s.[24] Even though she explicitly recognizes that there were Marxists in the CCF and the Trotskyist movement, she simply chooses to consider their Marxism irrelevant.[25] In effect, one is supposed to believe that Marxism in Canada was born and died at the same time.[26]

In this kind of scenario in which Marxism as a system of thought is essentially turned into a function of a particular party, there is not much room for writing about Marxists as individuals trying to maintain their own understanding of Marxism and corresponding programs of action. Canadian labour historians have overlooked the fact that Marxists of the third way got involved in the labour revolt of 1919 with little thought of the possible repercussions for their parties. These are not Marxists characterized by the political immobilism that plagued the leadership of the German Social Democratic Party, and the proof is the fact that both the Socialist Party of Canada and the Social Democratic Party were effectively destroyed in the years 1917–19. For Marxists of the third way, the issue in 1919 was the knowledge of socialism and preparedness of the rank and file workers to create a socialist society, not the acquiring of power at any cost. In the crucible of 1919 Canada's Marxism of the third way demonstrated its great strengths and exhibited its basic weaknesses.

The task, therefore, is to deal directly with Canada's Marxists of the third way and their ideas, to take them seriously as thinkers. The purpose of this study is to look more closely at the choices these people made, why they made them, and the structural restraints they encountered in doing so. It involves, as John Goode has said about E.P. Thompson's approach, treating consciousness as an historical agent. Consciousness is especially important when dealing with socialist thinkers who saw their primary role as helping to educate their working-class audience. The consciousness of the audience, like the consciousness of the theorists themselves, was always fractured, always characterized by ambiguity and contradiction.[27] Marxism must be approached as a system of ideas in constant transformation as it passed between leaders and followers, and as Marxist groups and individuals attempted to put it into practice.

Given the nature of the study and the relative paucity of sources, the number of individuals that could be chosen for such a study was relatively small. The individuals chosen had to be Marxists in the important sense identified by Paul Heywood, the belief that their political practice was "derived from theoretical formulations in a conscious manner."[28] In addition they had to be socialists who were activists, individuals who made a significant impact on the actual history of Canadian socialism and the labour movement in the first half of the twentieth century.[29] Because the biographies presented here are thematic biographies – that is, they involve a study of the ideas of Canada's Marxists of the third way and the efforts they made to put those ideas into practice – only individuals who left a significant body of personal correspondence or writings in labour papers and who were active over the span of the first half of the twentieth century could be chosen. The existing sources suggest that male British working-class immigrants from Protestant families, such as Edward Winch, William Pritchard, Robert Russell, and Arthur Mould, represented the historically most significant tendency in Marxism of the third way. They represent, if you will, the dominant sociological category in a broader political tendency.

This book is not a "definitive" history of Marxism of the third way. It identifies a powerful idea in the thinking of Canadian Marxists, and attempts to identify some of the roots of that powerful idea in the thinking of working-class British immigrants. The focus on this subset of Marxists of the third way does not mean that Irish Catholics like Jack Kavanagh and Jack Leheney, South Asians like Husain Rahim,

Jewish socialists like Sam Blumenberg and Max Tessler, women such as Helen Armstrong, Sarah Johnson Knight, and Elizabeth Morton, and Jewish socialist women like Sophie Mushkat were less committed to working class self-emancipation and less aware of their role as leaders. French, Yiddish, Ukrainain, Finnish, and other language sources will need to be explored in order to confirm or contradict the ideas advanced here in terms of other ethnic and religious sources for the ideas shared by Marxists of the third way. Ian McKay's path-breaking study of independent Marxist Colin McKay admirably demonstrates the vibrancy of the tendency in Maritime Canada, and we need to know more about where Maritime socialists such as Roscoe Fillmore, J.B. McLachlan, and Henry Harvey Stuart belong in this category. Albert Saint-Martin, the driving force behind the French Section of the Socialist Party of Canada in Montreal, was as committed to working-class education as any Marxist of the third way in English Canada and provides a key historical link between the socialist solitudes.[30]

In effect, this book is about striving, about being right and being wrong, about being human, about the attempt to find the path to socialism through the maze of capitalism. It is a chronicle of that experience Meridel Le Sueur so eloquently describes as "moving in the chaotic dark of a new creation."[31] Marxism of the third way was about individual socialists interpreting events in the material world through the lens of Marxist ideas and attempting to develop collective strategies out of that dialectical process. That vision, the self-emancipation of the working class, would remain a powerful ideal for Ernest Winch, Bill Pritchard, Bob Russell, and Arthur Mould throughout their socialist lives. This book claims that the socialists you will meet in these pages, for all their faults, remained for most of their lives truer to Marx's vision than most of their social democratic and communist contemporaries.[32] It is a claim that will be challenged, but if out of that challenge the debate concerning the history of Canadian socialism and the Canadian labour movement is broadened, deepened, and enlivened, it will have served its purposes, academic and socialist.[33]

Leading Canadian Marxists came from a relatively homogenous demographic background. Most of them were born into working-class families in the British Isles. Most were English, although Welsh, Scottish, and Irish socialists were also prominent. To begin with, Winch, Pritchard, Russell, and Mould all came from religious homes, although interestingly enough their parents belonged to four different Protestant denominations. While the religious roots of social democrats like J.S. Woodsworth on the one hand, and Communist Party members like A.E. Smith on the other, have been noted and analysed, little attention has been paid to the influence of religion on members of the SPC, the

SDP, and the IWW.[34] Usually born in the last three decades of the nineteenth century, these men, and some women, grew and were shaped by nineteenth-century events, politics, culture, and thought.[35] Their ideas were those of the British radical tradition – a questioning of hierarchical religious and secular authority structures, respect for skill, experience, and good work which cut across class lines, and a knowledge of and great appreciation for the literature, art, and music of Victorian England.[36]

It was this constellation of ideas, and not Marxism, that they usually brought with them to Canada. Some had read Marx, but they were not yet self-conscious Marxists, with the exception of individuals such as Bill Pritchard. More typical was Arthur Mould, who read Marx's writings but did not really understand a great deal of what he read. Ernest Winch had no identifiable background in socialist thought at all before coming to Canada. Bob Russell was aware of a whole range of socialist thought but was a member of the Independent Labour Party and a practical trade unionist, not a theoretical socialist.[37] Many Canadian Marxists came from skilled worker backgrounds. They were born into the now famous "labour aristocracy," the sons of master bricklayers, machinists, carpenters, typographers, and other skilled workers.[38] There were others, however, whose parents worked as labourers or semi-skilled operatives in the textile industry or on the docks. There was also a group with origins in the lower middle class, whose fathers were clerks or lawyers. From this latter group came leading socialist thinkers and writers such as Wallis Lefeaux, a long-time Socialist Party of Canada member who was a lawyer and real-estate salesman in British Columbia.

Regardless of their class origins, these individuals grew up like many young liberals and conservatives, believing in the superiority of the British parliamentary system – a belief many of them retained even as they became more influenced by Marxism. Their heroes were rebels, not the heroes of the socialist movements of continental Europe: they included Wat Tyler, John Ball, Robert Burns, the Chartists, and the Tolpuddle Martyrs. As youths, they tended to look to rebels who had been persecuted for their political and religious beliefs, not to the great revolutionary leaders of the past. Perhaps here we find the origins of the ambiguity about their role as leaders which informs their later involvement in the Canadian labour movement. They tended to see themselves as models for the workers, not as leaders to be followed, and this may help explain the role of a Bill Pritchard or a Bob Russell during the labour revolt of 1919.

Like Marx and Engels, they initially espoused a moral, not a scientific, critique of capitalism. As young people they encountered the class divisions, the poverty, the exploitation, and the hardships of working-class life in England, Scotland, Ireland, and Wales. Because most of the Marxist classics were not available to them in English translation, their response to working-class poverty was couched in the language and perceptions of Dickens, Gibbon, Macaulay, Buckle, Mill, Carlyle, Ruskin, and Morris, not Marx. Their bible was the Bible, not *The Communist Manifesto*.[39] Some of them were reading the first volume of *Capital* by the 1890s, but often they found it very tough going and preferred other sources.

Understanding Canada's Marxists of the third way is aided by Edward Thompson's important analysis of William Morris's relation to Marxism. Thompson disputes Stanley Pierson's position that Marxism became "superimposed" on Morris's Romanticism, arguing that Marxism became integrated with Morris's British radicalism, in particular his moral critique of capitalism and his utopianism.[40] Thompson's argument about Morris helps explain the attitudes of Canadian Marxists to key issues such as the role of leadership, the role of the trade unions, and the response in the early 1920s to the formation of the Communist Party. In addition, the Morris/Marx problematic has a great deal to say about the trajectory of Canadian Marxists in the 1920s and 1930s, and whether or not they remained Marxists at all. Thompson's analysis is invaluable, because it refuses to resort to labels or essentialist categories. He takes the position that Morris came to accept the basic tenets of Marxism, although he is hesitant to describe Morris as a Marxist *tout court*. In the writings of Morris the ideal and the scientific "continued to co-exist."[41]

Thompson's emphasis on nuance and subtlety provides an excellent model for the study of Canadian Marxists of the third way. On the one hand, they were firmly committed to the triumph of "scientific" over "utopian" socialism. On the other, they considered themselves part of the British radical tradition, often had a poetic sensibility, defended constitutional politics, and imbibed the ideas of a whole range of political and scientific theorists. By looking at individual lives, it is possible to explore how these ideas and sentiments developed into a critique of capitalism that co-existed with the scientific socialist defence of the materialist conception of history, the labour theory of value, and class struggle.[42]

Revealing how Marxists of the third way developed their critique of capitalism requires a reassessment of the genesis of Marxist thinking in a Canadian context. Most Marxists of the third way did not come to Canada as socialist crusaders. They tended to leave Britain because they were disgusted by the class divisions, poverty, and hypocrisy of their home country, were in search of better wages and working conditions, or wanted to provide a better life for themselves and their families. Many genuinely believed that Canada, a new country, would be free of these problems. Upon arriving, however, they discovered that cities like Montreal, Toronto, and Vancouver were in many ways just as class-divided and poverty-stricken as the areas they grew up in. How could it be, they wondered, that the conditions they had experienced at home were similar in this new land halfway round the globe?

It was in Canada that these British immigrants came face to face with the realization that capitalism was a system. This realization was brought home even more forcefully to those immigrants who had also travelled to the United States, India, South Africa, Australia, and elsewhere. Many began a serious study of Marx and his interpreters after they came to Canada. With some exceptions, their journey to an acceptance of the orthodox Marxism of parties such as the Socialist Party of Canada followed on the heels of long periods of political inactivity, support for independent labour parties, or membership in the Social Democratic Party. Many were not, strictly speaking, autodidacts; they had attended school as young boys and girls, and were able to improve their reading, writing, and speaking skills in the classes run by the SPC, SDP, IWW, and other socialist parties. Indeed, a few attended university, either in Canada or the British Isles.

Challenging the wages system meant educating the workers, and education became the key concern of Marxists of the third way. Parties such as the SPC saw election campaigns as vehicles for "propaganda," as a way of communicating their message more forcefully and meaningfully to the working class as a whole. They saw the party, therefore, more as a vehicle for socialist education than as an organizing centre of revolutionary activities. Leaders were the means by which socialist ideas were disseminated, but leaders and parties were not seen as the driving forces in the overthrow of capitalism. The overthrow of capitalism and the eradication of the wages system were the responsibility of the workers themselves.

In practice, ideas and education were seen as a predominantly male realm, as few women in parties such as the SPC and SDP became public speakers or led study classes. Women rarely became editors of the socialist press, and women who wrote for the socialist press generally did so for short periods of time. There were notable exceptions – Ruth Lestor, Bertha Merrill Burns, Sarah Johnston-Knight, Sophie Mushkat, Sanna Kannasto, and others – but it was not easy, and most male socialists did not go out of their way to encourage women thinking for themselves and engaging in theoretical debates.[43] As many feminist historians and historians of masculinity point out, in practice, if not always in theory, the "worker" being educated by Marxian socialists was assumed to be white, male, and heterosexual.

Like their counterparts in Europe and the United States, many Marxists of the third way were unable to shed the Victorian attitudes toward women propagated by the very bourgeois middle class they constantly condemned. They had difficulty coming to grips with the disturbing reality that their calls for the abolition of bourgeois private property meant the end of that quintessential product of bourgeois capitalism, the male-dominated nuclear family. They were much like the German American socialists of the late nineteenth century who, as Mari Jo Buhle points out, "believed in the sanctity of separate spheres for men and women and enshrined women's role as guardian of the proletarian family. No less romantic about womanhood than the proletariat, they sought to preserve feminine virtue against all threats, be they capitalism or a pernicious woman's rights influence."[44] Most Marxists of the third way could not break with the prevailing attitude toward women in the international socialist movement. Like many members of the American Socialist Party, they agreed with the position of the Second International that socialist women "were to cling to the party and resist the temptation to ally with the mainstream women's movement."[45] Marxists of the third way in the Socialist Party, who were always quick to condemn the Second International, revealingly failed to recognize that on the "woman question" they were at times more reactionary than many male European Marxists who supported the Second International.

In this respect Marxists of the third way resembled their counterparts in the United States, where socialists "transmuted 'scientific' principles into a reaffirmation of women's traditional role."[46] Mark Pittenger points out that the influence of Darwin, Spencer, and evolutionary thinking in general helped determine the attitudes of Marxists in this period toward women and workers of colour. Members of the Socialist Party of America "committed to science commonly regarded women ... as inferior products of evolution, and resisted their demands for equality in party affairs."[47] Influenced more by middle-class Victorian morality than by the writings of Marx, Engels, and Bebel, Marxists of the third way had a split perception of women. For them, women were oppressed when in the workplace but essentially performing their natural function when in the home. Many of them clearly were threatened by female activists who insisted on making the woman question central to socialist politics. It is on the woman question, therefore, that one finds the greatest gap between the theory and practice of Marxists of the third way, a gap that existed in the analysis of feminist socialists such as Ruth Lestor as well.[48] Like August Bebel and so many other "progressive" socialist thinkers, most Marxists of the third way "allotted woman no historical significance distinct from that of the proletariat."[49] Indeed, Marxian socialists in Canada may have been more conservative than their American or European counterparts, who tended to accept women's waged labour more fully than did many Canadian Marxists, their other prejudices concerning women notwithstanding.[50]

In the United States prominent female socialists, most notably Charlotte Perkins Gilman, Kate Richards O'Hare, May Wood Simons, and Josephine Conger Kaneko, had an impact for which there was no Canadian counterpart. There was no Canadian equivalent of the Woman's National Committee of the American Socialist Party, which by 1910 had gained access to the party treasury and space in the head office in Chicago.[51] As Mark Pittenger points out, "dissatisfied socialist women were less easily ignored than were blacks or immigrants, for political if not for theoretical reasons. Women had been party organizers and activists from the beginning, and were a self-organized constituency with their own clubs and press."[52] There had been no Seneca Falls convention in Canada, no process of politicization of women comparable to the involvement of American women in the abolitionist movement. One of the reasons women's issues were more marginalized in Canada than in Europe and the United States was because Canadian feminist socialists appear to have been less assertive in fighting for their concerns, more easily dissuaded by the opposition of male Marxian socialists. But this was not because Canadian feminist socialists were less intelligent, less dedicated, or less passionate; rather, it had to do with the political culture in which they operated. Canadian feminist socialists, unlike their counterparts in France or the United States, had few heroines to point to as possible models for proletarian womanhood. Nor could they draw as readily on the republican values of the French and American revolutions which, although exclusionary in practice, at least in theory promised full equality for women. Canadian feminist socialists, or at least the leading Anglo-Saxon ones, could make little headway by appealing to British constitutionalism or the rights of freeborn Englishmen, both entirely male-defined concepts. In effect male socialists controlled the definition and interpretation of both Marxist and British ideas of freedom, justice, and equality, leaving women in the socialist movement with little chance of even adding a gender dimension to the definition of proletarian or the socialist society of the future.

Many male Marxists, for their part, remained blinded to the importance of addressing the concerns of women socialists in the political realm. They also failed to recognize the domestic role played by their wives and daughters. While they were attending meetings, writing articles, and organizing workers, the women in their households struggled to put food on the table, keep the clothes washed, the children healthy, and the bills paid. It can easily be imagined that male Marxists often saw domestic concerns as a bothersome distraction from the more important tasks they were engaged in as trade unionists and socialist activists. During periods of political repression, or failing party fortunes, some of these men no doubt took out their frustrations on their wives and children.[53] As the lives of Ernest Winch, Bill Pritchard, Bob Russell, and Arthur Mould attest, the periods of financial hardship were many and protracted. The result must have led many a socialist wife to point out that while her husband was saving the working class from poverty and oppression, he was subjecting her and the children to poverty and oppression in order to do it. Winch, Pritchard, Mould, and Russell all endured the death of one or more children during their lifetimes. They paid a horrible price for their socialist activities, but their families often paid a higher one.

While this study recognizes, with the wisdom that comes with hindsight, that Marxists of the third way should have been much more supportive than they were of the women in their own lives and of women in general, it also seeks to counteract blanket dismissals of these men. The reader is reminded that many did fight for the economic independence of women in the workplace, and a small minority of Marxian socialist men wrote intelligently and insightfully on the "woman question."[54] In the space of a few months in 1912 in the *Western Clarion*, the journal of the Socialist Party of Canada, we find an anonymous author demythologizing the domestic realm and describing the double workday of working-class wives, A. Percy Chew describing Olive Schreiner's book *Woman and Labor* as "a great work, probably the most important contribution made to the literature of Sociology in the last quarter of a century," and George Paton of Alberta arguing that women are neither intellectually inferior nor physically weaker than men.[55] The record is mixed, and the purpose of this book is not to make sweeping generalizations or pass judgments but rather to further understanding of why Marxists of the third way believed what they did about the "woman question."

In spite of a generation of criticisms of their attitudes on race and ethnicity, the evidence suggests that Marxists of the third way were on the whole significantly less prejudiced than the political culture in which they lived.[56] This point has been obscured by the disparaging of Marxists of the third way in the Socialist Party, who are invariably compared unfavourably with their counterparts in the Social Democratic Party. Yet the entire body of literature on this question provides not a single credible reason for believing that the average member of the SPC was more racist or anti-immigrant than the average member of the SDP, the difference in the parties' positions on language locals notwithstanding. Given the existing literature, a reassessment of Marxism of the third way's record on this question must of necessity involve focusing on the Socialist Party of Canada, which was not as monolithically white, male, and Anglo-Saxon as has been argued. One of the members of the SPC's 1908 Dominion Executive Committee (DEC) was Finnish, and Abe Karme, another Finnish Canadian Socialist, was on the DEC for several years after. The SPC also had close relations at times with the South Asian community in British Columbia, with H.M. Fitzgerald and D.G. McKenzie being front and centre in the fight to end discrimination against South Asian immigrants. Husain Rahim, who attempted to organize a South Asian local of the SPC, was on the DEC for roughly two years and went on to become the party's expert on Freudian psychology. James Teit, one of British Columbia's leading anthropologists and a key organizer in the fight for native rights, was a longstanding member of the Socialist Party.[57] Marxists of the third way in the Socialist Party were well integrated into the ethnic community in Winnipeg as well. When John Houston ran on a Socialist Party ticket in the federal election of 1908, the meeting at which he was nominated was addressed by English, French, Finnish, German, Polish, Ukrainian, and Jewish speakers. Jack Leheney noted that a "campaign committee composed of one comrade from each nationality was elected with power to add to their number."[58]

Particularly striking are the close ties to the Jewish community, ties that became very important in Winnipeg during the labour revolt of 1919.[59] There appear to have been a number of reasons for the coming together of Jewish and non-Jewish Marxian Socialists. As Janice Newton points out, the anti-religious – in effect anti-Christian – stance of parties such as the SPC proved attractive to secular Jews.[60] Second, some socialists and labour people identified with the oppression of Jews and saw them as fellow victims of capitalist oppression. Third, Jews and non-Jews on the Marxist left shared a commitment to ideas and the forthright, unabashedly combative presentation of their political positions. One tends to forget, in an age in which being inoffensive is more important than being right, that this was a political culture in which former Christians like Bill Pritchard and secular Jews like Moses Baritz revelled in the thrust and parry of debate, skewering opponents on their own arguments, hoisting religious believers on the hypocrisy of their beliefs. Of Baritz's skill as a speaker and debater, Bob Russell said simply: "He was a hero."[61]

As a number of American authors have pointed out, Jewish immigrants, socialist and non-socialist, shared a commitment to science, the language of science, and the evolutionary thought of Darwin and Spencer. As David Hollinger observes, Jewish immigrants "undergoing secularization" were powerfully drawn to science:

> Science aimed, by definition, to enter a dialogue with the most universal and timeless segments of experience. Science sought truth of a sort that would command consent from persons of any national, religious, or ethnic background; it was concerned with propositions that were in no way culture-bound ... Science ... focused on what was least particular in the entire range of human experience; science thrust aside, in effect, those aspects of the Western tradition that served as barriers between nations, religions, provinces, and individuals. Science was potentially the basis for a fully secular ideology that would exclude no one from full participation in modern life.[62]

Because the religious background of non-Jewish Marxists of the third way has remained largely unrecognized, it has not been appreciated that they too underwent a process of secularization as young men and women. An almost unbounded belief in science was characteristic of most Marxists of the third way undergoing this process: they sought a vehicle for the transcendence of religious and national particularities, just as many Jewish socialists sought a vehicle for their internationalism. Science provided that vehicle for both Jews and non-Jews.[63] It offered a sense of certainty, if not inevitability, an assurance that capitalism's days were numbered, and a way of valorizing their own role as spokespersons for the future course of economic, social, and political events. While a Jewish liberal such as Morris Cohen enlisted science in his "nonideological pursuit of truth," Marxists of the third way, Jewish and non-Jewish, enlisted it in the cause of the unification and advancement of the working class.[64]

As Ian McKay points out, the most powerful word in this world of science for Marxists of the third way was evolution, much as culture was for many academics in the 1960s and 1970s, and discourse became in the 1980s and 1990s.[65] Herbert Spencer, not Charles Darwin, was its major apostle. Spencerian Marxists saw evolution as "a great, massive force, a universal principle, above all a *social and natural phenomenon* that was both the scientific *explanation* of change, the *process* of change, and the *politico-ethical practices* predicated on the awareness of this phenomenon of change."[66] The corollary of this powerful belief in evolutionary change was an equally powerful opposition to Spencer's individualism, which Arthur Morrow Lewis declared to be "defunct."[67] Marxists of the third way in Canada were greatly influenced by Lewis's critique of Spencer's individualism and constantly decried individualism as the outmoded ethos of a diseased and dying capitalist system.

Society, Marxists of the third way believed, was evolving away from individualist solutions to humanity's problems and toward collectivist ones. At first glance this faith in evolutionism and the attack on individualism appear to establish Marxists of the third way as precursors of the worst kind of state socialism. In taking a closer look, however, we discover that the critique of individualism is centred in a rejection of dependence on individual leaders, a position entirely consistent with a belief in the workers becoming more and more self-sufficient, and less and less in need of leaders. Bill Pritchard, commenting on his involvement in the Socialist Party of Canada, once said, "We don't count on leaders ... and chances are if one bobs up that looks like one, his head would come off."[68] Yet Marxists of the third way also agreed with Arthur Morrow Lewis that socialists "are not stupid enough to argue that because society can get along without a king, therefore an orchestra should have 'no head.'"[69] Marxists of the third way believed that dependence on individual leaders was becoming a thing of the past, but until the majority of workers were educated and organized they would continue to need support and direction.

The other problem, of course, was that Marxists of the third way were the inheritors of a British radical tradition and Protestant Nonconformism that made it very difficult for them to escape thinking of the creation of socialism as a kind of personal salvation. Like other modernists, they appear at times to believe that "only the integrity of the willful, autonomous self can afford them an escape from the general cultural condition that they abhor."[70] Their socialism was as much about desire as it was about the objective unfolding of natural and social forces, and it is entirely possible that had they shown this side of their personalities more openly and fully, their impact on the Canadian working class might have been even greater than it was. The influence of evolutionary thinking was profound, but it must not blind us to the fact that Marxian socialism in early twentieth-century Canada was also very much about idealism and the individual conscience.

Given their attachment to theories of evolutionary change there can be little doubt that Marxists of the third way will continue to be seen as "crass materialists" who believed that socialism was inevitable, the unstoppable outcome of material forces beyond human agency and control. If we look at the writers who influenced this generation of Marxists, however, we find reasons to take a rather different view of their ideas and inspirations. Antonio Labriola, whose *Essays in the Materialistic Conception of History* remains one of the great works of the historical materialist tradition, was one of the thinkers who influenced Canada's Marxists of the third way.[71] Labriola, building on Marx's positing of the importance of the individual to an understanding of historical materialism, states that "the perfect theoretical knowledge of socialism to-day, as before, and as it always will be, lies in the understanding of its historic necessity, that is to say, in the consciousness of the manner of its genesis." That consciousness, he says, "dates from the moment when the proletarian movement is not merely a result of social conditions, but when it has already strength enough to understand that these conditions can be changed and to discern what means can modify them and in what direction." Historical materialism "could not arise but from the theoretical consciousness of socialism."[72]

What is striking about Labriola's understanding of historical materialism is the signal importance of the role of consciousness, the fact that he begins with socialism as ideal. His conception is more Hegelian than Darwinist, and we can find Hegel's influence even in the Socialist Party of Canada, a party more identified with economic determinism and "vulgar" materialism. If we look at what SPCers were actually saying rather than at the stereotypes Canadian labour historians have pinned on them, what we find is a marked Hegelian and idealist influence.[73] H.M. Bartholomew, a leading theoretician of the Socialist Party who joined the Communist Party in the 1920s, evinced Hegel's influence in a 1915 *Western Clarion* article revealingly entitled "A Philosophy of Revolt." Quoting Hegel to the effect that "nothing is, everything is becoming," Bartholomew goes on to state that the socialist "comes, above all, with a clear vision of an orderly conception of what organized human effort can make of human life."[74] On a prior occasion Bartholomew had argued that "abstract investigation is the forerunner of all progress ... all advance is the inevitable product of thought and study."[75]

In order to understand the theory and practice of Canada's Marxists of the third way it is necessary to appreciate the fact that they lived and worked in a political culture in which the relationship between the ideal and the material and between inductive versus deductive reasoning were an integral part of a socialist understanding. The nuances of that culture emerge from a debate that took place in 1916 between A. Percy Chew of the Social Democratic Party and J.D. Harrington of the Socialist Party.[76] In that debate Chew accused the SPCers of being "inveterate deductionists," to which Harrington's response was that the SPCers "must plead guilty."[77] Chew's argument, based on the work of Joseph Dietzgen, was that the German-born working-class philosopher had argued that the proletarian method was the inductive method.[78] Chew's position was certainly defensible, given that Dietzgen had argued that scientific socialists "hold to induction on principle, that is we know that knowledge cannot be got by deduction, by drawing from pure reason, but *that it is gained through the instrumentality of reason from experience.*"[79] Harrington was correct in pointing out, however, that as a monist, someone who believed that thought and being were one, Dietzgen espoused both the inductive and deductive methods.[80] Harrington was pointing out that while Dietzgen opposed arguing from "pure" reason, that is to say, on the basis of *metaphysical* reasoning, he was not questioning the importance of deductive reasoning. Their differences notwithstanding, Chew and Harrington were part of a political culture in which ideas and dialectics were very much alive, a culture in which Dietzgen and Hegel could be as salient as Darwin and Spencer.

While they did tend to see science as the sole form of real knowledge, viewing socialism as ideal and using the deductive rather than inductive method of reasoning were quite characteristic of Marxian socialist thinking. Dietzgen, in spite of his claim to be replacing metaphysics with science, made "the Hegelian system of philosophy with its pronounced idealism the starting point of the materialist conception of history."[81] Even Friedrich Engels, again and again dismissed as a "vulgar materialist," argued in his tremendously influential work *Socialism: Utopian and Scientific* that scientific socialism is a science of movement, not of things. Marxists of the third way in Canada were not so much interested in what *is* as in what the what *is* is in the process of becoming. This is one reason why, as many critics of Canada's Marxian socialists have pointed out again and again, these socialists spent more time in abstract theorizing than they did in analysing the social, economic, and political institutions of their day. As Stuart MacIntyre quite rightly points out, "the historical contingency of the present order was a potent aspect of Marxism" for these socialists, an aspect Marx had derived from Hegel before Darwin would introduce him to a different but equally powerful argument for the contingency of the present.[82]

Marxists of the third way were dialectical thinkers who saw consciousness and, in particular, knowledge of scientific socialism, as the indispensable partners of experience garnered in the workplace. As Russell Jacoby notes, they espoused Marx's idea of science as the "knowledge of the social movement made by the people themselves."[83] Their willingness and ability to explore the dialectical relationship between knowledge and experience, while "unsophisticated" by academic standards, was nonetheless impressive. Indeed, their understanding of the relationship between theory and practice, between reason and experience, may have been more balanced than that of some of the leading neo-Marxists of the second half of the twentieth century.

As Perry Anderson points out in his critique of the work of Edward Thompson, experience was the "touchstone of the Thompsonian world."[84] It would be dangerous to accept Anderson's assessment at face value, of course, because Thompson gave many years of his life to adult education and was quintessentially a man of ideas. It remains true, however, that there was a strong anti-Hegelian, anti-theoretical bent in Thompson's thinking.[85] In his book on William Morris, another important influence for Marxists of the third way, Thompson observes that Morris six years before his death "was still placing far too much emphasis upon the inculcation of Socialist theory in the abstract; far too little upon the educative role of the struggle itself."[86] There were Marxists of the third way who evinced Morris's weakness, but it must also be pointed out that the decline over the course of the twentieth century in the commitment to worker self-emancipation has been accompanied by a decline in the left's valuing of worker education, especially in what SPCers called the Marxist classics. This is not, I would argue, mere coincidence.

For Marxists of the third way, education had a very important purpose. While certainly not Leninists, they considered violence a likely if not unavoidable outcome of revolutionary change, but they sought to avoid it more than they saw it as a weapon. Like Morris, they believed that revolution made education imperative.[87] When violence was involved, the working class needed to act intelligently. For Marxists of the third way, revolution was historically necessary and likely to be violent, but they were utterly convinced that a majority of educated, organized workers could keep that violence to a minimum. Bill Pritchard saw revolutionary violence as a sign of weakness in the working class, a result of workers hating the capitalist instead of hating the system.[88] In effect, the belief was that the socialist revolution could eradicate the capitalist system without necessarily eradicating the capitalists. The assumption was that significant numbers of capitalists would see the futility of resisting a well-educated, well-organized working-class majority and go over to the winning side. Unlike many Marxists who came after them, Marxists of the third way remained true to the vision of Marx and Engels, who argued that "in times when the class struggle nears the decisive hour ... a small section of the ruling class cuts itself adrift, and joins the revolutionary class, the class that holds the future in its hands."[89]

One of the decisive tests for Marxism of the third way was the labour revolt of 1919, and in particular the Winnipeg General Strike. In the thrust and parry of day-to-day events it did not much matter if Canadian Marxists drew their ideas of revolutionary change from Darwin or Dietzgen. The question of theory and practice came down to more fundamental questions having to do with trade union organization, leadership, direction, and the motivations of the rank and file of the working class. Although David Bercuson would have us believe that 1919 was just about wages and working conditions, it was about much more. As Gregory Kealey points out, "the Canadian bourgeoisie did not share Bercuson's perspective."[90] The Winnipeg of 1919 was a battleground of ideas.[91] The issue is, what ideas? Once again the focus must shift to Marxists of the third way in the Socialist Party, because only by critiquing mistaken assessments of their ideas and actions is it possible to explain what Marxism of the third way actually was in 1919. While Bercuson has described the SPCers involved in the labour revolt as syndicalists, Janice Newton has taken their gender bias to mean that their support for industrial unionism was essentially meaningless.[92] As these positions suggest, historians have been quicker to find labels or to criticize than they have been to seek plausible reasons for supposedly anti-trade union Socialist Party of Canada members guiding a revolt of organized trade unionists and taking a leading role in the formation of the One Big Union. It is necessary to explore more fully where Marxists of the third way got their ideas, and how they attempted to put them into practice, if we are to make sense of these apparent contradictions and understand what these individuals were attempting to do in 1919.

Contrary to the stereotype of them as being vehemently anti-trade union, these Marxists often came to parties such as the SPC from a trade union background and long experience in union organizing.[93] They came to "orthodox" Marxism in part because their actual involvement in the trade union movement convinced them that trade unions had to move beyond concern with wages and working conditions to challenging the wages system itself.[94] In effect, they joined the Socialist Party because they were trade unionists. The theoretical basis of their position is to be found in Marx's *Value, Price, and Profit*, a basic Socialist Party text containing Marx's explicit defence of trade unions as necessary but not sufficient guarantors of proletarian revolution.[95] In the years leading up to 1919, Marxists of the third way were not hostile to considering trade unions as centres of organizing resistance to capitalism; even most members of the SPC saw the trade union as historically necessary. As Bill Pritchard pointed out near the end of his life, his membership in the Socialist Party and his trade union activity were inseparable. Only "intellectuals" wanted nothing to do with trade unions.[96]

Indeed, it was the interaction between trade unionists and Marxian socialists that made the labour revolt of 1919 as widespread and effective as it was. The major product of that interaction, the One Big Union, was an attempt to unite the political ideas of Karl Marx with the economic power of the trade union movement. Canadian historians of all political persuasions have declared that the federal government's attempt to link the One Big Union with the Winnipeg General Strike was entirely mistaken, because the OBU had not actually been organized yet. This argument entirely dismisses the importance in May and June 1919 of the idea of the One Big Union, which aimed at the linking of socialist theory and trade union protest. The threat, of course, was real, and the recent attempts of Canadian historians to deny this linkage merely reflects the fact that state officials in this country take the power of ideas more seriously than do many academic historians.

Bercuson is not far off when he argues that the One Big Union was poorly conceived, badly organized, and unlikely to succeed.[97] What must be understood, however, is that there was a conscious and coherent basis to the OBU, the attempt by Marxian socialists to create a class union by uniting the functions of the trade union and the party. The confusion arose because Marxists of the third way were not in agreement on the actual relationship between the economic and political wings of class struggle. Bill Pritchard believed that there had to be both a socialist party and a class union; Bob Russell, in contrast, assumed that the party and the union would be one organization. What united Pritchard and Russell, and indeed all Marxists of the third way, was the understanding that without the increasing education and self-activity of the workers, any form of organization was doomed to fail. It was up to the workers themselves to put the One Big Union into practice. It would only succeed if the great majority of workers were committed socialists, thereby reducing to a minimum the violence of the counter-revolution.[98]

The events of the Winnipeg General Strike and sympathetic strikes across the country produced a debate about the understanding of Marxism and the tactics of revolutionary socialists that permanently split the socialist movement. Russell concluded from the strike that Marx's original formulation was correct, and that the strike's main weakness had been the paucity of rank and file people willing to step in to take positions of responsibility. Pritchard came to similar conclusions. Jack Kavanagh, Malcolm Bruce, and others, just as understandably, concluded that the main problem had been a lack of direction and disciplined leadership. The Winnipeg General Strike was the acid test of a Marxism based in the belief that Marxist leaders exist to guide and inform, not direct, the course of working class protest. It is instructive that in spite of the weaknesses in this position the Canadian Communist Party was never able to duplicate 1919, even during the labour upsurge of the late 1930s, or in the immediate post-World War Two period.

Sympathetic histories of the Communist Party have tended to portray the refusal of many Marxian socialists to support the Third International as reactionary, a refusal to respond in a "progressive" manner to a clearly superior Marxist politics. Ian Angus has argued that SPCers such as Bill Pritchard and Jack Harrington "preferred the academy to the class struggle."[99] There is some truth to these positions, but they refuse to recognize that the rejection of the Third International was based in a positive affirmation of an alternative Marxism, which placed greater stress on the role of the working class itself than on the role of the party. They also refuse to deal with the extent to which Bolshevism came to rely on the "great man theory" of history, an essentially nineteenth-century liberal world view that has informed much of twentieth century Communist practice, if not Leninist theory. Marxists of the third way continually and vociferously critiqued individualism and reliance on leaders. Like Fred Thompson, they were more than a little bemused by a twentieth-century Marxism that produced Leninism, Trotskyism, Maoism, Castroism, Stalinism, and a variety of other individual "isms."[100]

This position on leaders, and the activities of Canadian Communists, led Marxists of the third way to argue that the Workers' Party was undemocratic and led by a small minority that dictated policy to the membership. The position was not simply anti-Leninist but reflected an older and firmly held Marxist perspective. After 1919 Marxists of the third way continued to believe that socialism could only be brought about by an educated working class majority capable of stepping into positions of power and authority, thus destroying the need for bureaucrats and professionals. They continued to believe that the revolutionary "lead" had to come from the workers themselves, not from the party. These criticisms notwithstanding, most Marxists of the third way defended the Bolsheviks, the Soviet Union, and even the dictatorship of the proletariat. Wallis Lefeaux, who visited the Soviet Union in 1920, defended the militarization of labour in the context of external threat to the revolution's survival and the need to strengthen the Russian economy.[101] In Canada, however, Marxists of the third way had their own conception of the dictatorship of the proletariat; that is, they understood it as an exercise in self-discipline.[102] For them it was a period of class rule in which the workers were introduced to the responsibilities of power.[103] It was, in effect, an extension of the process of educating and organizing engaged in by the revolutionary socialist party prior to the actual seizure of power.[104] It was a period of class rule that required tremendous discipline on the part of the workers and their leaders, because the rule of the workers could not be more repressive than necessary to safeguard the revolution.[105]

Marxists of the third way who did not join the Communist Party remained faithful to Marx's stage theory of revolution, whereby a bourgeois revolution had to precede a socialist revolution. This argument they applied to the Soviet Union in their critiques of the Bolsheviks, who in their view had tried to leap an essential stage of history. In other words, they saw no necessary link between political revolution and the creation of socialism. They defended the Russian Revolution as historically necessary but were sceptical that it could lead to socialism.

With the decline of the Socialist Party of Canada after 1919 the standard of Marxism of the third way passed into the hands of the One Big Union.[106] After the Winnipeg General Strike the OBU became the main expression of the old SPC emphasis on worker education and initiative.[107] Martin Robin made this point in 1968, when he described the OBU as "the living embodiment of the class consciousness the socialist educators worked to create."[108] Since Robin made this key observation, however, the debate has tended to go in the wrong direction by even further accentuating the split between the "parliamentary socialism" of the SPC and the "syndicalism" of the OBU. Bercuson, for example, has contributed to the derailing of any serious discussion of the political ideology of the OBU by dismissing it as an essentially regressive, "syndicalist" organization that failed to see the future in industrial unionism.[109]

Describing the OBU as syndicalist serves to disguise the overwhelming Marxist orientation of the leading theoreticians in the organization. The first editor of the *One Big Union Bulletin* was John Houston, an old SPC member who wrote intelligent, insightful editorials.[110] The editor who replaced him, Frank Woodward, was also a Marxist theorist and member of the SPC. Woodward was followed in 1928 by Charles Lestor, a first-generation SPCer and one of the leading Marxist theorists in Canada. All attempted in their articles to maintain the emphasis on worker self-education and organization, while at the same time condemning the Communists as hypocrites who espoused rank and file democracy but embraced a form of party organization predicated on elite rule and enforcing obedience to dictates from Moscow.

With some exceptions, the politics of the third way fell on hard times in the 1920s. Arthur Mould, although not a veteran of the Winnipeg General Strike or the more extensive western Canadian labour revolt of 1919, maintained the integrity of the third way in the 1920s by seeking to preserve a worker-directed labour and socialist politics in southern Ontario that saw him launch searing critiques of both the Communist Party and reformist labour parties. In Winnipeg Russell, Houston, Woodward, and Lestor found some rootedness in the cause of the One Big Union. The situation was very different for Bill Pritchard and Ernest Winch, who in the 1920s tended to drift from job to job, with no long-standing involvement in any workforce or political movement. There was no longer a "centre" for them, because the working class itself seemed so fragmented, dispersed, disorganized, and disillusioned.

Even though Marxists of the third way directed their message almost entirely to the workers, their vision of socialist transformation was simply not feasible without the rise of "mental enlightenment" among non-working-class elements of society.[111] Who could or could not be a socialist was not bounded by class: this was a position that derived from a number of influential theorists. Antonio Labriola, for example, argued that only an "idiot" would believe that an individual's morality was a function of his or her economic position.[112] Enrico Ferrri argued that anyone could be a socialist, including members of the middle class and even aristocrats.[113] While Marxists of the third way espoused a Marxian theory of class struggle that saw the middle class as having little, if any, historical importance, their belief in the importance of individual conscience led them to seek the broadest possible audience for socialist ideas. In the years before 1919 Marxists of the third way directed their message exclusively to the wage workers, even though a number of leading members of organizations like the Socialist Party of Canada and the Social Democratic Party were professionals or small business people.[114] In the 1920s and 1930s, Marxists of the third way like Winch and Mould sought to build alliances with middle class socialists, "on strategic grounds as broadening the audience for socialist ideas."[115]

Yet they continued to believe, rightly or wrongly, that the leading role in any working class mobilization would have to be taken by the workers themselves. Like Karl Kautsky in Germany, they continued to defend Marx's original optimistic assessment of the leading role the workers would play in the revolution. This idealism on the part of Kautsky led him to insist again and again that the proletariat would not allow the victory of counter-revolutionary forces in Germany or Italy. Even after Hitler came to power in 1933 Kautsky continued to assert that the reaction could not be solidified.[116] Like Kautsky, Marxists of the third way in Canada believed that the workers themselves would respond to the challenge of fighting reaction and seek socialism under their own tutelage. Throughout the decade they waited for the mobilization of the workers, which would be the sign that revolutionary change was again on the agenda.[117]

The onset of the Depression in the early 1930s appeared to be what they were looking for and gave new life to Marxian socialists. Yet the responses of Marxists of the third way were many and varied. In Winnipeg the One Big Union was reinvigorated by its involvement with the unemployed and the railway workers who suffered a series of layoffs and wage cuts. Ernest Winch was a prime mover in British Columbia, spearheading the move to convert the Independent Labour Party to the Socialist Party of Canada (SPCBC). In June 1931 the Socialist Party of Canada was re-established in Winnipeg by George and Helen Armstrong, Alex Shepherd, Jim Milne, and Charles Lestor. Independent Marxists such as Mould, Elizabeth Morton, Bert Robinson, and Fred Hodgson formed the Ontario Socialist Party (OSP) in February 1932. More than twenty-five years after the formation of the original Socialist Party some of its members were thus still trying to create an alternative Marxist party. It was too little, too late, but on the eve of the formation of the Co-operative Commonwealth Federation and the long road to social democracy, they made their last stand.

Initially it appeared as if the creation of a nation-wide socialist party was possible. However, the movement found itself sandwiched between the twin pillars of communism and social democracy, its adherents pulled in one direction or the other. By the late 1930s it was no longer possible to establish an influential alternative Marxism on the Canadian left, although many Marxists of the third way continued to fight for their vision of socialism within the CCF, Communist Party, and various labour and socialist parties in Canada, the United States, and Great Britain. The One Big Union was unable to translate that involvement into a powerful movement. The old SPCers who refused to support either the CCF or the Communist Party struggled on in the Socialist Party of Canada, joined its sister parties in Great Britain or the United States, or forged linkages with the Trotskyist movement.

The Marxists who went into the CCF took a number of paths. Some left and joined the Communist Party. Some, like Winch, enjoyed long and distinguished careers as reformers in action, while insisting on maintaining Marxism as the party's theoretical base. Others, like Pritchard, left the CCF and later came to acknowledge that their support for the party had been a mistake. These "failures," however, have blinded historians to the fact that in the 1920s and 1930s these Marxists of the third way contributed important critiques of the economy and society of the Soviet Union and the economic and political policies of both the CCF and the Communist Party. With some exceptions – Pritchard, for example – they rejected the CCF's endorsement of government ownership or nationalization as state capitalism, the same analyis they applied to the political economy of the Soviet Union. In the late 1920s Marxists of the third way launched incisive critiques of socialists who endorsed nationalization, public ownership, and government ownership.[118]

Whatever may be said about Marxists of the third way, it cannot be argued they did not maintain an extremely critical and idealistic view of attempts to implement socialism. Even in their sometimes naive support of the Soviet Union they retained an informed critique of the specific mode of production in use there. Perhaps even more important, they remained incisive critics of excessively bureaucratic, top-down forms of socialism. They rarely succumbed to the technocratic, managerial ethos of Karl Kautsky, the right wing of the American Socialist Party, the Fabians, or the "brain trust" of the Co-operative Commonwealth Federation. They fought on in defence of worker self-emancipation and the dismantling of the capitalist state. They held to the Marx who opposed the division of human society into manual and mental workers, legitimating the class rule of a technocratic elite.

Against the background of political developments in the 1930s, and in particular the rise of fascism, they could not maintain their vision in practice. Neither the Communist Party nor the CCF was home for Marxists of the third way, but the alternatives were few. Following the Second World War, the third way became almost an impossibility in the era of the cold war. Yet a number of Marxists of the third way fought on for the politics they believed in, either as members of the CCF or Communist Party or as members of various Marxist and Trotskyist organizations. A lost cause? Perhaps, but history has not ended, claims to the contrary notwithstanding. The cause remains because capitalism remains, and as long as capitalism remains, the greatest fear of its defenders will remain the spectre of worker self-emancipation espoused by the Marxists of the third way you are about to meet.

1 Ernest Edward Winch: The Administrator of Class Struggle

The task Marxists of the third way set for themselves of facilitating the education and organization of the working class was a Herculean one. They had to contend with the hostility of the capitalist state and its allies in the government, press, and public institutions; they had to deal with numerous conflicts within the working class, most notably divisions between skilled and unskilled workers; and they had to fend off the attempts of employers, government officials, and press editors to convince workers that their best interests lay in serving the interests of capital. The fact that Marxists of the third way did not think of themselves as leaders did not change the fact that they often functioned as leaders. To do otherwise was to abandon the workers to both the allure and the iron heel of capitalism. In effect, Marxists of the third way engaged in a constant balancing act, attempting to guide without leading, advise without controlling, direct without dominating.

No better figure than Ernest Edward Winch can be found to illustrate the difficulties inherent in such a politics. By studying Winch's life on the Canadian left we are able to assess more thoroughly how effective Marxists of the third way were at involving rank and file workers in the process of creating a broad-based socialist movement, thereby putting their theory into practice. It is not a question of denying that Winch exhibited centralizing and authoritarian tendencies in his life as a labour leader and champion of socialism.[1] Rather, the purpose is to shift our attention away from the idea that this represented a "Marxist" type of behaviour to focusing on the real challenges facing Canadian socialists and labour leaders that made this choice one Winch felt he had to make. One of the key challenges of his life was, therefore, the attempt to find a way between abandoning the rank and file of the working class to the influence of the powerful forces of government, business, and media, and instituting in his own politics and practice the very authoritarian tendencies Marxists of the third way so strenuously opposed.

In the years 1910–40 Winch was one of the key figures in the labour and socialist movements in British Columbia, and he had a tremendous influence during that period in a number of left organizations. He was successively provincial secretary of the Social Democratic Party, secretary of the Auxiliary of the International Longshoremen's Association (ILA), president of the Vancouver Trades and Labour Council (VTLC), a leading member of the Socialist Party of Canada, secretary of the Loggers' and Camp Workers' Union (LCWU), a leading organizer of the Independent Labour Party, secretary and organizer of the Socialist Party of Canada (SPCBC) in the early 1930s, and a Co-operative Commonwealth Federation member of the B.C. provincial legislature for almost twenty-five years. His involvement in these organizations, often as the leading figure, provides clear evidence that the key members of the B.C. left were drawn from a relatively small pool. It serves as a reminder that although Marxists of the third way were committed to the education and self-organization of the working class, that emphasis really only bore fruit when these workers stepped into positions of power and responsibility. Marxism of the third way could only be realized when rank and file workers came forward to assume positions of leadership. When they did not, leadership inevitably devolved to a small group of men and women. Winch was one of that small group. In principle totally dedicated to rank and file participation and democracy, over the years he came to realize just how difficult that was in practice.

During the span of his career Winch was often accused of practising "machine politics," of controlling the supporters around him to ram through his own positions. He was also accused of taking the paying positions in unions and parties and jealously guarding them against all comers. He was, by all accounts, an "individualist" and a man who liked to get his own way. An understanding of theory and practice in his career hinges on the contradiction between his commitment to rank and file democracy and his apparently domineering and manipulative political practice. He was renowned, even into the 1950s, for his fiery revolutionary phraseology, defence of Marxism, espousal of class struggle, and insistence that he was but a humble servant of the working class. In practice, he often seemed much more concerned with promoting and controlling the particular party or union he was involved with at any given time – politics that usually led to an emphasis on reform, not revolution. He was committed to the creation of a socialist society, and selflessly dedicated much of his life to the working class of Canada. It is also true, however, that he liked to be in control, liked to be the centre of attention, and liked to be the one making the decisions. That contradiction is the measure of the man, and a key to understanding Marxists of the third way.

Ernest Edward Winch was born in Harlow, Essex, England, on 22 March 1879, the youngest of seven children. His mother, Emma, in addition to looking after her large family, was employed as a maid by the local squire.[2] The Winch home, a former Catholic charity building, was large and imposing. Pictures from the period indicate a well-dressed, well-cared-for family. Winch's later correspondence shows that he was close to his mother, brothers, and sister Carrie. He was born into the "labour aristocracy:"[3] his father, Charles, was a master bricklayer, as was his father before him.[4] Ernest went to a Church of England school, where he got a good basic education. He was by all appearances a Christian by belief if not by practice. When he left school he found a job as a railway ticket-office clerk, and in 1898 at the age of 19 emigrated to Canada.[5]

He came to Canada with knowledge of the bricklaying trade, but did not get to use it upon his arrival. He ended up in Churchbridge, Assiniboia, 250 miles northwest of Winnipeg. The farm work was back-breaking, and he left after two months to work for another employer. His brother Alfred joined him shortly after, and the two young men made their way to the West Coast.[6] In Vancouver Ernest held a number of jobs as a labourer, including the grading of Cordova Street. In his letters home he talked about doing temporary work as a carpenter, and helping to build a stone breakwater. He was employed in the Vancouver Club, perhaps as a busboy.[7] Afterwards he did some placer mining and prospecting in the Kootenay Mountains.[8]

Still young and unattached, he was not yet ready to call Canada home. In 1899 he went to Australia where he worked in the outback. Following a short stint there he returned home, where he learned the family business. In 1903 he went back to Australia, but sometime in 1904 or early 1905 he returned to England once more. In 1905 he married Linda Marian Hendy, who was born in Australia but raised in England. Shortly after Winch went into business for himself as a building contractor in the growing suburbs of London. He fell seriously ill, however, and lost the business. Tragedy struck the young Winch family in 1906 with the death of their infant son. Another son, Harold, was born in 1907, and a daughter Eileen was born in 1908.[9] In the fall of 1909 Winch left England alone to try his luck in Canada once more, to be followed some months later by his wife and young children.[10]

It was in 1910 that Winch began the long process of political education which would culminate in his involvement in the labour revolt of 1919. At the age of thirty-one, however, he had little, if any, background in trade unionism, socialist politics, or the study of Marxism. He came from Britain, but it was in Canada that he became fully conscious of himself as a member of the working class and began to understand and accept his links with his fellow workers and responsibilities to them. The most important changes involved his day-to-day observation of Vancouver's poor and unemployed, his first union experience, a change in his reading habits, encounters with socialist speakers, and the influence of persons he met in the labour and socialist movements.

In the late winter of 1909–10 Winch took a rather sudden turn toward socialist politics. In February 1910 he paid his initiation fee in the Bricklayers' Union. A letter he sent home at this time suggests that someone in the union convinced him to start thinking about getting involved in politics and helping society's disadvantaged. As a result, he suddenly switched from reading fiction to non-fiction. He began with a book called *The Evolution of the Japanese* but had difficulty concentrating on it.[11] He then read Robert Blatchford's classic *Merrie England*, which he found interesting but hard to follow.[12]

About this time as well he went to a socialist meeting in the City Hall. He was not impressed: he was "disgusted" by the speaker, who did not give "one single practical example of present day conditions & its cure." So incensed by the speaker's attack on religion was Winch that he wrote a letter to the Vancouver *Daily Province*, signed "AN EMBRYO SOCIALIST."[13] What the letter reveals is that Winch at this point was very much a temperate Christian.[14] His initial brush with socialism left him even more firm in his convictions: "Personally, I, a working man with a family, and who knows what it is to be down and out, would prefer to go through life working hard and yet poor, but holding to the faith that Christ, besides being the pattern for all Socialists, was before all the Son of God, rather than to live a life of ease and cheap notoriety by adopting a Socialism such as we heard at the city hall."[15] Clearly his pragmatism and Christian beliefs represented something much more profound at this point in time than a "superficial Tory crust."[16]

Although not specifically identified as a member of the Socialist Party of Canada, the speaker Winch heard was very likely from that party. Winch's initial revulsion would suggest that critics of the SPC are right to point out that such vitriolic speeches drove potential members away from the party. What is instructive in Winch's case, however, is that he had already made a commitment to socialism which was not deterred by his encounter with this particular speaker. He continued to go to socialist meetings and to read books related to the topic. He completed *Merrie England*, read a book he describes as *The State of Socialism in England* by Arnold Foster, and then began on Henry George.[17] His reaction to the speaker he heard at City Hall was not to abandon socialism entirely but rather to search for socialists who were concerned with present conditions and who were advocates of his personal understanding of the socialist cause.[18]

By the spring of 1910 Winch was already expressing interest in immediate reforms and taking the kind of socialist positions that led him to join the Social Democratic Party in 1911. Even in this earlier period he demonstrated the kind of concern with people in the here and now that would manifest itself so strongly in his career as a CCF member of the British Columbia legislature. Winch was primarily interested in the creation of a "Practical Programme," but socialist speakers did arouse his interest in the history of revolution. Prior to hearing socialist speakers his impressions of revolution had come from reading *A Tale of Two Cities*. Socialists introduced him to the Anabaptists, the French Revolution, and the Paris Commune, and he concluded that it was necessary "to study those three periods and see if they were satisfactory."[19] This practical rather than romantic view of revolution was reflected in his reaction to the ideas of a socialist acquaintance, whose opposition to all types of reform Winch considered to be "rot." In his view, there continued to be a great need for reforms.[20]

Winch's move to socialism does not appear to have been motivated by personal factors. Letters written to relatives at home during 1910 indicate a man not unhappy with his life. Since his arrival in Canada in 1898, he believed that wages for both skilled and unskilled workers were higher than in England. He thought there was "plenty of work" and was able to take advantage of his training as a bricklayer. In May he was building a brick kiln in New Westminster, and at other times did contracting work building chimneys. By October 1910 he was clearing trees on a quarter acre of land and building a house. There were now three Winch children, and Ernest Winch appeared to be a happy family man.[21]

Underneath the apparently calm exterior, however, Winch was rethinking his religious and political values, his economic situation, and his own role in society. By May 1910, mere months after his denunciation of sectarian socialism and his defence of Christ, he had begun seriously to question the existence of God and had become fed up with religious sectarianism and hypocrisy. He hinted at his impending acceptance of socialism in a letter to his brothers Walter and Alf: "I'm naturally inclined to get something in to my head & follow it out pretty hot without thinking to any great extent of the against side of the question."

As part of his transition from a Christian to a socialist perspective he began to see hell as something that was part of this earth. Where is hell? he asked: "I reckon some can tell us who are still rubbing shoulders against ours as we pass in the streets, for they are living in it."[22]

Winch's concern with the fate of his fellows was matched by the precariousness of his own economic situation. Wages in the lower mainland of British Columbia may have been relatively good, but that only mattered when you were actually employed. Work was seasonal in many occupations. In a letter written in the fall of 1909 Winch told his brother Alf that he had only worked eighteen hours that week.[23] A similar slowdown in the fall of 1910 may have led him to seek more permanent employment. On 6 December 1910 he withdrew from the Bricklayers' and Masons' International Union No. 1, perhaps to seek steadier, better-paid work elsewhere, perhaps because he could no longer afford the union dues.[24] In 1911 he shifted from wage labour to trying his hand at being an entrepreneur. The economy of British Columbia was in good shape, and Winch tried to make money building houses. The scheme was a fairly common one, whereby the builder constructed a house, mortgaged it, and used the money to build another house. It could all be quite lucrative, provided the payments were kept up on the first and then the ensuing mortgages. Winch did not make it work, however, and in the process lost his own house.[25]

More bad luck, or bad timing, followed him when he went back to England in 1912. Unable to make a go of the construction business there due to the pre-war depression, Winch returned again to British Columbia and took up residence in White Rock. He again tried the house-building scheme but defaulted on his mortgage with the Westminster Trust Company. According to Dorothy Steeves, the family was only saved from losing everything when the trust company took pity on Linda Winch and allowed the family to retain possession of one of the houses to live in.[26]

If Winch was rarely a success in business, he was almost always successful where his efforts to strengthen labour and socialist organizations were concerned. Interestingly, it was in the 1911–12 period, when he was self-employed, that he joined the Social Democratic Party. The SDP was originally formed in 1907 by Ernest and Bertha Merrill Burns, and ensued from Ernest Burns's expulsion from the Socialist Party of Canada.[27] The B.C. section did not have a significant impact on socialist politics on the coast, however, until the vast majority of SPC locals in Ontario broke away from the SPC, forming first the Canadian Socialist Federation, and then joining the Social Democratic Party.[28] The head office of the newly formed SDP was located in Berlin, Ontario, but the party became rejuvenated in far-away British Columbia as well.

The party was little more than a shell in the years 1907–11, but the provincial election of 1912 gave it two members in the B.C. legislature, former SPCers John Place and Parker Williams.[29] Prior to 1911–12 the SDP had drawn many of its members from the middle class and professions. According to Ernest Burns the SDP was reorganized in 1911, apparently with a view to increasing the working-class membership of the party.[30] Winch was one of those members from a working-class background. His concern with reform in the here and now and his tendency to see socialist and Christian values as complementary, not antagonistic, made him a more likely candidate for the SDP than for the SPC. It should be noted, however, that Burns himself considered Winch too radical and revolutionary for the SDP.[31]

Once Winch made the decision to become involved in socialist politics he plunged in with both feet. It is no coincidence that the SDP in British Columbia became a force to be reckoned with when Winch became one the party's leading proponents and organizers. By 1913 he was provincial secretary of the British Columbia SDP. He had become an active reader of *Cotton's Weekly*, the most widely read Canadian labour paper at that time. In the 1908–11 period, *Cotton's Weekly*, which has been described as "an independent organ of socialist commentary" in these years, was for all intents and purposes a Socialist Party of Canada paper which regularly published the party platform of the SPC.[32] Although *Cotton's Weekly* did become the organ of the SDP in 1911, it continued to feature numerous articles about Marxism and European socialism, and in all probability the Marxian socialism Winch learned from it pages influenced his later move to the Socialist Party of Canada.

Of more immediate import to Winch, however, was his involvement in the Social Democratic Party's attempt to convince the Socialist Party to dissolve itself into the younger organization. In the spring of 1911 the SPC was in crisis: in Ontario the party was ravaged when every local in the province except one or two left to join the SDP.[33] A majority of members in the Winnipeg locals of the SPC had already left to join the SDP, a decision officially taken on 24 July 1910.[34] The SDP was not long in seeking to take advantage of the SPC's weakened condition. In December 1912 the Woodstock, Ontario, branch of the SDP asked the SPC to send it fifty copies of the *Western Clarion* a week for one month.[35] The motivation behind the request is unclear, but it may have been part of an SDP attempt to find areas of common ground that could lead to a merger. The request was followed by a letter in the spring of 1913 from A. Jordan of the SDP, asking the SPC to hold a referendum on the question of uniting the two parties. Jordan stated, "I believe our differences are mostly imaginary."[36]

Jordan's initiative was later taken up by Winch. On 1 August 1914 a letter from him appeared in the *Western Clarion*, in which he informed the SPC that at the SDP's recent convention the membership had voted in favour of amalgamating with the SPC. Secretary J.H. Burrough responded, categorically rejecting the overtures.[37] The SPC's outward display of bravado notwithstanding, the offer must have been attractive to many members of the party. At the British Columbia SDP Annual Convention on 1 May 1914 Winch reported that the number of locals had increased 50 per cent and the membership by 125 per cent, presumably in the last year. Even at this early point in his socialist life, however, Winch recognized that numbers did not mean much in the absence of a "sound and clear understanding of Marxian economics and social questions," and the ability to spread that knowledge to the public.[38] Although he was a member of the SDP on the eve of the First World War, his insistence that Marxist education and the key role a socialist party plays in providing that education were more important than numbers placed him very close to the thinking of the Socialist Party.

By the end of the First World War Winch had decided that the Socialist Party was the key vehicle of Marxist education, but on the eve of that war he preferred politics that were practical and local, not international and revolutionary. In January 1914 he ran for councillor and school trustee in Ward 6 in Burnaby. His platform was essentially labourist and called for the public ownership of all public utilities, the initiative, referendum, and recall, and scientific accounting, efficiency, and "fullest public service" in government. Nominated by the SDP, Winch ensured his defeat by calling for sex education and stood on a platform advocating "Equal pay for equal work, irrespective of sex." Given that women were disfranchised in municipal elections, his campaign might best be described as suicidal.[39] It does demonstrate, however, that it took tremendous courage and principle for socialist men, their own sexism notwithstanding, to defend the rights of women, and call for changed attitudes toward sexuality, before a largely male, property-based electorate.

Winch's misfortunes at the local level were matched by the troubled state of the Social Democratic Party at the provincial level. Within months of the outbreak of war the fortunes of the Social Democratic Party changed for the worse. The war put tremendous pressure on both the SPC and SDP, opposed as they were to capitalist war and imperialism, and in favour of international working class solidarity. In the event, however, the SDP was much less successful than the SPC in maintaining the rank and file's adherence to that politics. In early to mid-October there were some 675 members in British Columbia's SDP. One month later there were only 450 members, a decrease of 225.

H. Martin, secretary of the SDP's Dominion Executive Committee, blamed the decline on unemployment and lack of funds.[40] That was part of the problem, but there can be little doubt that the primary factor was members abandoning the socialist position on the war.[41]

Ernest Winch had been quite successful in improving the fortunes of the Social Democratic Party, but by the fall of 1914 he did not have much to show for it. In spite of his foray into local politics, and his leading role in the SDP, he had slowly but surely been moving to the left in the years before the war. This leftward shift was strongly motivated by the depression that had hit Vancouver in 1913, leaving a situation Winch called "damnable." Writing to his brother Alf in the spring of 1913, he observed that he was already on his third job of the year. The influence of the SDP/SPC emphasis on Marxism emerges from his comments to Alf in reference to his brother Walter that "WW is still considerably at sea as to economics & the Scientific basis of Socialism ... we must hope that his Socialism of the Heart will in due time develop into True Socialism that of the head."[42] Even by the spring of 1913, therefore, when the fortunes of the SDP looked very bright, Winch was already well on his way to endorsing the scientific socialism of the Socialist Party of Canada.

On the eve of the First World War Winch was intolerant of those, including his own brother, who failed to recognize the need for "scientific socialism," yet his own political ideas and beliefs were drawn rather haphazardly from Christian and Marxist, evolutionary and revolutionary thinking. His membership in the SDP and his espousal of the scientific socialism of the SPC are indicative of the problems inherent in identifying the thinking of Marxian socialists in this period with the platforms of the organizations they belonged to at any given time. One characteristic of Marxists of the third way was seeing evolution and revolution as existing in a dialectical relationship, while in practice it was necessary to belong to either the "revolutionary" and "impossibilist" SPC, or "evolutionary" and "reformist" SDP. Ernest Winch's politics as war began were typical of many Marxian socialists whose beliefs did not conform easily with either option.

In his daily life, however, Winch was faced with a more immediate dilemma: how to maintain a family and his political activism on behalf of the working class on the earnings of a wage worker. Influenced perhaps by disappointment about the election results, or the impermanence of his employment, or the precipitous decline in SDP membership, Winch made yet another attempt to go into business for himself. In 1915 he moved to the Dewdney area, where he and a partner set up a business making shingles. Once more things did not go well, and Winch was forced to give it up; his partner stayed at it and did well.

While he was there Winch organized a local of the SDP in Mission, which nominated him to run in the provincial election of 1916. He left the area before the September vote, however, and gave up his candidacy.[43]

Winch returned to a Vancouver in which the importance of shipping war materials had greatly increased the demand for workers on the waterfront. Shortly before his return the longshoremen had won a wage increase that placed them among the better-paid workers on the coast. Winch was unable to join the International Longshoremen's Association, which was well organized and protected the jobs of its members, but did go into its Auxiliary, Local 38–52 of the Marine Warehousemen & Freight Handlers' Union. Although members of the Auxiliary were "longshoremen," they did not perform the same jobs or enjoy the same status as members of the main union. Longshoremen worked between the ships and the sheds, the Auxiliary workers between the sheds and the rail cars. J.S. Woodsworth, who was signed into the Auxiliary by Winch, wrote a short book about his experiences called *On the Waterfront*.[44] In it he described how members of the Auxiliary often stood for long hours in the cold and rain before getting a day's or even a few hours' work. Often they got no work at all. The longshoremen disdained working on the river barges, which were unloaded by the Auxiliary members; when work was in short supply, however, the longshoremen took precedence over Auxiliary members and were entitled to replace them. Needless to say, it was a daunting task for Marxian socialists and labour leaders such as Winch, Jack Kavanagh, and Bill Pritchard to forge a sense of labour solidarity in such a factious workforce.

By the summer of 1917 Winch was secretary and business agent of the Longshoremen's Auxiliary, and therefore entitled to delegate status on the Vancouver Trades and Labour Council.[45] In spite of his inexperience as both a longshoreman and a union leader, he proved immediately effective during the longshoremen's strike of July 1917. At the VTLC meeting of 19 July he reported that valuable concessions had been won by the ILA Auxiliary, and that the organization was growing rapidly.[46] In a letter back home he noted that prior to the strike the employers had offered 38 cents an hour for regular time and 50 cents an hour for overtime, the Auxiliary responding with a demand for 45 cents and 64 1/2 cents. When the union demands were refused, the ILA went on strike for a week and the Auxiliary followed with a spontaneous strike. The longshoremen emerged successful, and the employers agreed to go higher than 38 and 50 cents for the Auxiliary.[47]

Winch's return to Vancouver launched him not only into the affairs of the longshoremen but into national political questions as well. At a meeting of the Vancouver Trades and Labour Council in early July he seconded a motion to elect a committee to act to organize the anti-conscription forces of Vancouver.[48] He had returned to a Vancouver district very different from the one he had left less than two years before. The conscription issue was heating up, with organized labour across Canada disputing the need to conscript labour when the enormous profits made by war profiteers were not being conscripted. The Sunday evening meetings of the Socialist Party of Canada were now drawing thousands of workers to hear orators such as Bill Pritchard and Jack Kavanagh condemn the master class and call for militant action, most notably the general strike. Not all unions favoured the general strike option, but the Vancouver Trades and Labour Council agreed with the SPC's stand on conscription and agreed to put a general strike vote to the membership of affiliated unions.

In September 1917 Winch followed up his involvement in the longshoremen's strike and his support for the mobilization of the anti-conscription forces with an important contribution to the general strike debate. Prior to the British Columbia Federation of Labour (BCFL) Convention in September the VTLC had held a general strike vote, in which forty out of two hundred unions had taken part. Members in these forty unions had voted 1,841 in favour and 576 against calling the strike. Not willing to act on such a mandate, the VTLC referred the general strike question to the BCFL Convention. Winch claimed that he had come to the convention with instructions, presumably from the leadership of the Longshoremen's Union, to oppose the general strike. Winch, who believed that members who had not voted should be considered opposed to the strike, seemed to agree with that decision, even though the sentiment of those Auxiliary members who did vote was overwhelmingly in favour of it.[49]

Given his increasingly radical language at this time, his decision to act cautiously raises legitimate doubts about his motivation. One quite reasonable conclusion is that he had found yet another way to match his revolutionary rhetoric with reformist practice. On the other hand, it can be argued that his stance was a product of Marxism of the third way's genuine desire that all rank and file workers should have the opportunity to directly participate in radical change. In addition, many Marxian socialists, Winch included, remained rather ambivalent about general strikes, even during the labour revolt of 1919. Marxists of the third way supported industrial unionism and the general strike as a response to the repression of the capitalist state and the mobilization of the rank and file workers, but they were sceptical about its long-term benefits. The general strike raised in a very acute form the problem of when to act in the name of the working class, and when to act on the strictest adherence to rank and file democracy.

Some Marxists of the third way favoured the former approach, and some leaned toward the latter.

In the hurly-burly of day-to-day union activity, even honest efforts to act in the best interests of the working class could appear as dishonesty, hypocrisy, weakness, or lack of principle. Winch's advancement in the B.C. labour movement was rapid, but not as smooth or as quick as he might have liked, perhaps because his fellow trade unionists were also unsure of where he stood on the question of the general strike. In spite of the rise to prominence of the Longshoremen, reflected in the VTLC elections of January 1918, Winch himself did not benefit. On 17 January Gordon J. Kelly of the ILA was elected president of the VTLC, and Winch was defeated in the race for vice-president by F. Welsh of the Plumbers' Union. Winch also ran for secretary, but lost to Fred Knowles of the Letter Carriers. Also one of fourteen people who ran for four positions on the board of trustees, Winch was not elected for that position either.[50]

Not to be denied, he tried again for an executive position at the convention of the British Columbia Federation of Labour at the end of January. His persistence paid off, as he and W.R. Trotter were elected vice-presidents of the BCFL for Vancouver. Winch was immediately faced with a major decision affecting his class politics when the BCFL convention voted in favour of creating the Federated Labour Party (FLP). This organization was part of the same late war attempt to forge a broad electoral opposition to the Canadian government which saw the formation of the Canadian Labour Party in 1917 and the Dominion Labour Party in Manitoba in 1918. Legendary SPCer E.T. Kingsley became a party vice-president, and fellow party members J.H. McVety, R.P. Pettipiece, and A.S. Wells also joined. Former SPCers Dr W.J. Curry and J.H. Hawthornthwaite also threw in their lot with the new party. The platform of the new organization was essentially radical, and its parliamentary focus did not represent an essential break with the SPC past. However, when Hawthornthwaite stated that the FLP should not be a strictly labour organization but rather a party of all classes, he established a clear break with the working-class based Marxism of the Socialist Party.[51] Support for the creation of the FLP at the BCFL convention was overwhelming, delegates voting eighty-two in favour and eleven against, with fifteen abstentions. Voting against the formation of the FLP were SPCers Joe Naylor and Ginger Goodwin. Winch joined them in the minority opposition, thereby signalling to the B.C. labour movement his immediate political future on the B.C. left.[52]

His support for revolutionary industrial unionism and his uncompromising opposition to the capitalist class, both in evidence by early 1918, did not impede and may have aided his rise to prominence in the ensuing months. After being defeated in three separate VTLC elections in January 1918, he was elected president of the council on 18 July 1918. The contest was extremely close, however. Winch actually tied for the position but won because of the VTLC's system of voting based on proportional representation.[53] At his first meeting as president on 1 August he set the tone for the labour upheaval to come, stating that "he was particularly pleased that the council had elected officers who were uncompromising in their attitude to the capitalist class."[54]

Winch now bore little resemblance to the man who had slammed B.C. socialists and defended Christ in 1910. How had this transformation come about? How had he become president of the VTLC when there were many older and longer-serving B.C. labour figures? Call it ambition, call it intuition, call it opportunism, but Ernest Winch had an uncanny ability to be in the right place at the right time. Stan Lefeaux, who first met him in 1918, found him domineering and did not have too much use for him.[55] Ernest Burns, possibly the person who convinced Winch to join the Social Democratic Party, considered him "an individualist who always wanted his own way."[56] Perhaps assessments of Ernest Winch's importance in this period have been influenced by opinions such as these, and perhaps as well the fact that Winch was not a great platform speaker has influenced how he has been remembered. Old SPCers later recalled E.T. Kingsley, Bill Pritchard, Jack Kavanagh, Charles Lestor, and others as being key members of the party, but Winch's name rarely came up. He did not actually join the SPC until 1918 and gave his first speech under its auspices on 6 October of that year.

Yet even people who found him personally hard to get along with could not help admiring his tremendous administrative, secretarial, and organizational abilities. Helena Gutteridge remembered him as an excellent organizer and administrator, and Stan Lefeaux, who disliked him personally, remembered him as a hard worker. He was also a very generous man and not without courage. Burns recalled that Winch jeopardized his own job to get Pritchard and himself into the Longshoremen's Union.[57] Helena Gutteridge recalled that Winch, in spite of his own family's poverty, collected money for Pritchard's wife and children while Pritchard was in prison following the Winnipeg General Strike.[58]

Winch could also handle a crisis, and two weeks after he became VTLC president the Ginger Goodwin general strike gave him his chance to show it. Goodwin had been a miner in Cumberland and had then gone on to become an organizer for the Trail Smeltermen's Union. He was originally declared unfit for the draft because he had tuberculosis, but when he became active as a union organizer he was re-classified.

Like many workers of the day, Goodwin responded to the draft by taking to the woods. While living in the bush back of Cumberland he ran into Constable Dan Campbell, who was searching the area for draft evaders. What ensued is unclear, but B.C. labour has always argued that Goodwin was murdered. Predictably, Campbell was fully exonerated of any wrongdoing.[59]

The effect of Goodwin's shooting was electric. There were immediate calls in Vancouver for a one-day general strike, and on 2 August 1918 many B.C. unionists came out. The reaction of the anti-labour returned soldiers was equally swift. Some three hundred of them marched on the Labour Temple, smashed windows and doors, and destroyed books and furniture. In the most famous incident Victor Midgley was made to kneel and kiss the flag. The returned soldiers, Mayor Gale, and the Chamber of Commerce then demanded that Pritchard, Kavanagh, Winch, Midgley, Joe Naylor, Ernie Cotterell, and George Thomas leave the city until the war was over.

Perhaps because he had been warned ahead of time, Winch was not at the Labour Temple when the mob got there. The next day, however, the returned soldiers marched on the Longshoremen's Hall; getting hold of Winch was likely one of their objectives. Following a violent clash between soldiers and workers in which chair legs were used, Winch and a committee met with A.J. Devereaux, spokesperson for the returned men. Devereaux demanded that the seven labour leaders leave the city and argued that the radical leaders did not have the support of the rank and file. He told Winch that the VTLC should be able only to endorse, not recommend, strike action and that "action by labor itself must result from instructions of the rank and file of labor." There seemed to be a conscious attempt on Devereaux's part to render labour's leadership ineffective by manipulating its own stated belief in rank and file control. Winch was sensitive to the charge but was not about to see labour stripped of its leaders. He pointed out that the VTLC had voted 110 to one for the strike and that "while he was prepared as an individual to accept the responsibility of any views he held or action he took, still he was certain that organized labor would refuse to allow their executive officers to be penalized for carrying out the duties of their office."[60]

Winch's decision to put the question to a vote of the membership resulted in a special meeting of the VTLC. New elections were held, and almost all the old officers were returned. Fortified by this display of labour solidarity, Winch's inaugural address as president of the VTLC called for the six-hour day, five-day week in response to the influx of returning veterans. He also called for a switch from craft to industrial unionism. In March 1919 both proposals would be advocated by delegates to the Western Labour Conference in favour of organizing the One Big Union.[61]

By now we can see the kind of approach Winch took to the question of organizing a radical labour movement. He pointed out at the 3 August meeting that the VTLC was an administrative body with no power to call strikes, only to recommend action. However, as he maintained in his discussions with Devereaux, the leadership could not be restricted to merely endorsing strikes. He hoped that labour would soon dispense with labour leaders and "substitute officials and representatives who shall execute instructions and not define policy."[62] In the meantime, however, labour leaders had to have some ability to interpret what was in the best interests of the working class; hence the role of leaders and the party. Marxists of the third way were quite conscious of the relationship between party, leaders, and class, and attempts to portray them as part of a conspiratorial elite or as hopeless romantics with no sense of purpose are equally mistaken.[63] Winch's dealings with Devereaux and the returned soldiers demonstrates quite clearly that he was aware of the difficulties involved in maintaining rank and file democracy in the labour movement while ensuring that the workers were not left leaderless and defenceless against the powerful forces arrayed against them.

At some point during 1918 Winch gave up his membership in the Social Democratic Party and became a member of the Socialist Party of Canada. He had been moving into the radical camp since the summer of 1917, when he returned to Vancouver and joined the Longshoremen's Union. It was not until the fall of 1918, however, that he first spoke publicly on the platform of the Socialist Party. On this occasion he confirmed his position on the relationship between the party and the rank and file, arguing that it was the SPC that represented the true interests of the working class, and telling his audience that workers had to be class conscious.[64] In the event, however, he never became directly involved in the activities of the Socialist Party, his interests and talents tending more toward union organizing in this period.

As it turned out, his membership in the Longshoremen's Union was shortly to end. British Columbia, and indeed many areas of the world, were hit hard by an outbreak of Spanish influenza in 1918–19. In Vancouver and environs it struck the Longshoremen's Union particularly hard, one victim being Gordon J. Kelly, president of the Longshoremen's Pacific Coast District Council. Winch was one of the pallbearers at Kelly's funeral on 13 November 1918.[65] Winch, a physical culturist who ate what a later generation would call health food, was very conscious of his health, and he may have been frightened by the effects of the disease on the longshoremen.[66] Whatever his reasons for leaving the ILA, Winch was not long away from labour organizing. By January 1919 he was heavily involved with the B.C. Loggers' and Camp Workers' Union as secretary-treasurer. Over the traditional Christmas break in the coast logging industry Birt Showler and Helena Gutteridge had organized eight hundred loggers in Vancouver. They set up an office and an executive committee, including Winch, was elected.[67] Winch had a good reputation as an organizer and secretary, and his salary, at $50 a week, suggested that his abilities were appreciated.[68]

The creation of the union was a major accomplishment, because all earlier attempts to organize the loggers on a permanent basis had proven futile. The Industrial Workers of the World had some success in the years just before the First World War, but nothing lasting had come of it. In 1917 the Timberworkers' Union, affiliated with the American Federation of Labor, had tried again, but with no real success. The British Columbia Federation of Labour launched the next attempt in 1918. It was not much more successful until Showler and Gutteridge, who were members of the Federated Labour Party, organized the LCWU in January 1919.

The obstacles facing any attempt to organize the loggers were daunting. There were 270 logging camps on the coast, with many more located in B.C.'s interior.[69] Most of the interior loggers came from the prairies and were often farmers and their sons who worked in the bush during the winter months and then returned to the farm in the spring. Because they were not full-time bushworkers, the interior workers were transient and extremely difficult to organize. The coast workers were also transient, but many of them were full-time bushworkers with ongoing ties to Vancouver, where the hiring was done. Unemployed workers gathered there, as did employed workers during the breaks for Christmas and in July. They got together and discussed grievances, prospects for the coming season, and the desirability of forming a union.

By 1919–20 several factors made organizing the coast loggers more viable. The lumber industry was booming, with output peaking in 1920 at two billion board feet. Wages rose by about 50 per cent between 1915 and 1920, but inflation ate away the increase. The rise in wages also did not match the rise in lumber prices. Lumber companies were now larger and more impersonal; the old paternalist relationship between employer and employee was largely gone, and labour organizers were able to get an audience in isolated lumber camps.[70] The key issue, however, was camp conditions: poor ventilation, improper toilet facilities, lice-infested bedding, two-tiered bunk beds, and lack of medical supplies and care. It was also an issue affecting all workers, regardless of job, age, religion, or ethnic group. Another important factor, often overlooked by historians of the loggers' union, was the deportation of members of the Industrial Workers of the World from the United States. In 1917 Bill Haywood and 165 other members of the IWW were charged with criminal conspiracy in Chicago; among those charged was Harry Allman, who was deported to Canada and went on to become an organizer for the LCWU.[71]

Once the initial organizing work had been done and Winch took up his post as LCWU secretary, the new union grew by leaps and bounds. Membership in the union continued to grow at an incredible rate, hitting eight thousand by the summer of 1919. At the LCWU convention in Vancouver in July delegates decided to join the recently organized One Big Union. Instantly the LCWU, now called the Lumber Workers' Industrial Union (LWIU), became the most important union in the OBU and its greatest source of funds. While this was good news for the One Big Union, affiliation of the LCWU brought jurisdictional disputes and controversy concerning the proper form of organization. Already in April 1919 the LCWU had moved beyond organizing loggers and begun to organize construction workers. Harry Allman and several other LCWU members were leaders of a strike against construction companies in the Princeton area. A week after the strike started the men voted to join the loggers' union, with the understanding that they would later join the appropriate section of the One Big Union when it was organized.[72] The seeds of conflict were sown, and Winch, a leading exponent of the One Big Union, was about to find himself at the centre of several debates crucial to the future of Canadian labour and left politics.

By the spring of 1919 he had become one of the key figures in the coast labour and socialist movements. Not only was he re-elected president of the Vancouver Trades and Labour Council by acclamation but he was now secretary-treasurer of the fastest growing union in the country. His importance in the 1918–19 period has sometimes been underestimated because he did not take part in the Western Labour Conference held in Calgary in March 1919, at which the decision was taken to found the One Big Union. Thus he is rarely credited with being a founder of the OBU, although he was a fervent supporter and a paid-up member until December 1921.[73] He had been elected by the loggers' union to attend the convention, but he stayed in Vancouver to work on union business. The LCWU delegates who did go – Harry Allman, Tom Mace, and Alex Mackenzie – heralded the problems the OBU would later have in creating a viable organizational structure. Allman, a member of the IWW, would be fighting tooth and nail against Winch before the year was out. Mace, a very active OBU supporter, started out as LCWU organizer in the Prince George district and

Ernest Winch
Photo courtesy of University of British Columbia Special Collections

afterwards moved to Winnipeg where he became business manager of the OBU *Bulletin*. Mackenzie, LCWU organizer for the Kamloops district, was a Marxist theoretician and member of the SPC.

While Allman, Mace, and Mackenzie prepared for their journey to Calgary, Winch's espousal of revolutionary politics was attracting the attention of the capitalist press. An editorial in the Vancouver *Daily Sun* placed the VTLC president in exalted company by stating that he was "just as much the enemy of organized society as Lenine or Trotsky were till they seized authority themselves."[74] Five days later a letter to the editor entitled "An Insult to Socialism" described Winch in the following manner: "puffed up with the glory of his position, he seeks notoriety, and the pity of it is, he gets it." The author was obviously disturbed by the "colossal gall" of this anarchist claiming to be a socialist.[75] While the charge of anarchist was more than a little off the mark, Winch's rhetoric had begun to disturb even some of his fellow unionists and socialists. His resolute critique of capitalism earned him the criticism of VTLC delegates Welsh and Pritchard, who argued that Winch was providing employers with the ammunition they needed to portray the Vancouver working class as dominated by extremists. Jack

Kavanagh came to Winch's defence, claiming that the capitalist system not Ernest Winch, had created the class struggle. Winch could not be condemned, therefore, for simply stating the truth.[76] Winch defended himself by returning to the question of the relationship between leaders and followers. He reiterated his belief that the initiative in the battle against the capitalist system should come from the rank and file, but that as long as he remained in a position of authority he had the right to act according to his wishes. If the rank and file did not like what he was doing, then it was up to them to remove him.[77]

The growing assertiveness in his position propelled him to the forefront of the unfolding national labour upheaval that began to impinge on labour and politics in British Columbia in the spring and summer of 1919. On 15 May 1919 the Winnipeg General Strike began, and there were insistent calls on the coast for a sympathetic strike. What the Mounties called the "extremist faction" – Winch, Pritchard, Kavanagh, and Midgley – were caught off guard with no clearly thought-out plan of action. On 21 May 1919 the local superintendent wrote to the commissioner in Regina that the Vancouver labour leaders were "awaiting developments, holding themselves in readiness to jump into the fray, but hoping not to be called upon until the organization of the O.B.U. is completed."[78] On 27 May 1919 Special Agent No. 24 reported that Winch, Kavanagh, Midgley, and Pritchard were not personally in favour of a strike.[79]

The Mounties, however, believed that there was a great deal of radicalism at the rank-and-file level. Winch appeared to realize it as well. Inspector A.H. Vernon observed that the loggers and longshoremen advocated "stern measures," and Winch addressed them accordingly.[80] A week later special agents reported that members of the B.C. Ex Soldiers' and Sailors' Council had posted handbills in logging camps urging the loggers to create a Soviet-style government. Referring to these members as "Winch's rabble," the agents expressed concern that they could cause "much harm" by drawing veterans into the organization.[81]

Rather than clearing up some of the questions surrounding the events of 1919 in Vancouver, these reports tend to further confuse the issue. Why, for example, are members of the Soldiers' and Sailors' Council identified as being led by Winch? These same special agents would at the end of June also describe members of the Longshoremen's Union as "good Winch men."[82] Why was this designation used when Winch was no longer a member of the ILA, and Kavanagh, another radical, still was? There are no references in the reports of the Mounties and special agents to "good Pritchard men" or "good Kavanagh men." One part of the answer is that Winch was a man who tended to develop a large personal following in the organizations where he worked, and may have had that kind of following among the longshoremen. Another part is that Winch's rhetoric, and the response of the Vancouver press, likely led the Mounties and their agents to exaggerate his personal influence. This was certainly the case with the returned soldiers. Kavanagh, who had been in the British army for twelve years, was more involved with and better known by the returned soldiers than was Winch. The same might also be said of Charles Lestor, whose interest in the veterans may have been motivated by the fact that his son had been wounded in the war.[83]

The mistaken impressions of the Mounties notwithstanding, Winch's leading role in the loggers' union and his presidency of the Vancouver Trades and Labour Council most certainly made him an influential figure on the B.C. left. It also placed him in a rather awkward position. The contradictions were revealed at the meeting of the Trades and Labour Council on 29 May. When a number of loggers in attendance attempted to get representation on the strike committee they were told that they already had representation in the form of Winch and Victor Midgley.[84] The problem was that neither Winch nor Midgley was a logger, and had no first-hand knowledge of the situation in the camps. As a representative of the loggers Winch really had no basis on which to make a decision about the general strike and essentially took his stand as president of the VTLC. He therefore opposed an immediate strike in the camps and favoured taking a vote of the membership. Given that the vote could take two weeks, the strike might be over for the loggers before it had even begun. One logger at the meeting concluded that a general strike without the loggers was not a general strike at all.[85]

How could Winch, let alone the rest of the VTLC, even contemplate a "general" strike without the loggers, possibly the most radical union in British Columbia at that moment? There are four possible reasons, two theoretical and two pragmatic. On the theoretical level, the resolution adopted at the 29 May meeting explicitly recognized that capitalism was not yet at an end. The "extremist faction" knew that they were operating in a non-revolutionary situation. Why risk the tremendous growth of the loggers' union, as well as the chances for success of the One Big Union, in a general strike they believed could not be won? It may also be significant that Winch was not at the Western Labour Conference where some Marxian socialists called on delegates to accept adopting radical action with the support of the "active minority" in the labour movement. Had he been in Calgary he might have been more willing to call out the loggers without holding a referendum of the entire membership. On a more pragmatic level, there were two further factors. The first was timing. It made sense to hold off until late

June or early July when the coastal logging camps traditionally shut down for repairs and the loggers made their way to Vancouver. With the loggers in Vancouver, the general strike would be much more effective. The problem was that if they waited, the Winnipeg General Strike might already be over. The leaders of the B.C. socialist movement would have had great difficulty initiating a strike in sympathy with the Winnipeg strikers if the latter strike were already over.

Attempting to decipher Winch's motives in May and June 1919 is further complicated by the observations of the Mounties and the special agents. A report on the period 27–29 May concluded that Winch, Midgley, Pritchard, and Kavanagh were doing everything possible to get the workers to endorse the strike, including manipulating votes. The report also noted that Winch was "noticeably active in this work."[86] This report notwithstanding, there is no hard evidence to suggest that the "extremist faction" was engaging in any activity beyond the usual pressure tactics and manoeuvring which always characterized union politics.[87] Overt manipulation would have been inconsistent with the actions of Winch and the VTLC in 1917, when they refused to act on an overwhelming vote in favour of the general strike because a majority of rank-and-file unionists had not voted. In addition, even the RNWMP reports indicate that significant segments of the rank and file were more, not less, militant than the leadership. The activities of the strike leaders should be attributed to indecision and lack of planning, not malicious intent or a desire to misdirect the rank and file.

Winch's actions as secretary of the LWIU can also be explained. He was a Marxist at this time but a Marxist whose actions derived more from the day-to-day demands of labour organizing than from a theoretically driven commitment to revolutionary politics. Given the choice to go to the Western Labour Conference in 1919 or stay in Vancouver to work on union business, he stayed in Vancouver. He took a proprietary, protective attitude toward the unions and socialist parties he was involved in. In the summer of 1919 he was not willing to risk the upsurge in membership and radicalization of the loggers by immediately calling a strike with dubious prospects for success. More so than many other Marxists of the third way, Winch's interests were local and organizational, not international and political.[88] He was most definitely not a dogmatic, anti-union theorist divorced from the real world of labour politics.

His attitude toward the loggers' union was matched by the attitude of the strike leadership toward the sympathetic strikes and the One Big Union. As the Mounties were aware, OBU leaders in both Vancouver and Winnipeg saw the 1919 labour revolt as a potential threat, or at least obstacle, to the OBU's national success. They continued to be in the SPC tradition, believing that the key to overthrowing capitalism was education and organization. They were not syndicalists and did not agree with the syndicalists that a classless society could emerge from a localized strike evolving into a general strike. The revolution they envisioned occurred as much in the mind as on the picket line. To Winch the loggers, who had just begun to organize six months before, could not possibly be educated enough about the class struggle to launch an effective challenge to the capitalist system.

The events of the sympathetic strike in Vancouver and the actions of Winch must also be understood in terms of the political economy of British Columbia. Unlike Winnipeg where wages, working conditions, and collective bargaining rights were all central issues in both the metal trades and the building trades, there was less unity in various Vancouver and B.C. trades concerning the essential strike issues. Beyond sympathy with the Winnipeg strikers, there was little to unify them which arose from worker-capitalist relations on the coast. The years of socialist education were very important in maintaining a sense of class consciousness, but it could only carry the radicals so far, given the objective material conditions on the coast. The contradictory stances of the leadership, alternating between strident revolutionary positions and vacillation, was a product of a rank and file that shared that contradictory position as well.

During the course of the actual Vancouver sympathy strike, which lasted from 1 June to 3 July 1919, Winch literally disappeared from view. It is true that he was tied up with his work as secretary of the loggers' union, but it is also possible, given the dispute that took place at the 29 May meeting and the closeness of the vote, that he did not fully support the strike. There is even the possibility of a serious split between Winch and the rest of the VTLC over the loggers' role in the sympathetic strike. Otherwise it is difficult to explain why Winch disappeared from the pages of the *BC Federationist* in the month of June, even in reports on the loggers' union.[89] As president of the VTLC, however, and a member of the SPC, he garnered a great deal of attention from the police. On or about 30 June his house was raided by the Mounties.[90] Although a traumatic experience for Linda and their children, it was less so for Winch himself, because he knew the officers involved. According to Dorothy Steeves, he even made tea for them while they were conducting their search.[91]

Winch escaped the fate of his fellow Marxian socialists in Winnipeg, and following the end of the Vancouver strike he was back working hard to keep up with LWIU business. Camp delegates were sending in a steady stream of memberships, and strikes were breaking out all up and down the coast. There were thirty-one strikes in the camps in 1919, with fifty more to follow in 1920.[92] By April 1919 there were

150 members carrying delegates' credentials, and Winch described the camp delegate system as "the most vital factor contributing to the success of the organization." The system delivered into the hands of the workers a union in which Winch claimed there were no leaders or followers. It was up to the workers, he said, to write the laws and enforce them at the point of production.[93]

The camp delegate system was nothing new – it had been used by the IWW for many years in both Canada and the United States. However, both Winch and Bill Pritchard, editor of the *Camp Worker*, identified the system with the British Shop Stewards' movement, not the IWW.[94] Pritchard observed in the pages of the *Camp Worker* that the "camp delegate, as existing in the B.C. Loggers and Camp Workers' Union, is identical with the shop steward acting in the vast shops and shipbuilding plants of the Clydebank."[95] The system was essentially a reaction against the growth of trade union bureaucracy, which took the control of strikes out of the hands of the workers most closely involved and delayed decisions about strike action, sometimes for months at a time. The development of organization and quick-fire decision-making in the local context seemed perfect for the lumber workers. Characteristically, however, Pritchard went on to link organization in the camps with education, stating that "Organization without education is no organization at all. Education of the right kind makes for organization of the right kind." Winch's and Pritchard's endorsement of the camp delegate system was not "syndicalist" and did not imply support for the IWW as an organization, but they shared with the Wobblies Marxism of the third way's opposition to trade union bureaucracy and belief in educating and organizing the rank and file workers.[96]

In spite of charges that Winch himself was a trade union bureaucrat, he appears to have been sincere in his commitment to rank and file control. During a logging camp strike in Port Alberni in August 1919, the owner, a Mr Dent, contemplated bringing in strikebreakers. Before he did that, however, he went to Vancouver to see if Winch supported the actions of the men in the camps. Winch was in White Rock when he arrived, but a man at the office told him they would support a worker takeover of the camp. When Dent got hold of Winch on Monday, 5 August, the LWIU secretary said that he supported any action the men wanted to take.[97] The response of the Mounties to this incident was revealing: Inspector Newson concluded that the ultimate aim of the LWIU "appears to be that of taking over the various industries when they feel they are strong enough to do so."[98] The superintendent of "E" Division was even more forthright, telling the Commissioner that "it would appear that nothing short of taking over the means of production will satisfy them."[99]

As it turned out, of course, these fears were exaggerated. The Mounties knew that the threat was not isolated strikes but rather a general understanding in the working class as a whole of the need for working-class control of the means of production. Not only the Mounties but B.C. lumbermen as well began to recognize the threat and how to deal with it. By December 1919 the employers in B.C. had become shocked out of their complacency by the series of strikes hitting their camps, and they entered into an agreement which went into effect on 15 January 1920. The employers adopted a strategy of only negotiating with the men on issues directly arising from the affairs of each particular camp – issues brought in from the outside were not to be discussed. The effect was to isolate the disputes and to prevent the growth of industry-wide or working class-wide solidarity. In effect, the union's emphasis on local decision-making fed into the plans of the employers to head off a more broad-based labour revolt. There is no real indication that Winch or other LWIU leaders had thought out a strategy to counter the plan of the employers. Winch was not an armchair Marxist, and he and other Marxian socialists in the union did attempt to unite theory and practice in terms of education and organization. Too often, however, they viewed increasing membership and knowledge of Marxism as ends in themselves, and failed to develop a workable strategy for converting the growth and knowledge into effective action.

In the event, the employer counteroffensive was aided by a serious conflict within the union itself. In November 1919 Harry Allman published a list of sixteen demands in *The Worker*, at least half of them directed at the power and control of Ernest Winch. Allman demanded that full-time union workers not have a vote on the executive, that they refrain from participating in any political movement without the consent of the full membership, that no paid position be held for longer than six months, and that all officials return to work as loggers for a period of a year before running for another position. In addition, salaries would be capped and all decisions by union functionaries were to be under the strict control of the general executive.[100]

It would be tempting to turn the conflict between Allman and Winch into a battle between the competing left ideologies of the Socialist Party and the Industrial Workers of the World. It is true that the issue of *The Worker* in which Allman's demands appeared was the last one, leading Winch to begin publishing an LWIU page in the *BC Federationist* in December 1919. Alex Mackenzie added further credence to the idea that this was an SPC–IWW battle by claiming that some Wobblies had threatened to throw Winch down the stairs of the union's offices.[101] Were these democratic local organizers attempting to rid the LWIU of a bureaucratic SPC leadership? The problem with this explanation is that a number of camp organizers and district secretaries, including Burrough and Mackenzie, were members of the SPC. In addition, there were IWW members active in the union in Vancouver, including E. Lindberg, who succeeded Pritchard as editor of *The Worker.* Furthermore, Lindberg, at least publicly, endorsed Winch's position on the superiority of the industrial versus geographical form of organization, making them allies against centralizers in the leadership of the One Big Union.[102]

Winch could not have found Allman's demand for elections every six months unreasonable, because even the Vancouver Trades and Labour Council had six-month elections. In all probability he clung to the position for three reasons; one, he needed the money for his large and growing family; two, he felt he was the best person in the B.C. labour movement for the job, which he arguably was; and three, he believed that Allman was using the language of egalitarianism in an attempt to deliver the Loggers' Union into the hands of the IWW, not to promote the best interests of the rank and file workers. On the question of the relationship between leaders and followers, Winch was a Marxist of the third way: he was a genuine supporter of rank and file self-organization, but he was not about to abandon his fellow union members to a Harry Allman any more than he was willing to let A.J. Devereaux strip the rank and file workers of their representatives. The conflict within the LWIU took the form of a struggle between the SPC and the IWW, but in content it was actually a question of who was most faithfully carrying out the wishes of the rank and file. That question was about to surface in a much bigger dispute with much more serious consequences for the LWIU, and indeed for the Canadian working class itself.

The most threatening aspect of Allman's proposed changes was the suggestion that dues be paid directly to the OBU office in Winnipeg, a policy that would effectively kill the need for Winch's position as LWIU secretary. During 1920, therefore, the conflict between Winch and Allman evolved into the dispute between the OBU and the LWIU. The issue became one of centralization versus decentralization, geographical versus industrial forms of organization. Winch, given his record of maintaining a firm grip on the organizations he was a part of, and regional rather than national focus, was headed for a showdown with Victor Midgley and other OBU leaders.

While the dispute simmered, the union itself continued to grow by leaps and bounds. In January 1920 membership approached the sixteen thousand mark, and union organizers were contemplating a country-wide membership of fifty thousand. There were now nine organizers working in Ontario, and offices were set up across the country as far east as Montreal. There were even ambitious plans to expand into the Maritimes. In British Columbia the prestige of the union continued to grow, as workers won concessions dealing with wages and camp conditions. By the summer of 1920 fully 43 per cent of the One Big Union's funds were coming from the LWIU. As David Bercuson and Gordon Hak point out, in growing so rapidly the LWIU had become a threat to the leadership of the One Big Union, already seriously depleted by the imprisonment of Bob Russell and Bill Pritchard. It was up to men like Midgley to deal with Winch, and the old allies became embroiled in a conflict over the relationship between the two bodies. Midgley could not have helped being threatened by a union which was not only growing expansively in the bush camps but was moving toward organizing construction workers and agricultural labourers as well; Winch was certainly threatened by a dramatic drop in his wages or the elimination of his position altogether.

The actual split came at the OBU convention in Port Arthur, Ontario, in September 1920. At the convention the credentials of the LWIU delegates were challenged, including those of Winch. The initial charge was that the LWIU had not paid dues for June and July, which was true. However, there were other affiliated unions behind in their dues, and there was no justification for singling out the lumber workers, especially since they were the backbone of the OBU in terms of per capita dues. Next it was argued that the LWIU credentials were improper, but that charge was also dropped. Finally, it was argued that Winch's credentials, which were from Cranbrook, were not from the area where he actually worked. It was clear that the leadership of the OBU had decided to exclude Winch and other LWIU delegates on any pretext. By the time the credentials committee came down with a decision all but one LWIU delegate had left. Upon returning to B.C. Winch held a referendum, in which the LWIU membership voted overwhelmingly in support of his stand.

In 1921 Pritchard argued that the dispute had much more to do with personalities than with principle. He may have been right. Much of the rancour seemed to stem from Winch's dispute with Allman on the one hand and his clashes with Midgley on the other. After being released from prison, Bob Russell said that he saw no necessary conflict between the OBU and the LWIU, and that there was room in the OBU for unions organized on industrial lines.[103] Perhaps Jack Kavanagh came closest to understanding what was at issue when he pointed out that a district form of organization would have eliminated Winch's position.[104] The leaders of the OBU were justified in insisting that Winch put the interests of the working class as whole before the interests of individual unions. On the other hand, Winch was right, in terms of

Marxism of the third way's commitment to rank and file education and self-organization, to oppose what he and members of the IWW saw as the OBU leadership's excessive emphasis on centralization. Winch became, in this struggle, too much of a centralizer for the Wobblies, and not enough of a centralizer for the leadership of the OBU. As the labour revolt of 1919 merged into the reaction and downturn of the 1920s, he sat astride the horns of a major dilemma of Marxism of the third way.

Winch hung on for several months after the Port Arthur debacle, but the LWIU was already in the throes of a serious decline. The lumber workers' upheaval of 1919–20 was directed primarily toward camp conditions; there was no general dissatisfaction with wages or the employers. Once the food was improved, some provision made for better health care, the two-tier bunks removed, toilet facilities improved, and clean bedding provided on a regular basis, most workers were unwilling to remain on strike. Furthermore, the employers knew it, and were financially in a position to meet enough of the strikers' demands to defuse most threatening situations. The LWIU's failure to pay its dues to the OBU in June and July 1920 would suggest that members were already dropping out or failing to pay dues. In all probability Winch's generous salary was a victim of declining dues, and in January 1921 he left the union and went back to the docks. Like so many Canadian workers Winch was unable to maintain his commitment to the dream of one big unionism, and he left the OBU in December 1921. In August 1923 he left the Longshoremen's Union and went back to contract work in bricklaying. According to Dorothy Steeves, he was blacklisted in the long, bitter, and often violent longshoremen's strike in the fall of 1923.[105]

Life for the Winch family in the 1920s was often brutal and hard. Dorothy Steeves describes Winch being reduced at times to bringing home fish heads off the Vancouver docks to boil up for soup. Harold Winch, Ernest's son, recalled eating sheep heads until all the children were heartily sick of them. For a while in the 1920s the family lived over a shoe factory run by O. Lee Charlton, who had formed the Victoria Local of the Socialist Party in the early 1900s. The Winch family lived in one room separated by blankets. Much of the responsibility for keeping the family together fell to Linda, a task she may not have done as gladly as Dorothy Steeves suggests. Linda may have been one of the "unsung heroines of the class-struggle," but she found little sustenance in her husband's union activities or his Marxist beliefs.[106] She turned instead to religion, became a spiritualist and spiritualist teacher, and sought out like-minded friends who could provide her with the sense of meaning and self-worth she could not get vicariously through her husband's activities.[107] Indeed, Winch himself must have had many moments in the 1920s when he considered abandoning socialism. His son Harold later recalled one occasion on which his father was visited by prominent Vancouver businessmen who offered him a good job if he agreed to give up his socialist politics. Winch refused the offer, a decision his wife must have occasionally regretted, her support for her husband's political activities notwithstanding.

Like so many other labour radicals in the 1920s, Winch struggled to survive while retaining some ties to the labour and socialist movements. In 1926 his name appeared on a letter sent by the Vancouver Trades and Labour Council to J.S. Woodsworth, now the federal member for Winnipeg North.[108] The letter asked Woodsworth to look into the discriminatory hiring practices of the Shipping Federation of British Columbia. The defeat of the long and bitter Longshoremen's strike of 1923 had resulted in the destruction of the International Longshoremen's Union, thereby allowing the Shipping Federation to refuse to rehire union members active in the strike. Why Winch signed the letter is unclear, unless he had returned to work on the docks for a short period.[109] Nor does he appear to have been a delegate to the VTLC at this time. In all probability the VTLC was attempting to use his friendship with Woodsworth in 1918–19 to add a personal touch and some influence to their request.

How Winch reacted to the demise of the *Western Clarion* in the summer of 1925, and the effective collapse of the Socialist Party, has not been recorded.[110] He did not write to the *Clarion* in the early 1920s and does not appear to have been at all active in party affairs. Nor does he appear to have been among the ranks of B.C. leftists who rallied to fill the void. When delegates representing the Federated Labour Party, former SPCers, and the Labour parties met on 25 September 1925 to discuss the formation of an independent labour party, Winch was not in attendance. When the Independent Labour Party was formed at the end of 1925, former SPCer Angus MacInnis was its most prominent member.[111]

Winch does not appear to have been involved in the founding of the ILP, and the role he played in the organization in the late 1920s is rather shadowy. Dorothy Steeves claims that he led a small study group in Burnaby, and with the help of several other ILPers built a hall and organized the Burnaby ILP branch.[112] In fact, the leading member of the ILP in Burnaby would appear to have been Ernest Burns, the Burnaby ILP's head of the education committee and the man most often referred to in reports on the ILP in the *Labor Statesman*. Winch's name does not appear in these reports in the late 1920s. It is possible that the editor of the *Labor Statesman*, official organ of the by now AFL/TLCC-dominated Vancouver Trades and Labour Council, chose to ignore Winch's involvement because of his past association with the OBU. Winch's absence from *Labor Statesman* reports does not prove that he was not a major player, but it does render problematic any attempt to portray him as the party's leading figure in the late 1920s.

Winch did become a leading figure in the Independent Labour Party in the early 1930s. The crash of 1929 and the ensuing Depression of the early 1930s held special meaning for socialists trained in Marxist theory. The Depression represented the realization of the contradictions of capitalism, the arrival of that period in history when overproduction and underconsumption meant that only the social ownership of the means of production and production for use, not profit, could reconstruct the economy. Winch was not primarily a theoretician, but he did recognize that what Marx had predicted appeared to be coming true. He was less than overjoyed, however, because the left seemed strangely unprepared, in spite of the fact that it had been predicting this crisis of capitalism for decades. In a letter to Walter Nevison in the fall of 1931, he noted, "It certainly looks as if the capitalist system is developing – and collapsing – more rapidly than is the socialist preparation to deal effectively with the situation as, and when, it develops."[113]

The criticism Winch launched at socialists in general he could have directed at himself. He did not remain a major player on the B.C. left in the 1920s but was there in the early 1930s to take advantage of the rapid rise of the Independent Labour Party. On 21 June 1931 he was named party organizer, apparently because he was the only member willing to take the position.[114] He did an excellent job and at the party's Fifth Annual Convention was congratulated for his aggressive organizing work. He was elected secretary-treasurer at the convention, and $25 a month was set aside for organizing purposes.[115] In January 1932 he was appointed to a committee to set up an educational centre with classes in economics and other subjects.[116]

Once again Winch had risen from relative obscurity to being the key figure in a labour party which had been in a fight for its very life a year before. It was not the first time this had happened. In 1917 he had turned the ILA Auxiliary into a vibrant organization. He went from virtual obscurity to being president of the Vancouver Trades and Labour Council in less than a year. When the Loggers' Union was organized by Helena Gutteridge and Birt Showler in January 1919, he was there to step into the highest-paid position in the union. He had a history, therefore, of becoming involved with parties and unions organized by someone else, taking paid positions, and becoming the dominant figure. There can be no denying that he was a tremendously hard worker, fiercely dedicated, and compassionate when it came to the plight of the working class and the unemployed. Yet he also had a way of recognizing up-and-coming organizations, taking a lead role while times were good, and then bowing out of the limelight when times got rough. Whatever his motivations and his failings, however, he did what he did very well.

While it is true that that there was opportunism in Winch's politics, it is also true that he constantly struggled to keep the best interests of the working class as a whole as his ultimate guideline. That commitment to working class unity was strong enough to compel him to cooperate with the B.C. Communist Party, and to defend the united front. It was a courageous move in those days. With the entrance into the Third Period in 1929, the Communist International at Stalin's behest directed its member parties to resolutely and often viciously attack all non-Communist socialists as social fascists. The fact that Winch and other Marxists of the third way resolutely upheld the importance of Marxist ideas in organizations such as the Independent Labour Party, the Industrial Workers of the World, and the One Big Union did not save them from being identified as incipient fascists by Communist Party members and their press.[117]

In spite of these condemnations of his politics, Winch advocated cooperation with the CPC in the early 1930s. He paid for his stance with the opprobrium of many prominent B.C. socialists. His old friend Ernest Burns took the initiative in the summer of 1931, criticizing ILP speakers who attempted "to conciliate the communist elements of the working class." It was a question of methods; for Burns, the two camps would always be "mutually antagonistic."[118] Winch's response was at once overly optimistic and immensely perceptive. For him, there was no ultimate arbiter of "correct" tactics, no single party in a position to set out "the infallible line of political tactics to pursue." As a Marxist of the third way, he believed that the goal of working-class unity transcended party differences. Of CPC-ILP cooperation, Winch said that "conditions will compel them to cease magnifying the importance of their superficial differences and get together," thereby creating a broad-based socialist movement committed to worker self-emancipation. But he was realistic about the short term, arguing that the parties were "so distinct that it would be disastrous to attempt ... to bring them in to one organization." In the meantime, the two parties should be free to pursue their own tactics and goals, and Winch felt there were more important things for a Marxian socialist to do than attacking the Communist Party.[119]

For Winch, one of those important things to do was getting involved in electoral politics. He had run several times at the local level, most recently in January 1931 when he lost the second seat on the Burnaby school board by seventeen votes.[120] In August 1931 he was named to the ILP slate of possible candidates for the upcoming provincial election.[121] Now fifty-two years old and a proud man, he must have felt that he had not been rewarded for his many years of service to the workers of British Columbia. It was also time, perhaps, to make a permanent commitment to a party and to work for those changes he had espoused from his earliest days in the socialist movement. He dedicated himself to building up the Independent Labour Party, and at the Fifth Annual Convention held on 6 December 1931 he reported that twenty-four new branches had been formed and a thousand active members signed up. It was at this meeting as well that the decision to change the name of the party to ILP (Socialist) was taken, although it was not made official until the meeting of the Provincial Executive Committee on 13 February 1932. Needless to say, Winch was the driving force behind it.

During 1932 the party continued to grow by leaps and bounds. In July the name of the party was changed again to the Socialist Party of Canada. President Wallis Lefeaux, who had joined the old Socialist Party in 1905, wanted the new SPC to conform as much as possible to the traditions of the old one.[122] Critics of the change went further. Thomas Walton Jr of the South Hill Branch of the ILP implied that old SPCers had essentially rammed through the change against the wishes of many in the rank and file. As the leading old SPCer, Winch saw the change differently. He argued that the membership had voted "overwhelmingly" in the referendum in favour of changing the name. His interpretation of the change is important, because it elucidates the ways in which the new SPC was the inheritor of the old. Commenting on the change, he said, "the Socialist Party of Canada is distinctly revolutionary, being formed for the purpose of creating a working class consciousness, with a view of securing the collective ownership and democratic control of the means of wealth production, and the abolition of the wages system. This it proposes to accomplish through education, organization and action; the latter being governed by the degree of intelligence possessed by the working class when necessity and opportunity coincide."[123]

Winch's formulation for the new SPC includes all the strengths and weaknesses of the old party program. There is the same great faith in education, the same belief that the agency of the working class is the motive force of historical change. Yet there continues to be no serious consideration of how the working class is to effect that change, given the repressive power of the state and its supporters.The revolution will happen, Winch seems to be saying, when the working class is ready for it to happen. The question of structure, of what he calls "necessity," is left hanging. What does he propose in a situation where the contradictions of capitalism have made the system redundant, but the workers are not yet sufficiently class conscious? Is direct action, including armed struggle, "correct" at that point? Winch gives no indication that he has answers to these questions, and as of old he looks to education and increasing membership as the lead indicators of the growth of revolutionary politics on the B.C. left.

By 1933 it appeared that the SPCBC was on its way to becoming a major force in B.C., if not Canadian, politics. Appearances were deceptive, however. The party was almost as big as the old one, with between fourteen hundred and eighteen hundred members in the years 1932–34. It faced, however, a number of serious problems. Its leaders, including Winch and Wallis Lefeaux, were no longer young. Winch was now 54 and Lefeaux only slightly younger. The party had no trade union base, and was much further removed from the unions than the old SPC had been. More basic and more troubling was the party's theoretical confusion, which meant that its "revolutionary" stance had no structure, no tactical direction, and a rank and file membership that was older and more middle class. In fact, many locals of the SPCBC were little more than social clubs, with whist drives, dances, and lectures being the major activities.

Most troublesome, however, were forces pulling the SPC members in opposite directions. The Depression and subsequent unemployment had given great impetus to the Communist Party, which proved attractive to many on the left, even those who did not agree with the party's tactics or policies. The growing threat of fascism in Europe also made the CPC's anti-imperialist, anti-war position extremely popular and manifested itself in the number of non-CPers who worked with the League Against War and Fascism, the Workers' Unity League, and the Canadian Labour Defence League. An even greater pull, however, came with the formation of the Co-operative Commonwealth Federation. The organization had been launched in Calgary in July 1932 by a group of farmers, workers, intellectuals, small-business people, and socialists looking to form a broad-based coalition on the Canadian left. By the time of the CCF's first national convention in Regina in 1933 and the issuance of the Regina Manifesto, many B.C. leftists were already working for or attracted to the party. How was the SPC, without a base in the trade unions, and already becoming a battleground between constitutional socialists and Marxist-Leninists, going to survive?

One option was a national organization. Late in 1931 Winch, as secretary of the ILP (Socialist), began a correspondence with Bert Robinson, a former member of the Canadian Labour Party and now a member of the Ontario Labour Party. Their first letters dealt primarily with exchanging information about the respective movements. In

March 1932, however, Winch told Robinson that at the recent ILP (S) convention he had proposed the creation of a federal organization on a Marxian basis.[124] Robinson replied that the Ontario group wanted to create a Socialist Party, not an Independent Labour Party. By the time Winch wrote to Robinson in July 1932 the ILP had become the Socialist Party of Canada, with thirty branches.

While it is not possible to directly pin down the influence of Robinson on Winch's thinking, the timing suggests that Winch's support for renaming the party was in part inspired by Robinson's radicalism and was adopted with the intention of turning the SPCBC into a truly national organization. With the name change came a heightened rhetoric from Winch. He noted that "there are changes also taking place in tactics, all tending to clarify and stiffen the revolutionary position."[125] In an apparent reaction to the recent Western Labour Conference in Calgary he declared, "It is no use to build up a mushroom party of ignoramuses. Knowledge in Marxian Economics is the only basis upon which a real revolutionary movement can be built."[126] As we have seen, however, his own knowledge of Marxist economics was never extensive, and there is no evidence that he seriously opposed the SPCBC affiliating with the CCF, in spite of his concerns about that party's reformist tendencies. In one of his more astute predictions he observed that if the CCF survived, "it will become a mere office-seeking, vote-catching, reformist group of use neither to God or man (or at least not to those seeking emancipation from capitalist exploitation)." Radicals would have to work hard to make it a "straight revolutionary socialist movement."[127]

While Winch's rhetoric continued to be revolutionary, many of his thoughts and actions were confused and contradictory. He was at one and the same time secretary and provincial organizer of the SPCBC and secretary of the CCF provincial council. In the spring of 1933 he wrote to Bert Robinson, informing him that he was no longer secretary of the provincial council. He said he was fed up with disputes on the left and considered the provincial council too right wing.[128] At this point in his life Winch was searching, almost desperately, for a third way: "Man! Oh man! if only the Communists would embody the spirit of 'ism' & not intolerance into their movement what a glorious one it would be to get into," he told Robinson. Winch's indecision lends credence to his intemperate dismissal by David Lewis, who speaks for many social democrats and Marxist-Leninists when he describes Winch's revolutionary utterances as "meaningless and fatuous."[129] Granted Ernest Winch was prone to rhetorical excess, but no more so than David Lewis or Communist Party leader Tim Buck. The difference is that they are perceived by historians as speaking for recognizable, credible political tendencies, while Marxists of the third way are perceived as using rhetoric to hide their failure to support one of the winners.

Yet there is every reason to believe that Winch was guided by his own conception of the best way to fight capitalism and deal with the Depression, and he stayed with the CCF because he genuinely believed that it had radical potential and could be turned into a vehicle for Marxian socialism. Although not a theoretician, he was still Marxist enough to find it incomprehensible that any socialist could view what was happening to the economy and working class in Canada in the early 1930s and not see the validity of a Marxist analysis. He genuinely believed that the best policy was to go with the masses and try to turn them in a revolutionary direction. If Lewis and other CCFers had spent a bit more time thinking about the enormous difficulty of building a mass-based party of principle, and a bit less time dismissing the efforts of Marxists of the third way as opportunism, the fate of the social democratic left might not have been so dismal. There were times when Winch failed to match his Marxist language with Marxist actions, but it might be pointed out that the inheritors of David Lewis and Tim Buck no longer even speak the language.

Winch was buoyed by the events of the first national convention of the CCF in Regina in July 1933. He was not optimistic when he set out for Regina but came back convinced that there was reason for hope. At the convention he found an ally in William Moriarty, a leading Ontario Marxist expelled from the Communist Party in 1929. Both men opposed tying the CCF to constitutional action, with Winch arguing that the use of violence could not be categorically ruled out in effecting the transformation from capitalism to socialism. The two were soundly rebuffed on the issue, but Winch took solace in the final paragraph of the Regina Manifesto, which called for the eradication of the capitalist system.

Eugene Forsey's recollection of Winch at the founding convention of the CCF typifies the way in which Marxian socialists and their concerns have been trivialized by social democratic writers. Forsey does not deal with Winch's position on revolutionary violence, but he does note that the B.C. socialist suggested that the CCF come out in favour of nudism. Forsey says he "scotched" the idea, although his account suggests that he was more opposed to how it would look in the press than he was to the idea itself. Winch may have been serious, or he may have been joking, but it seems unlikely in any event that Forsey would have credited a Marxian socialist with a sense of humour.[130] His concluding statement about Winch is also revealing: "Ernie went on to become a very respected and beloved member of the British Columbia Legislative Assembly, where he was the champion especially of mental patients and dumb

Ernest Winch hard at work, March 1940. As labour leader, socialist activist, and parliamentarian he brought organizational skills, thorough research, attention to detail, and personal passion to the cause of defending the exploited and downtrodden. University of British Columbia Special Collections

animals."[131] That Ernie Winch – a child really, Forsey implies, and more than a bit misguided, not really up to understanding what it takes to create a social democratic movement destined to change Canada.

Winch's concerns with the CCF's politics and the attitudes of some of his fellow party members notwithstanding, he was not long in making himself a prominent figure in the new movement. On 2 November 1933 he became the CCF member for Burnaby in the B.C. legislature, and remained the Burnaby member until his death in 1957. Being elected, however, did not end his commitment to the need for Marxist education, organization, or the end of capitalism. Very much in the tradition of the old SPC, he believed that a socialist member of Parliament's primary goal was still education and organization, still the making of socialists. In his parliamentary report to the SPCBC in 1934 he said that "the real value in electing working-class representatives lies in their availability for unceasing propaganda and organization activities throughout the year." Complacency was a constant danger; members must continue to "participate in the every-day struggles of the working-class movement," especially amongst the unemployed.[132] In the mid-1930s Winch continued to stress the areas of agreement between the CPC and the CCF – social ownership of the means of production, and production for use not profit. There could be no middle ground between capitalism and socialism: the CCF must either "operate Capitalism" or challenge it, and that meant revolution. Continuing on, Winch stated categorically that "I know of no case in History where the ruling class has ever peacefully surrendered its power & privileges to a rising revolutionary class."[133]

By 1933–34 Winch could not have seriously believed that the CCF leadership shared his perspective. Even following the Regina Convention of 1933 he had described Agnes Macphail as "congenitally incapable of understanding and assimilating Socialism."[134] Correspondence in the mid-1930s between Bill Pritchard and J.S. Woodsworth, and between Victor Midgley and Angus MacInnis, clearly indicates that even Winch's old revolutionary allies were working to undermine his influence, head off any united front activities, and help dissolve the SPCBC into the CCF. Winch's report to the SPCBC on the 1934 CCF convention in Winnipeg described the event as "far from being revolutionary and tended further toward the right." He was even more acerbic the next year, saying that the gathering "would have been a disgrace to a third-rate Liberal convention."[135]

Perhaps Winch believed that the SPCBC, which the 1932 Western Labour Conference had recognized as the founding body of the CCF in British Columbia, could regain the initiative. The party was strong, with some forty-five branches and fourteen hundred members in 1934. It was literally swamped, however, by the membership of the CCF clubs, which were left social democratic at best, debating clubs for the latest monetarist panacea at worst. By the fall of 1934 the CCF leadership had been able to persuade the SPCBC to hold a referendum on affiliating with the larger movement. The referendum failed to get the required two-thirds majority, and the SPCBC continued to function as a separate body. In the winter of 1934–35, however, CCF leaders were given a new weapon with which to attack the SPC. On Sunday, 27 January 1935, a rally at the Colonial Theatre in Vancouver was addressed by representatives of the SPCBC, the CPC, the Young Socialist League, the Young Communist League, the Canadian Labour Defence League, and the Relief Camp Workers' Union. Winch spoke for the SPCBC, and called for the repeal of the amendment to the Dominion Franchise Act, which aimed to disfranchise the relief camp workers. Also prominent in the agitation was A.M. Stephen, an SPCBC member and one of the most knowledgeable Marxists in the country.[136]

In the ensuing months the Communist Party press was very favourably disposed toward the SPCBC's united front policy, while continually attacking the CCF. The CCF paper, *The Commonwealth*, edited and controlled by Bill Pritchard, was repeatedly attacked for its "anti-working class tactics."[137] Employing the party's social fascist rhetoric, the CPC claimed that Pritchard "drives on consciously or unconsciously to Fascism," because he insisted on telling the workers that socialism could come by constitutional means.[138] Pritchard, who had been attacking the Communist Party since the early 1920s, must have been furious with Winch and Stephen for their support of the CPC's united front strategy, and Angus MacInnis and J.S. Woodsworth felt the same way. Their intensified efforts to wrest control of the SPCBC rank and file from the Marxian socialists bore fruit when the membership voted to join the CCF in May 1935.

This was certainly the Communist Party's interpretation of events. In a perceptive article entitled "S.P.C. VOTES TO MERGE WITH CCF – Once Powerful Workers Party Commits Hari-Kari," J. Taylor observed that from the "very inception of the C.C.F. a carefully calculated policy of liquidating the S.P.C. was followed by the top leadership." Taylor knew the history of the party quite well, including how many locals had voted, and what the totals were. In all probability he got his information from Winch, or possibly Stephen. He described Winch as one of the "outstanding leaders" of the SPCBC and a "staunch supporter" of united front action.[139] Later on in the summer the CPC press pointed out that at the recent CCF provincial convention Winch had led "the progressives for unity with the rest of the workers in the fight against fascism and war."[140] Even as a member of the legislature, therefore, he did not allow himself to become divorced from the rank and file. He continued to defend the relief camp workers and the unemployed and recognized that to do it he had to work with members of the Communist Party. With the demise of the SPCBC, however, he and other Marxian socialists lost an important base of operations from which to counter the rightward drift of the CCF.

While there may still have been a chance to move the CCF to the left in the years 1932–35, that chance evaporated in the solidification of the right which took place in 1936–37. Several factors were involved in the split that occurred in the B.C. CCF in 1936, including a personal conflict between Winch and the Reverend Robert Connell, the B.C. CCF's provincial leader. Winch was still of the old school that demanded that parliamentary socialists spend all their spare time speaking and propagandizing for the party. Connell was not so dedicated that he did not sometimes wish for a break from the never-ending speeches and party meetings. To Winch, of course, this was akin to betrayal of the movement.[141] The conflict between the two men went back to late 1933, when Connell, and not Winch, was named parliamentary leader. At that time Connell had denied that Marxian economics formed the basis of the CCF program, a point on which Winch continued to be adamant, even into the 1950s. By 1936 the personal antagonism was exacerbated by an ideological clash, which centred around Winch's involvement in the League Against War and Fascism. Stephen, Winch's ally in supporting the united front, was now president of the League in British Columbia.

The situation came to a head at the 1936 CCF convention. By this time Winch was furious with Connell, who had added insult to injury by supporting a monetary policy closely akin to Social Credit. To make matters even more confused, both Bill Pritchard, editor of *The Commonwealth*, and Victor Midgley, Connell's secretary, supported Connell and were as furious with Winch as he was with the provincial leader. The old allies of 1919 had been on the outs for some time, but now the battle lines were much more starkly drawn. Within a month of the 1936 convention Connell had resigned and taken several CCF members including Pritchard and Midgley with him into his newly formed party called the Social Constructives. In the end the "Winch faction" triumphed over the "Connell faction"; both Ernest and his son Harold were re-elected in June 1937 while Connell and his allies went down to defeat. Within a year Midgley was in New Zealand and Pritchard had moved to Los Angeles where he remained for the rest of his life.

Yet it was not to be a victory for Marxism of the third way, for within a month of his re-election Ernest Winch moved to align himself with the mainstream of the party at the B.C. CCF's 1937 provincial convention. Winch was part of, not opposed to, the consolidation of the right-wing leadership of the CCF and the expulsion or whipping into line of recalcitrant members in 1936–37. Prior to Connell's defeat in the 1937 provincial election Winch had been very much a pariah, in large part because of his involvement with the League Against War and Fascism and his association with A.M. Stephen. The cause was very appealing to many rank and file CCFers, and Winch and Stephen were seen by CCF leaders as influencing impressionable CCFers to mistakenly legitimate the activities of the Communists. The CCF leadership feared losing control of the rank and file and moved to reassert themselves.

In British Columbia Connell attacked Ernest Winch as a "self-declared pro-Communist." Prior to the 1937 provincial election Winch did not seem overly bothered by Connell's attacks, but all at once he was. The defeat of Connell and his allies in the election greatly enhanced Winch's influence in the party, and he moved to consolidate his position by turning upon Stephen at the Fifth Annual Convention of the B.C. CCF in July 1937. When Stephen was expelled from the CCF for collaborating with the Communist Party, by a vote of ninety-six to sixty-one, Winch expressed personal sympathy but followed with a "vitriolic attack." It was necessary, according to Winch, if the CCF in British Columbia wanted to continue as a political force. In his haste to solidify the CCF and his role in it Winch condemned Stephen for the same involvement in united front activities he himself had participated in.[142] It was not his finest moment. Before 1937 he attempted to promote the cause of industrial unionism and supported causes he believed in, even if it meant being condemned by his own party members for cooperating with the Communists. Yet here, apparently, was an ugly manifestation of Winch's opportunism and self-serving politics, served up as an unprovoked attack on an old comrade.

As would be the case with Arthur Mould's decision to support the Communist Party, Winch's actions in attacking Stephen may have been prompted by the Communist Party's transition from the Third Period to the Popular Front in 1934–35.[143] Shifting from attacking all non-Communists as social fascists, the Communist Party attempted to build support for the Soviet Union and a broad-based anti-fascist movement by actively seeking the support of middle class allies. Early in March 1937 Stephen had declared that he supported "a broad people's movement comprising all progressive groups and parties."[144] Winch was not opposed, it appears, to the Popular Front per se. On Monday, 5 July, as the CCF convention was drawing to a close, a letter from the B.C. branch of the Communist Party was read to the delegates. It suggested that the CCF and the Communist Party get together to equip an ambulance to be sent to Spain and to otherwise aid the Spanish loyalists. Of all the convention delegates, only Winch spoke in favour of the proposal.[145]

In effect, Winch's outburst against Stephen may have been motivated more by a sense of personal betrayal than any philosophical rejection of the attempt to find a third way between the CCF and the Communist Party. The genesis of the shift in his politics may well have been Stephen's refutation of Marxian socialism and its class-based emphasis on worker self-emancipation.[146] Winch's political ambitions in the CCF notwithstanding, he was simply incapable of accepting the Popular Front if it meant abandoning Marxian socialism. In keeping with his commitment to Marxist education, he maintained that "quality is more important than quantity in membership" where party organization was concerned.[147] There were, of course, many enemies of Marxian socialism in the CCF itself, but it was still possible in 1937 to believe that the party of Woodsworth and Lewis promised a brighter future for Marxist education than did the Communist Party. This was especially true in British Columbia, where Frank Roberts, George Weaver, Wallis Lefeaux and other Marxian socialists in the CCF were still very much engaged in Marxist education.

Honours and recognition for Ernest Winch came only later in life. This picture may have been taken at a dinner held on 6 November 1954 to celebrate his twenty-one years of service in the British Columbia legislature. Linda Winch's eyes tell us a great deal about the reality of her life of public self-effacement. University of British Columbia Special Collections

It remains true, however, that Winch's attack on Stephen, and his decision to act in the best interests of the CCF as a party seeking electoral victory, marked a major turning point in his career. As the years went by, the class struggle retreated further and further into the rhetorical background. By 1939 it was not uncommon to hear socialists charge that Ernest Winch had gone over completely to the side of reformist politics. The charge was well founded. At the age of sixty, he had made his decision to help as many oppressed and disadvantaged people as the freedoms and restrictions of parliamentary politics would allow. He was a tremendous social democrat: no cause was too small, no person beyond his caring gaze. He fought for the homeless, for the mentally ill, the imprisoned, and the aged. He became a resolute opponent of capital punishment and a champion of prison reform. A lover of animals, he helped promote the conibear trap, fought for better cages for the bears in Stanley Park, and generally advanced the cause of better treatment for wildlife.

During the 1940s he continued to flail away at the capitalist system, but he no longer scared anyone with his rhetoric. By 1950 the divorce between rhetoric and action was brutally complete. At the CCF federal convention in 1950 M.J. Coldwell, David Lewis, and Frank Scott all denied that Marxism and the theory of class struggle had ever been the basis of the program of the CCF. Winch rose in righteous indignation on the floor, exclaiming that Marxism had always been the basis of the CCF and would continue to be so. When it came time to put his rhetoric into practice, however, he did not take up the challenge. The literature table at the 1950 convention was staffed by Evelyn Grey Smith, a B.C. radical who had maintained ties with the Trotskyist movement during the 1940s. Her table featured works by Marx and Engels and, most provocatively, Socialist Party of Great Britain literature critical of the British Labour Party. After an apparently staged provocation, David Lewis and Donald MacDonald confronted Smith and ordered her to stop selling what another CCFer referred to as "Trotskyist drivel." As Dorothy Steeves points out, Winch did not rise to defend Smith when she was censored by the convention.[148]

Nor did he get involved in the movement in British Columbia in 1950 to move the CCF to the left. In the summer of 1950 seventy CCFers, including the indefatigable Wallis Lefeaux, met to discuss their options. Rod Young, who joined the Young Socialist League in the 1930s and had a long association with the Trotskyist movement, argued that it was no longer possible to put forward Marxist ideas in the CCF. The group called itself the Socialist Fellowship, and set out to build a larger movement. No help was forthcoming from Winch, however, as he did not get involved.

As late as the early 1950s Winch nevertheless felt that something was missing from the CCF. He could still comment that he wished the party had some of the spirit and drive of the Communist Party. He also got himself in some trouble for signing the Communist Party's peace petition circulated in the early 1950s. In the darkest days of the 1950s, when even the most optimistic CCFer could see that the party might not survive, Winch continued to believe in the party's revolutionary purpose and the relevance of Marxism. Winch could not accept the revised party manifesto called the Winnipeg Declaration, which removed the last sentence referring to the CCF's goal of eradicating capitalism.[149] But he knew what was happening in the world. In an October 1956 letter he said: "We certainly need some refresher lessons in Marxian economics, but who will give them? It would be worse than useless to have the blind leading the blind & also who would attend?"[150] Two months later, however, he reaffirmed his commitment to the Marxian basis of CCF politics in a letter to national secretary, Lorne Ingle. No matter what the ravages of age and a changing world, it remained clear to him that "the CCF has now surrendered the stand which distinguished it from all other political parties and sounded its death knell as a vital and revolutionary force in the political life of Canada."[151] One month later, on 11 January 1957, he was dead.

Ernest Winch typified what was best in Marxism of the third way. He always kept in view the end of the capitalist system and the creation of a socialist society in which the needs of all would be met. He realized that this society had to be created by the workers themselves – it could not be given to them. Throughout his life he attempted to educate the rank and file, to bring them to a realization of their class position and what they had to do to change it. He was a social democrat in the best sense, a man who cared for the poor, the dispossessed, the exploited, the imprisoned, and the ill – all those he felt had been victimized by a system over which they had no control.

In his life on the left we see one of the central, and most difficult, dilemmas facing socialists in their attempts to overthrow capitalism and create a socialist society. Winch knew that the party, like the union, needed order, direction, planning, and a clear sense of purpose. On the other hand he was a fervent believer in the self-organization and mobilization of the rank and file, in rank and file democracy, and in the battle against trade union bureaucracy and the capitalist state. His life demonstrates that at its heart Marxism of the third way is the attempt to defend the working class from the deceit, manipulation, and oppression of the capitalist class, while at the same time seeking to nurture the freest and fullest development of the individual and collective identities of the great mass of workers. The need to continue that struggle, to find a third way, is as important at the end of the twentieth century as it was at its birth. The life of Ernest Winch stands as testimony to both its difficulty and its necessity.

2 William Arthur Pritchard: The Marxist as Worker Intellectual

Although he remained active on the Canadian left until the late 1930s, it was as a member of the Socialist Party of Canada's "second generation" that William A. Pritchard made his most important contributions to Marxian socialism. Like so many worker intellectuals in the years 1911–19, he toiled with both hand and brain, shared in and commented on the dreams and disappointments, victories and defeats of his fellow workers. Bill Pritchard assumed many roles – as political candidate, trade union organizer, journalist, teacher, and speaker. In whatever capacity he functioned, however, he was the eyes and ears of the rank and file workers, laying before them the reality of capitalism lurking behind its benevolent face. His role was to probe and dissect, offering up to the workers a capitalism exposed, shorn of its humanitarian appearance, reduced to its ugly core.

Socialists who wrote for the labour press, and editors in particular, assumed leading roles in the interpretation, explication, and criticism of capitalist society. Pritchard was a worker, but a worker with a grasp of history, politics, and economics which set him apart, and made him a "leader" in working class circles, his lifelong attacks on the deleterious effects of leadership in the socialist movement notwithstanding. As editor of the *Western Clarion* from 1914 to 1917, and a contributor between 1911 and 1919, he did much more than keep his nose stuck in Volume 1 of *Capital*. He carried out a continuous and comprehensive analysis of the popular press and contemporary journals in the fields of psychology, sociology, economics, history, and political science. Fordism, welfare capitalism, the latest developments in the field of psychology, women's rights, the League of Nations, increasing American control of Canadian culture and the Canadian economy, and many other topics occupied the minds and pens of worker intellectuals like Pritchard. The role and function of a Bill Pritchard cannot be frozen into functionalist categories like "professional revolutionary," "bureaucrat," or "orthodox Marxist." The influence he exerted over rank and file members of the Socialist Party and the thousands of other socialists and non-socialists who heard him speak or read his articles largely derived from his ability to interpret and critique capitalist society, present the case for socialism, and convince workers of the need for education and organization.

A generation of Canadian historians has criticized Marxian socialists in the Socialist Party of Canada for their dogmatism, their inability to deal with contemporary realities, and their academicism. Pritchard, like many SPCers, could indeed be arrogant, opinionated, and intolerant of opposing points of view. In spite of that, however, there was a very different side to the SPC approach, one based in an ongoing dialogue with the defenders of capitalism in public debate.[1] It is not true, as has so often been implied, that Marxists of the third way wanted workers to unquestioningly accept what they had to say. Nor did they attempt to create a self-contained alternative world view based in completely new categories and expressed in a new language. Marxists of the third way, for good or ill, took the theories, categories, and language developed in capitalist society, studied them, and attempted to modify them for use as socialist arguments. Psychology, for example, was not condemned outright as a bourgeois hoax; rather, Marxists of the third way like Husain Rahim attempted to develop the study of "working class psychology" to counter the uses it would be put to by the capitalist class.[2]

While it is true, as Ross Johnson points out, that Marxian socialists like Pritchard did not spend much time addressing the political, economic, social, and cultural issues that preoccupied provincial and federal politicians, it is not true that they were somehow totally divorced from the ideas and events of the world in which they lived. As interpreters of capitalist political culture, worker intellectuals were constantly on the lookout for the latest bourgeois attempt to mislead the working class. In this very important sense Marxists of the third way took their cue as much from the world of bourgeois science, culture, and politics as from the theories of Marx and Engels. Bourgeois ideas were not necessarily condemned outright; SPC intellectuals sought to interpret and use them in ways that would benefit the workers. It was a contest in which Marxists fought capitalists for the allegiance of the working class.

This jousting at the level of ideas was organically linked to the worker intellectual's view of the working class, education, and the organization of the party. For Pritchard the Socialist Party was more a vehicle for steadily increasing the number of workers with a knowledge of Marxism than the agent of a revolutionary program. The purpose of the party was to make sure that the workers were possessed of the knowledge necessary to act intelligently and responsibly when they, not the leadership of the party, were ready to overthrow the capitalist system. Predictably, Pritchard's response to the labour revolt of 1919 echoed that philosophy. Marxists of the third way in the Socialist Party knew that the vast majority of workers were not socialists in any meaningful sense. In such a scenario the role of the Socialist Party was to educate for the future when the workers would be ready. Given that a majority of socialists, not just in Canada but in the world, had to be socialists before the creation of a socialist society was possible, Marxists of the third way like Pritchard had absolutely no delusions concerning the revolutionary possibilities of Winnipeg in 1919. Nor were they about to "lead" the Canadian working class anywhere.[3]

With the defeat of the Winnipeg General Strike, the Canada-wide sympathy strikes, and the decline of the One Big Union, Marxism of the third way's attempt to locate the source of class struggle in the education and *prise de conscience* of the rank and file was superseded by the Communist Party's attempt to make the vanguard party the vehicle of socialist revolution. The Russian Revolution demonstrated that it was possible, and the role of the Marxist as educator and cultural interpreter had become problematic. Marxists of the third way had to make a choice, and Pritchard rejected the Communist Party's emphasis on the role of leadership in favour of continuing the SPC's emphasis on education and working toward the formation of a party composed of a majority of the working class. Having made that choice, and having given up the resolute Marxism of his *Clarion* days, Pritchard drifted away from revolutionary politics in the 1920s and 1930s. He remained a socialist committed to the eradication of capitalism, but he also shifted the focus of his educational efforts from the working class to the middle class.

His endorsement of the Co-operative Commonwealth Federation in the early 1930s, while not predictable, was not entirely surprising either. Like Ernest Winch, he evinced a dedication to both the principled, disciplined party of educated Marxists and to the creation of a mass-based socialist movement. Those two elements were often in conflict: some Marxists of the third way tended to emphasize purity, while others tended to emphasize growth. Pritchard, who leaned toward purity during the First World War, was impressed by the "mass" character of the

CCF in the 1930s. Yet it was a dramatic shift for him nevertheless, because his support for the CCF also involved the repudiation of some fundamental SPC positions. In the 1920s and 1930s, when the Communist Party spoke for Marxism in the minds of many Canadians and exhibited the revolutionary single-mindedness of the old SPC, Marxists of the third way like Pritchard slid much further down the slope of "reformism" than they themselves had ever thought possible.

In the last decades of his life lived out in California, Pritchard returned to the politics of his youth. As a supporter of the World Socialist Party of the United States, he continued to write and propagandize. His politics still emphasized education and organization and still called for the creation of a socialist society by a majority of the world's workers. He lived, therefore, the life of another kind of Marxist of the third way, one who trod the path, strayed from it, and then found it again. The trajectory of his life stands in marked contrast to that of the New York intellectuals who were Communists and Trotskyists in the 1930s, and became increasingly conservative in the 1940s and 1950s, never to return to their youthful radicalism.[4] Pritchard wavered in the 1930s, but his fierce engagement with the politics of his day and his outrage at the unrelenting depredations of global capitalism brought him back to the politics of his youth.

William Arthur Pritchard was born on 3 April 1888 in Salford, near Manchester, England, as typical an urban product of the industrial revolution as could be found. In all probability his father, James, moved with his wife, Priscilla, to Salford from Wales in search of employment.[5] For a time James Pritchard worked in the Ermen and Engels textile mill, one of whose owners was the uncle of Friedrich Engels. In the 1840s Engels described the city of 80,000 inhabitants as "dirtier than Manchester" and "really all one large working-class quarter."[6] By 1911, the year Bill Pritchard left Salford, the population had tripled to 230,000, but the essential character of the city remained.[7] Robert Roberts, a shopkeeper's son, echoed Engels's depiction of the "classic slum" in his book about growing up among Salford's working class.[8]

Although James Pritchard worked in the mines and textile mills of Lancashire, his son was not nurtured in a socialist or free-thought environment. Bill was raised in the Plymouth Brethren faith, and the major influence on his early ideas and beliefs was likely his mother, not his father. Judging by his later recollections, his religious training in the Brethren faith was extremely rigorous even by the standards of the day.[9] The Brethren were on the margins of Victorian Nonconformism, considered "unchurchly" even by fellow dissenters in the Methodist and Baptist congregations. They rejected an ordained clergy and believed that each person should be his or her own leader. The Brethren also tended to share the general Nonconformist emphasis on what Gerald Parsons, interpreting the work of R.J. Helmstadter, has called a "commitment to the moral priority of the individual conscience."[10] The animus toward leaders, typical of Marxists of the third way, may in Pritchard's case have been rooted in his religious upbringing. The importance in his thought of the individual conscience was also a recurring theme.

As Hugh McLeod points out, there was a distinct similarity between the "ultra-Evangelicalism" of groups like the Brethren and the radical political parties. Both groups "could dismiss the objections of their critics by branding them either as moved by class selfishness or as dupes of those who were."[11] While one would not want to posit too direct a cause and effect relationship between Pritchard's religious upbringing and his later socialist politics, McLeod's observation describes quite accurately the attitude Pritchard evinced as editor of the *Western Clarion*. At times he certainly engaged in what McLeod calls the "automatic rejection of criticism," and he was always ready to condemn any individual, party, or religious organization duped by the capitalist system. So there were, Pritchard's own denials notwithstanding, "religious" roots for his often single-minded defence of Marxian socialism.

It is important to note, however, that the close-mindedness of Nonconformist parents was often balanced by a tendency to allow their children to think for themselves. The process, which occurred in Pritchard's case, was fuelled by the importance Nonconformists placed on education and upward social mobility. Pritchard was not lacking in formal education, although throughout his life he portrayed himself as essentially an autodidact. He began school at the age of two and a half and was reading the newspaper to his mother when he was six.[12] He went to school in Swinton, near Manchester, leaving before he turned thirteen. Between the ages of thirteen and twenty he attended the Manchester School of Technology and the Royal Institute of Technology in Salford, where he learned shorthand, some German, and typing.[13] His formal education afforded him the opportunity to apprentice as a clerk in the building construction business. He served a seven-year apprenticeship as clerk of works on outside jobs and as cost clerk in the office.[14] As a result, he "knew lumber," and this helps explain his ability to get jobs in British Columbia as a longshoreman, shipper in a sawmill, and editor of the newspaper of the Loggers' and Camp Workers' Union. His last job in Manchester involved working with lumber in a big packing warehouse owned by Lloyd's.[15] He was a wage worker, but as a clerk he had both the time and energy at the end of the day to further both his formal and informal education. Even at a young age, therefore, he was of, and yet different from, the mass of skilled and unskilled workers in the industrial working class.

It is not surprising that in his move away from the religiosity of his home life and entrance into the world of work Pritchard should encounter the ideas of Karl Marx. By the mid-1890s H.M. Hyndman's Social Democratic Federation, an "overtly Marxist organization," was stronger in Lancashire than in any area of Britain with the exception of London. It was particularly strong in Salford.[16] Roberts claims that the SDF had "about as much political impact on the neighbourhood as the near-by gasworks," but his flippancy likely reflects opinions expressed in his father's store during a later period SDF of decline, not first-hand experience.[17] John Walton, on the other hand, suggests that the SDF in Lancashire was not dogmatic and sectarian and became very much part of the labour movement.[18] The salient point is that if Bill Pritchard was going to encounter Marxist ideas as a youth, there was no better place in England than Salford. Whether or not he began his socialist education with *Capital* is moot, but there is no denying the impact it had on him. His recounting of that experience is revealing: he later recalled that he came to *Capital* as an idealist, expecting from Marx a vision of the future. Instead, he was struck by the very first sentence, in which Marx began not with a prescription of the socialist utopia but rather with an analysis of the commodity. This was, according to Pritchard, "something different than I had been looking for, and I just took hold of it."[19] His embracing of *Capital*, therefore, was at least in part a reaction against the idealism and sentimentality of his religious upbringing, or his understanding of utopian socialism – probably both. Perhaps even his business training attracted him to Marx's more calculated and detailed analysis.

So what do we know about Bill Pritchard on the eve of his arrival in Canada? Unlike Ernest Winch, he did not come from a labour aristocracy background. His father was a labourer while the family lived in England, and he worked in the coal mines of Vancouver Island in the early 1900s. It seems almost certain that Bill's mother was the more religious parent, and that as Bill progressed toward adulthood the influence of his mother declined and that of his father increased. We do not know if James Pritchard was a socialist before coming to Canada, but his being a member of the Dominion Executive Committee of the Socialist Party is irrefutable evidence that he was a Marxist by 1908, and this may have been a major influence behind his son's interest in Marxism. In his youth, however, Bill Pritchard's intellectual interests appear to have been fairly eclectic, and he grew up in a home where learning in general, and reading in particular, were highly valued. It seems certain, however, that he was a Marxist by the time he left England in the spring of 1911.[20]

James Pritchard, Bill's father, as a member of the 1908 Dominion Executive Committee of the Socialist Party of Canada. Photo courtesy of William Rab

After a brief stay in Montreal, Bill Pritchard arrived in Vancouver on 19 May 1911. His father took him to the shop where the Socialist Party printed the *Western Clarion*, and he met party stalwarts E.T. Kingsley and D.G. McKenzie.[21] On 21 May 1911, his third day in Vancouver, he attended a Socialist Party meeting at the Empress Theatre where Wallis Lefeaux was speaking. Two days later on 23 May, he applied for membership in the party and was admitted a week later.[22] He thereby joined the party at the low point of its existence, it having been decimated by defections to the Social Democratic Party in Manitoba and Ontario.[23] The situation was not much better in British Columbia, where both D.G. McKenzie and James Hawthornthwaite, elected to the provincial legislature on an SPC ticket in 1907 and again in 1909, resigned from the party in 1911.[24] These defections and the consequent sharp decline in revenues struck a serious blow at both the party and the *Western Clarion*, which was not published between November 1912 and February 1913.[25]

Bill Pritchard joined the Socialist Party, therefore, when it was evident to all but the most "impossibilist" members that changes were needed. He belonged to the "second generation" of SPCers who were generally more committed to considering socialist options that went beyond education and elections, most notably industrial unionism. Initially, however, his involvement was along more traditional lines. In December 1911 his first article appeared in the *Clarion*. By May 1912 he was working with William Bennett on behalf of the unemployed protestors arrested in Vancouver in January 1912, which involved sending a letter of protest to the minister of Justice in Ottawa.[26] His consistent attendance at meetings of the Dominion Executive Committee indicates his increasingly important role in directing party policy.

His main contribution, however, was toward getting the *Clarion* back on its feet. When the SPC party organ reappeared in March 1913 it was a monthly not a weekly paper. The quality of the articles had declined, and there was a notable loss of energy and direction in its pages. In addition, the number of books and pamphlets on socialism sold by the party had declined during the recent troubles. Beginning in 1913, Pritchard was an integral part of the *Clarion*'s rising fortunes. He began his training under editor John Henry Burrough, who was to remain a lifelong friend and fellow socialist. Burrough stepped down in the fall of 1914 over the controversy created by an editorial in the *Clarion* by E.T. Kingsley, who described German workers as "so obsessed with militarism as to make them traitors to the international working class."[27] When a flood of protest issued from party members, Burrough accepted responsibility for publishing the article and resigned, and Pritchard took his place. At a salary of $15 a week he did not get rich, but he certainly put everything he had into the job. The *Clarion* slowly regained its readership, the quality of the articles improved, book reviews became a standard feature, and the list of books for sale by the party increased three or four times.[28]

In his years as editor of the *Clarion* Pritchard became a leading party spokesperson. He also earned a reputation for being outspoken and sectarian, and at times could be extremely arrogant. Critics of the party's position on trade unionism and women's suffrage and of its refusal to cooperate with other socialist parties sometimes singled Pritchard out as an impossibilist, thereby suggesting that he was a worthy successor to Kingsley.[29] There was a great deal of truth in the criticisms. Pritchard could be vitriolic, and the workers themselves caught the full brunt of his wrath. In a 1912 *Clarion* article he dealt with objections to socialism which came from the workers themselves. Addressing himself to "the fool working animal," Pritchard ridiculed workers for believing that socialism would wreck the family, destroy religion, and kill individual initiative.[30]

This one article provides a critical starting point for a more general analysis of Pritchard's thought. To begin, we see that one of Pritchard's abiding concerns was why the workers allowed themselves to be duped by the bourgeoisie and its press. As a result, therefore, he and other leading SPCers were often extremely critical of the workers themselves. But it was not, as Aileen Kraditor has argued, because they despised the workers or treated them as pawns and abstractions, but out of a sense of frustration.[31] It was painful to see the workers so mistreated and so misled when they had such enormous potential for permanently changing their conditions of life. Pritchard berated workers not because he despised them but because he cared about them so much. His socialism was about taking initiative, not destroying it, because only an educated, self-organized working class could create a socialist society.

Of note as well is his argument that socialism will not destroy religion. Pritchard and many other Marxists of the third way were atheists, believing that religion was irrational, and fighting against it tooth and nail because it was a major element in the bourgeoisie's efforts to pacify the working class. Pritchard was vitriolic in his condemnation of the "Religious freaks" and the "freaks of the Orange Order." He despised the inculcation of religious values in schools, an instruction he dismissed as "mental chloroform"; religion in the classroom had to be opposed, as well as the bourgeois class that supported it.[32] On the other hand, he pointed out that socialists favoured freedom of religion in the private realm. As a Marxist and historical materialist he recognized that it did not make sense to attack personal religious beliefs, no matter how irrational and reactionary, before socialism had removed the causes of workers turning to religion.

His defence of the family, however, is not so easily accorded a socialist rationale. Even though he was from a working-class family, he very much subscribed to the middle-class Victorian ideal of separate spheres for men and women. There is little if any evidence to suggest that he was greatly influenced by socialist or feminist writers who looked to the real or imagined equality of men and women in "primitive" societies as a model for the socialist future. For Pritchard, it was enough to rid family relations of their bourgeois content in order for working-class women to be happy and fulfilled. While he envisioned a socialist future without money and wages, he does not seem to have envisioned a world in which husbands and wives worked together inside and outside the home, sharing the same tasks. The family he wanted to safeguard for the workers from the attacks of capitalist exploitation was the male headed and dominated family of his Victorian youth. Why were Pritchard and many of his fellow Marxists of the third way such traditionalists on this question? Why may they have been even more "reactionary" than their American and European counterparts? Because, I think, their youthful attitudes toward women were formed at the height of Victorianism's power: that is, the explanation has more to do with the context in which they were raised than with their "maleness." Combined with that generation's almost evangelical belief in the necessity if not inevitability of socialism, it is tragic but not surprising that many male Marxian socialists came to see equality for women as a threat, not a means, to the realization of a socialist society. At such a moment, therefore, they saw the realization of socialism as based in the maintenance rather than the challenging of gender relations in the domestic sphere.[33] Equality in the family, if it came at all, would come after the revolution.

It is true, therefore, that SPC theorists such as Pritchard believed that the answers to workers' problems were to be found in the theories of Karl Marx and their application to current society, not in changing the attitudes and beliefs that were part of their cultural heritage. They saw their role as doing everything in their power to disseminate socialist ideas – rarely understood as mediated by race and gender – by means of the press, speeches, and literature. As Pritchard pointed out, it took more than favouring the collective ownership of the means of production to be a socialist. It also meant accepting the materialist conception of history, recognizing the class war, and understanding the labour theory of value and the source of surplus value.[34] All other considerations were of little importance if the workers did not understand these ideas and act upon them.

If class struggle was the "motor" of socialist revolution, then the fuel was provided by the agency of the workers. Critics of Second International Marxism, of both the right and left, have concentrated almost exclusively on its economic determinism, reformist tendencies, and capitulation at the beginning of the First World War. Lost in the criticism has been the enormously important emphasis socialists in this period placed on the leading role of the workers themselves. Pritchard's privileging of the agency of the workers began early in his SPC involvement and stayed with him in one form or another all his life. He did believe that capitalist society was inevitably proceeding toward collapse, but the collapse of capitalism did not necessarily imply the inevitable realization of socialism. He accepted the inevitability of crises of overproduction, and the consequent sundering of capitalism as a result of its own internal contradictions. The problem was not, however, that he privileged economic determinism over the agency of the workers but that he never fully worked out the relationship between the two.[35] In his earliest writings he placed the workers themselves at the centre of the socialist revolution. In the future society, he argued, it would be up to the workers to protect "liberties." Accomplishing the overthrow of capitalism "would be the result only of such an intelligent awakening of the class who produce all wealth, that they and their successors would be the first to resist any restraints imposed upon their full and complete liberty."[36] For Pritchard, therefore, the guarantee of a socialist future lay not in Marx's historical "laws"; rather, it lay in the consciousness and will of the workers themselves.

Yet he did not accept the argument that the class struggle did not exist until the workers became conscious of it. There was a class struggle in Canada before there was a Socialist Party, and before Canadian workers were involved in "a coherent and conscious striving after the reins of power."[37] But this did not mean that Pritchard was an economic determinist, because he rejected what he called "economic fatalism." Correctly interpreting Marx, he argued that what distinguished the class struggle since the advent of the industrial revolution was the creation, for the first time in history, of an underclass conscious of its class position and with the will to act upon that knowledge. For Pritchard there was no shortcut to emancipation – "nothing less than CLASS CONSCIOUS KNOWLEDGE and CLASS CONSCIOUS EFFORT will avail for the attainment of our object."[38]

For all of Pritchard's weaknesses as a theorist, his tendency to hyperbole and exaggeration, his excessively arrogant attacks on opponents, and his failure to theorize the working class as also comprising women and people of colour, it cannot be suggested that he was an economic determinist, blinkered Marxist, or Second International reformist. Nor did he analyse capitalism as if it were frozen in time. As he noted in his own inimitable style in August 1917, "Even to a man with a hat rack head piece it should be patent that capitalism in its complexity, differs very much from what it was fifty years ago."[39] During the war and after, he was very much in tune with changes occurring in the capitalist system.

At the cultural level, he followed assiduously the latest developments in Europe, Britain, Canada, and the United States. He was a voracious reader of newspapers, contemporary journals, and the latest works of non-fiction. In the pages of the *Western Clarion* he and other SPC members reviewed the work of Stephen Leacock, John Spargo, Jack London, O.D. Skelton, Charles Beard, Upton Sinclair, Paul Lafargue, and many other contemporary writers. Consistently Pritchard and others attempted to uncover the hidden motives of defenders of the capitalist system and lay them bare for the workers of Canada. The problem was that exposing the hypocrisies and brutalities of the capitalist class did not lead in a straight line, or even circuitously, to worker organization and the eventual creation of a socialist society. By 1917, therefore, when Pritchard left the *Clarion*, there was already an ill-defined realization among SPC leaders that they needed to enter more directly into the fray.

Pritchard had already demonstrated his worth to the Marxist cause, and both he and his wife, Eleanor, had endured the greatest pain parents can experience.[40] In the early winter of 1915–16 he was asked to go on a three-month "propaganda tour" of Alberta, a trip that involved speaking engagements in a number of small rural communities, as well as in Edmonton and Calgary. The choice of Pritchard was a testament to his dedication to the cause of the Socialist Party and to the standing he had acquired in a relatively short period of time as a writer and speaker. He returned to Vancouver in early April, and within days his youngest son, George Leslie, was dead. It is impossible not to believe that Eleanor associated her husband's absence during the trip with her son's death, and as contributing to the "harrowing experiences" that followed.[41] No doubt Pritchard himself was guilt-ridden, and when daughter Mildred was born the following year, his decision to leave the *Clarion* may have been influenced by his wife's desire that her daughter be better provided for than her son had been.

So there were personal as well as political reasons for Pritchard's entry into the labour force in 1917. If his personal motivation was providing for his family, his political motive was the need to link his analysis of the capitalist system and the SPC's educational function more firmly with changes taking place in the organization of industry. Socialist knowledge was being disseminated in the working class as a whole, but what were the tangible results? Pritchard, like Marx before him, seemed to assume that the process was cumulative, that more and more workers would become class conscious until the necessary majority had been created to take over the reins of power from the capitalist class. By about 1917, however, the leading SPCers were beginning to doubt the efficacy of such an approach, given the party's recent dismal performance in federal and provincial elections and the dominion-wide trend toward the formation of labour parties.[42]

Pritchard's ideas began to change when he left the *Clarion* to take a job as a shipper in a lumber mill. Until he began working in the mill, he does not appear to have been a member of a union. His experience apparently prompted an August 1917 article on trade unions, socialism, and the role of the socialist party – perhaps the most important article he ever wrote for the paper. In it he argued that the union could be a "powerful weapon," provided that it was "based upon class knowledge and undertakes class action." He also spoke out in favour not of an industrial organization but of an organization built "according to class and the needs of a class."[43] His involvement with the sawmill workers and his analysis in the *Clarion* article foreshadowed problems that he would face as an exponent of the One Big Union. He was calling for a class organization but was a member of the International Timberworkers, an affiliate of the American Federation of Labor. As an organizer in the mill where he worked, however, he was essentially attempting to build an industrial union that would include all workers in its ranks. Like the International Timberworkers' Union itself, he was unsuccessful. Within the mill his efforts were opposed by the sawyers and saw filers, who wanted to organize their own craft union. In the event, his organizational efforts were cut short when the mill shut down.

From the International Timberworkers he moved on to another AFL union, the International Longshoremen's Association. Like Ernest Winch, he ended up with the longshoremen because jobs were more plentiful under wartime conditions, and also because they were among the better paid workers on the coast. Radicalism in the ILA was not fed by bad pay, but rather by dangerous working conditions and the instability of employment. Pritchard did not experience the worst of the conditions, because his experience as clerk and accountant and also his ability to manage people and resources meant that he spent much of his time with the Dollar and Great Northern companies as either a checker or foreman. For a time he was also president of the Auxiliary, the wing of the ILA composed of dockers and warehousemen, whose secretary was Ernest Winch.[44]

Pritchard's membership in the ILA led him into further involvement in the Vancouver socialist and labour movements. He was obligated as a delegate from the longshoremen at the Vancouver Trades and Labour Council meeting of 5 April 1918.[45] It was not until seven years after he came to Canada, therefore, that he entered into active participation in Vancouver labour politics. Like Winch, he did not begin to significantly link the theoretical and practical, socialist and labour, elements of his involvement until the late war period. In making these linkages, he had to deal with the very real tensions that existed between his role as a trade unionist and his role as a member of the Socialist Party. While he was never anti-trade union, he had some very definite opinions about unions. As a union member, he believed a socialist should "point out the mistakes and shortcomings of the rank and file and the deliberate contortions of the leaders, functioning as master class hacks."[46] He never had much respect for trade union leaders, a point he made abundantly clear in a scathing review of the Trades and Labour Congress convention held in Vancouver in October 1915.[47] According to Pritchard, the workers "must be taught to work by themselves, not fooled to trust leaders. And that is the work of a Socialist party."[48] Even in his 1973 interview at the age of 85 with Norman Penner, he maintained that he detested leadership and that the labour movement continued to suffer from leadership.[49]

A young Bill Pritchard, the personal and political cost of a life of socialist activism not yet dimming his smile. Photo courtesy of William Rab

As the Canadian government became increasingly repressive in 1917–18, shutting down the ethnic press and instituting a no-strike provision, Marxists of the third way such as Pritchard, their dislike of leaders notwithstanding, were called upon to take a more aggressive role in leading the workers. They spoke out against conscription, condemned the ruling class and its executive in the government, and became increasingly active as promoters of industrial unionism. In July 1918 Pritchard himself was elected a trustee in the elections of the Vancouver Trades and Labour Council, further enhancing his influence in B.C. labour circles.[50] He did not see himself as a leader, but most rank and file workers certainly did, an impression fortified by his use of revolutionary ideas, language, and sentiments.

Yet even as he entered more directly into labour politics Pritchard was aware that political revolution in Canada was a long way off. Confirming the impression left by his earlier articles, his political writings in 1918–19 were premised on the belief that capitalism might last a long time. The evidence suggests that few, if any, Marxists of the third way believed revolution possible in Canada at the end of the war. They came to this conclusion based on empirical observation, their belief that too few Canadian workers were socialists, and their understanding of Marx's theory of revolution. In their speeches to the workers, however, they often gave the impression that revolution was just around the corner. Pritchard did not see a revolution happening in Canada in the immediate future, but it was "inevitable" that "before the relentless onslaught of the world's class conscious workers, before the impregnability of proletarian science, the devices of our masters and their apologists must fail."[51] This sounded like a real threat to the Canadian government, the police and military, and Canadian capitalists. As a result, the Canadian state responded to what socialists like Pritchard said they were going to do, not to what they really intended to do.[52]

Pritchard's rhetoric was misleading, because he wanted the transition to a socialist future to be as free of violence as possible, and there was no violent intent in his words. Never did he abandon his belief that in a country like Canada parliamentary politics had to be at least part of the process of creating a socialist society. Attempts to depict him as a syndicalist, beginning with Martin Robin in the 1960s, have left the impression that he abandoned his belief in parliamentary politics in the late war period, and tend to imply a link between syndicalism and the promotion of violence. Pritchard was never a syndicalist and repeatedly attacked both syndicalism and anarchism, which he identified with the Industrial Workers of the World.[53] The reasons for his actions in this period have been obscured by the state's reaction to his verbal assault on the capitalist system and the tendency of historians to identify him with left ideologies now synonymous in many minds with random acts of violence. It would have been utter folly, Pritchard argued in later life, to attempt to foment a full-scale revolution in Canada in 1919. Any successful attempt at revolution would have been forced to deal with the political and economic power of the United States.

The lead-up to the events of the spring and summer of 1919 have been well documented elsewhere.[54] The key occurrences began with the one-day Ginger Goodwin strike, which took place in Vancouver on 2 August 1918. Pritchard, unlike Winch, was not at the centre of events, because he was attending Goodwin's funeral in Nanaimo. Both Pritchard and fellow SPCer Wallis Lefeaux marched in the funeral parade and spoke at the gravesite. When Pritchard returned to Victoria to take the ferry to the mainland, he was met by another SPCer named Jimmy Hodgkinson who told him about the day's events in Vancouver, including the attack on the Labour Temple. When Hodgkinson suggested to Pritchard that he stay overnight in Victoria, Pritchard took his advice, and boarded the ferry to Vancouver the next morning.

But his absence did not prevent his name from appearing on the list put together by Mayor Gale, Vancouver business people, and the returned soldiers opposed to organized labour of labour leaders they wanted expelled from Vancouver for the duration of the war. Vancouver labour leaders in turn organized a group called the Four Ls, taking, as Pritchard later recalled, the same ground "occupied by the forces against us."[55] They presented Mayor Gale and Vancouver City Council with their own list of seven prominent community members, stating that if anything happened to an individual on Mayor Gale's list, the same thing would happen to the corresponding community leader on their list. The Four Ls, which had some three hundred members, fought to preserve free speech, and went so far as to tail Mayor Gale wherever he went. As Pritchard put it, the workers refused "to cringe before tyranny," and Mayor Gale and his allies "broke."[56]

It was this defiant attitude which B.C. and other western delegates took to the historic Trades and Labour Congress meeting held in September 1918 in Quebec City. The western delegates went with a mandate to convince eastern delegates to oppose conscription and the repressive policies of the employers and governments by doing more than forming a labour party. There was substantial support in the West for the organizing of industrial unions and backing up their demands by calling a general strike. The western delegates were in the minority, however, and all radical proposals were voted down. As Gerald Friesen points out, the western proposals won significant support from a minority of eastern delegates, but when the western delegates returned home they presented what had happened at the conference in regional terms.[57]

As a result, the western delegates returned from the East convinced that they could only forge ahead with radical action west of the Lakehead. The result was the historic Western Labour Conference held in Calgary in March 1919. At the B.C. Federation of Labour convention immediately preceding it, leading radicals such as Bill Pritchard and Jack Kavanagh supported organizing workers on the basis of industrial unions, which would enforce political and economic demands. There was no real belief in an imminent revolution but rather the basic SPC belief in the need to prepare workers for the eventual overthrow of capitalism and the running of the new society. In so doing Pritchard was not, as David Bercuson suggests, advocating syndicalism. He did not operate from the assumption of the French syndicalists that any strike, no matter how small or isolated, could grow and spread into a general strike, which might lead to the overthrow of capitalism. As Ian Angus points out, most SPCers saw "direct action" in the economic sphere as supporting, not replacing, the political aspect of the class struggle.[58]

The radicalism of the BCFL meeting was carried over into the meeting of the Western Labour Conference held 13–15 March. At that conference a historic decision was taken to organize the One Big Union along industrial lines. Pritchard, in Resolution No. 2, opposed "the sending of executive officers to plead before legislatures for the passing of legal palliatives which do not palliate." The Resolutions Committee proposed a similar substitute amendment; Kavanagh moved and Pritchard seconded its adoption.[59] Later in the convention Resolution No. 5 of the B.C. Federation of Labour proposed a much stronger position. It argued that "the legitimate aspirations of the labor movement are repeatedly obstructed by the existing political forms, clearly showing the capitalistic nature of the parliamentary machinery." This statement was followed by an endorsement of "the system of industrial soviet control."[60] The difference in the two resolutions is crucial, because Pritchard's statement may not represent a rejection of parliamentary politics per se but rather a rejection of sending labour delegates to lobby Conservative and Liberal members of the legislature, a common practice in the period. Anything Pritchard ever said, both before and after the Western Labour Conference, suggests that he did not personally agree with the replacing of parliamentary institutions with a soviet-style government.

Canadian historians have not identified the key issue in their attempts to link Marxists of the third way with syndicalism and the Russian Revolution. There can be no question that Pritchard and other Marxists of the third way were resolutely opposed to the way parliamentary government was operating in Canada in the years 1917–19. It is very unlikely, however, that the great majority of them rejected the need, even in a post-revolutionary situation, for a representative institution or forum for the expression of opinion by all classes in society. The syndicalist position on the trade unions was not unlike the Leninist position on the soviets; in theory, at least, they could be the organizational loci of a central government. But this was not Pritchard's position: any revolutionary act would have to be a political act. Undoubtedly he was impressed, in the euphoria of the years 1917–19, with the apparent success of the Russian soviets. His lifelong position, however, was that trade unions, workers' councils, or soviets could not form the organizational basis for a socialist society.[61] On the question of workers' councils he broke with the Dutch council communists Herman Gorter and Anton Pannekoek, whose ideas were quite influential in North America in the late 1910s and early '20s, and whose criticisms of the Bolshevik Revolution Pritchard and other Marxists of the third way shared.[62] Little wonder, therefore, that the actual organizational structure of the One Big Union was in such question, because some Marxists of the third way like Bob Russell were much more willing than others like Pritchard to model the OBU after bodies such as unions, soviets, or workers' councils.

Following the Western Labour Conference, Pritchard was busy promoting the One Big Union, a task that took him out of the country. It is important to note that right after the formation of the OBU, leaders like Pritchard recognized the necessity for international support. In mid-April he and Vic Midgley travelled to Seattle to solicit support from the Seattle Trades and Labor Council.[63] On 1 May 1919 Pritchard and Alf Budden addressed a meeting in Butte, Montana.[64]

More insight into Pritchard's understanding of labour organization, and its possible impact on his conception of the One Big Union, emerges from his involvement in the spring of 1919 with the Loggers' and Camp Workers' Union, which had been organized in January by Helena Gutteridge and Birt Showler. As editor of the union paper *The Camp Worker*, Pritchard argued that the head office of the LCWU on Cordova Street in Vancouver was "only a clearing house." The real organization was on the job, "where you meet actually the inescapable results of the system of production for profit." He claimed that the organization "is the sum total of the knowledge, the wisdom to apply that knowledge, and the unrelenting efforts of the membership."[65] In effect, his view of LCWU locals was much like his view of the Socialist Party itself – the organization was a function of the education, organization, and activism of the members. He identified the system of organizing in the lumber camps with the British Shop Stewards movement, and in particular its emphasis on rank and file control of decision making, indicating that for him the main issue was mobilizing the workers, not the actual form of organization that mobilization took.[66] It was this perspective he brought to his involvement with the One Big Union, and it helps explain why his focus was much more on the consciousness of the workers in the industrial union movement than on the specific form of organization that consciousness produced.

Pritchard's days as editor of *The Camp Worker* were cut short by his involvement with the One Big Union and the Winnipeg General Strike. The actual organization of the OBU took place in Calgary on 4 June, three weeks after the commencement of the Winnipeg General Strike, making it a rather anticlimactic event. Leading SPCers and OBU proponents in Winnipeg, most importantly George Armstrong, Helen Armstrong, Dick Johns, and Bob Russell, were entirely tied up as leaders of the strike. Johns, in fact, was not even in Winnipeg for the strike's duration as he was in Montreal organizing for the machinists' union. No record of the proceedings appears to exist, but without doubt West Coast delegates such as Pritchard played major roles in determining what the OBU eventually became. Many questions were left unanswered, especially those dealing with the relationship between large industrial unions and small geographical unions, and how members of craft unions already in existence could affiliate with the OBU.[67] A Bob Russell or Dick Johns would have dealt with these basic considerations more directly, but they were issues Pritchard rarely wrote about or perhaps even considered.

Whether or not the "structure and policies of the OBU were almost solely determined by the sterile and somewhat fuzzy ideas" of the SPCers as a whole is another question.[68] Marxists of the third way were always guided by Marx's maxim that socialism had to be the creation of the workers themselves.[69] That idea was the core of their politics, and they applied it to all organizations with which they were associated. There was, in other words, a positive affirmation of Marx's position in the formation of the OBU, however confused, naive, or poorly thought out the effort was. That idea may be entirely mistaken, viewed from a capitalist vantage point, but it is not sterile or fuzzy. Defenders of capitalism have known for a long time that workers coming to a realization of their class position and acting on that realization is much more dangerous than any particular organizational form that mobilization might take. Pritchard knew that as well, and as with all political ideas, it had both strengths and weaknesses.

The decision taken by convention delegates to have him go to Winnipeg to investigate the strike situation changed his life forever. It is not true, as the Canadian government tried to argue at his trial, that Pritchard was part of a Bolshevik conspiracy. Yet his argument that he only went to check out what was going on seems disingenuous.[70] He was in Winnipeg to promote the cause of the strikers, as he demonstrated in the speech he gave in Victoria Park. He had little to do with the actual conduct of the strike itself, although he did participate in a controversial meeting. Along with strike committee members Bob Russell, Andy Scoble, and Fred Tipping, he met with representatives of the returned soldiers. A man named Thompson, presumably one of the soldiers, later claimed that Russell and/or Pritchard had drawn an organizational plan on a piece of paper, while talking about "soviets." In his 1969 interview with David Millar, Pritchard described Thompson's story as "nonsense," but lingering doubts remain.[71]

It would be a mistake to take Pritchard's interpretation of this incident at face value. By the 1960s he was consciously attempting to dissociate himself from his earlier involvement in anything remotely connected to the Communist Party. Pritchard himself may not have done the talking and writing, but it is possible that Russell did. Russell did order five hundred copies of the *Soviets at Work* from SPC headquarters in January 1919, with the specific intention of distributing them to the returned soldiers.[72] Whether or not they arrived before the Winnipeg General Strike is unclear, but it is undeniable that more discussion of the soviets was taking place in the spring of 1919 than Pritchard later acknowledged.

On his way back to Vancouver he stopped to give a speech in Brandon, and then went on to Calgary, where he was arrested on 20 June. He was taken into custody, spending an unpleasant night in the Calgary city jail before being returned to Winnipeg. After six days he was released on bail, whereupon he returned to Vancouver to await his preliminary hearing. While awaiting trial he did not hold back his socialist views in order to help his cause. In July he spoke at the Empress Theatre and did little to help his case in the upcoming trial. In the speech he argued that revolution was part of the evolution of any society, because in order to produce something of importance something else must first be destroyed.[73] While he was speaking more of the future than about the Winnipeg General Strike, which had already ended, any talk about revolution and destruction could not help but set him up for a "legal" fall.

He continued to agitate and speak out for socialism, even though the thought of going to prison frightened him. In August he wrote:

> To place a man whose mind is keen
> Inside an iron cell,
> Is worse by far than damning him
> Into the Christian's hell.[74]

This poem was followed by two more Pritchard offerings entitled "A World within the World," and "Labor Day in Prison."[75] The tone of these poems conveys with great clarity the fear he must have come to trial with, possibly facing years of incarceration. It is in this context we must understand the remarkable defence he offered, and his two-day address to the jury which still stands as one of the great defences of socialism and the labour movement in Canadian history.

The trial began in January 1920. Bob Russell had already been sentenced in December, and Pritchard knew he was being charged with a crime against which there was no real defence. Even the charge itself was a spur-of-the-moment, trumped-up amendment to the Criminal Code. He sat in the docket while prosecution lawyers linked him and his co-defendants with every piece of socialist literature confiscated in raids across the country.[76] His lively, sometimes inspired defence won him the admiration not only of socialists and labour people but of the daily press and politicians from a wide variety of backgrounds.

The most important element in Pritchard's case was his speech to the jury. He spoke for two days, from roughly ten o'clock in the morning until ten o'clock at night. It was, like many of his extemporaneous speeches, a rather rambling effort, full of references to working class history, science, socialism, the union movement, current affairs, and famous figures from history.[77] Worthy of note is the fact that in it he does not locate himself in the tradition of the socialist left. He is highly critical of the French utopian socialists such as Proudhon and Saint-Simon. Nor does he see himself in the tradition of either the German Social Democrats or the Russian Bolsheviks. Instead, he links himself with the great persecuted thinkers of history, including Giordano Bruno and Galileo. He sees himself in a long line of searchers after truth, misunderstood and persecuted by the societies of which they were members.[78] We also see echoes of the individualism and sense of being on the margins that hearken back to his religious upbringing. He is obviously speaking on behalf of the Canadian and international working classes, but he is doing so as the lone champion, fighting a personal battle against the powers that be.[79] There is very much the sense of the individual conscience pitting itself against the overpowering might of a state which would pervert, silence, or destroy it.

A second key theme of the speech is his understanding of Marxism. Several times Pritchard talks about the tactics of a socialist party, and says that they must vary according to the historical context and the nature of the state. Referring to the SPC Manifesto, he quotes: "In one country it may be the ballot; in a second the mass strike, and in a third insurrection."[80] The basis of the position was Marx's famous statement that the workers could take power peacefully in Britain, Holland, the United States, and, by implication, Canada as well.[81]

Linked with this argument was Pritchard's conviction that an incorrect revolutionary strategy could lead to the "common ruin of the contending classes."[82] As a student of the *Commmunist Manifesto*, he was aware that Marx did not predict the inevitability of socialism; the failure to realize socialism would result in what Rosa Luxemburg called barbarism.[83] As a student of the French Revolution, the revolutions of 1848, and the Paris Commune, Pritchard was conscious of the potential destructiveness of the counter-revolution.[84] He was convinced that in a country like Canada, which permitted various freedoms denied the working class in countries like Russia, constitutional action could not only get the workers into power but would also significantly decrease the violence of the counter-revolution. The key to socialism, as always, was an educated, committed, working-class majority ready and able to accept the responsibilities of power.

In theory Pritchard had a strong position, but the events of 1919 had laid bare the weaknesses of his argument. The SPC had been telling the workers for fifteen years that no elite, including the capitalist state, gave up power without a struggle. Class struggle, after all, was the basis of their program. Yet when the Canadian state moved quickly and ruthlessly to crush both the Winnipeg General Strike and the One Big Union, Pritchard and the SPC were caught unawares, surprised almost that what they had predicted in theory had come to pass in reality. The Canadian state had responded exactly the way the SPC said it would, but the workers were obviously not ready to take over the means of production on a national scale. The SPC knew that, and made no pretense either during or after the Winnipeg General Strike to foment a revolution.

What they did do, however, was raise the class struggle in Canada to the level of ideas. In his address to the court Pritchard said, "the fight I carry on amongst my fellow-workers is a fight with ideas."[85] The One Big Union was the embodiment of that fight. As D.C. Masters astutely pointed out in 1950, the trial was not about the Winnipeg General Strike, it was about the One Big Union.[86] Many Winnipeg socialists were more heavily involved in the strike than Pritchard, but it was Pritchard who was arrested. He symbolized the attempt by the SPC and labour proponents of industrial unionism to create a class organization whereby the state and employers would have to deal with labour as a whole. Even as an idea, with no real organizational form, the One Big Union represented a threat to established patterns of capital-labour-government relations. It threatened to make the kind of class division in society envisioned by Marx a reality, with the sellers of labour power on one side, and the owners of the means of production on the other. On the table as well was the sanctity of private property.

The 1919 labour revolt was a fleeting moment, but it represents the most successful effort by political socialists in the history of Canada to force class struggle and revolutionary politics to the forefront of capital-labour relations. Whatever the weaknesses of socialist leadership, no matter how salient the regional, gender, and ethnic ambiguities and contradictions, 1919 must be seen, as Gregory Kealey has argued, in both its national and international contexts, for the simple reason that the shaking of capitalism's foundations that took place in 1919 resonated for decades to come.[87] Even the key Socialist Party leaders, however, did not fully realize the extent of their impact on the Canadian working class, from the mines of Fernie to the factories of Amherst, Nova Scotia. Perhaps even more surprising is that many of them do not seem to have fully comprehended just how threatened the defenders of capitalism were in that watershed year in Canadian labour history.

As Ian Angus points out, the great irony of 1919 is that the state realized the potential threat more fully than did many strike leaders themselves.[88] So much attention has been paid to the hysteria of the federal government and employers, so much written about the threat of foreign agitators, that many historians have lost sight of the fact that the threat itself was real. As fragmentary and little developed as the class consciousness of 1919 was, it was a major advance on the situation of five years before. The One Big Union, however ill-conceived and poorly implemented, was an attempt to institutionalize class conflict on an international scale, and the state knew it.[89] In many respects Pritchard symbolized that attempt. He came to Winnipeg as an outside agitator and a leading exponent of the One Big Union. He was a Marxist theoretician, one of the best-known speakers in Canada, and a former editor of one of Canada's leading socialist papers. He was sent to prison not so much because of who he was, or what he did, but for what he represented.

Although his prison term was a harrowing experience, Pritchard put it to good use. He looked after the prison store and taught recent immigrants to Canada how to read and write English. He kept himself busy with Marx and music. He indulged his love of the operettas of Gilbert and Sullivan, appearing in a production of *H.M.S. Pinafore* as the captain.[90] He was visited by Adolph Kohn, a member of the Socialist Party of Great Britain, who had been invited to Canada in the fall of 1920 to fill the void left by the imprisonment of four of the SPC's best speakers. Pritchard later recalled that Kohn "visited me in jail and brought the three volumes of Marx's *Capital*, passing them through the bars to me, and thus we had an economic class in jail."[91]

Pritchard served less than his one-year sentence, and was released on 28 February 1921. In the immediate euphoria of his freedom he had little time to look after his physical health or reflect on the decline of the One Big Union.[92] On 28 February, according to the OBU *Bulletin*, seven thousand people packed the hall to hear him give his first speech, and as many again were turned away.[93] Picking up where he had left off, he offered his audience a forceful defence of Marx and excoriated the international trade union leaders. He went after them with a vengeance, proclaiming in one of his typical rhetorical flourishes: "IT IS WAR! WAR TO THE KNIFE – AND THE KNIFE TO THE HILT, for when we have killed them, we shall have killed the finest weapons the master class ever had."[94] If he had fully realized the state of the One Big Union in early 1921, he might not have been so bold.[95] The OBU was already in serious decline and faced the concerted efforts of government, capitalists, and the American Federation of Labor to destroy it.

For the moment, however, Pritchard was the focus of attention on the Canadian left. When he arrived in Vancouver on 27 March 1921 some seven thousand people were there to meet him and his family at the station. The next day there was a mass meeting on the Cambie Street grounds, attended by a Who's Who of the West Coast left. The audience heard speeches from Pritchard himself, W.R. Trotter, Jack Kavanagh, Tom Richardson, J.S. Woodsworth, and Jack Harrington.[96] It was in many respects the high point of Bill Pritchard's life, although he was still only thirty-three years of age. He was not in very good physical condition, and it would appear that he spent some time recovering. His wife, Eleanor, who had stayed in Winnipeg while her husband served his prison sentence, was shaken physically and mentally by the experience, and was forced to sell their furniture for much less than they paid for it when her husband got out of prison.[97] Recollections of old SPCers also suggest that the family was in rough shape. Ernest Winch, in spite of Pritchard's criticisms of his role in the dispute between the Lumber Workers' Industrial Union and the One Big Union, and his own family's pressing need, was moved to anonymously give the family money.[98]

While this period of Pritchard's life is somewhat clouded, it appears he found his way back into the Longshoremen's Union some time late in 1921 or early 1922. As it turned out, it was to be his last major involvement as a union member on the Canadian left. It was not to be a very pleasant experience, because in the fall of 1923 he became embroiled in the long and bitter longshoremen's strike which began in October 1923. The ostensible main bone of contention, the union's demand for five cents an hour extra for workers unloading lumber, served as the pretext for an attempt by employers to break the International Longshoremen's Association, an effort that extended from San Diego in the south to Prince Rupert in the north. In Canada the union had been a centre of radicalism during the war, and had joined the One Big Union for a brief period. Although now back in the AFL fold, the ILA still presented a powerful challenge to employer control of the hiring process which, along with speed-up and the consequent threat of accidents, were the real issues in the dispute.

The driving force behind the strike was the B.C. Shipping Federation, a powerful group of employers which included the Canadian Pacific Railway. The B.C. longshoremen had a long history of cooperation with their fellow workers in the United States, and were fully aware that to lose the strike would mean the destruction of the union, employer control of hiring, and a return to the kind of speed-up that had existed prior to the formation of the union. It was clear from the outset that the radicals of 1919, Pritchard and Jack Kavanagh, although they most clearly saw the real motives behind employer intransigence, did not carry the weight they had four years earlier. When the four-member committee was struck to negotiate with the employers, neither Pritchard nor Kavanagh was on it. At the end of October the Shipping Federation was refusing to deal with the committee, because its members represented the ILA. The owners wanted to deal with the longshoremen themselves. Pritchard, the ILA's business agent, had something less than unshakeable faith in the longshoremen, stating: "I cannot say what the men will do, but I do not think they will accede to such a demand."[99] Once again he was caught in the classic dilemma of Marxists of the third way, wanting the rank and file workers to take the initiative in opposing the union-bashing of the employers, yet fully aware that most longshoremen did not fully understand either the extent or the ferocity of the employer assault. Like Winch facing the efforts of A.J. Devereaux to drive a wedge between the rank and file longshoremen and their leaders in August 1918, Pritchard and other ILA strike leaders faced the same dilemma in the fall of 1923.

As the strike progressed and grew more violent, and the longshoremen and their families came closer to starvation, Pritchard entered more forcefully into the fight, thereby admitting that he had to take on a leadership role, his own criticisms of leadership notwithstanding. He was one of four delegates representing the ILA at a Vancouver Trades and Labour Council meeting held in early November. At that meeting the VTLC endorsed the strike without opposition and called for support from all affiliated unions. Pritchard was the main speaker for the ILA, and emphasized that defeat for the longshoremen would imperil the collective bargaining rights of all workers. He also pointed out that the Shipping Federation was controlled by American interests and that these interests had broken the ILA all up and down the coast. Vancouver was the last stronghold. Pritchard's warning that "organized labor was in a death struggle, and should stand firmly together" brought an immediate response, with the street railway union voting $1,000 to the strike fund.[100]

In mid-November, however, the VTLC negotiated a settlement calling for a return to work at pre-strike wages and the open shop. The longshoremen's committee involved in drawing up the settlement did not include Pritchard and Kavanagh, and Pritchard predicted that the strikers would reject it. They did, by a vote of 1,007 to nineteen.[101] For the time being, at least, the rank and file of the ILA heeded Pritchard's warning, even though he himself was not directly involved as a member of the strike committee. As the weeks passed the situation became more desperate, and in hindsight a VTLC discussion in early December of a possible sympathetic general strike appears to have been a false show of bravado.[102] Less than a week later the longshoremen voted to return to work by a margin of 584 to 337. The workers had "won" the creation of a government employment agency – a pyrrhic victory to say the least, because it meant accepting that the ILA would no longer be recognized.[103] A month and a half later the Vancouver Trades and Labour Council received word that the ILA had officially disbanded.[104]

The brutal crushing of the ILA, as Pritchard had foreseen at the beginning of the strike, was a body blow to the entire West Coast labour movement. The strike, however, was more effect than cause. Union membership was on the decline, not only in British Columbia but throughout Canada and the United States as well. The One Big Union had failed to rally the Canadian working class to the banner of industrial unionism, and the ILA had been one of the early West Coast unions to disaffiliate and rejoin the AFL. High rates of unemployment ensured a reserve army of labour, and individual unions began increasingly to look to their own needs and survival. It seemed a long time since 1919, the moment of political socialism and looking outward. For Marxists of the third way like Pritchard, it was another object lesson in the strengths and weaknesses of relying on the initiative of the rank and file in countering the anti-union assault of employers aided by the direct and/or indirect backing of the government. As the 1920s progressed, Marxists of the third way receded into the background, while the emergent communist movement sought to convince the Canadian working class that resolute leadership and vanguard politics would deliver what the Marxian socialism of Ernest Winch and Bill Pritchard had failed to realize, the demise of the capitalist system and the creation of a socialist society.

Although the Socialist Party of Canada continued to publish the *Western Clarion* until 1925 and its members continued to play key roles in the trade union movement and the struggles of the unemployed, the formation of the underground Communist Party in 1921 heralded a new era in labour and socialist politics. The appeal of the Bolshevik victory in the Soviet Union and the call of the Third International for all progressive forces to unite behind it had torn the Socialist Party of Canada apart. It had also shattered old alliances within the One Big Union. Jack Kavanagh, Malcolm Bruce, and A.S. Wells, among others, answered the call. Winch, Pritchard, and Bob Russell did not, sundering forever the unity of 1919. Pritchard's reaction to the Third International and the formation of the Communist Party was swift and unequivocal. He considered the twenty-one points required for affiliation to the Third International a mistake and an insult to Canadian socialists and labour leaders who were familiar with how to operate in Canadian conditions.[105] In addition, he was not about to take directions from young party members, most of whom came from Ontario, about how to engage in socialist activity in the West.[106]

Pritchard's position on the Communists was stated in no uncertain terms in July 1921. He considered the decision to create an underground party a ludicrous one in a country like Canada, and referred to exponents of the Third International as "our friends of the rat-hole persuasion (by choice)." He was not without justification for his assessment: "As one who has reason to know a little of the present highly developed espionage system in existence today I protest."[107] It was not simply because the party wanted to organize an underground wing that Pritchard was upset; he was particularly scornful because party members were defeating the whole purpose of organizing such a party by running around the country telling anyone who would listen what they were going to do.[108]

In spite of this one vitriolic outburst his involvement in the sometimes bitter battle between communists and SPCers does not appear to have been extensive. He did have, according to police reports, a near fight with his old comrade Jack Kavanagh at a meeting of the SPC in Vancouver.[109] He was not, however, a major SPC spokesperson in the dispute with supporters of the Third International. The SPC banner in the *Western Clarion* was carried by Jack Harrington and Chris Stephenson, not by Pritchard. There is a great deal of truth to Ian Angus's contention that many SPCers, Pritchard included, reacted to the rise of the Communist Party and the decline of the Socialist Party by clinging even more tenaciously to their role as educators and propagandists.[110] In the early 1920s Pritchard's primary involvement with the SPC was as a speaker. Beginning with a speech at the Royal Theatre in February 1922, he spoke on average about once a month until July 1924, usually at the Star Theatre. The speeches combined the familiar SPC emphasis on Marxism and working-class history with critiques of more contemporary trends, and included topics such as "The Lesson of Marxism," "The Paris Commune," "Spiritualism," and "Socialism as a New Order."

His attacks on the Communist Party of Canada notwithstanding, Pritchard remained a defender of the Soviet Union. In a speech in February 1924 he defended the dictatorship of the proletariat in Russia as a necessary defence against the counter-revolution. He also considered events in the Soviet Union of great importance because they reminded the international working class just how difficult the transition from capitalism to socialism could be.[111] The Soviet experience confirmed what Marxists of the third way had suspected all along, that socialism could only be constructed under favourable material conditions and the combined efforts of an educated, organized, and politically mature proletariat. Not surprisingly, Communists took this affirmation of the leading role of an educated rank and file as a "reactionary" rejection of the importance of leadership and the vanguard party. In fact there was nothing reactionary about their emphasis on the absolute necessity of an educated working-class majority, because it had always been the very *raison d'être* of Marxism of the third way. By the early 1920s, however, it was also a position that was more form than substance, a rhetorical device wielded in the battle to demonstrate that the Communists put the aims of the party ahead of the welfare of the workers.[112]

After the failure of the labour revolt of 1919, and the decline of the One Big Union, even resolute Marxists of the third way like Bill Pritchard could not be as sure about the leading role of the rank and file as they had once been. Like Marx himself, the SPC had always operated on the premise that the coming to class consciousness by the workers would be a cumulative process. The early 1920s were a discouraging period for Marxists who could not accept what they perceived as Lenin's substitution of the vanguard party for the role previously reserved for the majority of the working class organized as a party. Pritchard rejected Lenin's formulation, but with the decline of the SPC and the One Big Union he had little else to offer in its place beyond an unquestioned belief in worker agency that at times seemed more like a kind of religious faith than the product of an historical materialist reading of the state of the working class in Canada and elsewhere in the 1920s.

Pritchard continued to present himself as a champion of rank and file initiative, a task legitimated by the almost legendary stature he acquired during his trial and incarceration. Yet in spite of protestations to the contrary, the old faith in the capacity of the workers themselves had been shaken. Pritchard recognized the change in the *Longshoremen's Strike Bulletin* which he edited during the 1923 strike. There was even a hint of moving away from a strictly class analysis in his comment that the "inhabitants" of Vancouver "have suffered a grievous decline in culture in so far as that term denotes ability in critical analysis industrial and social."[113] In the *Western Clarion* the weak, disorganized state of the Canadian and American working classes was a major topic of discussion in the early 1920s. In 1924, a year before the paper folded, J.A. (Jack) McDonald wrote from San Francisco to express his dismay that the *Clarion* was no longer the official organ of a revolutionary party and had become a mere compendium of points of view.[114] Canada's Marxian socialists were confronting, but not forcefully meeting, the challenge to educate and organize the rank and file workers in the age of mass culture.

By the mid-1920s, therefore, Pritchard had become a man adrift. Having found a niche as editor of the *Longshoremen's Strike Bulletin*, which then became the *BC Labor Bulletin*, and finally the *Labor Statesman*,[115] he remained editor of the *Statesman* for some three months, and was then replaced by H.W. Watts. Why Pritchard left is unclear, but it is quite likely he was forced out, possibly because of statements he made during the 1924 provincial election campaign.[116] He lost his job as editor of the *Labor Statesman*, and his old union, the ILA, had been destroyed. Election campaigns in 1916, 1921, and 1924 had ended in defeat at the polls.[117] Most telling, however, is the fact that when the *Western Clarion* died in the summer of 1925 Pritchard did not seem overly concerned. In an article in the last issue called "The Curtain Call" he attributed the demise of the paper to the reaction and conservatism of the age, citing Mussolini, the Palmer raids, the Ku Klux Klan, and the American Legion. The focus was on changes in capitalist society as a whole and the difficulties faced by socialists, not on proletarian science, the need for a class analysis, or the necessity of mobilizing the workers.[118] There was a tone of defeatism, a sense of being controlled by overwhelming forces that was rarely in evidence in the pages of the *Clarion* prior to 1919.

In his personal life as well the ties with the halcyon days of the Socialist Party were being broken. On 1 November 1926 Chris Stephenson, who had been Dominion Secretary of the SPC during the labour revolt of 1919, died a painful death of cancer. Pritchard recalled his passing in this way: "I remember as he lay dying of cancer some of us went to visit him knowing it would be the last time. As the rest of the boys left he called me back and looking at me with that quiet smile on his face, although in pain, he said: 'Billy! The real task now facing the socialist movement is to rid Marxism of its Hegelian weaknesses.'" A worker intellectual to the last, on his deathbed Stephenson's heart, mind, and soul remained dedicated to finding a way forward for Marxian socialism. The battle was still a battle of ideas, and Hegel was still beguiling scientific socialists with his idealism and ideas on the state. Perhaps Stephenson even sensed that Pritchard was headed in "statist" directions, but his dying words were to remain in the back of his old comrade's mind and have the desired effect, as later in life Pritchard observed that "through the years since I have pondered those last words of old Chris."[119]

In the late 1920s Pritchard remained politically active, but his analyis was no longer inspired by the theories and tasks that held so much meaning for the Chris Stephensons of his days in the Socialist Party. In the federal election of 1926 he pushed very strongly the necessity of electing labour members, not just Marxian socialists, to Parliament. Workers in Canada needed to fight for constitutional rights which they were denied, but which existed in Britain.[120] His emphasis on constitutional action had always been there, but now the class analysis and revolutionary Marxism that had accompanied his belief in constitutional action was very much in the background. He did, however, continue to emphasize the relationship between the power of the state and the consciousness of the workers. Constitutional rights are denied, said Pritchard, by "the power of your masters' state, which reflects only your own mental attitude."[121] But what must be noted is that whereas in the past the mental attitude of the workers stood in the way of the creation of a socialist society, now it stood in the way of achieving constitutional rights. New to Pritchard's analysis was the importance placed on the national context.[122] In what might be described as an early left nationalist position, he argued that only the program of a workers' party could make the slogan "'Canada for Canadians' a reality – to be attained through collective ownership."[123]

Pritchard's drift away from an explicitly Marxist position may in part be explained by his drift away from wage work. He later claimed that he had been "blackballed" during the 1923 longshoremen's strike, and there can be little doubt that it was not easy for him to find employment in Vancouver. In the mid-1920s he worked on barges for a man named McInnis, but it is difficult to find out more about his experiences.[124] By the spring of 1927 he was selling life insurance in North Burnaby.[125]

Involvement with the newly formed Independent Labour Party gave further evidence of Pritchard's gradual shift away from radicalism. The ILP was formed late in 1925 as a coalition of former members of the SPC, former members of the Federated Labour Party, and individuals opposed to Communist Party involvement in the Canadian Labour Party. It was a moderate champion of collective ownership of the means of production and was led by old SPCers and SDPers, including Angus MacInnis of the Street Railwaymen's Union, Wallis Lefeaux, and Ernest Burns. The party struggled along until 1930, when it got a much needed morale boost from the election of MacInnis to Parliament in the riding of Vancouver South. Pritchard's involvement with the ILP came mostly as a speaker. In July 1927 he gave a lecture to the North Burnaby study class on the materialist conception of history.[126] A month later he spoke to the North Burnaby ILP economics class, where he urged younger members to study social and industrial problems, "the solution of which demanded intelligent and united action by an enlightened working class."[127]

Pritchard's message to the young reflected his perception that socialism had become the creed of the middle-aged, and that most young Canadians were drawn to radio, dancing, and automobiles. He was now more willing to engage in self-criticism, pointing out that socialists in the past had talked over their audience's head, and used "peculiar language." He recognized that the need "to bring Socialism from realms of pure theory to practical life was imperative."[128] Still a Marxist theorist and working class activist, he had nevertheless come to question the legacy of the old Socialist Party of Canada and seemed convinced that the conservative tenor of the times demanded a rethinking of his old approach and positions. He had been humbled by his experiences, both personal and political, and seemed to think of himself as having matured somewhat with age. With that maturity came a recognition that Marxian socialists had failed to get their message across to the younger generation, and in this period he developed a concern with educating youth to the necessity of socialism, which was to remain with him his entire life.

What did not change is that he remained a very astute observer of the labour movement and retained his dislike for the leadership of the international unions. In a December 1927 article in the *OBU Bulletin* he defended the OBU and the role he played in 1919 in taking the Winnipeg Street Railway Union out of the AFL and into the OBU. He admitted that OBU membership had dropped substantially but went on to point out that AFL membership had also dropped "to an alarming extent." In his view, the AFL suffered from "antiquated machinery" and its leaders had become "an essential and integral part of the master class." Then he advanced the prophetic observation that once the AFL set out to become a truly effective organization, it would embark "that very moment upon the voyage of its own dissolution as at present constituted" – an uncannily accurate description of how the CIO would emerge from the AFL convention of 1935.[129]

Ironically, two weeks after this article on the labour movement was printed, Bill Pritchard was elected a councillor for North Burnaby; he attended his first meeting on 19 January 1928.[130] Precisely why he ran is not clear, although he liked to give the impression that he was talked into it.[131] It is more likely that after so many defeats in federal and provincial elections he tried his hand at municipal politics in an area where he was well known and had a good chance of winning.[132]

Pritchard's involvement in municipal politics in Burnaby meant that in the summer of 1928 he had to pass up a job he wanted, one that might have dramatically changed the future course of his life. The OBU in Winnipeg was in the process of looking for a new editor for the *Bulletin*, and the General Workers' Unit in Vancouver recommended Pritchard for the job. The Joint Executive Board of the OBU decided to write to Pritchard and to Ben Legere, asking both to apply for the position at a salary of $40 a week.[133] In his response Pritchard said that he "would like very much" to take the position, but the poor state of his wife's health prevented him from doing so.[134] It is significant that he cited Eleanor's health and not his position as a councillor in Burnaby as the reason why he could not take the job. It reflected, perhaps, a degree of concern for his wife which was not always there in his days with the Socialist Party. On the other hand, it is entirely possible that he was no longer fully committed to the cause of the OBU, for even his December 1927 article had been more about attacking the AFL than defending the OBU. His wife's health was a more acceptable reason for turning down the position. While it is not certain that he would have gotten the job in any event, it is unlikely that Ben Legere, who was from California, would have been able to take it. If Eleanor Pritchard had been in good health, they might have moved to Winnipeg where Pritchard would have been reunited with Russell, and in all probability would have become more directly involved in the labour movement. It is also possible that he would have responded differently to the formation of the Co-operative Commonwealth Federation in the early 1930s.

In the event, however, he settled into two rather uneventful terms as councillor in Burnaby, having been re-elected to serve in 1929. His two years as councillor were unspectacular, his major role being chairman of the Property & Publicity Committee.[135] In the municipal election of 1930 he ran for reeve on a program of "efficient and economic administration and sound financing." His slogan was "Method vs. Muddle" and reflected his turn toward a more Fabian emphasis on experts and planning of a socialist future which also proved attractive to the founders of the Co-operative Commonwealth Federation.[136] He won the election by 219 votes over A.K. McLean, to become the first resident of North Burnaby to be elected reeve.[137] It is unlikely that the working-class electors of North Burnaby were especially attracted by his call for efficiency and sound financing: in all probability they voted for Bill Pritchard the orator and hero of 1919.

As in the past Pritchard paid a high price for his successful entry into public politics. The late '20s were a very bad time personally for him, the most serious blow being the necessity of placing Eleanor in a hospital for the mentally ill.[138] During his campaign for reeve he had endured rumours that he was "deliberately and maliciously detaining his wife in a mental hospital, and refusing her access to the children." One couple associated with the rumours made a public apology, and admitted that they had spoken out after a visit to Mrs Pritchard but before they really understood the situation. Pritchard does not appear to have taken any action against them.[139]

Pritchard's questioning of his Socialist Party past, in evidence by the late 1920s and approaching a repudiation of that past by the early 1930s, arose in part from his personal problems. As his good friend Alex Shepherd noted in 1969, he went through a great deal of political turmoil and many family problems in the 1920s and 1930s, "perhaps the latter being most responsible for the former."[140] Marxists of the third way were much less willing, of course, to admit that their political commitments were responsible for family problems, especially the loneliness, sense of rejection, and lack of self-worth felt by their wives. Pritchard never seems to have fully admitted his own responsibility for his wife's problems, although he did recognize and regret the great stress she suffered during his trial and imprisonment. There seems little doubt that he blamed himself to some degree for Eleanor's illness, and associated it with his intensive involvement with the labour and socialist movements. However, being the child of a generation of male socialists who defended the complete separation of public and private lives, he never explored this relationship, either in terms of his own marriage or gender relations as a whole. Where private matters were concerned, one suffered in silence.

As his agonized private life remained out of the public eye, the man himself was increasingly in the public eye. Once he began to wrestle with the day-to-day problems of municipal politics, both the labour and the daily press modified their perceptions of him. The *Labor Statesman* noted that he "has learned the advantages of not getting too far in advance of the average citizen" and made friends "by dealing with municipal policies instead of theories of the millenium."[141] On the cultural level he had also become less of a threat to the status quo. It was difficult for even the most anti-Marxist editor or writer to see the leader of the Burnaby Male Choir and the director of productions of *H.M.S. Pinafore* and *The Mikado* as a dire threat to the continued existence of the capitalist system.

In his first year as reeve Pritchard dealt with two main issues. The first was ensuring that workers on relief in Burnaby received employment, which meant getting rid of overtime work and distributing funds as equitably as possible. The second issue involved convincing the federal and provincial governments of the severity of the unemployment situation, a reality many politicians refused to acknowledge in 1930.[142]

Pritchard was re-elected in 1931, and as the Depression deepened he took on new responsibilities. By all accounts he was one of the most progressive reeves in the country, with even the local Communist Party organizer admitting that the Burnaby Council was very cooperative with the unemployed.[143] In the spring of 1931, for example, the Burnaby Workers' Protective Association was given permission to hold meetings free of charge in the Public Hall.[144]

As spring turned into summer Pritchard came more and more into contact with federal and provincial officials. He was also in contact with Prime Minister R.B. Bennett and in July 1931 warned Bennett that failure on the part of the federal government to increase relief payments could result in "anarchy."[145] Pritchard's politics had changed, but his talent for the rhetorical flourish was still much in evidence. He was also corresponding regularly with Gideon Robertson, the federal minister of Labour and Pritchard's old foe during the Winnipeg General Strike. In September 1931 the two men met in Victoria. Pritchard asked the federal government for $720,000 and received $400,000. He also got permission to pay forty cents an hour, eight hours a day, five days a week, rather than simply providing relief workers with a "subsistence" allowance.[146]

Even the *Vancouver Sun* was impressed with Pritchard's actions as reeve of Burnaby. The paper observed that his recent election as president of the Union of B.C. Municipalities complimented a man "who commenced his public life in about [as] stormy and unfortunate a manner as could well be imagined." The *Sun* went so far as to mention his "remarkable defense" at the Winnipeg General Strike Trial and pronounced him one of Burnaby's best reeves. In what was probably a very astute analysis, it concluded that Bill Pritchard had not sacrificed his "strong labor sympathies" but had "modified his more extreme views."[147] This was well deserved praise, but it came as much because Pritchard no longer represented a threat to the interests the *Sun* spoke for as from any lasting respect for the man and his ideas.

The *Sun*'s assessment of Pritchard's politics was borne out by his actions during the long, bitter, and violent Barnet Mills strike, which began on 23 September 1931 and dragged on into the spring of 1932. Squeezed by declining markets in the early Depression, the Barnet company responded with four wage cuts in the space of a year, the one in September 1931 comprising 20 per cent of the original rate. The new rate would pay married men at the mill twenty-three cents an hour, little more than half the forty-cent rate Pritchard had just gotten for relief work in the municipality of Burnaby. The cuts were completely unacceptable to the workers, and they accordingly voted 195 to eight to go on strike.[148]

Pritchard's role in the strike was problematic from the beginning. He was at the mill the morning the strike started and was requested by the workers to take their case to Gideon Robertson, the minister of Labour. Given that the workers were represented by the Lumber and Agricultural Workers' Industrial Union (LAWIU), which was affiliated with the Communist Party, the choice of Pritchard suggests that the Communists were not a controlling influence in the strike committee at the beginning of the strike. Yet Pritchard immediately got himself into trouble with the Communist Party by saying that he would like to see the strike settled. As reeve of Burnaby, he knew that if the strike dragged on, many of the workers would end up on relief, and he and the Burnaby councillors were having enough trouble providing for persons already on the relief roles. It is possible to argue, therefore, that he was more concerned with heading off potential problems for the Burnaby council than with getting the best possible settlement for the striking workers. More problematic was the Communist Party's charge, based on a straight class struggle analysis, that Pritchard was siding with the company.

Pressure was coming at him from many directions, and he was no doubt influenced by the company's situation. F.E. Reid, the manager, did tell his foremen two days before the strike that the company had been losing money for a year. All employees, including himself, were subject to the most recent pay cut.[149] First of all, therefore, Pritchard did have some sympathy for the situation of the company. Second, although pro-union, he likely sympathized with Reid's refusal to deal with the LAWIU, because of the role of the Communist Party. Third, he was staring in the face a situation that had seen the number of persons seeking direct relief in Burnaby skyrocket from 935 in August to 2,153 in September. Finally, the Ministry of Labour was insisting that the Barnet strikers were not entitled to relief, while Pritchard and Councillor Lench insisted that they were.[150]

Trying to decipher Pritchard's motives in all this is a tricky business. There can be little doubt that he wanted to make sure that the Communist Party derived as little advantage from the situation as possible. The Communists themselves certainly sensed as much. When Pritchard declared the situation a lockout, not a strike, in order to justify the paying of relief to the strikers and their families, the Communist press went after him with a vengeance. It slammed him as a "labor renegade," "strikebreaker," and "capitalist Reeve." His contention that the mill did not intend to re-open was "calculated to weaken the morale of the strikers, draw them from the picket line, and so enable the company to re-open with scab labour."[151]

Whether or not this was the company's strategy, there can be little doubt that the heroic resistance of the strikers, in the face of heavily armed police, kept the company "honest." Yet even the Communists themselves could not sustain the charge of strikebreaker against Pritchard. Two weeks after he was denounced, the CPC's position changed dramatically. Suddenly the party was claiming that the strikers had "forced" the municipality to provide relief for families and single men with dependents.[152] Pritchard, on the other hand, claimed that the strike committee had originally told the workers not to apply for relief.[153] Suddenly the relief payments were a good thing, according to the CPC press, because strike funds which had gone to feed the strikers and their families could now be used to support the picket line. Nary a mention of Bill Pritchard, of course, but the implication clearly was that he had gone from being the destroyer of the picket line to the defender of the picket line in the space of two weeks.

Pritchard also proved to be right about the fate of the mill. In early December it was announced that the Barnet mill would remain closed indefinitely, perhaps to re-open in the spring.[154] The announcement may have been a ploy, because within the week the Burnaby council received a letter from the company, asking its members to use their influence to have the picket line removed. Reeve Pritchard and the councillors were not swayed, however, and the letter was filed without debate.[155] A month later the company filed for bankruptcy.[156] By April–May 1932, it appeared as if the strike itself had been called off.

Pritchard's conduct during the strike was certainly not that of the old class-conscious Marxist of Socialist Party days. He was working to change the system from within and was subject to all the ambiguities and contradictions that plan of action necessarily entailed. On the other hand, the reputation he developed for having lost touch with the working class during his period as reeve was not entirely warranted. During the Barnet Mills strike he defied federal and provincial government regulations which prohibited providing relief for the strikers and their dependents. Although he predicted that the mill might close, there is no record of his telling the workers to accept concessions in order to keep the mill in operation. Of particular note is the fact that there is no record in the press of public attacks on the Communist Party, although the party did everything in its power to provoke those attacks.

While Pritchard and the Burnaby councillors emerged from the strike crisis relatively unscathed, the numbers added to already bulging relief roles promised further trouble. In December 1931 Pritchard decided, with the support of his councillors, to pay relief workers with monies not designated for that purpose. To do so required a new by-law approved by the taxpayers of Burnaby. The reeve and councillors went ahead and spent the money on relief, an act which was illegal. The decision gave their local opponents an avenue of attack, and by February

1932 there were rumours that a group of Burnaby citizens was about to have the reeve and councillors removed from office.[157] In April they were served with a writ making the charges formal.[158]

Ironically, the challenge to Pritchard's actions as reeve came about at the same time that he was once again becoming known on the provincial and national scenes. In December 1931 he was named chairman of the Unemployment Committee of the Union of Canadian Municipalities.[159] In that capacity he attended the July 1932 convention of the Union of Canadian Municipalities in Winnipeg. While there he gave a talk on unemployment, broadcast on local radio, which he concluded by saying that he was "fully persuaded that the ultimate solution for unemployment can be nothing less than the complete elimination of the profit principle from the process of production" – the same argument he used in his dealings with R.B. Bennett.[160] Pritchard's condemnation of the capitalist system notwithstanding, he spent the first half of 1932 caught in the middle of a fight between federal and provincial officials over who was responsible for the payment of direct relief. Ottawa and Victoria were blaming each other for non-payment, and Pritchard, very much buffeted by the winds of capitalism attempting to right itself, was trying to ensure that the needy of Burnaby did not become victims of jurisdictional wrangling.[161]

By the late summer of 1932 the writing was on the wall for Pritchard's stay as reeve of Burnaby. A letter to the *Burnaby Broadcast* in August charged that the municipality was going down with the ship and that Pritchard himself, in obvious reference to his trips to attend various conferences, was guilty of "extravagance."[162] In November the Feedham vs. Pritchard case, which ensued from the April charges that the Burnaby Council had misappropriated funds, came to trial. The judge agreed with Pritchard and the other defendants, arguing that, although technically illegal, their decision to give money to the needy had defused a potentially dangerous situation. The case was adjourned, with Judge Gregory asking the provincial government to legalize the actions of Pritchard and the Burnaby councillors. Nevertheless, in December the B.C. Supreme Court issued a writ appointing a commissioner for the corporation of Burnaby. When it was discovered that the corporation had defaulted on a bond, the reeve and councillors were replaced. On 27 December 1932 Pritchard chaired his last meeting as reeve.[163]

It is impossible not to see his terms as councillor and reeve of Burnaby as a major turning point in his political career. As he himself observed, the negotiations concerning relief wages he conducted with the unemployed in Burnaby had put him on that side of the table for the first time in his life. Socialist companions from the pre-1919 period believed that between 1928 and 1933 Pritchard moved too far away from the workers. By the spring of 1933 even his speeches seemed to be lacking the old fire. In May an OBU correspondent, commenting on a recent speech given by Pritchard in Victoria, said that he "appeared far from well, and his old punch and pep were lacking."[164] In spite of his health, the recent loss of the reeveship, and changing politics, however, he was getting set to begin one of the most intense involvements of his entire life. In the summer of 1932 the decision to launch the Co-operative Commonwealth Federation took place in Calgary, and the movement toward the new party mushroomed in British Columbia. A key factor in the fate of the new party was the newly formed Socialist Party, of which Ernest Winch was the key member and guiding spirit. In order to be a success, the CCF in British Columbia needed strong support from old SPCers like Winch, Pritchard, and Wallis Lefeaux.

Pritchard's decision to become involved in the CCF was not without the kind of personal animosity he and other Marxists of the third way so decried during the heyday of the Socialist Party. There is reason to believe that he became involved in the Reconstruction Party, and then the CCF, specifically to attack Winch and the old Socialists. By the early 1930s Pritchard had come to believe that the approach of the old SPC had been a mistake, that its members had spent too much time talking at the workers and not enough time ensuring that the workers understood what was being said. In Pritchard's mind Winch epitomized this failing of the Socialist Party. Pritchard was right, of course, but what he never seems to have admitted, at least not publicly, was that he had been more guilty of this than Winch. He was also devastated by the choice of Winch as CCF candidate in Burnaby, a nomination he reasonably felt should have gone to him.[165] While he was justified in thinking he was a suitable candidate for the position, so was Winch, who had also paid his dues in local and provincial political struggles. It was almost as if Pritchard had forgotten why he was in the socialist movement and who the enemy was, for over the course of the next few years his motivation sometimes appeared to have more to do with repudiating his own past and saving the CCF from "doctrinaires" like Winch than with fighting for the working class.

Later in life Pritchard left the impression that he had come to see his involvement in the CCF in this period as a personal embarrassment, something to be forgotten. In his 1973 interview with Norman Penner he tried to claim that he had virtually nothing to do with the CCF in the 1930s. When pushed, he tried to suggest that he only became active in the CCF because Dorothy Steeves and others in the Reconstruction Party had cajoled him into doing it. In fact, he began his activities in the Reconstruction Party, a West Coast variant of the League for Social

Reconstruction, rather more willingly, and because he now espoused ideas that were not incompatible with the LSR's thinking. As reeve of Burnaby he had taken a Fabian turn and was now a man who often talked of planning, efficiency, and administration. He was drawn to the brain trust of the CCF, men like Frank Underhill and Frank Scott, and he was also a friend and ally of J.S. Woodsworth.[166] In effect, Pritchard began his involvement with the CCF as a supporter of the moderate social democrats in the party, not as a left-wing member of the Socialist Party, a fact he did not care to be reminded of later on.

For someone who claimed to have been talked into being involved with the CCF, Pritchard did quite well: by May 1933 he was chairman of the Reconstruction Party in British Columbia. In the same month he also launched *The Commonwealth*, a paper specifically dedicated to promoting the cause of the CCF. One of the first issues set the tone for CCF politics in the 1930s, attacking Colonel H.E. Lyon for setting up an Independent CCF party. Pritchard's editorial included the statement: "No individual is greater than an organization and individual insistence upon the viewpoint of any person is the very antithesis of good organization – in fact, it is just plain anarchy."[167] His criticism of Lyon, although consistent with earlier condemnations of the negative role played by leaders in labour and socialist organizations, also demonstrated his hypocrisy. In the past he himself had been accused of Lyon's crime and would be accused of it again in 1936–37. His critique also reveals the shift from the old Socialist Party days, when attacks on individuals were almost always based on their ideas, not so much on who they were or what role they played.[168] In addition, Pritchard's attack on Lyon quite clearly demonstrates that he was a leading spokesperson for party unity from the beginning, and as such gave either implicit or explicit approval of the policies of Woodsworth and other party leaders. He proved, if anything, less critical of the policies and actions of the CCF than he had been of the old SPC. It seemed, in an age of both personal and political uncertainty, that he made a leap of faith in supporting the leadership of the CCF and then only slowly began to assess the implications of that leap for his commitment to class politics and to Marxism of the third way.

By July 1933 Pritchard was heavily involved with the CCF and its formation. He was now president of the Associated CCF Clubs of British Columbia.[169] He attended the Regina Conference as official representative of the B.C. CCF Provincial Executive. At the CCF executive council meeting of 1 October 1933 he was named the party's provincial organizer.[170] He was a full-fledged CCF supporter and an advocate of electoral politics. In his Socialist Party days, of course, he had run for office, but he saw the campaigns as vehicles for the education of the workers, not as ends in themselves. Even in the heat of the electoral race he remained a committed Marxist, putting forward without stint the SPC's revolutionary critique of capitalism and its spokespersons. As Alex Shepherd said, it was in Pritchard's "SPC youth" that he "spoke what he knew was the truth."[171]

While he still hoped to free the "common folk" from the influence of the capitalist press and create a "public mind" which was independent and inquisitive, in the course of the CCF's first provincial election campaign this was not possible.[172] It was time to admit that the "old methods" did not work; socialist speakers had to realize that most people did not want to think for themselves. Pritchard concluded that "we must appeal mainly to the *feelings* of the public. The crowd, however intelligent its component units, does not think. Our candidates, and their campaign managers, should remember that."[173]

Pritchard's basic argument was leftist, in the sense that it was motivated by a desire to build a powerful socialist movement to head off the threat of nationalism and fascism. Yet in the act of opposing those forces, he embraced the very appeal to crowd psychology on which they were based. Such a perspective, of course, implied a crucial shift away from what was best in scientific socialism. Absolutely central to Marx's theory of class struggle was his belief that individual workers, having become conscious of themselves as a class, would act on that consciousness and seek to overthrow the capitalist system. Marx's optimistic assessment of the capabilities of the workers had been the indispensable cornerstone of the entire SPC approach and Marxism of the third way. To lose faith in the rationality of the workers, to endorse a clearly manipulative use of crowd psychology in order to elect a CCF government, represented a repudiation of the individual conscience so central to the educational philosophy of the SPC and the religious training of Pritchard's youth.

The change in his thinking did not go unchallenged in the labour press. One J. L. wrote to the *OBU Bulletin*, obviously disturbed about Pritchard's politics. What is Bill Pritchard doing in the CCF? he asked. Is there no other choice? What is a "scientific socialist" to do? Could it be Pritchard is "selling his birthright for a mess of potage?"[174] Pritchard's reply came a month later, and served only to further demonstrate that his critical skills had almost totally deserted him. The same man who in 1927 had brilliantly predicted momentous changes in the international union movement and continued to defend the One Big Union had now decided that industrial unions were becoming "increasingly impotent." It was now two years before the creation of the CIO, and four years before the industrial union upsurge of the late 1930s and early 1940s. Even more astounding was Pritchard's argument that the "cardinal fact of Canadian life is the overwhelming place agriculture has in the economic activities of the country," a situation which might last "for centuries."[175]

How to explain these positions? Could Pritchard not have known, even as he wrote this letter, that his arguments contradicted both his own long-held beliefs and the country's increasingly urban, industrial make-up? Perhaps the answer lies in his concluding statements, in which he ridicules "the pure and undefiled rigid, self-styled Marxians" for misleading the workers and unfairly attacking the CCF. The attack is directed at Winch in particular, and it is possible that Pritchard was so bent on discrediting the SPCBC and its leadership that he was willing to defend the CCF's agricultural base on the prairies at the expense of accurately assessing the situation. Pritchard went on in the letter to lump the SPCBC, the Communist Party, and the OBU together as guilty of Marxist orthodoxy, a ludicrous accusation that contradicted his earlier explicit and forceful distinguishing of the three organizations and indicated that he was embarked on a narcissistic, one-man crusade to rid the left of "doctrinaires."

The responses to the letter were swift and telling. William Morrison of Rabbit Lake, Saskatchewan, reminded Pritchard that while individual farmers could become socialists, as a group they would always be reformers. Morrison astutely pointed out that the composition of the CCF would define what it would be, and that social ownership of the means of production could only be brought about by the workers.[176] G. Sangster of Vancouver followed with an even more cutting critique: referring to British and American control of the economy, he pointed out that it was not just a "Canadian problem" but a question of the "universal capitalist economy." He suggested that Pritchard used to be very good at conveying to the working class the reality of capitalism behind the appearances, but wondered how the CCF was contributing to that goal.[177] The key to the situation, concluded the Vancouver socialist, was the study of Marx and Engels.

In October 1933 Pritchard possibly hit the low point of a long and distinguished socialist life. In a *Commonwealth* editorial about the upcoming B.C. election he stated that if the CCF were to win, "it follows as a matter of law that the vested interests must resign."[178] Pritchard had seen the supression of the left-wing press in 1918–19, had his own home raided, experienced the imprisonment of dozens of socialists and labour leaders, and been jailed following an amendment to the criminal code rammed through both houses of Parliament in a day. He had once advocated meeting the force of the Canadian state with the force of the working class. He understood elected politicians, as did Marx, to be the executive of the ruling class. But by December 1933 he was arguing that the fate of the socialist movement in British Columbia depended not on the education and organization of the working class but on the performance of CCF members in the B.C. legislature. Pritchard, of all people, admired the "moderation in speech" of Robert Connell, the newly elected CCF leader.[179] It just so happened that Connell's main opponent for the leadership had been Ernest Winch: Pritchard may have genuinely come to believe what he was saying, but there can be little doubt that his arguments were again influenced by his antipathy for Winch and the other old Socialists. Ironically, in defending the "moderate" leadership of the CCF Pritchard often exhibited the same unquestioning devotion to J.S. Woodsworth and other CCF leaders which he had reviled Communist Party members for in the early 1920s.[180]

It would be a mistake, however, to suggest that Pritchard had totally abandoned the working class and Marxism of the third way. Even in the fall of 1933 the *Commonwealth* was selling a pamphlet by SPCBC member A.M. Stephen entitled "Marxism, Basis for a New Social Order."[181] In a spring 1934 editorial Pritchard stated that it was wrong to dismiss "the obvious industrial progress of Soviet Russia." He also launched a spirited defence of Marx, who had "predicted with an almost prophetic sense the inevitable final crisis as the result of the recurring and unavoidable crises arising from the nature of capitalism."[182] At times it seemed as if the Pritchard of SPC days had gone forever; at other times it seemed as if he had merely gone into hibernation, to emerge on occasion like some irascible Marxist bear to defend his lair, only to slip back into a deep sleep once more.

Pritchard also maintained some links with the B.C. working class, but not on the basis of his earlier politics. In February 1934 he spoke out in defence of striking loggers, opposing a ban that prevented them stating their case on local radio stations. In the pages of the *Commonwealth* he demanded that they be allowed to make their case to the public.[183] It is instructive, however, that Pritchard made an appeal for public support rather than calling for the workers to educate themselves, organize, and act. His own actions consisted of presenting resolutions to the provincial government, the very strategy he and other delegates had decried at the 1919 Western Labour Conference. But he continued to be respected in labour circles, and in June 1935 he was chosen by the Bridge River miners to act as their representative on the arbitration board appointed by the Department of Labour in the Bridge River mines strike.[184]

In the summer of 1935 there was even a temporary thawing in the relationship between Pritchard and Winch. In July they both spoke at the opening of the Jubilee Labour Hall in South Burnaby.[185] The reason for the rapprochement was likely the impending merger of the Socialist Party with the CCF, a development that promised, perhaps even to the two men themselves, the possible healing of old wounds. At the CCF provincial convention held 27–28 July, the motion in support of the merger was moved by Pritchard and seconded by Winch.[186] Improved relations between the two old socialists, however, were not to last long.

The one gap that could not be bridged concerned the role of the Communist Party, to which Winch was much more sympathetic than Pritchard. In the spring of 1935 Pritchard, along with Wallis Lefeaux and Robert Skinner, had been appointed to a committee to develop policy related to the relief camp strikes and what the party referred to as "Communist Party Overtures."[187] Robert Connell, the leader of the provincial CCF, who was supported by Pritchard, considered Winch to be one of the CCFers responsible for bringing Communists into the party. The major vehicle for Pritchard's support of Connell and his attacks on Winch's relations with the Communist Party was the *Commonwealth*.

The conflict over control of the *Commonwealth*'s editorial policy had its roots in a number of factors. To begin with, Pritchard had proposed the creation of the paper, incorporated it as a limited liability company, and sold shares to CCF members and supporters.[188] According to Pritchard himself, the paper was incorporated under the Companies' Act of British Columbia, not under the Co-operative Act, which did not allow it to be run "efficiently and satisfactorily" – Pritchard's way of saying that it could not be operated at profit.[189] A provision was made for supervision by the B.C. CCF executive, but Dorothy Steeves is surely right when she says that there was only "a semblance of supervision of editorial policy" that was "purely nominal."[190] In the words of Steeves, "While the paper had been made financially possible only by CCF shareholders, subscribers and advertisers, the CCF found itself unable to control or even to advise on its policy."[191]

Pritchard told a rather different, and entirely plausible, story. A *Commonwealth* article of 28 August 1936 recalled his creation of the paper in this way:

> Eventually he proposed to the C.C.F. Executive of that time, that if they agreed that a paper for the movement was necessary he was quite willing to start it, his services could be used, and the Executive then could review the situation and do as they wished. The Executive did not warm to this proposal, owing evidently, to the problem of finance. The history of many labor papers was cited. Pritchard then proposed that he start a paper, allowing the Executive supervision of editorial policy, and the Executive remain free from any financial liability. That proposal set down in writing was accepted and the paper was launched. Thus was born The Commonwealth.

The real issue by late 1935, according to Pritchard, was that the paper had shown an operating profit in November and December of that year, and suddenly CCFers such as Winch, who had wanted nothing to do with the paper when it was losing money, wanted to control its editorial policy.[192] Late in March 1936 the Provincial Executive Committee passed a resolution to inform *Commonwealth* shareholders that Pritchard had "broken faith with the movement," even though committee members admitted that they had no control over the Commonwealth Publishing Company.[193] In effect, the attempt to end his control of the *Commonwealth* preceded his public support for Robert Connell and may have to some extent caused it. A motion to suspend Pritchard was passed by the Provincial Executive Committee of the CCF on 20 June 1936, two weeks before the convention of 3–5 July at which Robert Connell was overwhelmingly endorsed as party leader. Executive members must have known that Connell's leadership was not in serious danger, and that Pritchard's support for him was a reflection of rank and file opinion. In effect, if anyone was acting against the best interests of the movement and rank and file attitudes, it was the executive committee, not Bill Pritchard.

It was to prove a pyrrhic victory for both Pritchard and Connell, because several weeks after the convention, on 28 July 1936, Connell resigned from the party and formed his own party called the Social Constructives. Two of the party's leading figures were Pritchard and Vic Midgley, the old warriors of 1919. Connell announced that he could no longer support the platform and policies of the CCF. His resignation came complete with accusations against Winch of harbouring Communist sympathies and illegally electing a member from Victoria to the CCF executive.[194]

In 1937 the resolution came. Connell's breakaway party failed to elect any members in the provincial election of that year, and Harold Winch, Ernest's son, became leader of the provincial CCF.[195] Pritchard's days as a leading spokesperson for the Co-operative Commonwealth Federation thus came to an ignominious end. The *Commonwealth*, which he had once dreamed would become a socialist daily to rival the capitalist dailies, published its last issue on 18 September 1936. The end was hastened, according to Jim Milne of the Socialist Party, by the driving of four-inch spikes into the printing rolls and the throwing of bricks through the printing office's two large plate-glass windows.[196]

There was to be no respite for Pritchard in one of the darkest periods of his life. In the pages of the *Western Socialist* his old Socialist Party comrades mocked his involvement in the CCF, and it can have been of little consolation that they did so out of a grudging admiration and in hopes that he would come back to the fold. Nor can it be said that the mockery was without justification. Jim Milne was understandably merciless in his satirical comments about a claim Pritchard made in November 1933 that both Jesus Christ and Karl Marx would be members of the CCF if they were still alive. Commenting on Pritchard running as a Social Constructive in the June 1937 B.C. election campaign, one J.N. B. observed that Pritchard "has apparently forgotten all he ever knew about Marxian Socialism."[197] When Pritchard lost badly to CCF candidate Dr Lyle Telford, the Socialist Party noted that Social Constructives had spent much of the campaign being shouted down by "a hysterical mob" – a sad "fall from grace" for the "once lionized and popular" hero of 1919.[198] While it is not true that Pritchard had abandoned Marxian socialism, his championing of the CCF indeed ended in bitter denunciations by members of both Socialist Parties of Canada, the Communist Party, and his erstwhile allies in Canada's party of social democracy. He paid a high price for forgetting the lesson of his days in the Socialist Party and of 1919, that the lifeblood of Marxism of the third way is about what one is for, not about what one is against.

The late 1930s had been sad and dispiriting years in Bill Pritchard's political life, but it was in his personal life that he experienced the greatest sadness. On 22 September 1937 his mother, Priscilla, passed away.[199] Less than four months later, on 20 January 1938, he entered the bedroom of his daughter Mildred to find that she had committed suicide. According to Dorothy Steeves, Mildred Pritchard "got periodic fits of despondency and was afraid of becoming like her mother."[200] Her despondency may have been deepened by living in the shadow of her famous father. In January 1935 the *Commonwealth* had run a story on the women who worked in its offices; one of them was Mildred Pritchard, who told the writer that her biggest complaint was that people thought of her only as Bill Pritchard's daughter and not as herself.[201] Her father, whose politics were based in developing the self-confidence of workers and motivating them to establish an identity apart from the one imposed upon them by the capitalist system, was much less attentive to the needs of his own children to develop a similar confidence and identity. Pritchard was not a deliberately cruel or neglectful man, but as he himself admitted in later life, his family paid a terrible price in private suffering to make it possible for him to be an activist in the public realm.

For the moment, at least, most B.C. CCFers forgot the battles of the past and tried to find ways to help Pritchard survive his loss. He was dealing not just with his daughter's suicide but with his son Gilbert's attempt to stowaway on a ship bound for New Zealand as a way of relieving his family's crisis, one element of the situation being that the Pritchards "were down to their last cent."[202] On the strength of money raised by CCF members Pritchard left British Columbia for California on 8 February 1938. Originally intending to recuperate while living with his sister, he spent the next forty years of his life there.

According to Dorothy Steeves, there was a tragic and ironic twist even to his leaving. Rev. Robert Connell, who Pritchard had spent so much time defending, seemed rather indifferent to Pritchard's pain and the loss of his daughter. Yet Winch, the man he had been fighting with since 1918, gave money to Pritchard, but on condition that Pritchard not know where it came from. Pritchard may have known, however, because the day before he left Canada he commented to Steeves that "the so-called materialistic Marxians were always to be counted upon to be far more kind-hearted to a guy in trouble than any Christian."[203] It was a prophetic comment, heralding his return to Marxism of the third way and once again demonstrating how an experience in his private life influenced his political choices in the public realm.

It is not generally recognized that Pritchard spent more of his life in the United States than in either England or Canada. Our knowledge of his life there is sketchy, in part because Canadian historians have shown little interest in it, in part because his family and closest friends, for understandable reasons, have always been hesitant or unwilling to talk about him. We do know that he returned to Marxism of the third way by joining the World Socialist Party of the United States (WSPUS), a sister party of the Socialist Party of Canada. This was not the Socialist Party organized in British Columbia by Ernest Winch, but the Winnipeg-based party organized by former SPCers such as George Armstrong and Alex Shepherd.[204] The party published the *Western Socialist*, a "Journal of Scientific Socialism in the Western Hemisphere," until it was banned by the Canadian press censor during the Second World War. The journal was then moved to Boston where it was published by the WSPUS.

There were to be no more 1919s for Bill Pritchard, but in the United States he returned to the third way. In a series of position papers he wrote in the early 1970s he demonstrated the great breadth of his knowledge of western history and philosophy, his commitment to Marxism and historical materialism, and his adamant refusal to bend to the growing trend to question the applicability of Marxism to non-western societies. He rejected the argument that Marxism was Eurocentric and insisted, based on his belief that Marx's economic analysis and conception of history were inseparable, that Marx's analysis of the capitalist economy had universal applicability.[205]

By this time Pritchard had also returned, perhaps impelled by the dying words of his old comrade Chris Stephenson, to the anti-Hegelianism of the old Socialist Party of Canada. Pritchard firmly believed that Marx was being facetious when he referred to Hegel as a "mighty thinker." Reliance on Hegel's dialectic, Pritchard reasoned, had led too many socialists to believe that socialism was inevitable. He had now returned to emphasizing the crucial role of the workers themselves in the creation of a socialist society, the heart and soul of Marxism of the third way. We can tell the workers, he said, "that this system will not collapse but it can be superseded. This will take knowledge, and determination, and also require a majority. Only then can we perceive any possibility of great social change."[206]

By the time he gave a series of interviews in Canada in the late 1960s and early 1970s Pritchard had returned to the politics of his early days in the Socialist Party of Canada. He remained a devoted and knowledgeable student in the area of international politics and the nature of the capitalist system. He and his co-author, Bill Miller, produced either individually or in tandem at least forty-five position papers in the late 1960s and early '70s, on subjects ranging through Richard Nixon's trip to China, Hegel, the materialist conception of history, the Soviet Union, Czechoslovakia, Japan, Southeast Asia, and the philosophy of Marx.[207] In his later years Pritchard returned to the study of the socialist classics, analysis of contemporary developments in the capitalist system, and the importance of education – concerns that had been so central to his Marxian socialism in the pre-1919 Socialist Party.[208] As his comrades in the Socialist Party in the late 1930s had hoped, he was back where they felt he had belonged all along.

By 1975, at the age of 87, he had not lost his disdain for the violence and havoc wreaked by capitalism on nature and humanity. In a poem satirically entitled "Thanksgiving" he wrote:

> For this Predatory Economy, this Organization of Status,
> Where, over-night, Mere Mediocrity is catapulted
> Into the Category of celebrity.
> While Genius, disregarded, molds and withers
> In some foul and Darksome Garret,
> With Millions passing Blunted and Stunted Lives
> In the Grind of the Industrial Mill.

For Pritchard it was time to affirm the inherent talents and abilities of the producers, not the hype and glitz of his adopted city.[209]

The full sweep of Pritchard's life as a Marxist of the third way puts into perspective the roughly ten years he functioned as a worker intellectual in influential contact with the working-class movement. It was in those years that his theoretical ideas found the greatest resonance among workers and were in turn changed and shaped by the daily struggles of the Canadian working class. His movement away from a rigorous Marxist analysis in the 1920s and 1930s demonstrated the extent to which he was drifting away from direct contact with the workers, and the degree to which he was affected by the conservative tenor of the times. Like the Socialist Party of Canada as a whole in the early 1920s, he began to confront the reality that there were too few class-conscious workers in Canada and that they were increasingly taking their education from American capitalist culture. As a leading spokesperson for the Co-operative Commonwealth Federation, he appealed directly to the middle class to support the CCF movement, a dramatic shift from his politics in the SPC which argued that the middle class, for all intents and purposes, did not exist.

There exists in the current literature on Canadian working-class history no attempt to explain this transformation in the politics of one of Canada's most important socialists and labour leaders. Any effort to do so must begin, I think, by returning to the idea of worker self-emancipation, the belief that only an educated, intelligent, and disciplined working class was capable of overthrowing the capitalist state and creating a socialist society. Behind the power of the state, said Pritchard, lay the lack of education and organization of the workers. Yet in 1919 he was brought face to face with the realization that much more lay behind the power of the capitalist state than the disorganization and lack of knowledge of the working class. He realized, for the first time really, the extent to which the power of the capitalist state existed independently of what the working class thought and did.

In effect, the labour revolt of 1919 frightened Pritchard, because it unleashed repressive state forces and brought to the surface worker desires that he had only ever really known as theoretical constructs. He was not fully cognizant of the tremendous power of the ideas he fought for, what those ideas motivated ordinary workers to do, or able to admit that the labour revolt of 1919 was a legitimate threat to capitalist power. Least of all was he ever able to fully admit that the capitalist class responded in precisely the way he had said it would on so many nights in smoke-filled halls, filling the minds and hearts of Canadian workers with the dream of a society without wages, without money, and without capitalists. Workers were listening, and workers were believing. Pritchard never seems to have quite understood that the drama he acted in was not a Gilbert and Sullivan operetta, that the capitalists would not just bow politely and exit quietly as the curtain fell.[210] He forgot, at a crucial moment in his life, that he had not written the script.

Later in life he claimed that the Winnipeg General Strike had only been about collective bargaining and that the government's attempt to link the strike with the revolutionary ideas espoused by the Socialist Party, the Social Democratic Party, and the Industrial Workers of the World was a totally unjustified attempt to frame labour leaders like himself – a view he claimed was shared by "several historians with academic training."[211] It was a strange argument to be made by a man who had spent much of his life as a socialist mocking the pretensions of academics and claiming that the people with the real knowledge were workers steeped in the socialist classics. Winnipeg 1919 was about collective bargaining, but it was also about the power of the socialist vision, the idea of the One Big Union, the putting into practice of the belief that human society can be organized and run by the workers themselves. Pritchard was never fully able to come to grips with the leading role he and other Marxists of the third way had played in putting so many workers in the street. They were drawn there not by the sun, but by the vision of a new day in the sun, a new day promised by Marxists of the third way like Bill Pritchard.

After the failure of the Winnipeg General Strike Pritchard began to question the capabilities of the working class rather than engaging in an honest, searching analysis of his own role and that played by other Marxists of the third way. By the early 1930s he was claiming that socialists had to appeal to the feelings of workers, not to their reason. Having turned away from scientific socialism, and refusing to seek an alternative model in the Soviet Union and the actions of the vanguard party, Marxists of the third way like Pritchard were set adrift. Losing the Socialist Party of Canada itself was a serious blow but one that could be overcome; losing faith in the ability of a working-class majority to replace capitalism took the heart and soul out of everything that Bill Pritchard stood for.

In the 1930s, therefore, his words in defence of the CCF always had a hollow ring to them, and his old comrades knew it. In part he supported the CCF because he was someone who needed something to believe in, a sense of certainty, at a time when his personal life was so painful and the old verities seemingly gone and forgotten. In effect, he needed something to believe in more than he needed to remain committed to Marxism of the third way. With the lessons of 1919 still firmly planted in his mind, he comforted himself with the knowledge that he could support the CCF while J.S. Woodsworth, Angus MacInnis, and other leaders were responsible for the ultimate fate of the movement. His faith in the rationality of the working class badly shaken, he convinced himself that only with the support of the middle class could socialism be realized in an organic, non-violent manner. Old Marxian socialists like Winch, whatever their "machiavellian movements" in attempting to destroy Pritchard's hold on the *Commonwealth*, were a

Bill Pritchard at ninety, at the home of his good friend William Rab in the fall of 1978. "If I am remembered I hope it will not be for what I have done, but for what I tried to do." Photo courtesy of William Rab

constant reminder of his apostasy and a flesh-and-blood conscience he wished to be rid of.[212]

In his final years he wished to forget the personal tragedies and political choices of the 1930s, even as the ghosts still haunted him. On the other hand, he had also regained much of his sense of purpose and was more at ease with himself than at any point since his halcyon days in the old Socialist Party of Canada. Before he died, he was able to make two visits to Massachusetts to visit Isaac Rabinowich and his son, Bill Rab, long-time comrades in the World Socialist Party with whom he had corresponded for a quarter of a century. On these visits, one in the late 1970s and the other in 1980 or '81, Pritchard and Rab engaged in long, stimulating debates, mostly about music. Pritchard's socialist ideas in his last years were "classic," according to Rab, based on the World Socialist Movement's Declaration of Principles. Pritchard also remained a "classisist" in his musical tastes, although he "tentatively accepted" some of Rab's contemporary musical choices.[213] To the end, therefore, Marxian socialism remained Pritchard's guide in the world of politics, and he never stopped believing that music, by which he meant classical music, opera, and operetta, was "the highest and most imperious of the Arts."[214]

Bill Pritchard passed away, quietly and at home in Los Angeles on 24 October 1981.[215] His son, Arthur, and his daughter-in-law, Leah, spread his ashes in their backyard. A yellow rose bush planted in the ashes grew well and flowered. We are not yet in a position to tell if Pritchard's hopes and dreams for socialism will ever do as well. He once said, "If I am remembered I hope it will not be for what I have done, but for what I tried to do."[216] He was a Marxist of the third way, and even though he wavered in the 1920s and 1930s, never really abandoned the dream of socialism constructed by the workers themselves. Near the end of his life he continued to believe that "socialism will be impossible until an adequate majority and a very sufficient majority of people want it, understand it, know what they want, and demand it, and not until."[217] It was the commitment to worker self-emancipation, the legacy of "the Companionship of Comrades in Revolt," that Pritchard bequeathed to future generations of socialists.

3 Arthur Mould: The Conscience of Class Conflict

Marxists of the third way in Ontario were fewer in number and more difficult to identify than their counterparts in western Canada. Given the effective demise of the Socialist Party in 1911, and of the Social Democratic Party eight years later, the Communist Party seemed the only viable choice for Marxian socialists after the watershed year of 1919. Some scattered former members of the Socialist Labor Party, Socialist Party of North America, and Industrial Workers of the World attempted to maintain an independent Marxist politics, but most former members of these organizations who wanted to remain politically active on the left also joined the Communist Party.[1] During the 1920s, however, enough Marxian socialists remained apart from the Communist Party to re-emerge in the early 1930s as the Ontario Section of the Socialist Party of Canada (OSP), a party that also attracted members expelled from the CPC and adherents of the newly emerging Trotskyist movement. In the years 1931–34 they struggled valiantly to create a strong, viable movement based on Marxist educational classes, working class organization, united front activities, and a commitment to class struggle and worker self-emancipation.

Arthur Mould of London, Ontario, was in the forefront of that struggle. A figure of long standing in the London labour movement, he began his life of social activism in England as a lay preacher in the Methodist Church and completed his ideological journey by joining the Communist Party of Canada in 1943. At first glance, therefore, Mould seems rather different from Ernest Winch and Bill Pritchard, given the beginning and end points of his social activism and the fact that he was not a member of the pre-1919 Socialist Party of Canada. He was not as well read in Marx's thought as most Marxists of the third way, and he was more attracted by Marx's vision than by his analysis of labour in a capitalist society. Mould's class struggle perspective, unlike those of Winch and Pritchard, co-existed with his Christian-based critiques of capitalist exploitation and religious hypocrisy.[2] He did not find the "truth" in Marx's writings: he found some answers, and an internationalist outlook which explained why the conditions he sought to leave behind in England greeted him on his arrival in Toronto. He was less prone than many Marxists of the third way to impose a Marxist theory on Canadian society; rather, the objective class relations of Canadian society forced him to grapple with what he came to regard as the validity of Marx's teachings as echoed in the religious values he held as a young man in England.

What Mould did share with Winch and Pritchard was a similar cultural background, a Protestant upbringing, and a long history of "trying to understand and grasp the social and economic relations of our time."[3] Like other Marxists of the third way, he believed that the key to creating a truly human society was the idea that the emancipation of the working class must be the work of the working class itself. A forthright critic of organized religions, he was not so much committed to Christian institutions as he was to the human values that Christianity claimed to be based upon. Like other Marxists of the third way, he believed that Marxian socialists had to be forthright defenders of socialist politics in the trade union movement and relentless critics of labour bureaucrats and misleaders. Mould took a principled Marxist position, yet refused to believe that a resolute resistance to the capitalist system ruled out honesty, integrity, and a sense of fair play, both within the left itself and in relations with non-working-class members of society. Like Bill Pritchard, Bob Russell, and many other Marxists of the third way, he believed the enemy was the capitalist system, not the capitalists themselves.

Arthur Mould was born in Sawtry, Huntingdonshire, England, on 27 March 1879, and grew up in what he would later describe as "one of the drabest places in the drabest county I have seen in all England." His father, Simmons, a shoemaker, struggled to support his wife and eight children on fifteen shillings a week. His mother, Fanny, a woman Mould described as "patient, self sacrificing; and self effacing," was a major influence on him as a young man. There was little money for education, and at the age of eleven Arthur left school and went to work for a cattle dealer. Not long after, however, he found employment in the baking trade. During the 1890s and early 1900s it was his major occupation, and remained so until he left for Canada in 1905.[4]

Mould came from that most typical of Victorian radical backgrounds, that of the Liberal Nonconformist. His parents were Wesleyan Methodists and his father a Gladstone Liberal. Mould later recalled that his political consciousness began at the age of eleven, when local landowners, pursuant to the passing of the Land Enclosures Act, "attempted to steal our village green."[5] When his father fought to maintain the common lands, he became a hero in the eyes of his son, a feeling reinforced by the fact that young Arthur was reading about the Chartists at the time.

During the 1890s he worked in a number of English towns, but never left the baking trade for long. In 1894 he moved with his family to Peterborough, England, where his father attempted to become an insurance agent. Arthur did well, getting a job in the Cooperative Bakery at nine shillings a week, working ten-hour days. This was quite an improvement on the twelve-hour days he had worked in Sawtry and much more money than the three shillings, six pence a week he received in his home town. He was even able to begin night school, because he was now working days. Unfortunately his father's business venture failed, and the family moved to Bradford, Yorkshire, where the elder Mould went back to his old trade. Arthur did well again, getting a job in a bakeshop at fourteen shillings a week.

The Moulds arrived in Bradford at a critical period in the politics of British radicalism, and it was there that Arthur's political education began in earnest. Prior to the 1880s Bradford's leading industrialists and trade union leaders had been able to reach agreement "through the shared idiom of radical nonconformity."[6] By the late 1880s, however, growth in Bradford trade unionism, the attempts of exponents of the "new unionism" to organize unskilled workers, and the radicalization of craft workers threatened by technological change led workers to call for labour representation in Parliament.[7] Leading Liberal Party functionaries resisted the move, but the labour tide was hard to stem. In May 1891 the Bradford Labour Union was formed, and in the 1892 election Ben Tillett ran as an independent labour candidate. He lost but did very well. Labour clubs sprang up literally overnight, and labour in Bradford became an "independent force," albeit one with strong and enduring links with the Liberal Party. Mould's recollection that Bradford was "becoming labour conscious" in 1895 was quite accurate. Tillett did not poll as many votes in 1895 as he had in 1892, but his supporters were "more clearly socialist" than they had been three years earlier.[8]

While he was aware of what was happening in the labour movement Arthur did not, as a young man of sixteen, get involved in it. His main activity was still very much with the church, where the "linking up between Socialism and Christianity was to the forefront on the part of many preachers and lay preachers."[9] As a budding Christian Socialist influenced by this movement, he was more concerned with ethical behaviour than with changing social systems. Later in life he recalled being bothered by the hypocrisy of middle-class Christians who talked brotherhood but were less likely to give to the poor than were working-class people with very little. Delivering bread door to door, he was beginning to assess how people lived compared with how Christ's teachings said they should live, and was finding the middle class more wanting than the working class. His awakening social consciousness impelled him to criticize the hypocrisy of the rich rather than motivating him to become involved in organizing the poor.

It was in a socialist Sunday school that he began to study the socialist classics of the day. *Looking Backward*, the tremendously influential "utopia" of American writer Edward Bellamy, and Robert Blatchford's *Merrie England*, published in 1894, were being discussed. Mould was introduced to Marxism by a Sunday-school colleague who submitted Bellamy and Blatchford to a Marxist analysis. The experience prompted Mould to read Marx, but as he later observed, he made the youthful mistake of starting with *Capital*, a work he had great difficulty grasping. In the mid-1890s he read and got more out of J.S. Mill, Carlyle, Ruskin, William Morris, Kingsley, Malthus, Darwin, Spencer, and Henry Drummond. His Marxism was to develop very slowly over the coming decades, his embracing of scientific socialism always shaped by the values imbibed during a youth "steeped in orthodox Methodism-Christian evangelism."[10]

His job in Bradford came to an unpleasant end when the owner of the firm died, and he was dismissed by the former owner's sons. Fired for the first time and out of work, he reluctantly moved to Blackburn, Lancashire, where he got a job as a journeyman baker. When he was let go there, his employer got him a job in the fall of 1897 in nearby Accrington, Lancashire. But Mould was very unhappy: he was now living away from home, he greatly missed his family and friends in Bradford, and he disliked his job. The bakeshop was over a grocery store and there was "meagre equipment," not even a "proper oven." The job was made tolerable, however, when he became a foreman at nineteen, and the owner, realizing his youthful employee was so unhappy, raised his pay and bought a new oven. That first Christmas, and all the subsequent ones that he spent in the bakery in Accrington, Mould packed a big box of plum pudding and other Christmas treats, which he took back to Bradford. His mother was "overjoyed," greatly appreciating her son's thoughtfulness in relieving her workload and expenses.

When a bakers' union was formed in Accrington in 1900, Mould joined, although by his own later admission he did not know much about trade unions. His employer met the union's demands in terms of hours and wage scale, and there was no strike in his bakeshop. Union membership did not affect Mould's desire to go into business for himself, and shortly thereafter he entered a partnership. At the age of twenty-one he was still pursuing the entrepreneurial side of the Nonconformist dream. The rise of the union movement in the baking industry had little effect on him, and the desire to set up his own business was still his primary motivation. He did not become directly involved in the trade union movement or socialist politics – he remained committed to the church. Interesting as well is that although he was very lonely, he did not frequent pubs. Like other future Marxists of the third way, his religious upbringing led him to dislike the effects of alcohol. He was, however, understanding of workers who did drink.

In Accrington he again became involved in the Methodist Church. At the urging of the Sunday school leader he began to speak on religious topics in the Accrington market. But while the church wanted Mould to preach about individual salvation and workers receiving their reward in heaven, he wanted to talk about the communitarian teachings of Christ and what could be done here on earth. That temporal orientation led him to became heavily involved with the Young Men's Christian Association about 1899. At this time the YMCA was involved in a drive to organize chapters in the towns and cities in the north of England. Mould attended one of these organizational meetings, and joined up, although later in life he felt that he might just as easily have joined a working-man's club if he had been approached to do so by a labour man. (One possible factor dissuading him from joining a working-man's club was the fact that alcohol was permitted.) Mould became secretary of the Accrington YMCA in 1900 and drifted away from involvement in the Methodist Church. He felt freer to express his own ideas in the YMCA, which was not as bound by "creeds and dogmas." He took as his guiding principle the Sermon on the Mount, which implied a "revolution in society." He later recalled that the Methodists were horrified, but that the Anglicans in the YMCA, while not enthusiastic about his teachings and his opposition to the Boer War, were at least receptive.

The nature of Mould's opposition to the Boer War is difficult to assess. That difficulty is compounded by the fact that historians of working-class response to the war, such as Richard Price, have tended to see religious opposition to the war as essentially middle class and have not seen the churches as constituting working-class institutions.[11] Mould, because his opposition was essentially moralistic – that is, motivated by the Nonconformist conscience, Gladstonian Liberal anti-imperialism, and opposition to the making of profits by munitions makers – was more typically middle class than working class in his response. According to Price, "the main objection of the articulate working man to the war was that imperialism conflicted with social reform at home," a reason Mould does not give in his autobiography.[12] He was not aware at the time of his joining the YMCA the role it was playing, and would increasingly play, in the defence of British imperialism and the instilling of patriotism in young working-class Britons. Given that he spent some five years travelling to cities and towns all over Lancashire starting YMCA branches and speaking at meetings, he was clearly not disturbed enough by the social-control aspect of the organization's politics to leave it.

In the YMCA Mould was able to teach on subjects he did not feel free to discuss in the Methodist Church. The Bible classes discussed socialism as well as opposition to the Boer War, and he introduced Robert Blatchford's socialist paper, the *Clarion*, to the reading room. He and his students began a Ruskin Hall correspondence group, which developed into a Workers' Educational organization. The group set up an economics class, which was taught by a Marxist, a barber by trade. The whirl of ideas in young Mould's mind – Nonconformist, Gladstonian, and Marxist – was now made even more forceful by his growing pacifism, fuelled by his enormous respect for the writings of Leo Tolstoy. He was now reading a great deal of Tolstoy, developing a respect for the Russian author which lasted his entire life.

By 1904–05 he was becoming increasingly disillusioned with life in England, and was by this time unwilling to abide the hypocrisy he experienced in the church and the YMCA. He wanted to "start over in a new world, new surroundings, away from all the old shibboleths." This desire to start anew was spurred by his marriage to Alice Pollitt on 21 March 1904 after a courtship of five years. The young couple opened up a little store in anticipation of the end of the partnership in the baking firm, which came when Mould bought out his partner. This development, however, did not relieve his frustration with the "sordidness" of English society. By this time he was also disturbed by the way in which the leaders of the YMCA combined religion and imperialism, a tendency that intensified following the Boer War and the rise of the German naval threat. He wanted to get "away from Wars to a land of peace."[13]

In May 1905 he sailed from Liverpool aboard the *Tunisian*, while Alice remained behind with his parents to care for their daughter, also Alice, who was only months old. It would have been impossible to predict that the young man who debarked at Quebec City would one day join the Communist Party of Canada. He had read Marx but was not a Marxist in any meaningful sense. He espoused a kind of Christian

Arthur Mould and Alice Pollitt on their wedding day, 21 March 1904, in Accrington, Lancashire. Photo courtesy of Helen Mould Rawson

anarcho-communism, an amalgam of Christ and Tolstoy, but he had never been actively involved in the trade union movement or socialist politics. Nor was he a trade union organizer. He came to Canada to make his way in the world, not to radicalize the Canadian working class.

Almost immediately he realized that far from leaving his problems behind in England, he had found them in a different form in a new land. He had no trouble finding a job; the day after he landed he was back working in a bakeshop. When his pay turned out to be less than he had earned in England, however, he quit. In Toronto he ran into the bigoted anti-English sentiment prevalent at the time.[14] He sought refuge and friendship in both the YMCA and the Metropolitan Church but received what he considered an icy reception from both institutions. He had escaped some of what he saw as the sordidness of English society, but the newly arrived baker found that "Toronto the City of Churches spread a thin veneer of respectability over business practices, factory management, and racial discrimination that stunk to high heaven."[15]

His first job in Toronto was with George Weston, who founded what became under his son Garfield a virtual dynasty in the baking industry. Mould was not happy working in the shop, a feeling intensified by the arrival of his wife and their young daughter in the spring of 1906. It was a difficult life for Alice, trying to keep the baby quiet during the day while her husband slept. As a result the young couple had little time together, and at Alice's insistence Mould attempted to get a job on a delivery wagon. Failing to get a day position with the Weston Company, he quit. He then sold books, worked in a laundry, secured a job in a brickyard firing kilns and digging clay, and was a helper with a roofing and asbestos company. While holding down these day jobs, he also worked some nights in a bakery. He then went to work with a man from Accrington who had capital but not much knowledge of the baking trade. As Mould was working at night for wages, he could muster little enthusiasm for the business, and again with Alice's support left to find better work.

When he went back to the Weston bakery and asked for a job as a salesman, he was given a position as a bread deliveryman. Part of the company's attraction for Mould was his respect for George Weston who as a former deliveryman himself really knew the business. Weston was a self-made man who began as an apprentice in the baking trade, and worked ten hours a day, six days a week for little pay.[16] In 1882, at the age of seventeen, he bought two of his employer's bread routes and became an entrepreneur. By the early 1890s he had a two-storey plant on Sullivan street, seven bakers, six deliverymen, and two helpers. In 1897 he opened the Model Bakery with a staff of forty and fourteen horse-drawn delivery wagons. Two years later he had thirty wagons, and Weston bread was available in five hundred stores.[17] Weston knew that technological change and continual expansion were the driving forces of the emerging capitalist economy.

In the meeting of Arthur Mould and George Weston we find the full import of the contradictory legacy of nineteenth-century Methodist Nonconformism. They had a number of things in common: both men had fathers who were unsuccessful in business; both started in the baking industry as child apprentices, and were involved in unsuccessful partnerships in the baking trade. Their Methodist beliefs, however, led them to choose very different paths. Weston took from Methodism the entrepreneurial spirit that produced many of Canada's most powerful and influential political and industrial families, including the Flavelles, Masseys, and Eatons, while Mould travelled the route of J.S. Woodsworth, Salem Bland, and A.E. Smith into labour politics. Barring

Mould's labour sympathies and socialist leanings, he might have ended up as an important management figure in the Weston empire.

Exactly why Mould left Weston is unclear, but there are clues. As Charles Davies points out, Weston paid his workers as little as possible, treating them the way his employers had treated him.[18] There was little if any room in the Weston world view for trade unions. By 1906–07 Mould was beginning to become more politically conscious, starting down that long road to labour radicalism that irreparably sundered the world views of George Weston and Arthur Mould. On a more personal level, the birth of his son Alfred in 1907 put increasing pressure on Mould to be a better provider for Alice and a growing family.

In 1908 he became a salesman for the Prudential Life Insurance Company. In those early days of the insurance business, companies sought out persons such as Mould who knew a large number of people and were good at dealing with the public. He soon had a desk and six people working for him, and the future looked bright. But though he lasted a year or so, within three months he was beginning to feel like a "parasite." He found it "ghoulish" to tell parents that "it could be their Mary or Tommy next."[19] In spite of the money and promising future, he had difficulty selling insurance to working-class mothers and fathers. He was earning his living in ways that bore little relationship to the principles he embraced.

At this point in his life he wanted most to get away from the sordidness of his working life in Toronto; he was not interested in becoming involved in the labour movement and attempting to change things. In 1909, spurred by the birth of another son, Walter, he set out to realize a dream of becoming a farmer. He travelled to northern Ontario where he looked at partially cleared farming properties abandoned by settlers who had headed west to take advantage of the wheat boom. He found what he considered a promising two hundred acres near Mattawa, and returned home to tell Alice about it. He tried to make living six miles from the nearest neighbour sound as promising as he could, but Alice was not about to move. His dream of farming crushed, he went back to being a wage worker. For a time he was a shipper of parts at the Russell Motor Company, a CCM bicycle factory. Eventually he returned to Phillip Carey, the roofing firm that had earlier employed him as a helper, where he became a travelling foreman looking after product application. In 1911 a fourth child, Irene, was born. In September Mould moved his family to London and became district foreman of the local Phillip Carey outlet. He was to reside in the "Forest City" for the rest of his life.

But his sojourn in Toronto had left an indelible impression on his intellectual development. He continued to be a voracious reader, but now concentrated on socialist and Russian literature. He read Tolstoy, Gorky, Marx, Emerson, and a socialist paper from New York. The Mould home became a Sunday meeting place for all kinds of thinkers, theorists, and activists, drawn not just by debate but by Alice's roast beef and Yorkshire pudding as well. These regular gatherings became large enough that they were moved to a hall on Dundas Street. Not confined to the discussion of Marxism or even socialism, the meetings appear to have been a reflection of the wide variety of anti-establishment thought prevalent in Canadian society in the early years of the twentieth century, although as Mould noted, "we generally ended up talking socialism."

While his socialism continued to be an amalgam of Christ, Marx, and Tolstoy, he was now more aggressive in his defence of socialism than he had been in Bradford and Accrington. Now when he spoke in religious settings, he used the opportunity to steer the discussion toward socialist ideas or emphasize the more radical elements of a given thinker's ideas. He and a socialist friend attended men's Bible classes "in order to do a little missionary work ourselves." Invited to address a Sunday-morning study class in a Quaker church on the subject of Tolstoy, he chose to talk about Tolstoy's ideas in later life, not his literary works. He knew that Tolstoy's pacifism would be well received by his audience but that his attack on the social system and wealth would be unwelcome. Yet he was not ready to commit himself to supporting the Socialist Party, Social Democratic Party, or the Industrial Workers of the World, whose speakers he listened to on the streets of Toronto and whose platforms he understood quite well. He had been more at home in the College Street labour church organized by a retired Methodist missionary, where he heard addresses by "socialists, anarchists, single taxers, theosophists, Doctors, Lawyers and spiritualists." Now in his thirties, Arthur Mould continued to pursue the third way between Christ and Marx, not the class-based, worker-directed third way of the Socialist Party of Canada.

London, Ontario, in 1912 was one of Ontario's most conservative communities. London was a production and distribution centre for the surrounding agricultural areas, with woodworking, food, confectionary, garments, cigar production, and iron and steel being the major industries. In the labour movement the American Federation of Labor reigned essentially unchallenged; Marxian socialism and industrial unionism were virtually non-existent. As a result, the forces compelling cross-class alliances in London were quite strong. Unlike Winnipeg, where many labourers and factory workers were non-Anglo-Saxon immigrants, London workers usually came from the same religious and ethnic backgrounds as their employers. This situation helped some of the larger London employers become leaders, by the turn of the century, in developing strategies for commanding labour acquiescence.

As James Naylor points out in his study of southern Ontario labour in this period, London companies such as McClary's were leaders in the move toward welfare capitalism. McClary's stove works was the largest company in London. A pioneer in "welfarism," McClary's established an Employee Benefit Society as early as 1882. By 1910 the company had developed a "more generalized welfare system" that included a company store, library, private savings bank, medical care, and separate eating facilities for women. There was even an employee magazine called *McClary's Wireless*. Employees did much of the organizing themselves and set up sports' teams, dances, euchre parties, concerts, and moving pictures.[20]

This strong paternalist approach to labour helps explain the relative quiescence of London labour. When the trade union movement was hard hit by the recession of 1908–09, it produced a strong movement toward class collaboration. The Civic Federation, devoted to "promoting good relations between employers and employees," was formed on 13 November 1909.[21] In addition, London's blue-collar sector was not large, and at companies such as Northern Electric, McCormick's, Kellogg's, Westinghouse, and Bach-Simpson, a significant number of women were employed. Organizing women was not a priority of the Canadian Trades and Labour Congress before the First World War, and it is unlikely female workers could have received the organizational and financial support they needed to form stable unions. Even of the organized male workers Mould later observed that "very few trade unionists were trade union conscious let alone class conscious."[22]

Yet London had a long tradition of protest, and London labour could be surprisingly militant. In 1856 workmen in the Great Western Railway shops went on strike in order to have a fellow worker re-instated.[23] In the mid 1880s London workers swelled the ranks of the Knights of Labor, setting up seven Local Assemblies.[24] The London street railway strike of 1898–99 ended in the "riot" of 8–9 July 1899.[25] Naylor points out that even in the more progressive companies like McClary's, welfarism did not extend to the shop floor, where the wishes of the foremen remained law.[26] In London industry the carrot was used more often and more effectively than in the mining camps of the West, but employers knew where to find the stick if necessary.

Mould arrived in London just before the economic recession of 1913–14. Wages were low, with labourers earning $1.75 for a ten-hour day. There were no labourers' unions, and no roofers' union.[27] Like Ernest Winch, Mould built his own house, tearing down some old farm buildings and building a house from the logs on Merwin Heights. He and Alice moved in on 21 March 1914, their tenth anniversary. The year of the commencement of the Great War also brought the birth of their third daughter, Edith. Until 1917 Mould's work life was relatively stable, as he remained employed by the Phillip Carey Company.

The political culture he found in London should not have been entirely alien to him. On the eve of the war, labour was about to increase in size and importance, the way it had in Bradford and other English industrial towns in the 1890s. As in Bradford, advocates of labour politics "argued tirelessly that independent working-class political action was necessary to safeguard and expand Canadian democracy."[28] As in England at the turn of the century, advocates of independent labour politics were engaged in a constant struggle to maintain some degree of freedom, not only from the Liberal Party but from the Conservative Party as well.[29] Mould's recollections reveal that he became much more interested in the condition and fate of the working class in London than he had been in England or Toronto. The reason for this is not clear, but he came to the conclusion that he "should be in amongst the organised working class to help."[30] When the war, which he hated, broke out in 1914, his efforts were directed toward speaking out against militarism and imperialism.

He became involved in the Radical Club, a discussion group which attracted people from all classes, including ministers, doctors, lawyers, teachers, professors, workers, and soldiers. While Mould believed it to be a local venture, it resembled the "Open Forum" which had grown out of the Industrial Brotherhood in nearby Woodstock, Ontario. In the 1890s the Brotherhood's general secretary-treasurer was Joseph Marks, editor of the *Industrial Banner.*[31] According to Mould, the London Club was started by a Mr Lerner, a philosophic anarchist. There was "quite a group" of anarchists in London at this time, and some of them later formed a communist colony in the United States. The Radical Club met on Sunday nights, and Mould enjoyed the open and freewheeling debate. Speakers came from all walks of life and political persuasions, and there were no formal rules of order or parliamentary conventions.

His involvement with the Radical Club brought him into contact with non-Anglo-Saxons whose politics and religion set them very much apart. Mould's long-time friend Max Lerner, son of the founder of the Radical Club, was a Jew as well as an anarchist, placing him well beyond the pale of London's conservative politics. According to Mould's daughters Helen and Jesse, their father "was very, very close to many Jewish people ... he sympathized with the Jews."[32] His sympathy may have had roots in his family's identification as Methodists persecuted by the established church, with fellow religious believers also persecuted for their beliefs. Given as well that Max Lerner was a doctor,

Mould's sympathy was not class-based, but it was another element in his growing identification with the oppressed and exploited, soon to lead to his decision to become actively involved in the labour movement.[33]

What Mould and Max Lerner's father did share was a hatred of the war, and a commitment to dissent and freedom of debate, a freedom threatened by the crackdown on radical thought that intensified as the war dragged on. As early as January 1916 a Dr R.C. Barklie, described by the local press as a pacifist "as late as last week," stunned the club when he came out in support of the war.[34] When Moses Baritz, a British Marxian socialist who did lecture tours for the Socialist Party of Canada, spoke on the French Revolution and defended the use of violence, the pacifists in the club were shocked. Following Baritz's speech, according to the *London Free Press*, socialists, who "used to hold the floor of the club," now represented "only a few members."[35]

Given Mould's pacifism, it may be that he was numbered among the members upset by Baritz's oration. Mould was not a Marxian socialist at this time: he continued to espouse a kind of Christian anarcho-communism and was identified as the "leader of the Tolstoian party in the club," although he did not think of himself as an anarchist. He was critical of religious hypocrisy but found John Wesley's pacifism "commendable," and credited him with preventing a revolution in England. Mould approved of Wesley's influence in helping avoid "what might have been useless bloodshed." In effect, Mould was still closer in his thinking to Wesley than to Baritz. But Wesley wanted to restrict personal liberties, whereas Christ and Tolstoy wanted people to have their freedoms.[36] The problem with the church, said Mould, was its failure to teach "self-reliance of the individual."[37] Even at thirty-seven, then, he was still speaking in the idiom of nineteenth-century Liberal Nonconformism. His concern was still the classic liberal rights and freedoms, although there were hints that he was moving in a socialist direction. In May 1916, for example, he noted that international socialism had failed because it placed nationalism before socialism, national welfare before the welfare of humanity.[38]

Mould's shift to socialism may have arisen out of what happened to the club. At the 7 May 1916 meeting, secretary John A. Cottam observed that both civil and military authorities were watching the club; he suggested that an executive committee be formed "for the purpose of supervising the discussions of the club."[39] It was the beginning of the end. J.F. Thomson insisted on parliamentary rules of order and led a drive to change the club's name to "The People's Forum." According to Mould, the club was now forced to "conform to conformity," and it died out shortly after. Writing his recollections as a Communist during the Cold War, he looked back on this period with a great deal of nostalgia: even the press, he said, was freer then. If Mould was a Stalinist, he was a very special kind: he fought dogmatic positions and called for free speech in his disputes with the Methodist Church in England, he broke with the YMCA over its increasingly dogmatic defence of imperialism, and he looked back with nostalgia on the almost anarchistic ethos of the London Radical Club. During the year of the Russian Revolution he was a long way from the Marxian socialism of Ernest Winch and Bill Pritchard, but he did share their love of argument and defence of "liberties."

In 1917 he took a major step in his political evolution when he joined the Independent Labour Party, organized on 1 July 1917 under the leadership of Joseph Marks.[40] Mould also began a concerted effort to become a delegate to the London Trades and Labour Council (LTLC), an endeavour that raised strong suspicions among trade unionists on the council. It is not clear why Mould chose this particular moment of his life to become active in the labour movement, the same year both Pritchard and Winch too became heavily involved in the union movement for the first time. It seems likely, however, that his experiences in the Radical Club led him to realize that opposition to exploitation and injustice needed to be anchored in something more durable than the freedom of open debate and the defence of abstract principles. No doubt he was affected by the upswing in trade union organization and political activism, fuelled by inflation and opposition to conscription, that affected London as well as most other cities in Canada. The labour upsurge in London during the war years was different in degree but not in kind from that which occurred in western Canada.

As Naylor points out, however, the "few ardent spirits" in the Independent Labour Party were unable to prevent the London Trades and Labour Council from endorsing the Liberal candidate in the federal election of 1917.[41] Mould was greatly distressed by the fact that, even though the constitution of the ILP forbade cooperation with the "old line parties," some ILP members on the LTLC continued to support Liberal and Conservative politicians at election time. In effect, their continuing support of the "no politics" stance of the American Federation of Labor really meant no support for labour politics. They were members of the ILP, but when election time rolled around they were to be seen wearing the buttons of Liberal and Conservative candidates. Mould the Christian socialist reserved his most vehement denunciation for the "sordid record of those men who sold out their fellows for their 30 pieces of silver."

This was strong language coming from a man who had become self-employed in the summer of 1918. With the American entry into the war, the Philip Carey Company, which was based in the United States, began to cut back on its Canadian operations. Mould took on added duties in 1917, but in the summer of 1918, with the company unwilling to offer him a position in Toronto, he was let go. Mould's decision to open up his own roofing business may have been in part motivated by the birth in 1918 of his sixth child, daughter Helen. By his own reckoning his new business survived because there were enough Liberal and Conservative supporters in London who recognized that he did good work and were willing to overlook his politics. There were others, however, who would not hire him because he was "lining up with the wrong people." For one architect at least, the wrong people meant Jews.[42]

Being self-employed did not dissuade Mould from becoming further involved in labour politics, or from being openly critical of trade unionists who continued to support the Liberal or Conservative parties. There is reason, however, to question Mould's own commitment to the cause of labour at this point in time and his later interpretation of events. In the provincial election of 1919 the ILP elected Dr Hugh Stevenson, a former London mayor and a highly respected local figure. His victory, in which he garnered 13,008 votes, was impressive, given that in the 1914 election labour candidate John D. Jacobs had only been able to attract 417 votes.[43] Yet the ILP victory in London must be placed in the context of the Canada-wide labour revolt of 1919. The response of London labour to the Winnipeg General Strike and the formation of the One Big Union might best be described as apathetic. In May 1919 the London Typographical Union voted unanimously against joining the OBU.[44]

On the other hand, caution must be exercised in accepting Mould's later claim that in London "the organisation of the workers was chaotic."[45] Mould claimed that the Stevenson victory was produced by distrust of Conservative candidate Sir Adam Beck, not by support for the cause of labour. Mould was more critical of Beck in hindsight than he had been in 1919, and his dismissal of London labour has the ring of someone who saw himself as having set London labour on its proper course. In his memoirs Mould states that he was resolutely opposed to Beck in 1919, based on the fact that Beck owned a local box factory, paid very low wages, and was anti-union. Yet Mould, who campaigned hard for Stevenson and the ILP, expressed his admiration for Beck during the campaign. According to Mould, he had done much for the country, and the people admired him for what he had done in the development of hydro.[46] Beck himself claimed that his plans for hydro would benefit the workers, but there was a strong suspicion that big capital would be the major beneficiary. In effect, some London workers may have been more opposed to what Beck stood for than Arthur Mould was. Mould made his assessments of individual capitalists based on their characters and what they did, not on the basis of what class they belonged to. Like other Marxists of the third way such as Bob Russell, he saw no contradiction between being opposed to the capitalist system and at the same time respecting individual capitalists.

His own questionable labour credentials notwithstanding, he committed himself to steering the London labour movement in general, and the Trades and Labour Council in particular, toward involvement in independent labour politics. In the late 1910s and early 1920s it was a constant struggle for Mould and other political activists to enlist the support of organized labour in London. The London Trades and Labour Council refused to endorse the ILP, and Mould claimed, not without justification, that it was the efforts of the non-union members of the LTLC that prevented the trade unionists from swinging the council's support behind the Liberal Party in the election of 1919.[47] Among non-union members of the Labour Council, it was Mould who took a leading role in moving London's labour politics to the left.

Three important developments in the political arena set the stage for the growth of labour politics in London: first, the formation in 1919 of Federal Labour Union #16523; second, the election in the fall of 1919 of the farmer-labour government, a coalition created by the United Farmers of Ontario and the Independent Labour Party; and third, the election in January 1920 of an LTLC executive that favoured independent political action and supporting the ILP. These developments on the labour political front were accompanied by an increase in militance at the job site. Unlike the West, however, where the major upswing in labour protest took place in 1919, in London it took place primarily in 1920. In that year there were seven strikes in the Forest City, involving one thousand workers.

The key to understanding the relationship between the political actionists and the trade unionists in this period was the formation of Federal Labour Union #16523. Local craft unionists in the AFL/TLCC distrusted federal labour unions, because they permitted non-trade unionists to become members.[48] By joining the FLU, Mould and J.F. Thomson, who was active as an organizer of shop labourers, became eligible to become delegates to the Trades Council.[49] On 21 May 1919 the LTLC received the credentials of five delegates from Federal Labour Union #16523, including those of Mould and Thomson. At the same meeting both men were named to the LTLC organization committee.[50] As might be expected, Liberal and Conservative supporters on the LTLC were not exactly overjoyed to be dealing with forceful supporters of the ILP. As Mould later admitted, he consciously used the Federal

Labour Union as a vehicle for getting on the Trades Council in order to politicize it.[51] There is no evidence to suggest that Mould had read Lenin's argument that trade unionists on their own could only develop a trade union consciousness, but he clearly had come to the same conclusion through his personal experiences.

The hands of Mould and Thomson were immeasurably strengthened by the results of the provincial election in the fall of 1919. Not only did ILP candidate Hugh Stevenson win in London, but the Conservative government was swept out of office on a tide of support for the United Farmers of Ontario and the Independent Labour Party. Mould suddenly became a major figure in labour politics, and not just in London. He was a member of the ILP executive which met with the party caucus, and was involved in drafting legislation favourable to the workers of Ontario. He even learned that his name was submitted to the new Minister of Labour, Walter Rollo, for an appointment to the workmen's compensation board, a position eventually given to Harry Halford of Rollo's home town of Hamilton.[52]

Mould's influence in London labour circles was further enhanced by the results of the LTLC elections in January 1920. The new president and secretary were both supporters of the ILP, although the vice-president was a Conservative supporter. Mould now had the necessary support to launch two of his major contributions to London labour, the creation of a permanent meeting place, and the publishing of a labour paper. When he became a delegate to the Trades Council he immediately noticed that there was no permanent meeting place for labour. Individual unions met all over town, and there was little cohesion among them. Mould spearheaded an attempt to buy, build, or rent a building, and one was rented. Shares were sold in the Labour Temple Company, with Hugh Stevenson being the largest individual shareholder. Mould himself held sixteen shares and won a seat on the Labour Temple board of directors in January 1920. On 16 July 1920 he was elected president of the Labour Temple Company at its inaugural meeting.

Mould was also involved in the creation of the *Labour Herald*, published sporadically between September 1920 and December 1921. As one of the *Herald*'s three editors he expended a great deal of time, money, and effort to make it "one of the best progressive daily newspapers in Ontario."[53] In spite of his impassioned pleas at LTLC meetings for cooperation, an end to factionalism, and financial support, he was fighting an uphill battle in putting political action and education at the forefront of labour's agenda.[54] His battle became even more difficult following the Trades Council elections of January 1921, when a moderate slate was returned, including president Frank Burke, a Conservative Party supporter. When the *Herald* finally folded, Mould ended up paying employees' wages out of his own pocket.[55]

Attempting to sort out his motives in this period and assessing the relative importance of personal and political factors are not easy tasks. Like other Marxists of the third way, Mould could be arrogant and egotistical, yet profess the purest of motives. His protestations notwithstanding, it is difficult to escape the conclusion that by 1921 he was literally a one-man show attempting to get rid of "termites" like LTLC president Frank Burke who were attempting to wreck his efforts.[56] He sometimes paid the rent on the Labour Temple himself, "because of the desperate need I felt to stop the old gang getting back into power."[57] The source of this "desperate need" is problematic, but it was in part fed by personal egotism. Communist Party member Jack Scott, who met Mould in the early 1930s, remembered him as "an old English guy" who "thought a great deal of himself."[58] In his memoirs Mould tends to confirm the image, referring to London labour leaders as "so called Socialists" who "didn't know the first principles of Socialism, nor trade unionism." The Communist Party did not yet exist, and "the only people who knew the class struggle were in embryo."[59] Strong words from a man who was an employer of labour and a rather moderate socialist in the early 1920s.

As with Ernest Winch and Bill Pritchard, however, there was a deep, passionate commitment on Mould's part to the cause of the working class. He was no hypocrite – he had seen and experienced the grinding poverty of industrial England, knew the plight of the workers first hand, and appreciated, even as an adolescent, the struggles of his mother and father to keep the family together.[60] From 1917 on, he was not in, but was most certainly of, the working class. One of the reasons Mould engaged in the typical Marxist of the third way excoriation of trade union leaders was because he honestly believed that they were "misleaders" of the rank and file, men who had abdicated their responsibilities as socialist educators. In January 1919, the same month he was elected president of the London local of the ILP, he signed a resolution forwarded to the federal government protesting against the recent orders-in-council banning socialist literature. The resolution also opposed the removal of "sociological text books" from public libraries.[61] Mould was an aggressive, sometimes intemperate critic of labour leaders, a man who often failed to apply his tough standards to his own behaviour. Like Bill Pritchard, however, he was motivated by a very powerful, and very genuine, desire to advance the cause of the poor and oppressed, and was recognized as doing so by a wide cross-section of London society.

Mould was a major figure at the Third Annual Convention of the provincial ILP, held in London on 2 April 1920. He made no secret of the fact that his involvement in the ILP was fuelled by his belief that it was "the brains of trades unionism, both industrially and politically." He went on to claim that ILP members should not be "merely opportunists, but should stand out bo[l]dly for what they conceive to be in the best interests of the workers."[62] Mould may have been outspoken, even arrogant at times, but it was impossible to accuse him of failing to lay his cards on the table. Nor can it be claimed that his blunt honesty hurt him in the ILP; at the 1921 convention he was elected one of the provincial party's general vice-presidents.

The rather eclectic nature of his involvement at this time was reflected in the political content of his ideas. A speech he delivered to the Independent Labour Party on 15 May 1921 is conclusive evidence of his rather confused amalgam of Christianity and Marxism. He continued to be concerned with divisions within the labour movement and labour's lack of purpose. Labour should be actively engaged in "the struggle to produce a greater man living under ideal conditions." Going on to describe the labour movement as a religious movement, he stressed the importance of morality, for what is "morally wrong is never economically sound." In response to a comment from the audience, he described Marx as "far more religious than some of his expositors." In response to another question, he suggested that dogmatism should be avoided, as theories "are too often wrong."[63]

Mould's platform in the federal election of 1921 would also suggest that he was a moderate socialist, not a radical. He ran under the auspicies of the Canadian Labour Party in the election held on 28 October 1921, losing his deposit but receiving a very respectable 4,252 votes, winning several London subdivisions.[64] He made a direct appeal to women in the campaign and spoke to the Women's Council on 26 November 1921. Like Winch, he endorsed equal pay for equal work and discussed how women had been suppressed by men and the master class throughout history. His description of the oppression of women as being a gender as well as a class phenomenon distinguishes him from Marxists of the third way in the Socialist Party who sought to argue that the oppression of women was almost entirely class-based. One would not want to push the argument too far, because Mould's ability to see patriarchy as a systemic form of oppression may not have been any more developed than his ability to see capitalism as a systemic form of oppression. Earlier in his election campaign he had suggested that capital, rather than being expropriated, should receive its "just share."[65] His socialism was not so much governed by class struggle politics as it was guided by the "principles governing humanity" as a whole.[66] Even in 1921, therefore, ending the oppression of women and workers seemed to have as much to do with individual moral choice as it had to do with ending systemic discrimination by means of collective organization. Yet the mere use of the phrase "master class," a staple of Marxian socialists of more rigorous Marxist politics, suggests Mould's affinity with Marxism of the third way.

While the farmer-labour government was in power in Ontario, Mould was operating from a position of strength. By 1922, however, the UFO/ILP alliance was clearly in trouble, and the ILP itself was in serious decline. Mould's dream of an influential labour paper died with the *Labour Herald*. On the LTLC the supporters and opponents of independent labour politics continued to joust for position until the summer of 1923. In the 25 June provincial election Premier Drury and most of his UFO/ILP ministers suffered a crushing defeat. With the end of Ontario's experiment in "class government," the power of labour, and with it Arthur Mould's influence in the LTLC, declined significantly. His opponents moved quickly. On 6 July 1923 LTLC president Frank Burke wrote to Frank Morrison, secretary of the American Federation of Labor, complaining about non-trade unionists on the LTLC. According to Burke, international trade unionists in London over the course of the last four or five years, had "had a very strenuous time to keep the Red Element from gaining control of the Council." Some locals had withdrawn, and others were having difficulty getting delegates to attend LTLC meetings. The worst offenders came from Federal Labour Union #16523. Singling out J.F. Thomson and Arthur Mould, Burke wanted to know if self-employed men, doctors, accountants, and others had "a right" to be in Local #16523.[67]

Morrison responded to Burke's request by sending John A. Flett to London to investigate the books of the Federal Labour Union.[68] While the exact purpose of Flett's search is unclear, it would appear that Morrison hoped he would uncover some kind of irregularity which would justify revoking the union's charter, or at least lead to the expulsion of Mould and Thomson. Flett must have had mixed feelings about the assignment, because he had been instrumental in chartering federal labour unions in Canada in the first place, and surely did not want Local #16523's charter revoked. In fact, Flett himself had "initiated" Mould into the Federal Union.[69] In the meantime Burke was not taking any chances. Not having received Morrison's letter of 20 July, he wrote to the AFL secretary on 23 July, reiterating the charges of his earlier letter, but adding an important new one. The new issue concerned a clause in the LTLC's constitution passed in 1920, which stated that council members could only appear on the platform of the Canadian Labour Party (CLP) during elections, a provision now opposed by Burke and allies such as LTLC treasurer Fred Young.

The Canadian Labour Party had been formed in 1918 under the auspices of the Trades and Labour Congress of Canada. The CLP began as an attempt by the TLCC to steer the labour political movement into acceptable channels, responding to rank and file labour's call for independent labour action while blunting the appeal of political socialists like Mould. By 1921–22, however, the Canadian Labour Party had replaced the Independent Labour Party as the leading representative of political socialism in London. In February 1922 Burke's concerns were heightened when Mould and William Fleet were elected ILP representatives on the CLP executive board at the party's Third Annual Convention in Stratford, Ontario. By 1923 the CLP had become actively involved in provincial as well as federal elections, while claiming to have replaced the ILP as Ontario's leading political party of labour. In Toronto the labour campaign leading up to the Ontario provincial election was conducted by the Labour Representation Political Association, an affiliate of the CLP. Two of its candidates were Malcolm Bruce and Jack MacDonald, members of the Workers' Party.[70]

The CLP, which had appeared to be "safe" for AFL craft unionists in 1918, now seemed on its way to being taken over by Communists and left-wing elements in the ILP. To Frank Burke it appeared as if political socialists like Mould were about to make radical ideas at home in the house of labour and on the campaign trail, while he and other Conservative supporters were handcuffed in their own political endeavours. The "radicalization" of the CLP, combined with the defeat of the farmer-labour government on 25 June 1923, was enough to spur Burke to action.[71] He was successful to the extent that he received a favourable ruling from Tom Moore, president of the Canadian Trades and Labour Congress, that the CLP clause served "no useful purpose," and the LTLC could not dictate to members in affiliated unions on political issues. Then, in a masterpiece of bureaucratic obfuscation, Moore argued that trades and labour councils should support independent political action, but remain apolitical in terms of affiliated members.[72] Burke won, but it was a pyrrhic victory. He and ally Fred Young, LTLC treasurer, were on the defensive from the beginning, because they had appeared on Conservative Adam Beck's platform during the 1923 provincial election. It was they who had contravened the constitution of the LTLC, not Mould and the supporters of independent political action, a fact pointed out by London carpenters, machinists, and stove mounters.[73] Burke and Young won the right to appear on Conservative platforms; but Moore's ruling, given that FLU #16523's charter was not revoked, confirmed the right of Mould and Thomson to support labour parties. Ironically, Moore's ruling (unintentionally, one assumes) defended the rights of communists in AFL unions affiliated with trades and labour councils.

This incident, while of apparently little consequence in the overall history of Canadian labour, should not be lightly dismissed. What it demonstrates is that, even facing the might of both national and international officers of the AFL, local political socialists like Arthur Mould could be tremendously influential. The role of SPCers in the West, especially during the labour revolt in 1919, has been documented here and elsewhere. This incident demonstrates quite clearly that a similar situation existed in central Canada, where even powerful figures such as Frank Morrison and Tom Moore could not simply ride roughshod over political socialists in trades and labour councils. Mould may not have been a full-fledged Marxian socialist in 1923, but like Pritchard, Winch, and other Marxists of the third way, he knew the importance of labour and labour political organizations, places where left-wing ideas could compete with the everyday business of union affairs, where a class perspective could become firmly rooted.

In the 1920s Mould was busy with more than critics of his politics, and his wife Alice even more so. Daughter Jesse was born in 1920, daughter Mildred in 1922, son John in 1924, and son Robert in 1925, bringing to nine the number of Mould children. Helen and Jesse remember these as happy years, one of their fondest memories being of their father and mother taking them, and often some kids from the neighbourhood, for picnics on the Thames River. A highlight was the Labour Day parade, which their father played a large part in organizing. Helen remembers going to the parade with her sister Edith when she was six or seven years old, and in later years there were even trips to the big city of Toronto for its Labour Day parade. Jesse remembers that her father was always involved in their school and with the Christmas concert. He had grown up in a home in which grace was sung, and like many Marxists of the third way, he brought that love of music with him to Canada. To his daughters, therefore, he was, and remained, a family man and a religious man who went to church "on occasion" and sometimes spoke there.[74]

Certainly Mould remained a committed Christian in the 1920s, but by the middle of that decade there was a relatively new element of Marxist-based socialist thinking in his ideas. As we follow him into the late 1920s and early 1930s, however, it is important to note that his disputes with the AFL/TLCC and his involvement in the Canadian Labour Party do not indicate membership in or even strong support for the Communist Party. In the 1920s he was still very much an eclectic left thinker, a man who could switch with great facility from the ideas of Marx to the values of Christianity. Yet it is also true that Marxists of the third way in southern Ontario fell much more strongly under the influence of Marxism-Leninism than in the West, because the alternative Marxism fostered by the Socialist Party was much weaker in Central Canada. As a result, it was even more difficult to maintain the third way in southern Ontario than in Western Canada. What is clear, however, is that Mould attempted to do so, even as he increasingly came under the influence of the Communist Party. Indeed, he initially chose to challenge the strength of the Communist Party within the CLP itself. At the party's convention in London, Ontario, 2–3 April 1926, he stood for election against A.E. Smith, the popular incumbent president. Smith was re-elected party president by a vote of 99–72.[75] The result is difficult to gauge, but given Smith's much higher profile at the time, it appears to indicate a substantial anti-Communist sentiment within the ranks of the CLP, and reveals how well known and respected Mould had become.

Mould's opposition to the role played by the Communist Party in the CLP continued to grow in 1926–27. By 1927 he was described as a "right-winger" in *The Worker*, the Communist Party's paper. Yet by the mid 1930s he had become a supporter of the Communist Party. The problem he poses is common to labour history in general, which tends to encounter individuals at specific periods of their lives, characterizes them in terms of the party they belong to and the party they oppose, and does not look at their long-term commitment in terms of theory and practice. Two incidents involving Mould in 1926–27 shed some light on the importance of the long-term perspective, and a more in-depth analysis of theory and practice.

Mould's reputation as a right-winger arose from an incident at the convention called by the London Labour Party (LLP) to nominate a candidate for the 1926 federal election. At that meeting L.R. Menzies, secretary of the local Communist Party and member of the Communist Party of Canada's Central Committee, charged that right-wing LLP members were "crooks" who had rigged the convention.[76] According to *The Worker*, the meeting was supposed to be open, that is, both delegates and members of affiliated bodies were eligible to vote. Mould, who was the chairman, ruled that only accredited delegates could vote. His decision was upheld by a vote of twenty-five to seventeen, and the meeting adjourned in confusion.[77] At a subsequent meeting on 13 August, Menzies was asked to apologize. When he refused, he was unseated as delegate by a majority of four votes.[78] The Communists opposed the expulsion based on such a small majority, but the chairman, Mould, upheld it. The expulsion, however, did not stop Menzies's LLP supporters from nominating him to represent the LLP in the election. When all the other nominees declined, Mould claimed that Robert Foxcroft had agreed to run, although his name was not recorded in the minutes. Foxcroft then let his name stand and won the nomination.[79]

The Communists believed that Foxcroft had only run to keep Menzies from getting the nomination, and their suspicions were confirmed when he resigned at an LLP meeting on 24 August. Even the *Labor Leader*, the official paper of the AFL/TLCC, noted four days before Foxcroft's resignation that he would likely wait until it was too late to run a Communist candidate in his place and then step down. In the event the LLP was left without a candidate.

On 15 October 1926 the apparent "purge" was completed when an amendment to the London Labour Party's constitution banned Communist Party members from joining the organization. According to the report received by the Department of Labour, it was the London railway unions, not individuals such as Mould, who spearheaded the expulsion of Communists from the London Labour Party that October.[80] This makes sense, because Menzies and several other London Communists worked in the rail shops, and the attack on Communists in the LLP was likely an extension of attempts to destroy Communist influence within the railway unions.[81]

Deciphering Mould's actions in this incident is difficult, because the best source, *The Worker*, was clearly hostile to his positions. In addition, the Communist reporter in London made it sound as if the Communists were poor, innocent lambs being slaughtered on the altar of labour reactionaries. Mould's actions were anti-Communist and of dubious constitutionality, but he may have been reacting to Communist Party tactics that were far from innocent. It is entirely likely that the hall was packed on 28 July by members of affiliated bodies who had come for the sole purpose of voting for Menzies. Mould, who knew the London labour scene as well as anyone, would have recognized what was going on. His actions were not so much blatantly anti-Communist as they were motivated by his moralistic, almost self-righteous, sense of fair play, which was, under the specific circumstances, hard to distinguish from his getting his own way. Of his actions as chairman of the April 1926 CLP convention, the *Canadian Labor World* said that he "had battled for constitutional procedure throughout the convention."[82] If anything had surfaced during the Menzies controversy, it was as likely Mould's Britishness, Protestant conscience, and Pritchard-like appeal to constitutional politics as a reactionary distrust of all things Communist.

It is tempting, given his "anti-Communism" in this period, to see him as little different from J.S. Woodsworth, a fellow Methodist who fought long and hard against Communist influence in the Co-operative Commonwealth Federation. Indeed, an article Mould published in *Canada Forward* in this period appears to make the linkage explicit. The article, entitled "The Labor Political Situation," argued that a

Canadian labour movement could not be based on models developed in Britain or Russia. Mould continued:

> Don't start to holler, my British or Russian friends. I appreciate both your arguments, and recognize capitalism is the same any place. But I recognize, also, heredity and environment, and they are not the same here as in Britain or Russia, therefore, the plant will not grow the same way. We recognize the working class movement the world over, but its growth is governed by its environment just as much as the wheat kernel. Therefore, if we are really scientific socialists we will cease to try and foist any system made in London or Moscow, but build a movement suitable to Canada that we may link hands with those others.

It is the desire to create a Canadian brand of socialism, predating Woodsworth's call in 1933 for the same thing, that appears at first glance to be the most significant element of Mould's argument.

On closer inspection, however, the differences are evident. These words could easily have been written by a pre-1914 member of the Socialist Party of Canada: the emphasis on scientific socialism and the Spencerian equation of change in human society with biological processes are particularly striking. Woodsworth was anything but an exponent of scientific socialism; Allan Mills is close to the mark when he describes Woodsworth as a "militant anti-Marxist."[83] The continuing influence of Spencer, whom Mould had read as a young man in England, stands in stark contrast to Woodsworth's turn-of-the-century dismissal of the nefarious influence Spencer had on the British working class. Woodsworth at that time bemoaned the gullibility of Methodist radicals and the inability to think logically that led them to fall for Spencer's ideas.[84] He became, of course, much more sympathetic to the cause of labour in the ensuing years, but there is little to suggest that he ever developed much faith in the capabilities of the rank and file of the working class. As Mills points out, Woodworth's conception of socialism was statist and characterized by a "relentless technological determinism" that saw socialism, in the manner of right-wing members of the pre-1919 American Socialist Party, as a result of the supposed efficiency produced by monopolies.[85] There was not, in other words, much room in Woodsworth's call for a distinctive brand of Canadian socialism for the self-emancipation of the working class, a key element of Mould's conception. As Mould would discover in 1934, Woodsworth did not think much more of Methodist radicals than he had in Britain thirty-five years earlier.

Mould's most famous "anti-Communist" action took place at the annual convention of the Ontario Section of the Canadian Labour Party in 1927. In a separate caucus he and about forty other delegates met and expressed their desire "to help the movement to fall in line with the rest of the workers in Canada." Toward that end they called for an organization that would "reflect a distinct labor and socialist view point."[86] Delegates opposed to the revolutionary resolutions adopted by CLP conventions and concerned about the exodus of trade unions opposed to "Communist domination" thus decided to revamp the Independent Labour Party. On 11 November 1927 they met again in Toronto, where fifty-three delegates representing fifteen organizations discussed possible strategies. One group favoured attempting to regain control of the CLP, while another favoured leaving the Communist Party with an empty shell. Delegates decided to defer a decision until the next meeting, which would give them time to discuss the situation with the local organizations.[87]

Mould was instrumental in the split with the Canadian Labour Party. Jimmy Simpson was not at the Eighth Annual Convention in Hamilton, leaving Mould the key figure in breaking away from the CLP. Simpson was at the organizational meeting in Toronto on 11 November, but it was Mould who was chairman. He was also elected president of the re-organized ILP.[88] As Martin Robin points out, the labour party that was formed in 1927 with Mould as its leading spokesperson was "an avowedly socialist organization," something the old ILP definitely was not.[89] In effect, Mould's primary concern with Communists in the Canadian Labour Party was not that they were too radical but rather that the party's basis of representation gave the Communist Party more influence than the number of workers it represented warranted. In all likelihood Mould agreed with the Jewish National Workers' Alliance, which charged that the Labour Party had become an adjunct of the Communist Party.[90] As his 1926 article in *Canada Forward* demonstrates, he refused to concede to the Communist Party its claim to being *the* party of the working class, the same argument Winch was to make in the early 1930s. Mould's actions in 1926–27 did not make him anti-Communist but rather indicated his continuing belief that there had to be a principled socialist path between labourism and Marxism-Leninism.

The years 1928–31 were not auspicious ones for Canadian labour or radical politics. There were 132 delegates at the Ontario CLP convention held in Toronto in April 1928, but that was a significant drop from the 218 delegates who attended the 1927 convention. By 1929 the Ontario section of the CLP did not even meet. In 1928 the First Annual Convention of the Ontario Labour Party (OLP) was held in Toronto on 6–7 April. The forty-four delegates representing eighteen local organizations who again elected Mould to the presidency cannot have been fired with socialist prospects, as there was no convention the following year.[91] The Second Annual Convention held in Toronto, 18–19 April 1930, was more promising, attracting seventy-three delegates and once again electing Mould president.[92] Noteworthy among the thirty bodies represented were six socialist and fraternal bodies, indicating that the onset of the Depression had generated a revived interest in socialist politics, as well as increased trade union interest in political action.

Yet there is a great deal of truth to Jack Scott's observation that the Ontario Labour Party "was Arthur Mould and that was about it."[93] Mould's contribution to the Ontario left in a difficult period for the labour movement and political socialists was significant and lasting. While the Canadian Labour Party died a slow death, and the Communist Party tore itself apart in factional disputes, the OLP at least provided a home for political socialists and reached out to new constituencies. By the time of the 1931 convention the party had locals in the northern Ontario towns of Kenora and Cochrane, and the Joseph Mazzini Branch gave the party a presence in the Italian community.[94]

As in British Columbia, the onset of the Depression in Ontario produced two related but ultimately antagonistic tendencies on the left. The first tendency resulted in a renewed attempt to create a socialist party dedicated to the eradication of capitalism, based in Marxian economics and able to steer clear of the Communist Party of Canada while maintaining the centrality of class struggle and worker self-emancipation. As in British Columbia, Ontario socialists created a socialist party that gained strength in the years 1932–34, only to be swallowed up by the surging CCF movement. The Ontario section of the Socialist Party of Canada (OSP) was not, as Gerald Caplan claims, the same as the pre-war Socialist Party based in British Columbia, but its platform bore many similarities to the party of Bill Pritchard and Ernest Winch.[95] The second tendency was to create a broad-based coalition of labour, farm, and petit bourgeois elements resulting in the formation of the Co-operative Commonwealth Federation in Calgary in 1932. In Ontario as well as British Columbia, socialists believed they had a key role to play in maintaining class politics as the basis of the CCF political program, while the national CCF leadership was equally convinced that any and all linkages with Marxist-based parties and organizations that cooperated with the Communist Party had to be destroyed in order to attract farm support and votes in provincial and federal elections.

Mould, because he was both a member of the OSP and a supporter of the CCF, found himself in the centre of a fierce battle for control of the future of the Ontario left. Like Winch in B.C., he saw the CCF as a chance to create the mass workers' movement he had endeavoured so many years to build. He and others insisted, however, that it must be firmly based in Marxian economics, that the workers' party must be free from all entangling alliances, and that the eradication of capitalism must always remain firmly in view as the ultimate goal of the socialist movement. For their insistence, he and other Marxian socialists have been dismissed by Gerald Caplan as "a destructive crew: inflexible, uncompromising, utterly dogmatic, elevating intransigence to the level of a sacred principle. They held a conviction of their righteousness and a delusion of their self-importance which were totally unshakeable."[96] Given what we know about Mould's political past, his religious beliefs, and his ongoing attempts to maintain fair play in the labour movement, Caplan's diatribe more accurately describes the leaders and main organizers of the CCF than the Christian-turned-Marxian-socialist from London.

The Ontario Section of the Socialist Party of Canada was initiated on 7 February 1932 at a meeting in Toronto of thirty-five delegates representing nine organizations. The composition of the OSP ensured that the leadership of the CCF would be leery of its involvement and influence right from the start. Correspondence from J.S. Woodsworth indicated that the CCF leader was already aware of the movement to create a socialist party.[97] When the Young People's Socialist League's proposed program of a future socialist state and plans for the transition from capitalism to socialism were adopted, the party leadership's suspicions were no doubt confirmed. Yet former members of the Communist Party, most notably Jack MacDonald and William Moriarty, were not involved in the founding of the OSP.[98] Their influence, and that of the Trotskyists, who did have a presence in the Young People's Socialist League, became important, but neither group controlled the OSP or occupied executive positions.[99]

The organizational meeting of the Ontario Section of the Socialist Party in February 1932 was followed in March by the Ontario Labour Party's convention. One hundred delegates were in attendance, including eleven members of the Socialist Party. It was the beginning of the important role OSP members would play over the next two or three years in championing the cause of labour in Ontario. Mould, again elected president of the party by acclamation, thereby solidified his position as one of the key Ontario socialists and labour figures who needed to be won over by the leadership of the CCF.

Following the Calgary Conference in July 1932 Agnes Macphail and Elmore Philpott were selected to rally support behind the CCF idea in Ontario. Woodsworth also assumed a leading role. A key result of their efforts was the Ontario Conference of Political, Labour, and Socialist Groups which met at Cumberland Hall in Toronto on 27 November 1932. Forty delegates representing twenty-three organizations, none of them unions, met to discuss linking Ontario socialists with the CCF. Mould was at the centre of organizational efforts, serving on the credentials committee and as convenor of the Agenda Resolutions committee. He accepted the CCF manifesto on behalf of that committee and was also elected convenor of a provisional committee to arrange the next conference, a body that included the University of Toronto's Frank Underhill.[100]

The Labour Conference organized by Mould and his comrades took place on 26 February 1933 at Cumberland Hall in Toronto. Of the sixty organizations represented there were only five socialist parties, but their members played a much more important role than their numbers warranted. The 159 delegates came from thirteen labour party units, thirteen independent labour parties, the five socialist parties, seven other socialist groups from the Jewish community, four workers' associations, five miscellaneous groups, and thirteen trade unions. Mould as chairman of the meeting put his influence behind having all labour and socialist groups affiliate with the CCF through the Labour Conference, a proposal that left the United Farmers of Ontario section and the CCF clubs free to proceed in their own manner, without any real commitment to socialist principles or solidarity with labour. After a long debate, in which the Toronto Labour Party supported limiting the voting power of the CCF clubs, the original motion proposed by the resolutions committee was passed.[101]

As James Naylor points out, the Socialist Party supported the inclusion of middle-class elements in the Labour Conference in an effort to give socialist ideas a wider audience.[102] This position appears to indicate a major break with the Marxian socialism of the pre-1919 period and raises questions about defining Mould as a Marxist of the third way. It must be remembered, however, that although SPC theorists rarely broached the subject directly, their position that there was no middle class implied that all workers who worked for wages, regardless of income or occupation, were working class. In addition, a number of leading SPC members, including Wallis Lefeaux and Husain Rahim were, like Mould, self-employed. Naylor insightfully observes that "detractors of the 'dogmatists' have entirely missed the extent to which Marxists struggled with new conditions and sought to build an ideologically pluralist, yet staunchly working-class political movement and eventually, even, to formulate a basis upon which cross-class alliances might be built."[103] One needs to be careful, however, with the concept of cross-class alliances. It was not so much a case of recognizing the middle class as a distinct, objectively existing class as it was of defining as "working class" those non-wage workers who supported the working class cause in their ideas and actions – a perspective entirely consistent with the position Marx and Engels set out in *The Communist Manifesto*. Arthur Mould was self-employed, but still working-class in so many ways, still a fighter for a "staunchly working-class political movement." In the mid-1930s, his religiosity notwithstanding, he was more firmly attached to the third way than Pritchard, who temporarily strayed from it by arguing that the socialist movement had to be *based* on middle-class support. Pritchard thereby lent credence, even if unintentionally, to the British Fabian "suspicion of independent working-class identity" – something Mould did not – and thus adopted a position incompatible with Marxism of the third way and the Marxian socialism he espoused for much of his life.[104]

Not large or likely ever to be, the Ontario section of the Socialist Party nevertheless played a key role in the mobilization of labour in the early 1930s. According to OSP secretary Bert Robinson, it was OSP members who took the initiative in convincing labour organizations to come to the Labour Conference. The party also ran three candidates in Toronto's municipal elections, participated in May Day rallies, and provided speakers for other socialist and labour groups in the province. With the CCF now becoming a broad-based electoral party, Socialist Party members saw their role as forming the policies of the CCF, guiding its actions, and ensuring that class politics and the ultimate goal of socialism did not get lost in the search for parliamentary seats.[105]

It was a tall order for a small party, given the rapidity with which events unfolded in the spring of 1933. On 8 April 1933 a May Day Conference called by the Labour Conference (CCF) attracted sixty-seven organizations, including labour parties, trade unions, socialist parties, the Canadian Labour Defence League, the League for Social Reconstruction, Jewish and other language federations, CCF clubs and other groups. On 14–15 April the convention of the Ontario Labour Party was held. President Arthur Mould, at this time a vocal champion of the new party from the West, was instrumental in opposing attempts to block affiliation with the CCF. He was re-elected president, and OSP members made their continued influence felt by placing six party members on the provincial executive of sixteen.[106] On 23 April 1933 the Labour Conference meeting held in Cumberland Hall in Toronto attracted 110 delegates representing fifty organizations, including six new affiliations.[107]

In his address to the Labour Party of Ontario convention held in Brantford, Mould expressed his opinion that the CCF was the movement the workers of Canada had been waiting for. He suggested that the "Banner of Socialism has been raised higher by the C.C.F. than ever before in Canada." He saw in the CCF "no modification or cramping of our Party but an enlargement of our vision and scope and the possibility of a wider field." At the same time, however, he was an exponent of "mass action," of going to the workers by whatever means presented themselves. Noting that labour had "sniped at Capitalism for the last 20 years," he believed the time for action had come. The workers could "learn to march in step for Socialism" long before they could "understand Karl Marx." For Mould, the letters CCF stood for "Class Conscious Fighters." The time for bickering and back-stabbing within the left had ended – it was time to confront capitalism. As he so clearly put it, "Any hesitation on the part of Lenin and the Czar would still be on his throne."[108]

Mould's decision to back affiliation with the CCF earned him some bitter rebukes from members of the Ontario Labour Party. The 3 May 1933 issue of the *Toronto Star* reported that one George Bennett lambasted Mould for his stand at the April convention. Bennett was also outraged by the singing of the Red Flag, and resigned from the party. Incensed by what he considered Mould's high-handedness, he called him "this little Hitler; this little dictator." The *Star* also reported one Percy Fisher claiming that Mould "had double-crossed his followers by sliding down to Sarnia, where he started a Co-operative Commonwealth Federation club instead of a party branch."[109] Fisher's attack was entirely credible, because Mould had obviously decided that the CCF was a more suitable vehicle for mass action than the OLP. His intentions may have been honourable, but as events were to show, he was laying the groundwork for a CCF capture of Ontario's labour political movement.

By the spring of 1933 the leadership of the CCF and the Ontario section of the Socialist Party were destined for a final showdown. Woodsworth, based on his long-time association with Communist Party members, categorically refused to engage in any united-front activity with the CPC or its "front" organizations.[110] He was unlikely to come to any kind of understanding with OSPers like Bert Robinson, who saw the successful affiliation of the Labour Conference to the CCF as freeing up OSP members to shift their focus to supporting the Communist Party in its efforts to advance the cause of the working class. The Labour Conference's resolution on working-class unity called for "the complete abolition of the capitalist system and the establishment of a socialist commonwealth." It considered the conference "expressive of the first hesitant steps of the workers toward class consciousness," and said its members would "endeavour to adjust our theoretical basis upon socialist principles until we achieve the historic mission of the working class."[111] At the Regina conference CCF leaders would adopt a similar goal, only they felt they could do it without Marx, without a party based in the working class and union movement, and without the

Communist Party – in effect, an admission that they had no intention of doing it at all.

Mould, Robinson, Elizabeth Morton, and other OSP members must bear some of the responsibility for leading the Labour Conference into a party whose leaders saw the termination of their involvement as necessary to the success of the party. It all seemed so obvious to Marxists of the third way. In the winter and spring of 1933 capitalist society appeared on the verge of collapse. How could the CCF be anything but a mass working-class movement? Given that Mould, Robinson, and Morton all wrote respectfully to J.S. Woodsworth, it is clear that they expected him to do the "right" thing. They also expected to continue being "the leading force in the C.C.F. movement for a revolutionary socialism."[112]

By the summer of 1933 Mould found himself once again caught in the contradictory politics of the third way. His support for the CCF won him the enmity of Ontario Labour Party members who wanted to remain distinct from the CCF. He got himself into further trouble by fighting for a leading role for the OSP in the CCF, specifically in the form of representation on the provincial council. The OSP had been denied official representation, although it already had seven members on the council through other affiliations.[113] Mould, who had defended the CCF clubs at the Brantford convention in April, was now forced to listen to club members accuse OSPers of being disruptive, a position that amounted to a denial of any role for a Marxist perspective in the CCF. The dispute came to a head at a CCF club meeting on 22 June and resulted in Mould and his supporters walking out.

Mould's attempt to defend the OSP brought a stiff rebuke from C.W. Heath, president of the London CCF Club. He argued that, because the CCF was composed of labour, UFO, and CCF club groups, it was only logical that the OSP should be excluded. He also rejected Mould's position that OSPers were the "intelligentsia of the whole movement" and that CCF members had to be socialists.[114] The conflict escalated when Mould and the OSPers opposed the nomination of Norman Campbell as CCF candidate in upcoming federal and provincial elections. Campbell, in the estimation of the socialists, was not left wing enough. The OSP meeting which decided to oppose Campbell also proposed that the OSP put forward Mould as the party's candidate.[115]

The continuing conflict proved too much for Mould. The 30 June issue of the *London Free Press* reported that his doctor had recommended dropping all involvement in politics for six months. Now fifty-four, he was said to be suffering from a "severe illness" related to health problems encountered two or three years before, when he was "faced with a nervous breakdown." In the meantime he was to ask for a leave of absence from the labour organizations to which he belonged.[116] It did not take London critics of the Socialist Party long to exploit his medical problems. At a CCF council meeting on 11 July 1933 his old ally J.F. Thomson charged that the central executive of the Ontario CCF was "dominated" by Socialist Party members. He did not make clear, apparently, how seven socialists were able to dominate an executive of thirty-six members, but his attack was indicative of the approaching ouster of socialists from prominent positions in the CCF. In Mould's apparent absence OSP secretary Fred Hodgson took up the defence of the Socialist Party. Hodgson, with more than a little truth, shot back that the socialists were prominent because they were active all the time and did not just show up for meetings. Rather than responding to Hodgson's argument Thomson charged that socialist dominance ensued from the "machinations" of the Ontario Socialist Party's secretary Bert Robinson.[117]

Mould was not able to stay out of the fray for long and by the end of August was making public statements certain to antagonize the CCF leadership. When during a 27 August address to London socialists Elizabeth Morton talked about the confiscation of private property, he interjected that the word should be "restitution." Demonstrating the characteristic Marxist of the third way tendency to see such questions from the working class perspective, he claimed "that the C.C.F. desired only to restore to the masses that which had been already confiscated by the capitalist class."[118] He remained in some ways a Christian socialist at this time, but the number of Christians in Canada, especially church leaders, who were willing to endorse this kind of class politics were few and far between indeed. More importantly, this kind of class politics sent shivers up and down the spines of most CCF leaders.

By September 1933 Mould and other OSP members were beginning to realize the danger of their position. Fred Hodgson commented, "Arthur doesn't believe that the clubs will be on the Socialist side," indicating that Mould had already become leery of anti-Marxist elements in the CCF.[119] In October Mould wrote to Woodsworth, concerned by Elmore Philpott's attempts to promote amalgamation, rather than federation, of the UFO, the clubs, and the Labour Conference. He expressed confidence in Woodsworth's leadership but made known his concern about the new people coming into the party who had no real socialist beliefs. Echoing the overall strategy of the OSP, he noted that it is "no use kidding ourselves that this battle against Capitalism is so easy that we can let the last recruits change our policy and strategy at will."[120]

The "battle against capitalism" took on a new form at the Provincial Council meeting of the CCF in early November 1933. The meeting passed two resolutions: the first eliminated the Labour Conference as a separate entity entitled to equal representation with the UFO and the CCF clubs; the second banned former members of the Communist Party from membership in the CCF. On 17 November 1933 the Labour Conference responded in a letter under the letterhead of President Arthur Mould, Secretary Elizabeth Morton, and Treasurer A.M. Barnetson. The socialists found the new changes unacceptable, because they did not recognize that labour had a "historical role to perform" in the creation of a socialist society. Furthermore, it could not be accomplished by the labour elements in the middle-class controlled CCF clubs but had to be the work of "politically organized class-conscious" labour.[121] Marxists of the third way like Mould, Morton, and Bert Robinson, who saw the CCF as a "means of spreading socialistic doctrines," were still seeking a third way between the anti-Marxists in the CCF and the Communist Party, but they were quickly running out of time and options.[122]

Mould's final decision to ally himself with the Communist Party was prompted by personal as well as political factors. He hinted at financial problems in his letter to Woodsworth of 10 October 1933, telling the CCF leader, "I have nothing left to lose, I have lost all after 29 years in Canada, and may not even have a home this Winter."[123] The following month Arthur and Alice were forced to move out of the house on Merwin Heights which Mould had built himself. According to his daughters Helen and Jesse, they could have moved into a house across the street also built by Mould, but he was unwilling to evict the tenants at the height of the Depression, and they moved instead into much more cramped quarters in their brother Alfred's house. The business downturn, combined with the refusal of some Londoners to hire Mould because of his political beliefs, resulted in his becoming involved in relief work. At the age of fifty-five, he was doing pick and shovel work on the roads and, because he had a truck, driving the workers to and from work.[124]

When Fred Hodgson, secretary of the London OSP, heard about Mould's relief work he commented: "No damn wonder he's a bolshevik."[125] If Mould was a bolshevik, he was not the bolshevik of legend. One of his daughters' most vivid memories is of the Friday night gatherings that used to be held in the Mould home on a regular basis, where square dancing was the main activity, and fun was had by all without the benefit of alcohol. It was at these soirees that Mould learned to call square dances, and when times were tough during the Depression he made a little extra money calling dances in the London area. Life for him during the Depression was not consumed by revolutionary politics – there was always time for music, sociability, and fun.

It is true, however, that by February 1934 he supported the activities of the Communist Party with some misgivings. When A.E. Smith was arrested for stating at a public meeting that a recent assassination attempt on the life of CPC leader Tim Buck, who was in the Kingston Pentitentiary, had been organized by someone in the federal government, Mould pointed out to Woodsworth that it was the clubs, not the Labour Conference, that had initiated cooperation with the Canadian Labour Defence League in its attempts to defend Smith.[126] Mould told Woodsworth, "I detest the tactics of Smith et al. as much as you," but it could not be overlooked that Smith represented a working class organization which had "done some share in the struggle." It was up to the CCF, according to Mould, to take the initiative from the CPC, not to oppose it. The Communists could be emulated, because they were better at sensing "the rallying point of the worker." Then, once again searching out the third way, he said that Communists should be disciplined for causing problems in the ranks of labour, but so should right-wingers in the CCF who refused to take an active part in the struggle.[127]

The leadership of the CCF had a very different course of action in mind. CCF leaders at the time, and party defenders since, have tried to put as democratic a spin as possible on what happened in March 1934, but the fact remains that they were determined to abolish the Labour Conference and rid the party of Marxian socialists like Arthur Mould. Their opening came when the United Farmers of Ontario and the CCF clubs requested action against the Labour Conference by the National Council. Woodsworth referred the matter back to the Provincial Council with, according to Gerald Caplan, the "expressed hope it could settle its own differences."[128] A more likely scenario is that Woodsworth, Angus MacInnis, and other CCF leaders were doing everything possible to keep the issue from being settled at the provincial level, thereby justifying dissolution of the Provincial Council. When the UFO representatives conveniently failed to appear at the 10 March meeting of the Provincial Council, a deadlock ensued between the Labour Conference and the clubs.

The absence of the UFO came as no surprise to Agnes Macphail and Woodsworth. When the entirely predictable deadlock between the club and Labour sections ensued, council members turned to leading CCFers for a solution. Woodsworth "had apparently been prepared for just such a move for after a short discussion he produced a document signed in advance by his national council outlining the problem and what was to be done about it." D.M. Lebourdais justified the dissolution by suggesting that the OSPers "have no Canadian background and lack political sagacity," adding that they "had a lot of European Marxian doctrine and sought to impose their Marxian ideas on Canadians who would not accept them."[129] Both claims were nonsense, of course: Mould was just as Canadian as J.S. Woodsworth, and it was anti-Marxists in the CCF, not "Canadians," who were the more unwilling to accept Marxist ideas. But some justification had to be found for the kind of hypocrisy and double-dealing that CCF leaders like Woodsworth constantly claimed only the Communists were guilty of.

Lebourdais's comments made crystal clear what had been evident for some time – there was no place in the CCF for Mould, Morton, Robinson, Moriarty and many others. From its earliest days, therefore, the CCF demonstrated that it would go to any lengths to expel Marxists from the party, while maintaining that its actions were exemplary and democratic. It was a sorry episode. Elmore Philpott, the CCF's foremost champion of socialism in Ontario, resigned from the party on 12 March, two days after the Labour Conference was expelled. In March 1935 he rejoined the Liberal Party. Gerald Caplan has suggested in a masterpiece of understatement that it would be "invidious" to attempt to ascertain Philpott's motives.[130] A more critical assessment would suggest that Philpott was a hatchet man enlisted by Woodsworth and the National Council to destroy the Labour Conference.

Mould's initial response to the expulsion was remarkably low key, admitting that Woodsworth's decision was supported by the National Council. In a surprisingly reticent tone he told a *London Free Press* reporter that the Labour Conference would have to accept the decision, because the National Council had the power "to do what it wishes on matters of that kind."[131] By mid-April, however, Mould was describing the conference as a farce.[132] The resignation of Philpott, the most prominent "Johnny-come-lately" in the party, must have infuriated him. In all probability he came to the conclusion that if these were the kind of tactics employed by the CCF, then it was impossible to believe that Woodsworth's party was more democratic than the Communist Party, which was at least honest about its intentions.

By becoming a supporter of the Communist Party, Mould left the third way in the sense that he gave up trying to build a socialist movement that steered a middle course between the CPC and the CCF.[133] It is important, however, to follow his involvement in the CPC, because in most ways he remained true to the spirit of Marxism of the third way until the very end of his life. While he has left no record of his reasons for becoming a Communist, having seen his fellow Methodist J.S. Woodsworth betray those values most dearly held by the Protestant conscience, there was no reason any longer for him to accept that the CCF was as pure, or the Communist Party as evil, as Woodsworth and other social democrats said they were. In effect, if Bill Pritchard could accept Christ as a member of the CCF, Arthur Mould could see Christ as a Communist.

In the absence of his own reasons for becoming a supporter of the Communist Party, it is possible to speculate that one had to do with the creation of the Popular Front in 1934–35. Abandoning the sectarianism of the Third Period, in which all non-Communist leftists had been branded social fascists, the Communists attempted to create a broad-based anti-fascist movement that, as James Naylor points out, "saw class distinctions as a barrier to anti-fascist unity." The Popular Front's appeal to potential middle-class allies meant that the Communists "increasingly shifted their focus from the defence of the working class to the defence of the Soviet Union."[134] Mould, who did not come out of the British Columbia tradition of Marxian socialism, was more likely to respond positively to the Popular Front than was Winch. As Maurice Isserman points out, the Popular Front "restored a measure of democratic content to Communist ideology." In the message of the Popular Front could be found two ideas that had long been at the heart of Mould's activism: that "war was a ghastly pursuit," and that "ordinary people had the potential to control their own destinies."[135] When Marxism of the third way ran out of organizational bases in the mid to late 1930s, it was possible for its adherents to be both supporters and critics of the Popular Front, with no fundamental abandonment of the third way's central tenets.

Yet as always with Mould, his decision to join the Communist Party came very slowly, although he publicly allied himself with it in late 1934 or early 1935. At the London May Day rally in 1935 he appeared on the platform with Sam Scarlett, a former leading member of the Industrial Workers of the World and Communist Party member.[136] In January 1936 Mould spoke to a gathering of two hundred people at the Ukrainian Labour Temple in London on the anniversary of Lenin's death. His admiration for Lenin was evident: "Lenin was brought to the front in the greatest struggle the working class has ever seen. No leader in history will stand out as strongly as Lenin as time goes by." The best way to eulogize Lenin, said Mould, was "to put into action the things he taught."[137] This admiration for Lenin was unusual among Marxists of the third way, but it should not be forgotten that the Socialist Party of Canada defended the Russian Revolution, and on the eve of the Depression, Marxists of the third way like Charles Lestor retained great admiration for Leon Trotsky.[138] It is unclear, however, if Mould ever fully accepted Lenin's theories of the vanguard party. He turned to the Communist Party because it was the only left party, in his estimation, making a serious attempt to put the ideas of Marx and Lenin into practice.

Although he did not become a Communist Party member until 1943, Mould backed the official positions of the CPC once he broke with the CCF. He was a delegate and chairperson at the First Canadian Conference of Friendship with the U.S.S.R., held in Toronto on 29–30 June 1935. At that meeting he was reported as stating that he was a Communist.[139] By 1941 he had become a Communist willing to follow the "party line" of the Communist Party of Canada. Although he had been anti-war all his life, when the Second World War broke out he opposed the isolationist stance taken by Woodsworth as CCF leader. Following the Nazi invasion of the Soviet Union on 22 June 1941, Mould supported the Communist Party's call for the defence of the Soviet Union and labour backing for the Canadian war effort.[140]

Early in 1942 Mould was involved in the National Conference For Democratic Rights (NCDR), a Communist-led organization fighting to free interned Communist Party members, including leader Tim Buck. He was one of 173 delegates who attended the organization's convention held at the Chateau Laurier in Ottawa on 22–23 February 1942. A delegation of twenty-five from the convention, under the leadership of A.E. Smith, and including Mould, met Justice Minister Louis St Laurent. The statement given to St Laurent claimed that the NCDR represented seventy-six organized bodies with 140,000 members, including forty-three trade unions representing ninety thousand members.[141]

Given his record over the previous eight years, it is somewhat surprising to discover that an RCMP report in March 1942 came to the conclusion that Mould "has never been known or suspected of being a Communist or even an ardent supporter." The report recommended that his file be closed. If it was, it did not stay that way for long.[142] In the summer of 1943 the Communist Party, which was still illegal, formed a new party. It was a euphoric time for Canadian Communists: the successful Soviet defence of Stalingrad against Hitler's apparently unstoppable military machine was cause for celebration by Communist and non-Communist alike. On the home front the Communists scored impressive electoral victories in the Ontario provincial election, with A.A. MacLeod elected in Toronto – Bellwoods and J.B. Salsberg in Toronto–St Andrew. If Mould had not already made his politics public, he now did so in no uncertain terms. At an August meeting in the London Labour Temple he said "that it was the first time he had publicly allied himself with Communists pointing out, 'As I grow older I become more radical not more conservative.' "[143]

The new party, the Labour-Progressive Party (LPP), came into being at a meeting of some five hundred delegates in Toronto in August 1943. Clearly the Communist Party considered Arthur Mould the kind of leftist they had hoped to attract, because he was one of the speakers

Arthur Mould, possibly taken for his 1945 election campaign. Photo courtesy of Helen Mould Rawson

on this historic occasion. He stated that he had been present at the birth of many labour organizations, but that none had given him more pleasure than this one. He was to prove true to his assertion that he was committed to the party "with everything I have left in my life." The delegates cheered his words "as the expression of their own faith, an avowal of their own resolve."[144]

In 1945 he ran in the federal election as a Labour-Progressive candidate in his home town of London. Given that both A.A. MacLeod and J.B. Salsberg were re-elected in the provincial election, held one week before the federal election, the 196 votes Mould received can only be described as extremely disappointing. That political disappointment in his public life was soon followed by tragedy in his private life, the death in 1946 of his son Alfred at the age of thirty-nine. Mould was grief-stricken, his loss made even more poignant by the fact that of all his children, it was Alfred who had been most interested in the Communist Party. In the late 1940s Arthur Mould remained active, but failing eyesight and a business in decline prevented him from being more active in the London LPP local. His main activities involved attending socials, raising funds for the *Canadian Tribune*, and being chairman of meetings. In 1949, however, he ran municipally and did much better than in the federal election of 1945, although he failed to win a seat on council.

In 1950, at the height of the cold war, Mould became more active than he had been for some time. He returned to his old passion, the anti-war movement. As chairman of the London Peace Council he was involved in the distribution of "Ban the Bomb" petitions.[145] In the fall of 1950 he went to England for the first time since he left forty-five years earlier. There were two reasons for the trip: one was to visit relatives and friends in Sawtry and Accrington; the second was to attend, as an accredited delegate of the National Council of the Canadian Peace Congress, the Second World Peace Congress held in Sheffield from 12–19 November 1950.[146]

Involvement in the peace movement seems to have brought back some of the drive and dedication Mould lost in the late 1940s. It had been fifty years since he opposed the Boer War while living in Accrington, but he still considered peace "the heart cry of the world."[147] Given the end of the Korean War, and the failure of the Communist Party to enlist widespread support for its peace initiative, however, he returned to more routine activities. His health was again a problem, and in the years 1953–55 generally confined his activities to attending socials and meetings of the local LPP, along with writing his autobiography.

The events of 1956, however, inspired him to make some of the most important theoretical contributions of his long career on the left. The Twentieth Party Congress of the Communist Party of the Soviet Union (CPSU) revealed that Joseph Stalin, not the Central Committee, had ruled Soviet society for the last twenty years of Stalin's life. CPC leaders Tim Buck, William Kashtan, and Leslie Morris attempted to limit the potential damage to Buck and the party by blaming the deviation on the "cult of the individual" that had grown up around Stalin. They failed, and the full impact of the revelations of the Party Congress hit London, Ontario, months before the National Executive Committee of the CPC was able to organize a conference in Toronto. The accusations against Stalin were hotly debated in a series of LPP educational meetings held in the London Public Library in the spring and summer of 1956. By June 1956 Mould had come out, as he had done all his life, with a forceful position, yet one that sought a third way between the pro- and anti-Buck forces in the leadership of the CPC, and hearkened back to long-held positions typical of Marxists of the third way.

Unlike many leading members of the CPC, Mould quickly and forthrightly admitted that he had been impressed by Stalin, and that the revelations were a shock to him. He argued that in "our admiration of

Stalin and the Soviet Union, we too often forget we are Canadians and that Marx's scientific socialism belongs to the world and is not the product of the Soviet Union, although the Soviets are its greatest demonstrable proof." Echoing Pritchard of some thirty-five years before, Mould declared that Communists should learn from the successes and failures of the Soviet Union, not emulate it. Our faith, he said, should be in "the compass of our goal," not in Soviet leaders.[148]

He continued this line of argument in the *National Affairs Monthly*, which had been opened up to a debate within the party on the Stalin revelations and the future direction of the party. He argued that Khrushchev and the other Central Committee members of the CPSU could not be excused for Stalin's crimes; echoing the findings of the National Committee of the CPC, he asked: what kind of Marxist explanation places the blame for such atrocities on one individual? The CPSU Central Committee was most culpable, because it was on the scene, but Mould concluded that "we are all to blame." Once again echoing Marxists of the third way who did not join the Communist Party, he noted: "It took me years to rid my soul of hero worship, therefore I always resented making leaders into gods. I don't propose now to fall into the mistake of transferring individual cults into executive cults – or priesthoods."[149] In launching his critique he had forgotten, or was covering up, the fact that he had once eulogized Lenin, and that from the late 1930s to the mid-1950s he had been as unquestioning of Stalin's leadership as most other members of the Communist Party. His own culpability notwithstanding, however, his analysis was direct, to the point, and of great validity.

By the fall of 1956, therefore, it would appear that Mould was in the same camp as Norman Penner, Stewart Smith, J.B. Salsberg, and other "oppositionists" who wanted major changes in the CPC. Indeed, Mould appeared to be in agreement with Penner, who "proposed changes that would make the party independent of the Soviet Party and would allow its own interpretations of Marxism."[150] At the same time Penner was putting forward his ideas Mould was suggesting that the party be called the Canadian LPP, and was espousing an essentially federalist relationship between the CPSU and the Canadian Party. In his plans for the future direction of the CPC Mould went back to the days of the farmer-labour government of 1919–23. He concluded that there had been too much cynicism in the past about reforms and "palliatives," and that he and other political socialists had been with the workers but "not of them." The task, said Mould, was to correctly apply the tremendous advances in theoretical knowledge that had taken place since 1919, a process that had to be much more cognizant of Canadian conditions and the wishes of the workers themselves.[151]

In the fall of 1956 it appeared that Arthur Mould was prepared to endorse Norman Penner's position that the CPC stop opposing CCF-labour political action and condemning the leadership of the CCF as the enemy of the workers.[152] When the "oppositionists" in the leadership of the party began resigning, however, Mould's response was swift and devastating. Commenting on comrades who were leaving the party, he said, "other than the basic principles of Marxist socialism, they could never have been fully convinced of the party, its aims, policy or principles, otherwise they could not so easily step out, instead of remaining to fight for what they believed should be done." The problem was not the party itself, but that certain leaders had forgotten that they existed to serve the party and its cause, not the other way round. What must not be forgotten was that parties "live and die when they reach their goal."[153] For Mould, as for Bill Pritchard, the party was an indispensable vehicle in reaching the final goal, not an end in itself.

Mould saw taking it easy on the CCF and its leadership as no option at all – he had experienced first hand, in the early 1930s, the conception of leadership and socialist unity espoused by CCF leaders. In 1959, when the New Democratic Party was in formation as the "New Party," Ontario CCF leader Donald MacDonald suggested that it would act as a buffer between the workers and the monopolies. Mould was having none of this kind of leadership. He pointed out that Keir Hardie and J.S. Woodsworth, for all their faults, "were at least sincere in their desire to improve the conditions of the working class." If the new party of the workers was to be a buffer, rather than a fighter for the cause of the workers, "then the CCF is giving up the struggle."[154]

Now eighty years of age, Mould had not renounced the struggle, and in the waning years of his life he continued to press the politics of Marxist education and class struggle, as well as resistance to war. On Labour Day 1958 he published an anti-war poem in the *Canadian Tribune*:

> In Eighty years I've not had time enough
> To do the things I'd hoped to do.
> I dreamed to plan a perfect State
> In which I'd build man's social day
> Wherein he'd live in perfect peace ...[155]

That perfect peace was not to be, of course, even in Mould's own family. Alice's health began to fail in 1957, and in 1959 she fell in the yard and dislocated her hip. Faced with the possibility of putting her in a nursing home, Mould brought her home, where he and his daughters cared for her. He had not been able to drive for some time because of his eyesight; unable to get out to meetings, he took to gardening. It was a difficult fate, because he had spent his life in the company of friends, social and political; and now, according to his daughter Helen, "people just ignored him ... when you're no use to them, they don't want you, and he felt it."[156]

As Mould moved out of the orbit of public life, new bonds and understandings developed in his family life. It was in these final years that Helen really got to know her father. All those years of reading the papers had convinced her that his involvement in the Communist Party had been "awful," but now she came to better understand him and what he stood for. As she says, "there was a lot of things that I didn't understand about him because you just didn't sit down and talk to your father." Her comments are a poignant reminder that divisions between socialist fathers and daughters in this period were based both in the gender roles sanctioned by society and in society's class bias against involvement in socialist politics.

Mould himself gained an important understanding in these final years of the extent to which his public life in the workers' movement had been sustained by his wife's familial responsibilities. He realized that "the fact of not being free to come and go places like her husband could, and did, must have made the bonds of homes as rigid as the iron bars of a prison." The years he spent at home with Alice humbled him: "In my downcast moments, when unable to come and go as heretofore, I thought of these things and realized what little thought men give to the years of self sacrifice and devotion women give to their home and children."[157] Yet it remained the case that he was able, even in his final years, to get away for a few hours to have a beer or two with friends. Alice, on the other hand, became bed-ridden in April 1961 and in October passed away. Less than two months later, his companion of fifty-seven years gone, Arthur Mould died.

In the summer of 1961 just months before his death, *Marxist Review* published Mould's personal tribute to Leo Tolstoy.[158] What he most admired about Tolstoy was his attempt to grapple with the great questions of his time, to find a way through the trials and tribulations of life. Mould could relate to Tolstoy. Even Leslie Morris, who tried very hard to make Mould a committed Marxist-Leninist forged in the heat of the Russian Revolution, had to admit in the end that he was primarily a searcher after truth.[159] His "Stalinist" years notwithstanding, he was a forceful but not excessively dogmatic man. He insisted that socialists be active in the struggle, that they do more than vote and show up for meetings. He recognized that the working class must not categorically renounce the use of measures, including violent ones, which the state did not hesitate to use against its own citizens. He could be as critical of the Communist Party as he was of social democrats. He refused to endorse Communist Party tactics which appeared deliberately dishonest, petty, or gauged primarily to advance the cause of the party at the expense of working class unity. He sought to put the needs of the workers ahead of concern for party advantage or the careers of individual leaders.

As a socialist he was not free from weaknesses. The obvious faith he placed in J.S. Woodsworth in the early 1930s, and in Joseph Stalin in the ensuing years, was the faith of a man who sometimes overlooked or chose not to see that he himself was at times incapable of the discernment he expected from the workers themselves. Yet he understood that without a class struggle perspective, without a commitment to worker self-emancipation, without the daily battle to eradicate capitalism, the socialism of the CCF could only be warped, twisted, and finally destroyed by parliamentarism and middle-class opportunism. At the same time he recognized that Stalinist bureaucracy and the cult of the individual could only serve to crush the working-class initiative so central to a Marxist politics. If the socialist movement in Canada is to find a new sense of purpose for the twenty-first century, its adherents might do well to listen a little more carefully to Marxists of the third way like Arthur Mould, and a bit more critically to the defenders of the social democratic and communist traditions.

4 Robert Boyd Russell: The Search for a Third Way

In Winnipeg, Manitoba, the emphasis of Marxism of the third way on education and self-directed working class action underwent its greatest test. During the Winnipeg General Strike of May–June 1919 the workers of Winnipeg were called on to demonstrate their superiority over the ruling class of the city by showing restraint, not participating in violence, and proving their ability to run the affairs of the city as well as, or better, than the employers and their capitalist allies in government and the press. One of the momentous protests in the history of North American labour, the Winnipeg battle saw thirty thousand workers off the job for six weeks, tremendous organization and control, and thousands of workers performing various functions from working on the strike committee to collecting food for strikers' families. In the process the Canadian state was presented with the spectre of a working class saying, both directly and indirectly, that it was capable of running a functioning society without the aid and authority of the ruling elite. Regardless of the strikers' good humour, lack of weaponry, or intent to overthrow legally constituted authority, that was a revolutionary stance.

For leading activists of the Socialist Party of Canada – Bob Russell, Dick Johns, George Armstrong, Helen Armstrong, Sam Blumenberg, and Max Tessler – and other Marxists of the third way, the Winnipeg General Strike represented a test of the resolve and capabilities of the working class. There was no intent to foment a political revolution, but Marxists of the third way in general, and members of the SPC in particular, did see the strike as a proving ground for their ideas. They wanted to win the strike, but as Marxists they were also interested in more and more workers becoming cognizant of their class position, seeing through the lies and deceptions of the capitalist class, and working towards the creation of a broad-based class organization. At the time they did not see the Winnipeg General Strike in the kind of apocalyptic terms we see it in now, as a decisive turning point in the history of the Canadian left. For them revolution was part of evolution, and the Winnipeg General Strike was a building block, albeit an especially important one, in the long-term construction of a socialist society.

Going into the Winnipeg General Strike, however, Marxists of the third way had little real understanding of how they could transform local manifestations of labour protest into a wider collective struggle against the ruling class. Leading figures in the SPC were groping toward that form of organization by creating the One Big Union. While it was thought of as both an industrial and a class union by its supporters, the OBU was not a form of syndicalism, being an attempt to combine the educational function of the Socialist Party and the class struggle politics of a radical union. Although Marxist in conception, the One Big Union at least implied dissatisfaction with the organization and politics of the Socialist Party, and this led many SPCers who were initially in favour of the organization to abandon it in the months and years following the strike. Yet disagreements between OBU supporters and the SPC faithful notwithstanding, both organizations continued to consider Marxist education and organizing the workers on a class basis to be the central socialist tasks, whatever conflicts existed as to the relative importance of those two activities. Like the SPC, the OBU was dedicated to working-class education and the necessity of workers fully understanding their class position. The OBU, like the SPC, was vehement in its condemnations of what it considered the arrogance, extravagance, and corruption of the American Federation of Labor and its leaders in the United States and Canada. Egalitarianism continued to be a touchstone, as OBU leaders were to be paid no more than a machinist's wage, thus preventing them from getting too far away from the world of the rank and file. It continued to be an article of faith that change could occur from the bottom up, that an educated rank and file, freed from the influence of capitalist propaganda and traitorous labour bureaucrats, would create a different kind of organization, led by a different kind of leader.

Robert Boyd Russell was a key figure in the Winnipeg General Strike, the Socialist Party of Canada, and the One Big Union. As a leading organizer for the railway machinists during the First World War he ceaselessly pushed the creation of industrial unions, emphasizing the necessity of approaching the employers from a position of strength. During the strike itself he was a central personage on the strike committee, engaged in numerous rounds of negotiations with government and business leaders, and helped set the tone of the workers' response during the six-week duration of the strike. After his release from prison Russell came to embody for literally thousands of workers in Canada the hopes and aspirations of One Big Unionists. He acted as secretary-treasurer, spokesperson, writer, organizer and promoter of social and cultural events, as guide, conscience, and inspiration.

His life and work presents us with the most comprehensive picture of the strengths and weaknesses of the SPC-OBU and Marxism of the third way. A fearless defender of the rank and file, a committed socialist and antagonist of capitalism, Russell was nevertheless caught in a series of contradictions that at times led him to expose workers to dangers which he was not in a position to protect them from. A leader who constantly attacked other leaders for their failings, he was often less than honest in admitting his own. A Marxian socialist who envisioned a socialist future of freedom and equality for women as well as men, he failed to confront, and at times endorsed, sexist attitudes towards women in his daily politics. Invariably he sacrificed family responsibilities to the good of the cause, at times to the point of cruelty and neglect of his wife and children. He did not make the organizing of workers of colour one of the goals of one big unionism, but like many other Marxists of the third way he was willing to fight racism and ethnic chauvinism in situations where the vast majority of socialists and trade unionists remained silent. His vision of class unionism was flawed, but not so flawed that we cannot in good conscious choose to learn and understand, rather than close our minds and condemn.

Bob Russell lived in an era in which many Marxist unionists, rightly or wrongly, considered the major threat to working-class solidarity to be the divide between skilled and unskilled workers. Being a machinist, he was right in the middle of momentous changes in the nature of work on the shop floor, and he was acutely aware of the advantages to the employers of convincing the skilled workers that the labourers, not the bosses, were threatening their jobs and skills. He was acutely aware of processes of de-skilling in his trade and the dilution of skilled machinists with unskilled and semi-skilled operatives. Rather than feeling threatened by this development, and attempting to further safeguard craft privilege at the expense of the labourers, he responded by trying to organize the unorganized and to bring the benefits gained by skilled workers through years of struggle to the unskilled. In the early 1930s he remained committed to this politics, fighting attempts by workers with jobs to abandon the unemployed to their fate. Only in this way, he believed, could labour solidarity be achieved. In that belief lay the triumphs and tragedies of a long and invaluable life.

Robert Boyd Russell was born in Glasgow, Scotland, on 31 October 1888. His father, who worked in a brass foundry, was able to apprentice his son as a machinist. Young Russell learned his trade in the Glasgow shipyards of John Brown, the largest ship manufacturer on the Clyde.[1] While not a great deal is known about his early political career we do know that he was a member of the Springburn local of the Independent Labour Party. No doubt his father, a socialist and member of the ILP as well, was a formative influence.

His mother's influence, about which we can only speculate, was almost certainly religious and must be seen in the context of developments in Scottish Presbyterianism in the last half of the nineteenth century. There were two basic tendencies in the Presbyterian Church: the Moderate tradition in the Church of Scotland and the Evangelical tradition in the Free Church. At mid-century, however, the majority of members in both wings of the Presbyterian Church were essentially conservative. By the 1870s liberals were gaining ground in both camps. Evangelical revivals in 1859 and again in 1873–75 stimulated the popularity of hymns and hymn-singing. By the 1880s the adoption of organs and hymn-singing was part of a move "away from the old tradition of objective and intellectual Calvinism and towards a subjective and emotional form of Christian faith."[2] Along with this changed attitude toward Calvinism came an increasing awareness of social problems. By the 1880s and 1890s the questioning of both Calvinist predestination and classical political economy led to an increased emphasis on the "environmental factor" in explaining bad housing, urban slums, and working-class poverty. Along with this went a "marked weakening of traditional Presbyterian opposition to socialism," and a new sympathy for trade unions.[3]

Bob Russell grew up listening to his father argue the case for socialism with two of his brothers, who were Presbyterian ministers. It can easily be imagined that the young lad's mother often sided with her brothers-in-law in these discussions. Like so many Marxists of the third way, therefore, Bob Russell grew up in a home where religion, which in his grandparents' generation had generally served to bond parents and children, and husbands and wives, had become a source of discord. As the father's commitment to socialism deepened (as it did in the home of Bill Pritchard as well), it was likely that he would see his wife's religiosity as questioning his authority, threatening his beliefs, and clinging to "bourgeois" values. Certainly in Bob Russell's own future marriage, as in that of Ernest Winch, such a rift existed. In effect, Marxists of the third way like Russell were prone to see women as threats to socialism, not allies in the struggle, in part because of their childhood experience of their parents' relationship.

Russell's father proved a more lasting influence than his mother, and his uncles were unable to translate the Presbyterian Church's newfound sympathy for the working class into increased religiosity and church attendance on the part of their young nephew. Like many other Scottish workers, Bob Russell turned to secular pursuits; his interests became socialism, horse racing, and football, "the new opiate of the people."[4] However, like Bill Pritchard and Arthur Mould, he retained from his religious upbringing a lifelong love of music and singing, but he indulged that love in the Clarion Scouts, a socialist choir, not in the church choir.[5] He may have picked up his basic philosophy that people are a product of their environment from religious thinkers, but it led him to Marx, not to an attempt to change the beliefs, activities, and goals of the Presbyterian Church.

Before he came to Canada Russell was by no means a radical, the Independent Labour Party at that time being more a labourist than a socialist party.[6] At Glasgow Square he listened to every answer for the ills of the day imaginable, from the Marxism of the Socialist Labour Party to anarchism, spiritualism, and the single tax. A major counter-influence in his journey to socialism was Margaret Ritchie Hampton, the young woman he took with him to the Glasgow Square meetings. She was quite religious and did not share Russell's enthusiasm for socialism. When she followed him to Winnipeg and they married, religion was her main source of strength in this bitterly cold country where she had few relatives and friends. Margaret Russell missed the religious fellowship of her home in Scotland; in response, her husband and a group of workers from the Canadian Pacific Railway shops built her a Presbyterian church.[7] Although respectful of his wife's religious beliefs, Russell himself stopped going to church at some point in 1912 or 1913. His move away from the church is evidenced by the fact that the first Russell child, Margaret, was baptized, while the second, a son, David, was not.[8]

In moving away from the church Russell was moving in a socialist direction, later observing that he "was always inclined" to Marxian economics.[9] He had not immediately become involved in political socialism on arriving in Canada in 1911: he joined the Socialist Party of Canada in 1914 after a brief three-month membership in the Social Democratic Party.[10] In all probability he initially joined the SDP for three reasons: one, because it was closer in philosphy to the Independent Labour Party, which he had belonged to in Scotland; two, because the SDP had closer ties to the trade union movement in Winnipeg prior to the First World War; and three, because of the influence of his good friend and prominent SDPer John Queen, whose family lived across the street from the Russells. Russell respected the SDPers' knowledge of

Marxian economics but came to believe that their approach was "too piecemeal," and that they had a tendency to lose sight of the necessary revolutionary transformation. He believed that the Social Democrats took an evolutionary approach, while he, like most members of the Socialist Party, understood revolutionary change as a "complete" evolution. Given these kinds of subtle distinctions, it is not surprising that like Ernest Winch and many other Marxian socialists, he could be a member of both the SDP and SPC.[11]

Bob Russell was part of a "second generation" of SPCers in Winnipeg who became much more heavily involved in the union movement during the First World War. However, there is reason to question his own claim that in the early days of the SPC its members were "all academic" and that it was young immigrants like himself who "changed the Socialist Party of Canada's attitude to one of testing their theories in the world of experience."[12] A check of the early SPCers in Winnipeg would suggest that, contrary to this argument, most of them did come from working-class backgrounds.[13] These members included Max Tessler – a Jewish Marxist, member of the Tailors' Union, and delegate to the Winnipeg Trades and Labour Council – who as a young man had aided the revolutionary forces during the 1905 Russian Revolution, and upon his arrival in Canada in 1906 joined the SPC.[14]

Russell was not wrong, however, in claiming that he, Dick Johns, and other Marxists of the third way built up a stronger following in Winnipeg's trade unions than had their predecessors.[15] He observed that "the rank and file of the Unions, when it came to the electing of shop committees and negotiating committees, it was always a Socialist they picked out, you see, whether they were Social Democrats or they were Socialist Party of Canada."[16] On the shop floor, and in the labour press, he used every opportunity to advance the socialist cause and to convince rank and file workers that they could never attain the full value of their labour within the capitalist system. That argument took on added effect during the First World War, which offered up the example of munitions manufacturers making enormous profits while Canadian workers had their rights taken away and died on the field of battle. Just after the war began Russell offered this analysis of the conflict to his fellow machinists:

Of all the causes of the war I have heard defined I think Edward Carpenter, the Socialist poet and philosopher, hits the mark when he brings it down to the insane commercial and capitalistic rivalry, the piling up of power in the hands of mere speculators and financiers, and the actual trading for dividends in the engines of death, all these inevitable results of our present industrial system. This is the cause of the war and while on this subject would like to call the brothers' attention to the fact that this is a capitalists' war, so why should we let ourselves be gulled to fight their battle?[17]

From this time until the Winnipeg General Strike, his column in the Machinists' *Bulletin* would alternate between discussing Marxian socialist politics and organizational questions in the union, as he struggled to unite socialist theory with trade union practice.

Russell's involvement in the International Association of Machinists (IAM) and the socialist movement prior to the Winnipeg General Strike can be divided into two periods. The first runs from his entrance into the IAM in 1911 to the end of 1917. He moved on to a new phase of his involvement in January 1918 when he became a delegate from IAM Local #122 to the Winnipeg Trades and Labour Council. In February 1918 he stopped working on the shop floor and became a full-time paid official. Prior to 1918 his time and energy were largely dedicated to trade unionism and labour organizing, not to the propaganda activities of the SPC. He rose to prominence in the IAM much more quickly than he became a leading member of the SPC.

Russell was very much a machinist and was keenly aware of the stature of his trade in the Manitoba labour community. When he came to Winnipeg the machinists, and to some extent the building trades and street railway workers, were the labour core of the city. They had a long history by western labour standards, and Russell's IAM Local #122 was the first railway shop union organized in Winnipeg in 1893.[18] By the outbreak of the First World War the railway shops had become even more central to labour radicalism in the city. Prior to the war the machinists in both the railway and contract shops were challenged in importance by the building trades workers. Construction was booming in Winnipeg in the years 1911–13, when the city saw the establishment of 130 new industries.[19] In the years 1913–15, however, a crippling depression in the construction industry dealt a severe blow to the size and influence of the building trades unions. The advent of the war expanded the need for machinists but had relatively little effect on the construction industry.[20] By the end of 1915 there were eight Winnipeg and area companies engaged in shell production.[21]

By the time Russell joined the SPC he had already become heavily involved with the International Association of Machinists as a shop committee member. By February 1913 he was vice-president of Local #122.[22] He and his allies began to lobby for the end of separate lodges for machinists' helpers, who were considered labourers, at the annual IAM conventions. They had sympathizers in many American cities as well, including Seattle, Washington, New York, and Chicago, lobbying leading machinists to support making helpers members of the machinists' lodges. Gradually, according to Russell, "we got the helpers sneaking into the machinists' lodge."[23] The efforts were rewarded in 1916, when the union became the International Association of Machinists, Boilermakers, Specialists and Helpers Local #122. By 1915 Russell had instilled enough confidence in his co-workers to be named Local #122's delegate at the Winnipeg convention of the CPR Systems Federation, and in the fall of that year he was elected to the executive board of Section No. 1 of the IAM.

In September 1915 Russell attended the annual convention of the Trades and Labour Congress in Vancouver. He was by no means a prominent figure, but he did spark one of the most heated debates and gave notice that even as a first-time delegate he would not shrink from supporting Socialist Party positions at TLC conventions. On the first day the executive council presented a report which had a section on the war. It called on labour to "lend every assistance possible" to the Allies in order to secure "early and final victory." On the third day Russell moved that the clause be deleted. Following a lengthy discussion the amendment was defeated by a vote of 103 to twenty-eight. Russell's championing of the Socialist Party of Canada position on the war may help explain why he was not one of the six nominated delegates to be elected for the three positions on the Manitoba Executive Committee of the TLCC.[24] It was a temporary setback that did not in any way dissuade him from continuing to fight for Marxian socialist ideas within a sometimes hostile trade union movement.

In 1916 his profile heightened in both labour and socialist circles. That summer he attended a meeting of the Winnipeg Trades and Labour Council as a visitor, although not yet as a voting delegate from IAM Local #122.[25] By December he was chairman of Section No. 1 of district #2 of the IAM.[26] In September he had attended the Trades and Labour Congress convention in Toronto as a delegate from IAM Local #122, where once again he became involved in one of the most controversial political issues. On the sixth day the Ontario Provincial Council of the Carpenters submitted a resolution calling for the "elimination" of Asiatic labour from Ontario. Alex Lyon, from Toronto Local No. 2642 of the Carpenters, and a Marxian socialist, challenged his own governing body by stating that he was quite willing to work with Asiatics "so long as they were paid the same rates of wages and accept the same working rates that union men had to work under. He thought there was far too much race hatred and he did not sympathize with it." Russell supported Lyon's comments by also opposing the Carpenters' resolution.[27]

His stand against the exclusion of Asian workers was consistent with attitudes he demonstrated from his earliest days as a machinist in

Canada. The IAM in Winnipeg had accepted his membership in the Amalgamated Society of Engineers as proof of his status as a skilled machinist – he simply had to say the oath in order to become a member. But for Russell this presented a problem, because the oath required him to state that he would nominate for membership in the union only sober and industrious white machinists. Russell and the other members of his group, which included future SPC ally and fellow machinist Dick Johns, refused to take the oath. The president of the union later permitted them to join by simply swearing to be loyal to the IAM.[28] While there is no evidence to suggest that Russell made the organizing of "ethnic" workers and workers of colour one of his goals, he took principled stands against racism in the labour movement and in 1918–19 joined with his fellow unionists in welcoming workers of colour into the house of labour.

As was typical of Marxists of the third way, however, the inclusion of women in Russell's conception of the working class came much more grudgingly than did his inclusion of non-Anglo-Saxon workers. In this sense he was typical of machinists across Canada, whether they worked in the Angus Shops in Montreal or the Ogden Shops in Calgary. There was radicalism in the shops, but it was a very masculinist radicalism. Late in 1916, when women were hired in the Angus Shops in Montreal, their fellow workers and machinists across the country demanded that they be removed. A similar demand was made in Winnipeg, and in his column in the *Bulletin* of the IAM Russell joined the chorus of voices demanding their removal.[29]

There can be no doubt that Russell and his fellow machinists felt threatened by women in the skilled trades, and many an anguished cry about male machinists wearing skirts and female machinists wearing pants echoed off the walls of machine shops across the land. In reality, however, the issue was rather more complicated. According to Angus union officials, women were first introduced into the shops as car cleaners and washers. They were then brought in on the locomotive side to work on turret lathes, drills, and screwing machines, the men already working on those machines being transferred to the erecting shop.[30] The union demand that the hiring of women be stopped and that those already hired be removed at the end of the war was indefensible, but male unionists had every reason to suspect that the replacing of skilled male workers was a prelude to the lowering of wage rates. Even in the Calgary shops where male unionists threatened to go on strike if the women in the Angus Shops were not removed, women were employed in the car and coach shop by 1918. A columnist in the *Bulletin* who wrote under the pseudonym "Ogden Scribe" responded to the hiring of women by noting that to immigrant workers "that have been exiled from the old sod through economic pressure, this is nothing new, but who ever thought that this rotten business would be introduced in this glorious land of freedom."[31] On the one hand Scribe and other male machinists demonstrated their failure to appreciate the enormous challenges faced by women workers as women; on the other, however, their class analysis – which focuses on "economic pressure," not victimization by women workers – demonstrates their ability to see the problem as the capitalist system, not women per se. It was one of those moments which demonstrated both the strength and weakness of Marxian thought where women workers were concerned, as well as the linkage of class and gender in the Canadian working class.

While Russell's reasons for opposing women in the shops remain obscure, it seems reasonable to assume that they were those of other machinists – a combination of male insecurity, assertion of the "virility" of the skilled worker, and fear that this was another capitalist ploy to lower wage rates. What is most significant, however, is that Russell was willing to challenge the union culture to which he belonged when the issue was racism, war, or economic exploitation, but not when the issue was women working in the shops. Russell the machinist was not able to surmount the sexism of his union culture, but it is not true that his commitment to industrial unionism and the working class itself was fatally marred by his sexism. Nor can his failings on this question be used to sustain an argument that Marxism played a regressive role in this period of Canadian labour history, or that the ideas of parties such as the SPC were merely the "progressive" sheep's clothing on a "reactionary" wolf. Marxism of the third way would have better days, even on gender issues, and Marxist ideas would play a key role in making those days better.

It was in the Machinists' Union that those Marxist ideas received their greatest test, and how they became manifest must be analysed in terms of the political economy of Winnipeg during the war years. As David Bercuson points out, the cost of living was a key issue in the politics of the Winnipeg left during the war. His major finding is that machinists were the group least affected by wartime inflation. In the years 1914–18, when the general increase in the cost of living was 40 per cent, wages in the railway shops increased 49 per cent, and in the contract shops they increased 62 per cent.[32] In contrast, the wages of carpenters increased by a meagre 9 per cent. Bercuson notes, "the greatest increases went to the very group who usually led the most militant strikes and provided the most radical leadership – the contract and railway shop machinists."[33]

Having made that important observation, however, Bercuson does not go on to explore the reasons for it. Russell himself was keenly aware of one major reason: the pride machinists had in their traditions and skills – skills being threatened by labour-saving technology and seemingly endangered by the hiring of semi-skilled machine operatives. Machinists also had a long history of asserting workers' control at the point of production.[34] Wartime demand for their labour made them amongst the most sought-after workers in the country. In addition, their central importance to the war effort gave them the courage to take a leading role in 1917 against conscription, the issue that really galvanized the Canadian left and drew together strands of radicalism that were dispersed in the first years of the war.

The neglected factor in explaining machinist militance has been the role of ideas – in particular the impact of Marxist theory. According to Russell, tradesmen in Winnipeg "realized that their wages were depressed according to what the basic wage was ... for the common labourer, which is the basis of all wages."[35] This was a position derived from Marx, and one which Winnipeg bricklayers, carpenters, electricians, and masons, as well as machinists came to out of their working experience, where most of those on the jobs they worked at were labourers. Russell, Dick Johns, Alex Shepherd, and other Winnipeg machinists were not lulled into complacency by their relatively high wages: instead, they saw the low wages and insecurity of employment of the labourers as presaging their own futures. They used Marx's argument concerning the basis of wage rates in a capitalist economy to convince machinists that they had to see their commonality of interests with unskilled workers and to act in concert with them to defend the interests of the working class as a whole.[36]

The significance of Russell's involvement has been obscured by the tendency of some Canadian labour historians to associate AFL craft unionists with conservatism, and frontier labourers and the unskilled with radicalism and industrial unionism.[37] During the war, however, Winnipeg machinists like Russell and Dick Johns were at one and the same time machinists and at the forefront of the move to industrial unionism. As a member of IAM Local #122 Russell became a fervent exponent of industrial unions within the AFL. The growing acceptance of industrial unionism in the metal trades paralleled and fed the insistence of the Marxists on united working-class action and political solutions. Rather than retreating into craft exclusivity, Russell looked outward and worked to unite the machinists, boilermakers, specialists, and helpers in the railway shops.

By 1916 he was already headed toward supporting a "one big union" type of organization. In January 1916 the CPR Systems Federation, which included boilermakers, helpers, and specialists, was formed.[38] In contract negotiations the CPR refused to deal with the demands of individual unions – they wanted a collective agreement. As Russell and the defence lawyers pointed out during the Winnipeg General Strike trials in 1919–20, it was this demand by the CPR that served to legitimate the formation of the Systems Federation.[39] From there Russell developed the idea of one big union of railway workers, and eventually of all labour.[40] By 1917 there was a growing audience for the message of Bob Russell and the other Winnipeg exponents of breaking down craft divisions in the labour movement, one of the factors behind a dramatic jump in the number of strikes that year.[41] In May 1917 the announcement of compulsory military service brought a degree of cohesion to the Canadian working class, both east and west, which set the Canadian government and Canadian capitalists scrambling to find ways to head off the growing labour radicalism.

Not surprisingly, however, Russell continued to focus his analyses of the changing situation in terms of capital-labour relations on the railways. He saw the CPR Systems Federation as a step in the right direction, but he was opposed to the craft basis of its organization. Decisions made by the federation were based on craft autonomy: individual crafts such as the boilermakers or blacksmiths did not have to abide by majority decisions of the federation. Russell wanted to make "a nearer attempt at the one big union idea" by creating "one central body."[42] As early as 1915 he had talked about "the amalgamation of all the workers in one big army."[43] As a first step in creating that army, the various craft federations needed to follow the lead of the machinists and "sink their individuality" in order to bring about amalgamation and the creation of an industrial union. According to Russell the current setup was so complicated that not only the rank and file workers but even the officers of the various federations did not know how it worked. Such a system prevented recognition that "we are but one – a working class, enslaved."[44]

This background is crucial in understanding the academic debate concerning the relationship between syndicalism and the One Big Union. Generally speaking, the One Big Union has been described as syndicalist because of its espousal of industrial unionism, assumed rejection of parliamentary politics, and support for the general strike. The problem is that labour historians have correctly identified "classical" syndicalism with the French labour movement but usually without realizing that it was based on craft, not industrial, unionism.[45] French syndicalism was based in smaller unions of skilled artisans, and reflected the generally less centralized nature of French industry in the late nineteenth century.[46] It was not until 1906 that the Confédération Générale du Travail, the syndicalists' umbrella organization, decided to organize on the basis of industrial unions. Even then craft unions already in existence were allowed to remain organized on that basis.[47]

The key to the original form of French syndicalism was that local unions were not bound by the decisions of CGT conventions. This was precisely the kind of "individuality" that Bob Russell was trying to get rid of in his plans for the creation of an industrial union for railway workers. If he was influenced by syndicalism while still a native of Glasgow, there is little evidence to suggest that influence was still alive during the First World War period.[48] His espousal of both industrial unionism and class unionism was not linked to a syndicalist conception of the general strike. As a member of the Socialist Party, which constantly emphasized that action on the political field was more effective in the long run than action on the economic field, he did not tie his support for one big unionism to a rejection of parliamentary politics. Perhaps there is a syndicalist "spirit" in some of Russell's positions, and the idea of one big union came from the Industrial Workers of the World, but his main connection with that organization may be that he knew the words to some of the songs in the IWW's *Little Red Song Book*. His own writings demonstrate that he was guided by his understanding of Marx's call in the *Communist Manifesto* for a party composed of the majority of the working class. Like Marx, however, he never worked out exactly how this organization would operate – one of the reasons he continued to describe the One Big Union as both an industrial union and a class union.

How widespread the influence of Russell and other Marxian socialists was by 1918 is difficult to assess. Many Winnipeg workers, even in the machinists' locals, remained largely untouched by their educational and organizational efforts. What is undeniable, however, is that in the Machinists' *Bulletin*, which Russell became the editor of in April 1918, a surprising number of railway workers wrote in to expound on topics related to their jobs, and in the process drew on Marxist categories and ideas.[49] Russell and other Marxists of the third way had machinists thinking about their class position, the extraction of surplus value, and the ways in which capitalism divided the workers from each other.[50] Nor was their impact only on the working class: one of the company representatives whom Marxian socialists in the rail unions negotiated with was Grant Hall, western vice-president of the Canadian Pacific Railway. According to Russell, Hall had read *Capital* and was able to debate Marxism. Unlike some company negotiators, who were thrown when the machinists began demanding wages based on the relationship between what they produced for the company and the profits the company made, rather than on a strict dollar basis, Hall was able to engage the labour representatives on their own terms.[51] As in British Columbia, where the language of Marxism made its way into the capitalist class and the discourse of the Mounted Police, Marxist ideas in

Winnipeg played a role in the actual confrontation of labour and capital in the shops and at the bargaining table.

While we may never be able to assess the actual impact of socialist ideas on Winnipeg's working class in this period, it is evident that Russell's Marxism in no way impeded, and likely spurred, his growing influence and popularity. In January 1918 the Winnipeg Trades and Labour Council accepted his credentials as a delegate for IAM Local #122. In February he stopped working on the shop floor, and became a full-time union official and trade union organizer.[52] By early April he had succeeded Bob Ward, who had died suddenly, as secretary-treasurer of IAM Local #122.[53] Within weeks he also became secretary of the Metal Trades Council. In May 1918 he and fellow SPCer Alex Shepherd began organizing machinists in the contract shops.[54]

In September 1918 Russell attended the Trades and Labour Congress meeting in Quebec City at which the fissure between the western and eastern wings of the Canadian labour movement widened into a major political breach. Russell, along with Jack Kavanagh and R. Livett, signed a minority report of the Committee on Officers' Reports, the first time this had happened in TLCC history.[55] The report condemned the actions of the labour delegation, composed largely of international union officers, which had met with the War Cabinet in January 1918.[56] Objections were also raised to the National Registration Scheme and to the membership of TLCC secretary Paddy Draper on the National Registration Board. The report, following a sharp debate, was voted down.

While this aspect of the congress is now "common knowledge," another key aspect has gone strangely unnoticed. On the sixth day eight resolutions in favour of industrial unionism were introduced, with all of them, not surprisingly, being turned down. Nor was it surprising that all eight came from western Canada. What is crucial, however, is that all eight came from Winnipeg – five from machinists' unions, one from the Machinists' Joint Executive, one from the Winnipeg Trades and Labour Council, and one from the Transcona Trades and Labour Council. While there is little direct evidence, undoubtedly Bob Russell and Dick Johns had something to do with some, if not all, of these resolutions. This evidence serves to refute David Bercuson's argument that Russell's role in the labour revolt of 1919 has been exaggerated by left-wing labour historians such as Gregory Kealey and Nolan Reilly. Bob Russell was the key figure, not just in Winnipeg but in western Canada as a whole, in the effort to organize industrially and thereby break down some of the barriers that had historically divided the working class. As part of that attempt, Russell spoke out against racism in his own union, fought to bring labourers into it, spoke out against the exclusion of Asian workers, and opposed the war and conscription.

Russell, like Bill Pritchard, would be quick to refute any attempt to portray him as the individual hero of the Winnipeg General Strike, and to the extent that the "new" labour historians do so they are wrong.[57] Yet Bercuson's characterization of Winnipeg's skilled craft unionists – Russell, Dick Johns, and Alex Shepherd included – as racist, sexist, labour aristocrats who did not care about anyone but themselves is egregious. Claims that they "made virtually no effort to organize the truly downtrodden of Winnipeg," and "tried to keep their union locals as lily white as they could," fall to the ground when faced with the actual historical record.[58] Russell, who counted fellow Jewish Marxists Max Tessler and Sam Blumenberg among his comrades, did not espouse the widespread anti-Semitism to be found in Winnipeg in this period, and both he and Alex Shephed fought to organize downtrodden workers, including Ukrainians in the contract shops. On 7 January 1919 Russell was at the meeting of the Winnipeg and Trades and Labour Council when the sleeping-car porters asked for affiliation, a request that was "unanimously and heartily endorsed." Of note is the fact that secretary Robinson expressed surprise that the porters "were not accepted by the railroad trades but are treated as a subsidiary organization."[59] It was a contradictory moment for white labour, demonstrating its ignorance of racism against black workers within its own house, while accepting black workers in a way they had not been accepted before. The moment would not last, but while it lasted white unionists demonstrated that their ability to defend the downtrodden was not categorically defined by their identity.[60]

Nor is it true that the growing radicalism and swing to industrial unionism of the late war period excluded women workers in its vision of a new labour solidarity. At the September 1918 Trades and Labour Congress convention, representatives of the Winnipeg Trades and Labour Council, among them Bob Russell, asked the congress to place women organizers in the field. Russell and secretary Robinson's report of the convention to Winnipeg unionists quite dramatically demonstrates that women workers were included in both the plans of organization and the vision of the new working class of the future. Following praise for Rose Henderson's speech at the convention, Russell and Robinson wrote:

It was an inspiring sight to see so many delegates in attendance at the convention and one could see in imagination the many, many thousands of men and women whom these delegates represented and who are taking their part faithfully and well in the great industrial movement of the Dominion ... the magnificent possibilities ahead of our movement if and when those men and women of the rank and file, filled with a knowledge of their own position in society, realizing that they are the producers of the wealth of the country, determine to leave no stone unturned, no effort spared, to stamp out of existence a state of affairs where the few get the good things of life while the many are denied even the necessaries of life.[61]

Russell continued to demonstrate a more open attitude toward women in the labour movement than he had in 1916–17 as a member of the Winnipeg Trades and Labour Council. On 18 December 1918 the Women's Labour League requested affiliation with the WTLC. There were arguments for and against, Russell's contribution being to point out that it would be hypocritical to turn down the request on the grounds that the women were non-unionists, since a precedent had been set with the admission of the Ministerial Association. On vote the Women's Labour League was accepted.[62]

Even the increasingly repressive measures of the Canadian state in 1918–19 served to unite labour and socialist radicals. Within weeks of the 1918 Trades and Labour Congress convention Robert Borden's Union government passed a series of orders-in-council that took direct aim at "alien" workers in general and their socialist organizations in particular. On 25 September, P.C. 2381 prohibited the use of fourteen "alien" languages, and on 28 September P.C. 2384 declared fourteen "alien" organizations unlawful.[63] On 11 October P.C. 2525 banned strikes and lockouts in industrial disputes, in the process launching an attack on organized labour as a whole and helping to bring Anglo-Saxon and non-Anglo-Saxon workers together in common cause. Many left-wingers in the ethnic community belonged to language groups affiliated with the Social Democratic Party, but raids on SDP offices and the banning of its ethnic press left many radicals looking for a place to go. Ironically, given that the ethnic federations had broken away from the SPC in 1910 and joined the SDP, a number of ethnic radicals, including the Lettish local of the SDP, now joined the party of Russell, Johns, and Helen and George Armstrong.

Even in Winnipeg, however, the banning of strikes and lockouts and the attacks on the ethnic socialists did not translate into immediate control of the labour movement by radicals. In the December 1918 WTLC elections, James Winning, a moderate, defeated Bob Russell in his attempt to become president of the council. The ascendance of the radicals did not really begin until the Walker Theatre meeting of 22 December 1918, but even at this point there is no reason to believe charges by critics of the Socialist Party that the meeting was an SPC "conspiracy." Russell spoke at the meeting under the auspices of the Trades and Labour Council, not of the SPC.[64] In the *Western Labor News* the meeting was advertised as being under the auspices of the council.[65] The meeting, addressed by members of both the SPC and SDP, was characterized by strong rhetoric and open discussion of the Russian Revolution. Russell earned his reputation as a radical by introducing the motion to condemn the allied intervention in the Soviet Union, an act of aggression in which Canada was taking part.[66]

Events moved rapidly following the Walker Theatre meeting. In early January 1919 Russell, Fred Tipping, and W.H. Logan were appointed by the WTLC to organize a meeting dealing with reconstruction and the returned soldiers.[67] Initially the intent was to work in conjunction with the SPC, but when the council pulled out, the SPC went ahead and organized a meeting for 19 January. In spite of his being an SPC member for five years, the Majestic Theatre meeting was the first time Russell spoke in public under the auspices of the Socialist Party. He made good use of the opportunity. He laid into the Dominion Labour Party and all other parties which believed that capitalism could be reformed. Turning his fire on the capitalists, he assailed the Canadian Reconstruction Association for preaching harmony between labour and capital. Only a new system controlled by the working class, he argued, could save society from the devastating unemployment that was coming with the return of the soldiers. He added an internationalist perspective, praising Rosa Luxemburg and Karl Liebknecht for their efforts to overthrow the right-wing social democratic government of Germany and establish a socialist society.[68]

January 1919 saw Russell shift significantly to the left. In spite of protestations to the contrary during his trial, it is undeniable that he considered what was happening in the Soviet Union as a possible model for Canada. He wrote to SPC dominion secretary Chris Stephenson asking for five hundred copies of the *Soviets at Work* to distribute to returned soldiers, a clear recognition that the veterans must be won over in any attempt to challenge the Canadian state and also proof that Russell was at least thinking about how a socialist society would function after the overthrow of capitalism. He knew, however, that a socialist society in Canada was a long way off, and his political involvement continued to focus on the needs and desires of Winnipeg workers. When he raised the possibility of a general strike at the 21 January 1919 meeting of the Winnipeg Trades and Labour Council, he had in mind forcing the owners of the metal shops to accept collective bargaining, not storming the barricades.[69]

In March 1919 Russell's focus and that of other Winnipeg radicals shifted to the Western Labour Conference being held in Calgary. The Winnipeg delegation was strong and included four leading members of the Socialist Party; Bob Russell and Dick Johns represented the Labour Council, George Armstrong was a delegate from Carpenters' Local

#343, and Helen Armstrong was there on behalf of the Women's Labour League. The important role of these Winnipeg delegates has been almost entirely overlooked in the histories of Canadian labour in 1919. Both Robin and Bercuson have focused on the role played by Bill Pritchard and Jack Kavanagh during the course of the conference. Highlighting the importance of Kavanagh is warranted, but as we have seen, Pritchard made only one speech of any significance. His topic, which was how much money unions should be initially asked for to get the One Big Union off the ground, was influential, but in no way key to the convention's proceedings.[70] At the crucial last session, on the morning of 15 March, Pritchard's only input was to second the passing of two motions. Kavanagh made a major contribution, but he did not have the clout of R.J. Tallon, who chaired all the sessions. The "reds" were better organized than any other group, but there is virtually no evidence to prove that they were in a position to railroad the convention.[71]

The Winnipeg delegates were not part of a conspiracy, but they did firm up support for the One Big Union, which was beginning to slip by the last day of the conference. Into the breach stepped George Armstrong, Johns, and Russell, perhaps buoyed, or shamed, by the example of fellow delegate Helen Armstrong, who had made a courageous speech earlier in the session on the important role played by women in the labour movement.[72] Russell followed George Armstrong's call for decisions to be based on the will of the "active minority" with a similar argument. Once again basing his analysis on his experience with the thirty-thousand member Division 4 of the railway unions, Russell lashed out against the craft unions and their defenders, calling the latter "serpents." He accused delegates who attempted to question the unanimity of the decision to form the OBU of seeking press attention, and he expressed complete confidence that "the majority of the active workers" would endorse the OBU. Those not voting were to be counted in the affirmative.[73] Following an endorsement of Russell's position by Vic Midgley, Dick Johns rose to state that the workers who did not vote in the referendum to form the OBU and/or call a strike would have to follow the majority who did.[74]

For SPCers like Russell the Western Labour Conference represented a major turning point. Marxists of the third way, especially members of the Socialist Party, prided themselves on being democrats, spurning the elitist trappings of the international craft unions, and being more responsive to the needs of their fellow unionists and the working class as a whole. In Calgary, however, there was a great willingness, evinced strongly by George Armstrong, to concentrate on the majority of active union members, not on the majority in the entire union. Even in 1919 many Canadian workers remained apathetic, and leaders such as

Russell were increasingly under pressure from the active workers to take a more militant stance. Something had to give, and in this case Russell, like Pritchard, Kavanagh, Midgley and other SPCers, opted to pursue the promise of the One Big Union, thus temporarily de-emphasizing the task of educating the majority of the working class to class consciousness.[75]

Upon his return to Winnipeg Russell set about promoting the One Big Union, both locally and nationally. Early in April he mailed twenty thousand copies of the proceedings of the Western Labour Conference to Vancouver, Edmonton, Regina, Brandon, Fort William, Cochrane, North Bay, Toronto, and Montreal.[76] A great deal of time was also taken up with raising funds for the new organization. Russell's organizing work for the OBU was cut short, however, by the impending clash between the metal trades and the big three employers in Winnipeg: Vulcan Iron, Manitoba Bridge, and Dominion Bridge. The companies consistently refused to deal with the Metal Trades Council, and the council insisted that it must deal with the companies in its fight for better wages and working conditions, and union recognition. As secretary of the Metal Trades Council and delegate to the Trades and Labour Council, Bob Russell was front and centre in the struggle.

On 1 May both the metal and building trades went out on strike. Russell, like many leading SPCers on the coast, was initially opposed to the strike, because he felt it would interfere with the efforts to organize the One Big Union.[77] Support for the strikers in Winnipeg was widespread, however, and on 9 May the WTLC held a referendum on a general strike vote. The response was overwhelmingly positive, with 11,112 union members in favour and a mere 524 members opposed, with seventeen unions still to report.[78] On 15 May twenty thousand more workers walked off the job, including a significant number who were not unionized. Although initially opposed to the strike, Russell fully committed himself to it once it had begun. On 4 May he spoke to between four and five thousand workers at the Industrial Bureau.[79] As he had so often done in the past, he linked the strike demands of the workers to the functioning of the capitalist system as a whole, exhorting the workers in the audience to seek out the real cause of low wages and unemployment. If they did, he argued, they would recognize that civilization was toppling because the foundations were faulty. It was their task to rebuild society on a new foundation.[80] Part of that faulty foundation was, of course, craft unionism and its attendant divisions, the new foundation being one big unionism and international solidarity. At the WTLC meeting held two days later Russell gave a rousing speech in which he set the Winnipeg General Strike in its international context, urging Winnipeg labour to stand firm for workers everywhere.[81]

The charge was made, and would be made again and again during the strike trials, that Russell and other radicals were outside agitators forcing their ideas on the rank and file. Russell was well aware of the accusation and its intent. His response was to take his case to the workers, and he made one of his most vehement attacks on the charge before five thousand people in a meeting at the Industrial Bureau on 18 May. During his speech he argued that leadership was "dictated" by the rank and file: leaders were merely the "mouthpieces" of the workers.[82] What is striking about his position is that it is virtually identical to that espoused by the Polish revolutionary Marxist Rosa Luxemburg. In the last paragraph of her classic *The Mass Strike* written in August 1906, Luxemburg argued that in revolutionary struggles the masses would be the chorus and the leading bodies merely the "speaking parts." The role of leaders was to act as the "interpreters of the will of the masses."[83] The similarity between Luxemburg's and Russell's positions is striking, and helps identify why labour historians have had difficulty explaining Russell's socialism and the politics of the One Big Union. In effect, what labour historians have habitually identified as syndicalism was really a minority tendency in Second International Marxism.

Bob Russell may have been a mouthpiece during the actual course of the strike, but he was most definitely a leading mouthpiece of the workers in negotiations with Mayor Charles Gray, Premier Norris, and federal government officials. On 13 May Premier Norris appointed Russell to the ad hoc committee to negotiate a settlement.[84] Initially Russell was one of five members of the Winnipeg Trades and Labour Council appointed to the Central Strike Committee, and the only member of the SPC. The Central Committee was then joined by 195 other members, three from each striking union, to form a Central Strike Committee of two hundred.[85] This committee proved too cumbersome, and on 22 May it became the General Strike Committee. The new, much smaller Central Strike Committee of fifteen members included Russell, again the only SPCer in the group.

Perhaps Alex Shepherd exaggerated somewhat when he called Russell the "ringleader of the strike," but he was almost always at the centre of the action.[86] It was usually Russell who reported on the ad hoc committee's negotiations to the daily meetings of the Strike Committee. Russell also dealt with the daily entreaties from company representatives that they be allowed to transport perishable goods and operate vital industries. He enjoyed his role as a leading member of what Bercuson calls "labour's government."[87] He commented to Vic Midgley that it was enjoyable "to see employers coming to the Labor Temple, asking permission to operate their various industries."[88] In spite of that pleasure, however, Russell harboured no illusions about the General Strike being revolutionary. He recognized the tremendous amount of educating and organizing of the workers left to do. For that reason he saw the strike as impeding the progress of the One Big Union, the organization he felt certain would be the vehicle for a mass working-class mobilization across the country and the eventual creation of a socialist society.

The Canadian state, however, was not interested in what Russell was actually doing during the strike. Government and employers wanted an example made of the strike leaders, and the proof of conspiracy to overthrow the government had been provided by labour leaders and socialists on the public platform. Statements made or alleged to have been made at the Walker Theatre and Majestic Theatre meetings, combined with the revolutionary literature dispensed by the Socialist Party, provided the basis for the state's case. In the early hours of 17 June 1919 the strike leaders were taken from their beds. Russell faced the most severe charge and would be tried separately before the other seven leaders were tried as a group, but he was able to publish his views while awaiting the setting of a trial date.

In July he set out the lessons of modern industry in a long article in the *Western Labor News*. Reiterating a point he had made many times before, he argued that "good leaders" were no longer needed in the labour movement, because leaders were only mouthpieces. It was time to abandon the "great man" theory of history and realize that the rank and file workers had to do the job themselves. Labour officials were no longer in touch with what was happening in the shops, because they were too caught up in protecting their own jobs. Like so much of Russell's thought, the argument was both insightful and confused. He appeared to believe that labour officials selling out their own rank and file was a new development, one which could now be corrected by organizing on an industrial basis, breaking down old distinctions, and developing a rank and file movement. Why workers in 1919 were more aware of the betrayal of the officials than they had been a generation or two before Russell did not explain – he just assumed it. Nor did he give any reasons why unskilled or semi-skilled workers should be any more activist or willing to oppose the activities of their leaders than were skilled workers.

The weaknesses in his analysis notwithstanding, his continuing focus on changes at the point of production, and his awareness of the effect of the Canadian state and its laws on organized labour, produced insightful analyses. Increasing skill dilution, he believed, was weakening the craft unions, which could no longer be the basis of effective strikes. The need now was for the sympathetic strike, because it included all workers in a particular area, both skilled and unskilled. As Mary Jordan points out, a key element in his thinking was that a one big union type of organization, in which workers in a given city, or eventually the entire country, were members of the same union, regardless of their occupation, could go on strike and the state would not be able to ban it as a general sympathetic strike.[89] His solution was naive, because it failed to recognize that the capitalist state had the power to change the law if threatened by this new type of organization, but Russell's ability to link theory and practice, and to link changes at the point of production with solutions for the organization of labour, was impressive. In his sometimes crude way he was dealing with the same problems of the relationship between economic and political action, and between objective and subjective manifestations of class, which have occupied academic Marxists and labour historians for decades. Bob Russell was no Edward Thompson or David Montgomery, but the questions of structure and agency, leaders and followers, and changes in the capitalist mode of production and resulting working-class consciousness were all questions he not only analysed but tried to provide answers for in the material world of labour organizing.

This one article is also very revealing because its analysis is entirely devoid of any reference to the Winnipeg General Strike, less than a month old. Russell had a highly ambivalent relationship to the strike. While he did see 1919 as a crucial turning point, it was only a moment of revolutionary potential in that much longer evolutionary process Marxists of the third way saw as the basis of all change in the organic world and in human society. The creation of a new kind of labour movement was an evolutionary process, and the OBU, not the general strike, was its vehicle. Yet given his impending trial and likely incarceration, Russell faced great difficulties in helping with the early organizing work of the One Big Union. On 5 August he was elected secretary-treasurer at the inaugural meeting of the OBU's Central Labour Council, but there was little time to tackle the tasks at hand.[90] A week later he and the other strike leaders were committed for trial, and a request for bail was denied.[91] He then spent several weeks in jail. Eventually, however, the efforts of the Defence Committee were rewarded, and the strike leaders were granted bail on 10 September 1919.[92]

Russell's actual trial was launched in November with an address to the jury by A.J. Andrews. The composition of the jury, twelve citizens from rural Manitoba, gave an early indication that the verdict was already in. The defence had only one real chance: to prove that the assessment of guilt or innocence should be based on Russell's actual actions as a trade unionist during the strike, not on what he said as a member of the Socialist Party. Robert Cassidy, the lead defence lawyer, portrayed him as a trades unionist who worked from the bottom up and was not an outside agitator.[93] Cassidy hoped to demonstrate that Russell's actions involved "the legitimate expression of trades unionism on the political field."[94]

The crown was having none of that argument and went to enormous lengths to prevent Russell's defence lawyers from even introducing his past union involvement as evidence. The crown, interested only in what Russell claimed in his speeches, not in what his actions were, considered this evidence inadmissible. In his summation, Andrews put the crown's case succinctly: "We say ... that their intention was to bring about discontent and dissatisfaction and what would be the logical result some day – revolution – some day attempted revolution – some day overturning the government, but it was not necessary to charge and we did not charge anywhere that they attempted in the first instance to overthrow the government."[95] As Gerald Friesen points out, there was some foundation to the crown's case. Members of the Socialist Party of Canada and other Marxists of the third way were preparing for revolution, although much educating and organizing had to take place before it could be realized. Winnipeg in the spring of 1919 was not to be the time, but the leading Marxian socialists had every intention of living to fight another day.[96]

For Bob Russell and the other imprisoned strike leaders, that day would arrive when they had served their prison sentences. Russell went to prison with the satisfaction of knowing that the vast majority of workers of all ethnic and religious backgrounds supported his actions. Fellow SPCer Max Tessler held a party at his home for Russell just before he entered prison on 26 December 1919, indicating the respect and affection Jewish socialists in Winnipeg had for Russell.[97] Early in 1920 a Winnipeg worker praised him for his "great sacrifices," stating that he had not sought personal gain but was guilty only of doing "just what we wanted him to do."[98] It was the kind of praise Russell must have cherished, given his insistence that the role of the leader was to interpret and honestly implement the express wishes of the rank and file.

Russell served about 350 days of his two-year term, and was released on 11 December 1920. Like Bill Pritchard, he received a rousing welcome back, with four thousand people attending a reception for him at the Industrial Bureau on 27 December 1920.[99] There was little time, however, for celebrations. Ten days after his release from prison Russell was named general organizer for the Winnipeg District of the One Big Union.[100] It was not the One Big Union he had hoped would be in existence by the time he got out of prison. The organization he had envisioned as the future hope of the Canadian working class was already in serious decline. In Vancouver, where most of the major leaders of the

OBU lived and worked, the organization was in disarray. Lumber workers, B.C. metal miners, and the coal miners of District #18 had taken their leave of the organization, and only in Winnipeg, where the OBU had 4,438 members, did it have a strong base from which to build.[101]

As an independent industrial union it faced an extremely difficult structural problem involving the combined hostilities of the international unions, the companies, and the state. Repeated linking of the two organizations over the years notwithstanding, the OBU and the Industrial Workers of the World were entirely distinct organizations, but the OBU encountered many of the difficulties the IWW had faced for years. Originally formed to organize unorganized workers, the IWW increasingly found itself forced to organize workers under the jurisdiction of AFL unions. Unorganized workers proved a hard organizational nut to crack. They were often transient, divided by race, ethnicity, and religion, and very poor. Craft workers provided much more fertile ground for unions because they usually had cohesive union structures, relatively large treasuries, capable leaders, and a shared attachment to their skills.[102]

The OBU was in trouble once the economic downturn of the early 1920s combined with the hostility of both government and the AFL unions made it very difficult to unite unorganized workers. Left with little choice but to "bore from within" established AFL unions, the OBU was caught on the horns of a dilemma. Given that it categorically rejected calls for Lenin's program of organizing within the existing craft unions, it was left to do precisely that while calling it something else. It was virtually inevitable, having lost the lumber workers, coal miners and metal miners, that it would have to concentrate on workers such as the machinists and carpenters in major western cities, especially Winnipeg.[103]

Within a month of his release from prison Bob Russell found himself attempting to carry out in practice policies which he had always condemned in theory. At a meeting of the unemployed in the Roblin Hall on 10 January 1921, he observed that building trades workers in Winnipeg were suffering the most from discrimination in AFL unions.[104] He attempted to defend a number of carpenters, supporters of the OBU, who wanted to get jobs helping to construct the new Eaton Mail Order building in Winnipeg. They were dismissed from the site for refusing to join the United Brotherhood of Carpenters and Joiners (UBCJ), an AFL affiliate that controlled the hiring and firing of carpenters on the job. The dispute placed Russell and the OBU in an impossible position. If they did not defend their members, who had to work to eat, they risked discrediting and speeding up the OBU's demise, even in Winnipeg. If they defended the OBU carpenters, they were in effect calling for an open shop on the Eaton job site. Swallowing his pride and laying aside principle, Russell went to the Joint Council of Industry, an arbitration body he once condemned as a sham, with a charge of discrimination against the UBCJ.

The council had been created by the provincial government of Manitoba in response to the Winnipeg General Strike. It consisted of two representatives from the Employers' Association and two from labour, including the secretary of the Winnipeg Trades and Labor Council. The chairperson was Charles W. Gordon, better known by his pen name of Ralph Connor. Gordon, who had acted as an arbitrator for the federal government in a number of strikes, was proud of the fact that the council ruled on 107 cases and came to 107 unanimous decisions.[105] These decisions may have been unanimous, but they were certainly not about to go in favour of the OBU. Given that the council was explicitly designed to prevent the kind of capital-labour conflict that produced the OBU, and that the Trades and Labour Council was now controlled by supporters of the AFL/TLCC, the OBU had no chance of getting a favourable ruling. Russell must have suspected this, and his insistence on going to the Joint Council can only serve to underline the desperate situation the OBU was facing. Needless to say, the council rejected the charge of discrimination against the Carpenters' Union.

When James Winning, a former colleague of Russell's on the strike committee, accused him of favouring open shop principles and setting aside the principle of collective bargaining, he did not respond.[106] Two years later, however, the OBU was openly following a "scorched earth" policy, arguing that any strategy that weakened the hold of the AFL in Canada should be used. Russell claimed that vicious discrimination in the railway and building trades made the open shop not only acceptable but the preferred option.[107] In his defence it should be noted that his approval of the open shop was not as surprising and contradictory as it might seem. There were those in the Communist Party who were opponents of the closed shop and a compulsory dues check-off. Jack Scott, for example, has argued that the union shop must be based on voluntary membership. In the late 1930s the CPC "was in principle against the compulsory dues check-off. And the reason was simple: compulsory dues check-off put a firm financial base under the labour bureaucracy."[108] Given that the entire raison d'être of the OBU was to free rank and file labour from the clutches of the labour bureaucrats, an open shop position was at least consistent with the "spirit" of the OBU. The reality was, however, that while workers wanted the fullest possible rank and file democracy, caring for the economic needs of their families made the protection of the closed shop a more pressing need, even for many supporters of the OBU.

In effect, Russell and the OBU were attempting to realize a form of workplace organization, and political organization, that was simply not possible without a mass base in the unions. With the OBU under fierce attack by the state, employers, and AFL/TLCC officials, its rank and file supporters were not in a position to abandon the security of the AFL/TLCC, no matter how fervently they believed in what the OBU stood for. As a result, in the mid-1920s Russell and other OBU leaders did not have the support of the critical mass of workers who had made the Winnipeg General Strike possible. During the course of the strike Russell experienced a degree of freedom to implement the ideas he espoused that he would never again experience as Canada's leading exponent of the One Big Union. He was never able to realize in the OBU the kind of solidarity, sense of purpose, and confidence that the working class really was capable of running society that he had experienced in those inspiring days and weeks of May and June 1919. He knew that the organization he envisioned for the working class was made possible by the widespread labour militance that had characterized 1919, a moment in time when it was possible to dream of a labour movement without hierarchy and bureaucracy. The Winnipeg General Strike held more meaning for the fate of the One Big Union than even Russell himself suspected at the time.

By the spring of 1921 the dilemma had been laid bare. An RCMP report stated that in the dispute with the UBCJ the OBU did not have "a leg to stand on." The "secessionists" were beginning to fight among themselves, and the OBU clearly had "its back to the wall."[109] Perhaps hoping to find that the situation elsewhere in western Canada warranted fighting on, Russell and Johns embarked on an extended organizing tour in the spring of 1921. Russell claimed that the response was good in Moose Jaw, Swift Current, Saskatoon, and Edmonton, where he and Johns spoke to "a crowded house" in the Empire Theatre on 15 May 1921.[110] They also spoke to a crowd of six hundred in the Victoria Pavilion in Calgary on 22 May. There Johns was well received, but Russell was apparently "very hard to follow." He was rather vague, suggesting that workers subscribe to the *OBU Bulletin* and become educated, and eventually strength of numbers would lead to working-class victory; the capitalists were class conscious, and the workers had to become so as well.[111] In effect, Russell was once again evincing the major weakness that had characterized the Socialist Party for so many years prior to 1917–19 – an inability to develop a plan of action for translating the education and organization of the working class into an effective force for combatting and eventually overthrowing the capitalist state.

In spite of some well-attended meetings it was clear that Russell was discouraged, almost despondent. A 23 May Calgary meeting was "a total failure" and prompted him to describe Calgary workers as a "dead bunch."[112] At a meeting of railway workers the same day he predicted that the OBU would be back to its former strength within a year but could not come up with a reason why that should be so.[113] He told Comrade Flye of the OBU that his old ally Jack Kavanagh was "alright but he is helping to kill the O.B.U. in Vancouver." Russell tried to put a brave face on the situation, but he was so discouraged by external attack and internal division that twice he sent the OBU Central Labour Council letters of resignation.[114]

The reasons for his decision to resign are not entirely clear, but some of the answers came to light at the 5 July meeting of the Central Labour Council. At that meeting Russell, who had returned to Winnipeg, accused individuals in the party of "self aggrandisement." He also noted that "he had been thinking anyway for a long time about going back to the tools." The first charge was often made about Jack Kavanagh in OBU circles, and may also have referred to Ernest Winch, a key player in the split between the Lumber Workers and the OBU. Russell was not entirely without justification, because the actual creation of the OBU had been spearheaded from the coast, and now that times were bad, everyone appeared to be leaving the ship. It is possible that he really did want to go back to the shop floor, although a guilty conscience about his status as a paid official may have had more to do with his wishes than did any real desire to engage in manual labour.

His disillusionment with the OBU existed alongside his growing estrangement from the Socialist Party of Canada. There was by this time discussion in SPC circles about statements he had made since his release from prison – some members even wanted him expelled if it was found that he was no longer a socialist.[115] Russell moved to mend some fences, claiming that the SPC was still, presumably in contrast with the OBU, the "scientific organization" of the workers, and that he would begin to direct his energies toward helping the SPC.[116] However, given that he was to leave the SPC early in 1922 it is difficult to see this endorsement as genuine.[117] He knew that the SPC was in as much, if not more, trouble than the OBU. While they remained personal friends, Russell and Alex Shepherd, his old ally in the IAM, were slowly drifting apart for political reasons. W.H. (Bill) Hoop, who had been in the SPC when Russell first came to Winnipeg, was now a leading supporter of AFL craft unionism. In the municipal election of 1920 he ran as one "Who stands uncompromisingly opposed to the One Big Union and its Direct Action Policy."[118] The One Big Union was Russell's life: barring its complete collapse, it was no longer possible for him to work with old SPC comrades who supported the AFL and were thus unwilling to fight for the OBU's survival.

Although publicly he seemed reluctant to stay with the OBU, it is almost certain that he never intended to leave, that what he really wanted was some recognition and reassurance. Like Winch, he was good at playing the humble servant of the workers and accusing rival labour leaders of unethical, self-seeking behaviour of which he, of course, was incapable. In fact, he always had a keen sense of his own importance, and knew that the One Big Union would be rudderless without him. There can be little doubt that he was appropriately assuaged when Comrade Wooler said that his resignation "would mean the last of the O.B.U." Russell's motives notwithstanding, Wooler may have been right.[119]

While Russell decided to stay with the OBU at least temporarily, the threat to the organization's survival remained very real. It was rescued, strange as it may seem, by two rather startling developments. The first was launched in November 1921 when the OBU leadership decided to run a lottery in the *Bulletin* in which readers would receive cash prizes for correctly guessing the winners in English football games. When the football season ended, the contest switched to major league baseball. The scheme was an immediate success, and tens of thousands of dollars rolled into the OBU treasury. There were protests both within the OBU and elsewhere in labour circles that this was an act of heresy for a working-class organization. Much of the protest was little more than rhetoric: imitators followed, including the *Western Labor News* and the *BC Federationist*.[120]

When the contest was ruled illegal in June 1922 by the Manitoba Court of Appeal, the OBU got around the ruling by making the lottery coupons free and taking the money as subscriptions. When the contest was again ruled illegal in March 1925, the *Bulletin* switched to a weather-guessing contest, which immediately dropped the prize money from $8,100 a week to $4,000.[121] The OBU continued to challenge the authorities, however, and in the spring of 1931 the lottery switched from the weather to baseball. The last contest appeared in October 1933, following two raids on the *Bulletin* offices in the space of a month. By then the OBU had spent tens of thousands of lottery dollars on organizing work, relief for Nova Scotia miners and their families, the British General Strike of 1926, and the OBU summer camp for working-class children.

Just two months before the launching of the OBU lottery, the second development occurred, one certain to solidify Russell's distrust of Canadian Communists and bolster his waning commitment to the OBU. His disillusionment with the OBU apparently continued into the fall of 1921 when, for the first and only time, he decided to run for the House of Commons in the working-class riding of North Winnipeg.[122] Had he been elected it is very likely that he would have remained the sitting member for many years. In that event the One Big Union would likely have folded much sooner than it did.

One of the main reasons he failed in his attempt represents one of the strangest tales in the history of the Canadian left. In mid-September 1921 Fred Kaplan, still a member of the SPC but a supporter of the Communist Party, asked Russell to go to the Ukrainian Labour Temple to speak to a group of people willing to support his election bid. At this meeting Kaplan, John Navis, Boris Devyatkin, and Mathew Popovich agreed to deliver the Ukrainian vote to Russell if he entered into a written agreement with them.[123] Russell responded by saying he had to think about it, and left the meeting, agreement in hand. His next step was to lay the agreement before a special meeting of the Socialist Party. Kaplan, as well as the other three signatories to the agreement, denied that the meeting had ever taken place. He was expelled on the spot. In response he, Navis, Devyatkin, and Popovich convinced Jacob Penner to run against Russell. The votes cast for Penner would not have given Russell the win, but a combined effort from the outset of the campaign might well have pushed him over the top.

The terms of the deal were such that Russell could not possibly have accepted them. He was to pay the four men $1,000 a year for every year that he sat in the House of Commons. They would control all of his speeches and publications, including speeches to be given in the House of Commons. He was also required to sign any documents submitted by them. In return they were to do whatever it took to get him elected.

While it is only possible to speculate about the impact of this incident on Russell, that speculation seems crucially important. He did not make the document public in 1921, thereby lending credence to the idea that he was implicated in the deal by agreeing to it. It is possible that he agreed – quite likely before having seen the actual terms – and then turned on the Communists when the terms became known to him. Even then his primary motivation seems to have been to use the document to defend the embattled Socialist Party, without betraying the Communists to the capitalist press. The deal notwithstanding, he was not nearly as hostile to the Communists in 1921 as he would become over the course of the 1920s and into the 1930s. In all probability he sought to use the deal to turn the tide of SPC defections to the Communists, while at the same time avoiding the airing of the left's dirty laundry in public.

The timing of the document's public release in 1931 can be more easily explained, coming as it did during the Third Period, when all non-Communist leftists were being condemned as "social fascists" by the

Communist Party. The revelation also came in the wake of the Winnipeg Civic elections of 1931, in which the Communist Party attacked the One Big Union and Independent Labour Party with a virulence unknown since the formation of the Communist Party in 1921. *Bulletin* editor Charles Lestor, commenting on the day of the document's publication, was furious that "this self-styled group of Simon Pures accuses all and sundry of being guilty of corruption, while as a matter of fact they themselves are the most corrupt organization that ever masqueraded under the name of labor."[124] Given that *The Worker* remained silent when the document was revealed in December 1931, and did not respond to Lestor's accusation, it would appear that Russell's version of events was essentially accurate. The staff of *The Worker* followed events in Winnipeg, and it is extremely unlikely that the paper would have passed up an opportunity to condemn Russell and the OBU if at all possible.

Throughout the 1920s, therefore, Russell and the OBU possessed a document they could hold over the heads of the Winnipeg Communists. In response to charges of OBU corruption and improper activity, Russell could summon up an incident that appeared to demonstrate that leading members of the Communist Party were just as willing to sell out the workers for personal advancement as anyone else on the left. The deal was so damning because the money in question was to go to the individual Communists, not to the working class as a whole. The Communists always bragged about the fact that members who had paid positions of any kind always donated a large part of it to labour causes, and the deal with Russell appeared to make a mockery of that claim.

In spite of this incident Russell remained sympathetic to the Communist Party throughout 1921 and into 1922. In the spring of 1921 he had been offered a chance to go to Moscow as the Canadian representative at the founding of the International Congress of Revolutionary Trade and Industrial Unions (Profintern). He declined the offer, and Joe Knight went in his place.[125] Knight reported on his trip at the OBU's Third Annual Convention, held in Winnipeg from 26–29 September 1921. Even though the convention was held after Russell had been involved in exposing the election document to the SPC, he endorsed Knight's call for the affiliation of the OBU to the Profintern as soon as possible. Yet he must have been uneasy about Knight's admission that the Profintern completely opposed secessionist organizations, which the OBU clearly was. He tried to get more information to clarify the situation in his own mind but without much success.[126]

The issue came to a head at the meeting to form the Workers' Party in Toronto on 17 February 1922. The Workers' Party was to be the legal, above-ground wing of the illegal underground Communist Party. Russell arrived late and did not like what he saw, afterwards reporting that the important decisions had already been made. He opposed the party's plan to "bore from within" the AFL unions, portrayed it as reactionary, and fought for the OBU as the only progressive way to organize labour. The repudiation of Russell was swift and overwhelming. Almost every leading supporter of the Workers' Party, including Jack MacDonald, Maurice Spector, Michael Buhay, Becky Buhay, and Russell's old ally Jack Kavanagh condemned him for his "reactionary stance" and refusal to support the new party. In his report to the OBU Russell responded to these attacks by describing the convention as "confusion worse confounded." It may never be possible to say at what point he made up his mind, but it is quite likely that he had no intention of supporting the Workers' Party, even before he went to the convention. If there really was a chance of his involvement in this new Communist politics, that hope was dashed when Spector announced, "We are not confronted with the question of educating the workers today, that is not necessary." For a Marxist of the third way to be attacked on questions of organization was one thing, but to question the ongoing need to educate the workers was something else again.[127]

A couple of scenes were still to be played out in the drama. At the Central Labour Council Special Meeting held on 12 March 1922 Russell was accused of being "hostile" to the Workers' Party by its supporters in the One Big Union. He replied that the report of the convention would back up his position. When the report was read, Workers' Party supporters walked out of the meeting. This incident was followed by a series of meetings held in April and May 1922. Supporters of the Workers' Party had momentum on their side, the ability to point to the Russian Revolution and the attempts to build socialism in the Soviet Union as proof that any policy other than outright support for the Third International was "reactionary." Russell struck back by pointing out the contradiction in the Workers' Party position, on the one hand condemning the AFL and then telling its supporters to work within it. By this time he also had the increasingly bitter attacks appearing in the Communist press as proof of the Workers' Party's strategy of destroying the One Big Union.

The OBU leadership rejected affiliation with the Workers' Party, but the battle was just beginning. Throughout the summer of 1922 Third International supporters in the OBU, including Joe Knight, Sarah Johnston-Knight, Jack Kavanagh, and Malcolm Bruce, were actively "boring from within" the OBU. Finally, in November 1922 Bob Russell, *Bulletin* editor Frank Woodward, and other OBU faithful expelled Workers' Party supporters from executive positions in the organization.[128]

The OBU looked death in the face and survived. It would be tempting, given the events of 1921–22, to believe that its survival was based on a major blunder by local Communists, a resort to gambling in the *OBU Bulletin*, and Russell's stubborn refusal to recognize that the OBU was doomed to become a magnificent failure. Such an assessment, however, neglects the commitment Russell and other OBU leaders had to the One Big Union as ideal and the Marxist ideas on which that ideal was based. In November 1922 *Bulletin* editor and SPC member Frank Woodward responded to an editorial by fellow SPCer Alex Shepherd. Entitled "Signs of the Times," Shepherd's article took the "impossibilist" position on trade unions, arguing that they were non-revolutionary, bread-and-butter organizations. In his response Woodward, quoting *The Communist Manifesto*, stated that Marx and Engels saw the unions as more than bread-and-butter organizations, that what mattered to them "was the consolidation of the workers as a class, the elimination of various craft divisions and sectional outlook, and the recognition by them of the identity of working class interests." Taking the classic Marxist of the third way position, he rejected both the impossibilism of the early SPC and the Communist emphasis on the vanguard party, stating that "the workers organized as a class are a political party."[129]

When the *Bulletin*'s Book Department was launched in December 1922, made possible by lottery proceeds, the emphasis on the classic works of Marx and Engels was pronounced. Titles included the three volumes of *Capital*, *The Critique of Political Economy*, *The Civil War in France*, *The Poverty of Philosophy*, *The Eighteenth Brumaire of Louis Bonaparte*, *Revolution and Counter-Revolution*, *Wage-Labor and Capital*, and *The Communist Manifesto*.[130] The OBU educational classes announced in the fall of 1923 included working-class history, evolution from the workers' point of view, and Marxian economics.[131] By 1923, therefore, Russell and the OBU leadership had staked out territory as a Marxist-based class union which maintained the SPC's emphasis on working-class education and self-organization, while rejecting any significant role for leadership in general, and labour bureaucrats in particular. After a brief flirtation, Russell turned definitively away from both E.T. Kingsley and Lenin. That he rejected the Communist Party and left the Socialist Party in the same month indicates his forthright embracing, in practice, of the third way. Unlike Pritchard, Winch, and Mould, he would try in future to combine the role of the party and the role of the union.

One of the major weaknesses of the post-1919 OBU was self-inflicted – the failure to bring women into full participation in the leadership of the organization. As Todd McCallum points out, Pritchard and other male OBUers insisted that voting rights be restricted to wage earners, effectively excluding women who worked in the home. Shortly after the Winnipeg General Strike the Central Labour Council of the OBU voted twenty-three to eighteen to deny full affiliation of the Women's Labour League.[132] The marginalization of women in the OBU continued into the 1920s, the all-male leadership willing to accept women in the rank and file but not willing to elect them to positions on the executive.[133] While one response to sexism and discrimination in the OBU is to decry its masculinist, male-centred politics, another is to point out that the closeness of the vote on the admission of the Women's Labour League indicates much stronger support among male members of the organization in 1919 than either before or after. It quite dramatically demonstrates that the sexism of working-class men was conditioned by the society, culture, and family structure in which they had grown up, was susceptible to change, and cannot simply be attributed to identity – male or Marxist. The real tragedy of the situation is that influential OBUers like Russell and Pritchard, had they swung their full support behind women in the OBU, in all probability could have swayed the membership in favour of voting rights for female members. They were right to fear all manner of threats to the continued existence of the One Big Union, including employers on the right and Communists on the left, but sadly mistaken to see women in the OBU as one of those threats. Without women in influential positions on the Central Labour Council to direct the leadership's attention to women workers in home and factory, the OBU continued to look to its traditional support base in mine, mill, and factory for salvation.

The notable exception to the OBU disregard for women workers was the effort to organize hotel and restaurant workers in Winnipeg in 1925, a year in which most of the OBU's efforts and money was being poured into the campaign to organize miners in Nova Scotia. While the effort to protect young women working in the service industry was no doubt in part inspired by the organization's failures in more traditional workforces, the effort was genuine and not without success. There was a determined, albeit paternalistic effort to protect female employees in restaurants from sexual harassment; many young women became actively involved in union work for the first time, and the Hotel and Restaurant Workers' Unit of the OBU engaged in effective strikes and boycotts, cleaned up conditions, shortened hours, and procured one day's rest in seven for workers in almost forty establishments.[134] Mary Jordan notes that Russell "was happy and enthusiastic about what he was doing for the immigrant girls."[135] For a moment the OBU even recaptured the inclusiveness of 1919 – albeit a masculinist and chivalric inclusiveness – when the *Bulletin* counselled: "Remember this, fellow worker, it may not be your sister today that is subject to these conditions. You may not have a sister for that matter, but whether you have or not, these girls are members of the working class and that's what counts."[136]

The OBU's chauvinism notwithstanding, the harsh reality is that in the 1920s the One Big Union was not going to organize the Canadian working class on the basis of successes in the service sector. The One Big Union could have been larger, stronger, and more vibrant if women had been treated fairly and equally, but that factor alone could not have realized the vision of Bob Russell and other OBU founders. By 1923 the One Big Union desperately needed an organizing success in mine, mill, or factory. Another speaking tour of western Canada convinced even the usually indefatigable Russell that the OBU's prospects were slim at best.[137] Even the Workers' Party had written off the OBU organizers, with Tim Buck telling his western supporters to "ignore them and concentrate on those organizations and individuals who are a real menace."[138] Ironically, given its western roots, the OBU in the 1920s threatened to be most successful, and thus a "menace" to the Communist Party, in Nova Scotia.[139] In Canada's easternmost province the economic downturn resulted in the end of the wartime inflationary spiral. Prices dropped significantly in 1920–21, then levelled off until the end of the decade. If Nova Scotia miners had been able to maintain their wage levels, their real wages would have risen substantially. The British Empire Steel and Coal Company (BESCO), the largest employer in Cape Breton and Nova Scotia, had other ideas. The company wanted to cut wages by one-third, a decision supported by the United Mine Workers of America and their leader, John L. Lewis.

During 1921 an increasingly bellicose BESCO management clashed with a militant rank and file. BESCO officials blamed falling markets, but the workers were quick to point out that cutting wages did not produce markets. They argued that production costs could be lowered "through elimination of needless officials and exorbitant executive salaries," and greater efficiency in mining operations.[140] The company remained resolute, and in January 1922 instituted the one-third wage cut. This produced stark deprivation for miners and their families, with those on short time literally facing starvation. By June 1922 the miners were obviously in a militant mood: they re-elected Workers' Party member J.B. McLachlan and elected "Red" Dan Livingstone to the executive of District #26. They also called for a 100 per cent strike, which began on 15 August 1922.[141]

When the men returned to work on 5 September it was with mixed feelings. They had managed to reduce the average wage cut from 33.6 per cent to 18.9 per cent, but were not happy with the lack of support coming from the international leadership of the United Mine Workers of America.[142] Most of the UMWA's funds were being expended in the American fields; in addition, union president John L. Lewis gave little support to Communist leaders in District #26. It was the rank and file workers, sustained by tremendous support from the local communities, who had restricted output and closed mines during the strike. The *Halifax Citizen* noted that it was "a solid strike, with leaders ordered to take orders from the rank and file or get off the job."[143]

In the summer of 1923 militance spread, as the steelworkers of Sydney were added to the ranks of Maritime workers facing a wage cut. They responded by seizing part of the steel plant. On 1 July 1923 a squad of provincial police on horseback charged into a crowd in Whitney Pier, the working-class neighbourhood near the plant where many of the workers lived. The attack led to a mass meeting that called for a general strike, and the resulting work stoppage on 3 July was supported by a sympathetic strike by the miners in the UMWA. This action was not sanctioned by Lewis and the UMWA leadership, which replied by revoking District #26's charter and replacing McLachlan and Livingstone.[144]

As Bercuson points out, the situation was tailor-made for the One Big Union. There was a great deal of disillusionment with the UMWA's international leadership, and a militant rank and file in the mining industry was willing to engage in sympathetic strikes with the steelworkers, creating fertile ground for the OBU's appeal for class unionism.[145] Russell was quick to see the possibilities. At a mass meeting in Victoria Park in Winnipeg to protest the sending of government troops to Nova Scotia, he took on both the AFL and the Communist Party. He argued that the UMWA leadership was selling out the miners of Nova Scotia, and the Communists were helping by telling the workers to stay in the AFL. According to Russell, the Communist position was breaking the solidarity of the strikers and was anything but a revolutionary strategy.[146] It remained to be seen if he had a revolutionary strategy of his own, but in the fall of 1923 the OBU demonstrated that it was very serious about challenging the Communists and the UMWA leadership by flooding the mines and steel mills of Nova Scotia with OBU literature.[147]

By 1924 the OBU was in a position to take advantage of the situation. On 15 January District #26 miners went on strike against another BESCO wage cut. When an agreement supposedly based on pre-1922 wage rates proved to give the workers very little, there was a virtual revolt in some locals. On 24 March UMWA headquarters replaced Silby Barrett with William Houston as head of District #26. In mid-May the locals rebelled and called a meeting of unauthorized representatives in New Glasgow. They struck a committee to explore the options and made plans to call new elections.[148] By that summer, therefore, the OBU felt the time was right to send in an organizer. Ben Legere, a veteran of the Lawrence, Massachusetts, strike of 1922, began a tour of Cape Breton amidst great hopes of success.[149] The *Workers' Weekly*, published in Stellarton, Pictou County, was enthusiastic about the One Big Union from the beginning, noting that "the miners of Pictou County are sick and tired of the dictatorship brand of industrial leadership and the mess that has resulted therefrom."[150]

The response of the pro-Communist *Maritime Labor Herald* was perhaps even more startling. In June 1924 the *Herald* argued that a union was "only a tool" for getting results from its members; whether the workers were organized by the UMWA or the OBU mattered little. The paper had "not the least doubt but the O.B.U. can get hundreds of dissatisfied miners" to join the organization, but in reality a split would serve the purposes of BESCO and Lewis. In the long run the miners would be better off in the UMWA.[151] The *Herald's* recognition of the OBU's appeal and right to organize Nova Scotia miners notwithstanding, hostility to the OBU was not long in coming. Legere's attempts to organize unorganized steelworkers in Sydney were unsuccessful, which led to an organizing campaign among the miners of Pictou County.[152] Once again the age-old failure to organize the unorganized forced the OBU to concentrate on workers who were already in unions. By focusing on the miners of Pictou County, Legere and the OBU were getting themselves into trouble. As the *Herald* pointed out, the old Provincial Workmen's Association, founded in 1879, had been torn apart by the efforts of the United Mine Workers to take over its jurisdiction. As a result, the mineworkers were divided in the years 1908–18, and the *Herald* concluded that "we have no stomach for a like experience." The OBU could organize the steelworkers but should leave the miners alone.[153]

The OBU was not dissuaded, however, and there can be no disputing its impact. On 10 September John L. Lewis wrote to William Houston and called for a convention to restore the autonomy of District #26. New elections were to be held, but with those officials expelled in July 1923 not allowed to run for office. Local unionists were caught by surprise; *Workers' Weekly* called the convention call "a bolt from the blue."[154] There was not a doubt in Russell's mind what was going on. In a speech to a Glace Bay audience of three hundred on 20 September, he confidently concluded that "we know perfectly well the organization of the O.B.U. coming into Cape Breton has forced Lewis to restore the District autonomy."[155] Whether or not the OBU "forced" Lewis to call the convention is a mute point, but there is no doubt the organization had local labour leaders running scared. On 18 September Ben

Legere was arrested by immigration officials, charged with violating the Immigration Act, and held for deportation pending a review hearing. It is quite possible that someone in the UMWA or the Communist Party tipped off the authorities about his arrest during the Lawrence textile strike of 1922, but no substantiating evidence has yet been found. Legere beat the charge when the government could find no reason to deport him, and he resumed his organizing activities with Russell, who had come east to help.[156]

Russell arrived in Nova Scotia in September 1924 and spent two and a half months organizing for the One Big Union. He immediately began hammering away at his favourite theme, that "man is the product of environment." John L. Lewis could not be condemned as an individual, he said, because he was put in his position by a rank and file that did not realize that electing "good men" to office was not the answer. All union officials, paid $8,000 to $10,000 a year, getting used to sleeping in the Chateau Frontenac or Royal Alexandra, would be corrupted. Like Pritchard, Russell based his analysis on Eugene Debs's famous counsel, stating that "if any man can lead you from your misery to emancipation, he has also got the power to lead you back to slavery once more."[157] In a speech delivered in Sydney on 26 September Russell reiterated this message in his by-now classic speech on the One Big Union. Criticizing the tactics of the Workers' Party, he presented the OBU as an alternative, a genuine rank and file union. Workers, he said, should trust no leaders – an extremely appealing message to Nova Scotia miners and steelworkers who were themselves disillusioned with the existing leadership. The only solution, according to Russell, was for the miners to take organization work into their own hands.[158]

The OBU had little success on Cape Breton Island, but in Pictou County the response was encouraging. The Stellarton local withdrew from the United Mine Workers by a vote of 528 to 261. In Thorburn the vote was decisive, going 282 to 48 in favour of the OBU.[159] When the Westville local followed suit, the three locals formed the Pictou County Central Labour Council.[160] Yet the organizational successes of the OBU did not translate into a changed policy on BESCO's part. The assault on the workers continued apace, and near the end of November the company proposed a 20 per cent wage cut to take effect in the new year. It eventually wavered in the face of militant opposition, and reduced the proposed cut to 10 per cent. The workers were unwilling to accept the pyrrhic victory, however, and responded by staging a general walkout on 6 March 1925.[161]

Russell himself was back in Winnipeg by December 1924. There he took up the task of explaining and interpreting the events in Nova Scotia for the workers of western Canada. He informed readers of the

Bulletin about telling the striking workers that the problem was one of leadership. Echoing a position he had taken in 1919, he argued that Maritime labour officials had become victims of their own environment – that is, they liked their new privileges and associating with the company bosses. The problem with the miners, he said, was that they looked to their leaders rather than organizing themselves. The workers, according to Russell, "had never heard a philosophy like this taught before."[162] He was convinced that he had found the message that would save the OBU and continued to hammer away at it into the new year. As in the past, he pointed out that the Communist Party's "whole policy is bound up in the Great-Man theory." There was nothing for BESCO to fear from the Communists, Russell said, as long they continued to keep the workers dependent on party leaders. The only thing BESCO and other Canadian corporations feared was a rank and file movement, one without leaders who could be corrupted.[163]

There was a great deal of truth to Russell's observations, but they belied an inability to analyse his own role as an organizer in Nova Scotia. Miners in Nova Scotia could not stay around for a couple of months and then go back to another job in Winnipeg. They had to gain their bread and butter where they stood. Russell's ideas sounded good in theory, and many Nova Scotia miners were indeed angry enough about their leaders to be attracted to the OBU. The problem was what the OBU was offering in the long term. Russell never seems to have realized that just by being in Nova Scotia, and being the influential, almost legendary figure he was, he was creating the kind of dependence on himself that he continually attacked when it involved Communist Party or international union leaders. He too was a product of his environment, not having punched a time clock since February 1918. Russell was a classic Marxist of the third way – a Marxian socialist always quick to spot the hypocrisy in the actions of other leaders, but often unwilling, or unable, to see the hypocrisy in his own. His commitment to rank and file organization and self-education was passionate and genuine, but he was often blind to the very real concerns that rank and file workers – whether miners in Nova Scotia or OBU women in Winnipeg – had with his personal politics and the ability of the OBU to protect their economic, political, ethnic, and gender interests.

The weakness of the OBU in Nova Scotia did not end there, as the organization had a very serious problem on its hands getting accreditation for OBU locals. It was trying to break into a long-standing relationship between labour leaders such as John L. Lewis, his Canadian lieutenants, and the federal and provincial governments. Neither the United Mine Workers nor the company had any intention of giving it a chance to establish itself. If Russell had been honest with himself and the miners and steelworkers of Nova Scotia, he would have dealt with the problem head on. Instead, there is little evidence to suggest that he, or other leading OBU members, worked out a strategy for establishing the new organization legally. In the euphoria of 1919 it was assumed that government, companies, and rival unions would have to deal with the OBU based on its sheer size, and that it could operate without reference to the courts and the labour relations system. Once it was reduced to a struggle for survival, however, it had to try to establish itself in the very system of labour relations it initially set out to destroy. Unfortunately for the miners of Pictou County, they ended up caught in the middle of the OBU's attempt to discredit the UMWA and its leadership, an attempt with little real chance of success.[164]

To its credit, the OBU attempted to put the needs of the workers and winning the strike ahead of strengthening itself, but this was impossible during the long, bitter, and violent BESCO strike of 1925. Bercuson claims that the OBU attacked the Communist Party and took the UMWA to task for its poor financial support of the strikers, but that it would have been "foolish and perhaps fatal" to attack the leadership of District #26.[165] Given that a number of its leading local executive members were Communists, it would have been rather difficult for Russell to attack the Communist Party without attacking the leadership of District #26, which he in fact did, especially in Pictou County.[166] His supposed foolishness notwithstanding, criticizing the leadership of both the UMWA and the Communist Party was indispensable to the OBU's overall strategy. It is true, however, that on Cape Breton Island he tended to back off, exhorting the workers to win the strike first and then to switch to the OBU.[167]

He was forced to attack the local leadership as a result of his involvement in the Dominion and Nova Scotia Relief Committee, based in Winnipeg. The relief effort, spearheaded by the One Big Union and really made possible by the efforts of OBU women, represents one of the great instances of working-class solidarity in the history of twentieth-century Canada. From all over Manitoba and the West, money, food, and clothing poured in. The lumber workers and trappers of The Pas, Manitoba, raised $175.59; the OBU unit in Nanaimo raised an additional $367.62.[168] At one point eighty-one bundles of clothing valued at $15,000 were sent to Nova Scotia as part of the enormous outpouring of support for the striking workers.[169] According to the OBU leadership, a total of forty tons of clothing was shipped from Winnipeg during the strike.[170] Alex McKay, secretary of District #26, and secretary of the Glace Bay CPC, made his contribution to the effort by accusing the Relief Committee of only helping miners and their families in OBU areas of Pictou County. The charge was a blatant lie, quite rightly provoking the outrage of Russell and the OBU, and may have resulted in McKay's expulsion from the Communist Party.[171]

The efforts of the western working class helped prevent striking miners and their families in Nova Scotia from starving or freezing to death, but it could not produce a victory. On 10 August 1925 the miners went back to work. They and their leaders were exhausted, a period of inactivity hit the Nova Scotia mines, and the OBU's grip weakened in Pictou County. On 31 August 1926 the Acadia Coal Company, a BESCO subsidiary, banned two hundred miners from work until they signed the UMWA check-off. Four OBU supporters who refused were fired, and the OBU's strength in Pictou County "melted away."[172] As had been the case in western Canada, the organization was squeezed out by the UMWA check-off and BESCO support for the American-based international union. Within a year the OBU stopped holding public meetings.[173]

It would be a mistake to evaluate the OBU's contribution to the Nova Scotia working class in this period simply on the basis of organizational success. It donated an amazing amount of financial assistance to striking miners and their families, a material expression of labour solidarity. At the Fifth OBU Convention in May 1927, it was announced that since the previous convention held in 1923, the OBU had raised $12,088.16 for the Nova Scotia Miners' Strike, $1,000 for the Minto Miners' Strike, $1,226.61 for jailed Nova Scotia miners, $410 for miners discriminated against in Nova Scotia, and $3,000 for the Inverness strike.[174] In the same period it also raised $13,934.07 for the British Miners' Strike.[175] Perhaps the OBU was waging a "hopeless fight for survival," as Bercuson has put it, but it certainly made a major contribution toward alleviating the suffering of the miners of Nova Scotia and their wives and children.[176]

Like many other Marxian socialists of his generation, Russell often seemed more concerned with the working-class wives and children across the country than he was with his own wife and family, who suffered because of his constant organizing work. In 1924 he had been sent to Edmonton and Calgary to replace organizer Tom Cassidy, who died of tuberculosis on 13 February 1924.[177] According to Mary Jordan, Russell saw his newborn daughter Pearl "for a few hours" on his return from Alberta, and then went right back. Meg Russell was "bitterly lonely and hurt" by her husband's departure, and her feelings must have turned to anger and anguish when the little girl died shortly thereafter. It can have been of little consolation to her and the other children that they had made their terrible sacrifices for the good of the movement. Nor was there to be any sympathy for Russell, who when he heard the news left Edmonton for Winnipeg without telling the

OBU's General Executive Board. His reward was to be "severely criticized" for his actions at the OBU's annual convention.[178] Russell, who did not get up on the floor to defend himself, was much like Pritchard, a socialist who believed that one's personal sufferings were to remain in the private realm, with no understanding or compassion sought or expected. Meg Russell did not even have the comfort of knowing that her private pain was compensated for by public recognition of her husband's dedication.

Bob Russell's personal tragedy had its counterpart in his political life, as within weeks of the collapse of the BESCO strike in August 1925 the last issue of the *Western Clarion* marked the effective demise of the Socialist Party of Canada. Defections to the Communist Party, changes in the political economy of Canada, the formation of the One Big Union, and the rise of farmer-labour politics in the 1920s, following the state repression of 1919, resulted in the increasing marginalization of a party with only pockets of strength outside British Columbia. Russell remained publicly silent about the death of his infant daughter, and there was to be no public lament from him in the *Bulletin* concerning the passing of the Socialist Party. He remained a trade unionist first and a political socialist second. However, he had been, and continued to be, a fervent believer in the educational role of the Socialist Party, and its demise must have signalled to him the further slipping away of the euphoria and promise of 1919. Taking his cue from Joe Hill, he chose in both his private life and his public activism to organize rather than mourn. With the OBU he would rise or fall.

By supporting the OBU in 1919, then rejecting both the Socialist Party and Communist Party in 1922, Russell made a fundamental break. More so than that of Pritchard, his Marxism of the third way was based in the conviction that the working class needed an organization whose political action derived from the point of production. He slowly came to accept and more fully understand the dialectical relationship between the economic and political aspects of class struggle, but his predilection was always to see the economic as the "base." Even after the failure of the BESCO strike he continued to believe that the One Big Union was the only possible vehicle for the realization of a working-class majority committed to the creation of a socialist society. He also continued to emphasize the importance of the organization and education of the rank and file and kept up his attack on what he perceived as the treachery of the international trade union leaders. When he critiqued Lenin's book *Soviets at Work* in the *Bulletin* in August 1925, a Brandon Communist accused him of being an anarcho-syndicalist.[179] Communist Party members used the word pejoratively, continuing their failure to appreciate Russell's positive affirmation of an alternative vision of Marxism, and also thereby bearing witness to the fact that Marxism of the third way continued to appeal to the Canadian working class.

By the spring of 1926, however, it was apparent to even the most die-hard OBU member that sacrifices would have to be made in order to create a broader-based movement with a national focus. In May the General Executive Board decided to make the initial move to create a Canadian-based trade union organization.[180] A number of smaller unions were interested, but the key union was A.R. Mosher's Canadian Brotherhood of Railway Employees. Russell's grudging support for the move may have been prompted by the presence of the railway workers, a group he remained keenly interested in. The unity conference was held in Montreal on 16 March 1927, and Russell was one of four OBU delegates who participated in the creation of the All-Canadian Congress of Labour. The OBU's major sacrifice was accepting the affiliation of both industrial and craft unions. The sacrifice was more apparent than real, however, because many OBU locals were craft unions, not industrial unions, and always had been. In spite of the OBU's apparent abdication of its most fundamental tenet, therefore, affiliation was endorsed at the union's Fifth General Convention.

It is beyond question that the One Big Union was in a seriously weakened condition by 1927, a situation which prompted the support for affiliating with the ACCL. According to Bercuson, the OBU paid dues on only sixteen hundred members in 1927.[181] According to Russell's report, the OBU "represented" seventeen thousand workers, and was financially healthy – he even claimed that the OBU's membership was increasing.[182] Assessing the organization's actual strength raises the question of the best basis on which to make the assessment. As both the Winnipeg General Strike and the OBU organizing work in Nova Scotia had demonstrated, the OBU was almost more important as an idea than it was as an organization.[183] The Nova Scotia experience demonstrated that there were many thousands of workers in Canada who continued to support the OBU philosophy but were prevented from becoming dues-paying members by the opposition of the government, courts, companies, and AFL unions. On this basis Russell's figure of seventeen thousand may not be entirely out of line. How many of those seventeen thousand could be mobilized to organize for, or even support, the union was another question.

Russell's year-end review indicated that the OBU was still out there fighting and making an impact in one of the worst periods for labour in recent memory. The OBU was active in the Avon Coal strike in Minto, New Brunswick. There was now a Rank and File Unit in San Francisco. Organizing work had been done with the Montreal packing house workers and the Point St Charles CNR railway workers, but nothing permanent appears to have been established. The Montreal Gas Company Workers joined, and its organizers were attempting to bring the furniture workers of Stratford, Ontario, into the fold. Four organizers were active in the metal mines of northern Ontario and western Quebec at various times during the year, and Tommy Roberts organized two hundred building trades workers in Regina.[184] Even in the late 1920s Russell was reaching out, publishing pamphlets in French and planning a French-language *OBU Bulletin*.[185]

As had been the case since the early 1920s, however, the OBU was rarely able to establish permanent unions with a solid core of rank and file activists. It continued to respond to specific local requests for an organizer or specific events that galvanized the workers. Brief flourishes of support in scattered areas of the country, however, could not be translated into sustained growth. Nonetheless, the One Big Union remained committed to the rank and file workers of Canada and to the international struggle to defend labour's allies and challenge the capitalist system. On 10 August 1927 Russell wrote to the governor of Massachusetts on behalf of the OBU, charging that the state of Massachusetts would be "legal murderers" if Sacco and Vanzetti were killed.[186] The OBU continued its commitment to the creation of a working-class culture at home, the Central Labour Council declaring that "labor is capable of providing its own education, its own amusements, its own entertainments, its own sport and physical training and satisfy[ing] all of its desires in social life."[187] And in November 1927 the OBU sent greetings to the Soviet Union on the tenth anniversary of the Russian Revolution, Russell observing that the Canadian working class needed to understand what was going on in the Soviet Union, "in order that they can avoid many of the hardships our fellow workers in Russia have gone through."[188] As with all Marxists of the third way, he gave critical support to the Soviet Union but held firm to the belief that the creation of a socialist society would be done by rank and file workers in their own way in each national setting.

By 1928–29 the OBU was down, but the dream was not dead. In October 1928 the editorship of the *Bulletin* passed to Charles Lestor, a leading member of the SPC prior to the First World War. Still a household name in Canadian socialist circles, Lestor brought not only his reputation but also a vast knowledge of the Canadian and international labour movements, Marxism, and the political events of the day to the editor's desk. The OBU was not "broke," as Bercuson has argued, and continued to publish the *Bulletin* on a weekly basis for five more years.[189] The lottery continued to bring in substantial sums until October 1933. It is true that the organization could no longer disperse money with the almost reckless abandon which characterized the

1922–26 period, but there was enough money, enough commitment, and enough need in the ranks of Canadian labour for it to rally if the opportunity arose.

Canadian historians have ignored the role of the OBU in the early 1930s, when it was growing stronger, not weaker, for a few years. Most labour historians have concentrated, with the exception of the Workers' Unity League, on the latter half of the 1930s, as the rise of the CIO and militant industrial unionism galvanized the Canadian left. The early '30s were, in fact, a period of great importance, for it was in the years 1930–35 that major realignments took place on the left, most notably the formation of the Co-operative Commonwealth Federation. The Great Depression also provided the One Big Union with one last chance to mobilize the Canadian working class, and gave Russell's commitment to finding a Marxist third way a final short breathing space. The OBU stood to benefit from the early years of the Depression, because its message of working class solidarity and insistence that rank and file workers had been sold out by capitalist and trade union leaders alike promised to have a greater and greater appeal as the Depression worsened.

In the event a very different pattern emerged. With the onset of the Depression came new organizations on the left and the rebirth of some old ones, creating an impetus of fragmentation amid the trend to solidarity. The early 1930s saw the re-formation of the Socialist Party, the creation of the CCF, and the early beginnings of the Trotskyist movement. In June 1931 the Socialist Party of Canada was reorganized in Winnipeg, with George Armstrong, Helen Armstrong, Charles Lestor, and Russell's old comrade Alex Shepherd taking leading roles.[190] Shepherd notes that when the SPC was reorganized, the OBU "allowed us meeting rooms practically rent free." Since 1919, however, Shepherd and Russell had "slowly parted ideologically," Russell feeling that the SPCers were not sufficiently committed to the cause of the OBU.[191] Indeed, some leading pre-war members of the SPC were actively defending the AFL craft unions the year after the OBU's formation.[192] While Russell remained good friends with SPC members, he now believed that the goal of worker self-emancipation was to be realized by the One Big Union, not the SPC. Theory and practice needed to be more firmly united than they were in the SPC, and as always, he looked to the OBU and economic changes in his own industry to show him the way forward.

Russell decided that fighting the capitalist Depression, uniting the working class, and strengthening the One Big Union necessitated coming to grips with the plight of the unemployed and forging links between them and workers, railway shopmen in particular, struggling desperately to fight against wage cuts, poor working conditions, and massive lay-offs. On 28 February 1931 an unemployed conference in Winnipeg appointed him to a committee to lobby other labour organizations to join the conference.[193] He and the other committee members did their job well: at the second conference, held on 7 March 1931, fifty-eight delegates representing thirty-five unions supported a moratorium on the expulsion of unemployed and semi-employed workers from their homes for debt.[194] The 7 May 1931 issue of the *OBU Bulletin* reported that at least eighty-seven workers' homes had already been saved from foreclosure.

While his support of the unemployed continued, Russell became increasingly involved with the plight of the Winnipeg shopmen. On 21 September he spoke at an OBU meeting of five hundred CPR workers who were facing an indefinite lay-off following the closing of the CPR shops.[195] In October, with the Street Railwaymen facing a 10 per cent wage cut, he urged them to join the OBU. His answer to capital's onslaught was to eliminate "the craft viewpoint" completely. The deplorable condition of the railway workers had been brought about, he said, by "their craft organizations and the machine tactics of their executives."[196] It was certainly an opportune time for him to appeal to rank and file organization, but as in the early 1920s, he did not explain how mobilization against the craft union leaders strengthened opposition to capitalism or kept workers from being laid off.

In spite of the enormous possibilities for militant action, Russell's activities in the early 1930s consisted of the very tactics he and other militant industrial unionists had denounced in 1919. In February 1932 the unemployed conference met with Manitoba premier John Bracken, with Russell acting as chairperson of the meeting.[197] The non-confrontational tactics continued in the following months, with a mass meeting of railway shopmen on 26 February, and another on 20 March 1932.[198] In spite of the weaknesses in Russell's strategy, however, by the spring of 1932 it appeared that the One Big Union was on the verge of mobilizing a massive protest against lay-offs on the railways. In April a mass meeting of eight hundred CNR shopmen was held in Winnipeg. The meeting agreed to endorse "whatever action" was necessary, including a strike, to force the Canadian Railway Association to meet its committees. There was also a call for the six-hour day to save the jobs of 1,157 workers.[199]

On 15 April 1932 another mass meeting of CNR shopmen was held. In one of his most fervent speeches in years Russell called for cooperation between employed and unemployed workers: "Unless the employed workers acted together with the unemployed workers," he said, "it would not be long until the one section was used against the other to the detriment of our class as a whole." He attacked the salaries and perks of CNR officials and asked the workers why they should take job cuts when Sir Henry Thornton was making so much money. Russell also called for cooperation between the returned soldiers and foreigners, reminding his audience that, with the exception of the Indians, they were all foreigners.[200] The mere fact that he had to call for cooperation between returned soldiers and "foreigners" in 1932 indicates that the old divisions that haunted the Winnipeg working class in 1919 returned to the surface in the early 1930s, as workers turned inward and desperately clung to their jobs. Russell's appreciation that people from the British Isles were "foreigners" themselves and his recognition of native people were exceptional among men of his generation, but they were not enough to overcome the structural roadblocks in his path.

He was painfully aware of the dangers, and his warning that the working class as a whole would be split along employed-unemployed lines proved prophetic. As it turned out, Division #4 refused to agree to work sharing and argued that the laid-off shopmen could affiliate with the unemployed associations in their municipality, bodies the OBU had been instrumental in organizing.[201] It was a terrible irony for Russell. In the end all his efforts to unite the employed and unemployed workers on a class basis resulted in the unemployed organizations acting as an excuse for the leadership of Division #4 to reject work sharing.

Russell must have been desperately discouraged, but he refused to give up on the self-organization of the workers as the key to the creation of a socialist society. By "trial and error," he argued, "we have learned to organize new forms of struggle to correspond with the new forms of the exploiting process which capitalism has developed." The employed and the unemployed must realize that they were "class brothers" whose interests were identical "from a class standpoint." Echoing an old, old theme, he stated that it was "not a question of leadership, but of getting the workers to understand so that they will trust themselves."[202] Somewhere deep in his heart he must have known that for most members of the Canadian working class the One Big Union was, by the 1930s, an old, not a new form of class struggle. He could have made it new by realizing that much of the mobilization of the early 1930s was the responsibility of class sisters, not class brothers, but like so many Marxists of the third way, Russell continued to think of the working class in gendered terms. But on the core idea of Marxism of the third way, that a socialist society can only be created by a confident, educated, committed, and organized working class, egalitarian and self-led, he never wavered.

In a sense he had come full circle. On 14 May 1933 he spoke to over five hundred railway workers at the Dominion Theatre. In an obvious attack on the Communist Party he stated that the emphasis on leadership had produced apathy and fear in the rank and file, a product of the "rotten philosophy that the working-class should have leaders." His animus towards leaders was also fuelled by his belief that the unemployed, with no experienced leadership, had shown more spirit than the employed, who did have leaders. In conclusion he put forward the proposition that "a working class not capable of organizing itself for the every-day struggle is not capable of bringing about a new social order."[203] He had returned to the politics of the old SPC, criticizing the working class for its ignorance and inability to take its fate into its own hands, sounding for all the world like Bill Pritchard.

Given Russell's emphasis on mass rank and file movements, it might seem reasonable to assume that he would support the newly launched Co-operative Commonwealth Federation. Even before the Calgary convention of 1932, however, he clearly indicated that he would not support a political movement that did not make industrial unionism the basis of its politics. At a June 1932 meeting of the Central Labour Council's Joint Executive Board one of the comrades suggested that industrial organizations were "helpless" and that political action was necessary. Quoting from a speech Marx gave at the Geneva Conference of the International Workingmen's Association in 1866, Russell forcefully defended Marx's proposition that political organizing had to flow from the defence of the trade unions as "indispensable" organizations in the abolition of the wages system. He carried the day, with comrade Dunn suggesting that the supporter of political action had made "various errors" in his argument.[204] Together Bob Russell and Karl Marx, still a material force in the OBU in the early 1930s, had won this battle, but they were not about to stop the drift to social democratic politics.

Even Russell was forced to bend a bit, because in July 1933 Fred Fix took an OBU resolution to the Regina Convention calling for the fledgling organization to officially support industrial unionism, and Ernest Winch helped him get it placed before the Resolutions Committee.[205] On the floor of the convention, however, Winch laid low, choosing not to speak in favour of it. In any event his support would not have made a significant difference, because the opposition of J.S. Woodsworth, Angus MacInnis, and other CCF leaders would have killed it.[206] Exactly why the OBU submitted the resolution is unclear, although its acceptance might have initiated a movement in the organization to merge with the CCF. Even after rejecting the resolution, the CCF presented a threat to the OBU because of its broad-based support and populist appeal. While identifying a clear cause and effect relationship may never be possible, it is worthy of note that the OBU's gradual rise in membership, which characterized the late 1920s and early 1930s, stopped in

1933–34. It is also suggestive that the OBU *Bulletin* ceased publication in the spring of 1934, just about the time CCF publications such as *The Commonwealth* in British Columbia and the *New Commonwealth* in Ontario began to attract a wide readership.

By late 1933 and early 1934 even Russell's drive and enthusiasm could not stop the drift to the CCF, conflicts within the OBU, or the deepening rift between the OBU and the Socialist Party. In May 1932 friction had erupted in the OBU concerning the endorsement of George Armstrong as the SPC's candidate in the upcoming election. Russell, while saying that he would support his old friend personally, could not support "a group which was doing everything possible to destroy the effectiveness of the O.B.U." – as much a comment on Armstrong's affiliation with the AFL as a critique of the Socialist Party. Charles Lestor also spoke against supporting the SPC campaign, stating that "if we supported this so-called bunch of Socialists we would not be true to ourselves."[207] By January 1933 the breach reached the point where the *Bulletin* stopped publishing SPC meeting and activity notices.[208]

The worst blow, however, came late in 1933. Russell's son-in-law, Sam Sykes, and Jack Clancy, the two of them among the OBU's oldest and best organizers, were accused by an Investigating Committee of secretly discussing OBU financial matters at the St Charles Hotel with non-OBU members. As a result, Sykes was expelled from the Central Labour Council, his unit, and the OBU itself.[209] The actual dispute in question was a symptom, not a cause, of the OBU decline. The organization was again facing financial difficulties, and it was simply too ingrown, too prone to personality disputes. In addition, the minutes of the Central Labour Council indicate that the newly organized CCF, whose dynamism contrasted with the stultification of the OBU, continued to act as a magnet for experienced political and trade union activists.[210]

By February 1934 Russell had truly become the One Big Union. He was now General Secretary, secretary of the Labour Council, and editor of the *Bulletin*, and he felt that it was "physically impossible" to carry on. It seemed to him that "the Council was at all times willing to exploit the only real workers in the movement, and so far as he was concerned, while he at all times was willing to do more than his share, he refused any longer to be exploited sixteen and eighteen hours per day."[211] He knew that his dream, if not the greater dream, was dead. Commenting on this period Mary Jordan, Russell's friend and secretary for many years, made an observation which could stand as his epitaph: "If the working-class did not want the One Big Union then the working-class of Canada did not want him."[212] Without the One Big Union, which for Russell was the only true expression of the desire of the

Bob Russell in later life, the years of labour radicalism behind him. Provincial Archives of Manitoba/Robert Boyd Russell Collection, N10134

working class for education, self-organization, and the creation of socialism, he was rudderless. A year before the war broke out his fate was captured by a harsh yet accurate Mounted Police report that stated that he had "degenerated into an agitator of secondary importance."[213]

By the outbreak of the Second World War the time was past for the One Big Union to fulfil its historic mission. A new champion of industrial unionism was abroad in the land, and workers rallied to the magical letters CIO, not OBU. For a time Russell left not only his province but his class, taking a job as a superintendent in a Toronto war munitions plant. He could not stay at it very long, however, and less than a year later he was working for the Unemployment Insurance Commission in Toronto. In the spring of 1944 he returned to Winnipeg, where he took up his old post in the One Big Union. Just months earlier, in February 1944, the Liberal Cabinet had approved P.C. 1003, for the first time providing legislative backing for the principle of orderly collective bargaining and rules, procedures, and supervising agencies to ensure that workers could choose a bargaining agent and enter into negotiations. While P.C. 1003 led to scores of collective agreements with companies that had resisted unions for generations, it also embodied anti-labour provisions and was, as Bryan Palmer points out, intended "to regulate the class struggle."[214] It was also another sign that the day of the One Big Union had passed, and with it a Marxist and class-based philosophy of opposing the capitalist state.

In the fall of 1944 Russell participated in a Labour Weekend at the Marlborough Hotel in Winnipeg, organized by the Prairie School for Social Advance. He chaired a session entitled "The Economy of Abundance and Its Challenge to Labor," in which he demonstrated that in theory he still held fast to the old socialist positions in spite of his activities in the work force and role as conciliator in capital-labour disputes. In spite of the weakened state of the OBU, Russell clearly did not accept the bureaucratization of labour relations which was going on during the war, and stated that labour could not confine itself to organizations already in existence because of their limitations. In a second session entitled "Beyond the Labor Code," he warned that the labour code "*has within itself, state control of labor organizations.*" Continuing on, he stated: "I am afraid that what stands before us beyond the Labor Code is a servile state ... In our efforts to break down fascism we, ourselves, have had to build up a dangerous state apparatus. It has control of the labor organizations." In the year of P.C. 1003 he saw to the heart of increasing state control of labour organizations, and offered in its place a central tenet of Marxian socialism. It was necessary, he said, for unions to continue to challenge the ownership of property: if they did not, the result would be the same "divided aims, petty jealousies, and short vision" that characterized the union movement after the First World War.[215]

Yet even socialists have to eat, and Russell himself became a part of the new capital-labour relationship in the post-war world when he was appointed to the Manitoba Labour Relations Board in 1947. While it would be easy to say that he had sold out, it would also be misleading, given his past actions as well as another characteristic of Marxists of the third way. Russell had always maintained a great respect for individual employers, and he judged capitalists as individuals, not as functions of their class position. He essentially acted as a mediator during the Winnipeg General Strike and saw no reason why a sense of justice and fair play should not rule while capitalism continued to be the context. Indeed, he believed that if enough workers could be educated to socialism, and the workers operated from a position of overwhelming strength, it might even be possible to convince the capitalists to surrender without a violent struggle.

In spite of the One Big Union's slow and painful decline in the late 1940s and early '50s, Russell continued to defend what was best in Marxism of the third way. In 1947 he became one of two vice-presidents of the Winnipeg Labour Committee Against Racial Intolerance, which was organized to carry on an educational campaign against racism.[216] He also refused to be cowed by capitalist reaction and the cold war. In the summer of 1951 Local 430 of the International Union of Fur and Leather Workers (IUFLW) was refused certification, ostensibly because membership rules did not allow laundry workers to join. The refusal, of course, had much more to do with the fact that the IUFLW was a "known" Communist union. When Russell supported certification, an act not lacking in courage at the height of the cold war, the Mounties reactivated his file.[217]

Opposing state controlled labour-capital relations, fighting racism, and standing up against McCarthyism were all noble endeavours, but they were not enough to bring workers back to the One Big Union. The official end of Russell's dream came in 1956, when the unions of the American Federation of Labor and the Congress of Industrial Organizations united to form the Canadian Labour Congress. It was all over quickly and quietly, with Russell not betraying the emotions he must have felt inside. Old wounds had healed and old battles were only vaguely remembered. As Alex Shepherd pointed out, however, Russell was still a respected figure, and on 6 June 1956 he became secretary of the now united Winnipeg and District Labour Council.[218]

Unlike Pritchard, Russell lived long enough in one place and made enough contributions to the city of Winnipeg to be accorded recognition during his lifetime. His labour colleagues honoured him at a testimonial dinner in 1961, but from that point until his death in September 1964 the honours came from the legal profession and the provincial government. When he died, a short editorial in the *Winnipeg Free Press* recalled that he had been involved in the Winnipeg General Strike and was a prominent Winnipeg labour man, but there was little sense of the historic importance of Bob Russell or the generation he represented. He was now remembered for advancing labour law and for his work on labour-management relations. The Marxism of his youth, his decades-long fight for the One Big Union, and his critique of capitalism belonged to a political culture that no longer threatened the class he had opposed so forcefully in those heady days of 1919.[219]

Following the Winnipeg General Strike and his release from prison Russell did a courageous thing – he decided to remain faithful to

Marxism of the third way in a decade in which business, government, craft union leaders, and the Communist Party of Canada all dedicated themselves to the destruction of the One Big Union. The decline of the OBU in the 1920s, his personal and political problems, and the sacrifices of principle notwithstanding, it is a tribute to both Russell and the dedication of Canadian workers to the idea of worker self-emancipation that the organization made it through the decade and was still alive and kicking in the early 1930s. It is significant, I think, that Russell's dedication to the OBU survived the 1920s, but not the 1930s. In the decade of the Depression both the Communist Party (particularly as it manifested itself in the Workers' Unity League) and the Co-operative Commonwealth Federation claimed to be creating mass-based organizations dedicated to rank and file democracy and worker-directed socialist politics. Russell need not have felt a sense of betrayal, because many workers joined the CPC, the CCF, and the CIO in the 1930s in search of the very thing he and other Marxists of the third way had been seeking for two decades. In the end both the social democrats and the Marxist-Leninists were to prove unable to maintain their theoretical commitment to rank and file democracy in the workaday world of socialist and union politics.

If the One Big Union that Russell led is dead and gone, the idea behind it is very much alive. Workers all over the world, of all creeds and colours, are still searching for a way to be human, still convinced that freedom is to be found in this world, not the next. The legacy of the Bob Russells of this world still has something to say to these people, still has the power to inspire. If we can look beyond Russell's weaknesses and failures, if we choose to learn from rather than condemn the contradictions of his theory and practice, we find one of the most powerful attempts of our age to realize Marx's goal of the self-emancipation of the working class. To study and learn from the history of Russell's involvement with the One Big Union is to come away with one overriding realization – that worker self-emancipation, and the creation of a truly human society, can only be accomplished by a revolutionary transformation of the capitalist system. The all-out assault on the Winnipeg strikers and the One Big Union demonstrates more dramatically than any theory could that there is nothing defenders of the capitalist system fear more than a commitment to worker self-emancipation and leaders who cannot be bought. Bob Russell could not have left a better, or more fitting, legacy to workers of the world attempting to unite.

Conclusion

History has not been kind to Canada's Marxists of the third way. They are now largely forgotten, their search to put an end to the essential inhumanity of the capitalist system and their faith in the self-emancipation of the working class seeming like little more than the delusions of a bygone era, youthful enthusiasms discarded by a world grown older and wiser. Their generation is now synonymous with elitism, dogmatism, arrogance, intolerance, and the crushing, not the fostering, of Marx's original commitment to egalitarianism and worker self-emancipation. In a cruel irony, many of the dreams that nurtured Ernest Winch, Bill Pritchard, Bob Russell, and Arthur Mould were turned to dust by men and women claiming to be Marxists, claiming to be seeking, indeed creating, a more human society. But it was to be the mechanical, state and party-sanctioned scientific socialism of Joseph Stalin that triumphed in the twentieth century. Joseph Dietzgen's advice to scientific socialists to "above all be human" was lost in the death camps and pogroms of a Soviet Union more driven by a death struggle with western capitalist nations than a Marxist-inspired effort to create a truly egalitarian society.[1] In the process the legacy of the Dietzgens, Rosa Luxemburgs, Karl Liebknechts, and Bob Russells became muted and marginalized.

Michel Foucault believes much of the blame can be placed at the feet of "universal" intellectuals, Marxists such as Bill Pritchard and Bob Russell, who saw themselves as individual representatives of "a universality whose obscure, collective form is embodied in the proletariat." Since the Second Word War, according to Foucault, the eclipse of this "faded Marxism" has given way to a new relationship between theory and practice, one in which the "specific" intellectual has become grounded in particular sectors of human society – the asylum, the university, the home, family, and sexual relations – but not, apparently, the factory or sweatshop. As a result, this transformation has given the intellectual "a much more immediate and concrete awareness of struggles."[2] John McGowan comments:

> Associating theory with the claim to universal applicability, Foucault proposes instead the nontheoretical work of the specific intellectual, whose work is directly related to a particular social struggle ... The specific intellectual's work pertains only to the situation at hand and is placed at the service of those in the struggle. Crucially, Foucault is wary of the intellectual's offering any recommendations for action ... we might say that Foucault is deeply troubled by the whole concept of an intellectual and would prefer that we think of intellectual work as being done by anyone who happens to be in the particular circumstances that call for such work.[3]

The claim that specific intellectuals are more in tune with the struggles of the workers and the dispossessed than were Lenin, Luxemburg, and Canada's Marxists of the third way flies in the face of history and common sense. Foucault's theory might be credible, except for one nagging anomaly – the "death" of the universal Marxist intellectual is directly responsible for the fact that for much of the post–Second World War period there has been no struggle for the specific intellectual to be in tune with. What struggle there has been has been carried out on the basis of an acceptance of the continued existence of the capitalist system. In effect, Foucault's distinction serves as little more than a condemnation of revolutionary Marxism and a justification of social democracy.

Winch, Pritchard, Russell, and Mould can no longer speak on the street corner or in the socialist halls in order to defend themselves, and influential critics such as Foucault have had more or less free rein to tell us why the revolutionary Marxists of their generation were so mistaken in their theory and practice. Being in the "particular circumstances" that call out for their defence, in this work I have taken the liberty of believing that Foucault would not begrudge me the role of the specific intellectual in coming to their defence, in order to remind the reader of the hypocrisies, misreadings, and distortions of their critics, and, I hope, thereby creating the same space for them that they fought so long and hard to create for the workers of Canada. It is revealing that in a political culture in which the glorification of feminist, black, native, and gay and lesbian leaders and spokespersons is taken for granted, and their politics are taken to have "universal" meanings, working-class Marxist intellectuals, even the ones who were themselves from the working class, are portrayed as "misleaders," phonies, and hypocrites – indeed, as little more than con artists.

But we do ourselves a disservice if we relegate Winch, Pritchard, Russell, and Mould to the rubbish heap of history. Far from being marginal figures in Canadian history, they deserve to be numbered among those individuals Matthew Arnold calls the "great men of culture." It seems strange to enlist Matthew Arnold in defence of Canada's Marxists of the third way, given that Arnold himself was very critical of British Nonconformists whose opposition to the "establishment" he believed to be based in a narrow sectarianism. Yet Marxists of the third way, many of whom came from Nonconformist backgrounds, fit Arnold's two definitions of culture quite well: one being "the scientific passion, the sheer desire to see things as they are," and the other "the impulses towards action, help, and beneficence, the desire for removing human error, clearing human confusion, and diminishing human misery, the noble aspiration to leave the world better and happier than we found it."[4] Canada's Marxists of the third way would not have disagreed with Arnold's definitions, and even agreed that one made the world "better and happier" by teaching the "best" ideas. They would have pointed out, however, that the ideas Arnold espoused were the best ideas for the ruling class, not the working class. They spoke for the working class, and the workers they spoke for had other best ideas.

Their best idea was that the humanity and freedom they sought could not be realized within the confines of the capitalist system. In searching for answers, often over the course of many years, Marx provided most of the pieces for the puzzle of the realization of human freedom, but Hegel, Christ, Spencer, Engels, Morris, Labriola, Tolstoy, Darwin, and many others contributed their own pieces, some large, some small, to solving it. With varying degrees of success Marxists of the third way attempted to meld the ideas of these writers with a practice that combined a British-based respect for constitutional action, justice, and fair play with a resolute commitment to the overthrow of the capitalist system by the world's workers and their allies. They took good care of Marx's legacy by continually attempting to historicize capitalism – by explaining its origins, exposing its apologists, and acting to bring it to an end. Winch, Pritchard, Mould, and Russell, their weaknesses notwithstanding, lived lives worth remembering and learning from, because they never forgot that the rank and file workers themselves must be possessed of socialist knowledge and the willingness to act on that knowledge. They knew that the defenders of capitalism fear nothing more than an educated, activist, working-class majority determined to end the exploitation that is at the heart of the capitalist system of production.

If Marxists of the third way had a serious flaw, it was that they never fully appreciated or implemented Kant's argument that "the subject is active in the constitution of experience itself."[5] While theoretically committed to Kant's model, in practice these Marxists too often saw the workers as agents of a seemingly impersonal transformation rather than as subjects directly involved in forming and shaping a new way of being. They validated only those ethical, social, religious and political choices workers made that directly challenged the capitalist system. In theory as well as in practice, women were too often relegated to the margins of this concern with class struggle, their fight for personal dignity and respect considered ancillary to the "real" struggle.

Critics of Canada's Marxists of the third way have been right in arguing that they too often perceived women as a threat to the development of unity of purpose in the socialist movement. These Marxists did tend to see women's difference as implying disunity and challenging coherence.[6] They were too willing to believe, as Joan Scott points out, that men who worked outside the home "acquired class consciousness and engaged in rational political struggles; women were tied to the domestic sphere and religious reform movements that together functioned to 'compromise or subvert' class consciousness."[7] Even when there was a theoretical commitment to women's equality, it was not always adhered to in practice. The concerns of women as women rarely resonated in the socialist and union halls in which they were active.

Marxists of the third way were not intolerant of women because they were men or because they were Marxists. They were even more critical of labour bureaucrats and bourgeois economists than they were of women who emphasized gender over class. As historical materialists, they tended to dismiss women's activism for the same reasons they were critical of trade unionism and reformist politics — for the failure to embrace the revolutionary task at hand. There was too often a self-righteousness in their manner and message, an intolerance of those who failed to see the correctness of their ideas.[8] But it was difficult for many workers to accept their position, because it was founded on the idea that a socialist society could be forged out of the material world in which workers lived and struggled. As Karl Mannheim points out, the socialists of their generation expounded "a glorification of the material aspects of existence, which were formerly experienced merely as negative and obstructive factors."[9] Marxists of the third way were attempting to convince workers that the material world provided the vehicle for their future emancipation – that same material world which workers, especially women and workers of colour, experienced as hemming them in, holding them back, and victimizing them.

Yet, as we have seen, Marxists of the third way themselves were never able to make a complete break with the religious values and cultural influences of their youths. Pritchard was an historical materialist, but there was a place in his soul that only classical music and the operettas of Gilbert and Sullivan could fill. Russell also loved music, including Christian hymns, and his Scottishness and sentimentality found a home in his love of the poetry of Burns. Even as a Communist and defender of Stalin, Mould could not discard the Christian verities of his youth or feel himself complete without the utopianism and pacifism of Leo Tolstoy. In effect, Marxists of the third way were never able to make the break that they routinely expected the rank and file workers to make. One cannot know, but nevertheless suspects, that the vitriolic denunciations Pritchard sometimes directed at the workers for failing to study Marxist economics, to think about their class position, and act to overcome their exploitation, were in part prompted by dissatisfaction with his own inability to fully commit to the cause he espoused.

For Marxists of the third way the search for certitude in religious salvation became the search for certitude in the historical materialism of Karl Marx and Friedrich Engels. As we have seen, however, the scientific socialism of Marx and Engels, and of their interpreters like Antonio Labriola and Joseph Dietzgen, was a much more nuanced phenomenon than critics of these thinkers have claimed. Indeed, the historical materialism of the thinkers of this generation, including their positing of the relationship between the economic base and the ideological and cultural superstructure, remains much more credible than the alternatives offered by their modern-day critics of both the right and the left. Historical materialism, and its defenders, will long outlive the challenge of the "new true socialism" of Chantal Mouffe, Ernesto Laclau, and Gareth Stedman Jones.[10] As Ellen Meiksins Wood points out, the new true socialists are so driven by the desire to prove that the working class is no longer the subject of history, and so eager to replace the working class with the "people" and the new social movements – notably the feminist, anti-racism, environmental, and gay-rights movements – that they first displace the workers as the agents of socialist transformation; and then the need for the transformation from socialism to capitalism itself is dispensed with.[11] Abandonment of the anticapitalist struggle is made necessary by the desire to discredit historical materialism, a goal that demands "the dissociation of politics from class; the establishment of the non-correspondence between the economic and the political."[12] Unwittingly, one assumes, they have proven the validity of what they set out to disprove. The entire logic of their critique is that Marx was right – capitalism can only be overthrown by class-based struggle, and by accepting correspondence between the economic and the political.

Had the new true socialists been truly committed to the cause of human emancipation, not the task of discrediting Marxism, they might also have noticed that they were attacking the wrong people. Their critique will not stand the test of time, not because it is without merit but because the non-correspondence principle on which their critique is based is anti-capitalist as well as anti-Marxist. It is the defenders of liberal capitalism like Francis Fukuyama, who assert the victory of economic liberalism and the "universalization of Western liberal democracy as the final form of human government," who are the "vulgar" materialists.[13] It is now the defenders of capitalism, not the defenders of Marxism, who are the champions of finality. Labriola's advice was not always heeded, but he had warned historical materialists to guard against "any form whatever of finality."[14] Following decades of attacks on Marxian socialists for asserting a "vulgar" materialism in which ideas are merely a superstructural reflection of the economic base, Fukuyama and the defenders of liberal capitalism assert an all-encompassing base/superstructure model that would have made Pritchard and Russell, not to mention Marx and Engels, cringe. We live in a society in which there is a widespread belief that political democracy is a plant that grows naturally from the fertile soil of free market capitalism. When this kind of Spencerian analogy was employed by Marxists of the third way, it was evidence of stupidity. When employed by the defenders of the capitalist system, it takes on the aura of revealed truth.

Karl Marx and his adherents, including Canada's Marxists of the third way, were system builders, but so of course are economic liberals past and present. As Elaine Freedgood argues in her analysis of the work of Harriet Martineau, classical political economy's "promise of meaning and predictability suggests that it functioned as a cosmology." That cosmology was limited by the attempts of the classical political economists "to totalize too tidily a particularly recalcitrant social reality."[15] If Canada's Marxists of the third way are to stand condemned as system builders, we need to recognize that they lived in an age of system builders. Anyone who has read – or, more likely, tried to read – Mackenzie King's *Industry and Humanity* has encountered system building at its best, and will recognize that King's corporatism faced the same dilemma of a "recalcitrant social reality."[16] Capitalism's recalcitrant social realities – racism, poverty, and homelessness in America, slavery in the Sudan, child labour in India, and the destruction of native peoples and degradation of women the world over – provide stark evidence that Canada's Marxists of the third way were not the only ones who constantly wrestled with a social reality that refused to conform to their theoretical understanding.

The purpose of this study has not been to deny that Marxists of the third way were system builders, or that they were influenced by determinist ways of thinking, or that they too often attempted to deal with a "recalcitrant social reality" by attacking their critics and attempting to assert (rather than prove) the validity of their ideas and world view. The purpose has been to demonstrate, however, that in an age in which these ideas were pervasive in western society, among liberals and conservatives as well as Marxian socialists, Canada's Marxists of the third way remained remarkably committed to the goal of worker self-emancipation and human freedom. The enormous influence of Darwin and Spencer notwithstanding, and the constant temptations faced by Marxists of the third way to become socialist evolutionists, they remained committed, as Bryan Palmer has stated of Edward Thompson, to the "systematic elevation of human agency."[17]

Marxists of the third way shared a tremendous faith in education and the influence of environment on the actions of the workers. That ethos is not entirely dead, even in the late twentieth century; but there is no disputing that it was of an intensity in the late nineteenth and early twentieth centuries that is difficult for the late twentieth century mind to comprehend.[18] One can only marvel at their faith in this period to believe that even an uneducated worker could learn the history of class relations in Greece and Rome, the reasons for the rise and fall of feudalism, and the origins of industrial capitalism, and that a miner in British Columbia could trace his relationship to the means of production directly through that history. It was this marvellous historical sense, this belief in the rationality of even the least educated worker, that stands as the enduring legacy of these worker intellectuals. They built a socialist movement of thousands of educated and motivated political activists whose political and economic knowledge was second to none, and they did it while being attacked, not subsidized, by the state.

This emphasis on education, self-activity, and self-organization had roots in utopian socialism, Protestant Nonconformism, and Marxism itself. It is the belief in worker self-emancipation that is the enduring legacy of Marxists of the third way. In a century in which, as Peter Beilharz points out, "all forms of mainstream political thinking become statist," their commitment to agency remains an enduring legacy.[19] This was possible because they were Marxists, not in spite of the fact they were Marxists. Even those like Arthur Mould more influenced by Christ than Hegel were nurtured in a socialist culture essentially monist in its assumptions, a culture that saw thought as part of being, a culture in which the great evolutionary transformation from capitalism to socialism was at its most basic a transformation of thought. Without education, without a change in the consciousness of the workers, without William Morris's making of socialists, it would all be for nought. The thought of Marx and Engels has been so bastardized in the twentieth century that it is now almost impossible to make anyone realize that Engels, when he talked about the material world having its own laws of motion, simply meant that the unfolding of events in nature and human society were not directed by God or some unseen spiritual force. Marxists of the third way took that idea and said that the workers of the world, taking their fate into their own hands, could be that force. Marx and Engels opened up the future, and made it possible.

In describing the thought of independent Marxist Colin McKay, Ian McKay insightfully captures Marxism of the third way's commitment to education, worker self-emancipation and opposition to finality:

> One reason why workers needed to understand evolution and the historical background of capitalism was precisely in order to combat the fatalism inherent in bourgeois ways of thinking, especially those centred on the supposed universality of supply and demand ... Lacking any sense of history, many workers developed a purely fatalistic attitude toward the world ... Only if they were taught how to look at things from a more critical and longer-term perspective would the workers' fatalism be overthrown. Rather than leading to a sense of helplessness, a grasp of evolution and social history would reveal the transitory nature of capitalism and open up a vivid sense of the possibilities for radical change.[20]

McKay's evocation of the thought of Canada's Marxian socialists reminds us that in the late twentieth century capitalism has become frozen in time, a system without a history. Capitalism appears as a system beyond the reach of the education and self-organization of the workers, an ethereal colossus bestriding a world in which only the right has agency.

Historians of Canada's Marxian socialists have been quick to point out determinist and statist elements in their thinking, and much less willing to acknowledge the centrality of agency and the individual in their world view. Like D.G. Ritchie, whose work *Darwinism and Politics* was read by Canada's Marxists of the third way, they were as likely to describe history "as the development of thought" as they were to see it as "the succession of time."[21] The legacy of Canada's Marxists of the third way will remain alive as long as the consciousness of the workers themselves is an indispensable part of the fight against the capitalist system.

Conservative critics of Canada's Marxian socialists tell us that they rode roughshod over the thoughts and wishes of the rank and file workers, while Marxist-Leninists would have us believe they were too concerned with what the workers were thinking. The historical record provides evidence to support both positions: what we need is a clear understanding of the enormous difficulty of what they were trying to do, and an appreciation of the depth of their commitment. It is true that their efforts to reflect the wishes of the rank and file were sometimes too honest, their willingness to interpret the will of the workers rather than lead them altruistic to the point of placing the workers in potential danger. Yet, just as Winch faced the mob at the Longshoremen's Hall and refused to abdicate his responsibilities as the representative of the workers, Marxists of the third way fought to give rank and file workers the space in which to develop their own capabilities and come to their own determination to overthrow capitalism and create a socialist society. The shadow of Marxism's Stalinist past notwithstanding, their example makes it possible to believe that a new generation of Marxist leaders can step forward, provide resolute leadership, and at the same time build on and expand the commitment to rank and file democracy and the inclusion of workers of all identities in the socialist movement of the twenty-first century.

Marxists of the third way attempted to fulfil their responsibilities as socialist leaders and educators, yet never forgot that socialism had to be created by the workers themselves. It is that ethos that emerges so forcefully from Arthur Mould's response to 1956: If Stalin committed horrendous crimes, he asked, how can we exonerate ourselves? We put those leaders there, we made them what they were and allowed them to get away with what they did. We should look to ourselves, to our own failings, not blame this person or that person. Nor should we leave the party or the movement, because the party and the movement are not to blame. We should listen to the rank and file more, and to leaders less. We should go back and think about what it was we intended to do when we set out.

In the latter days of the twentieth century it is important to recall the legacy we have been left by Ernest Winch, Bill Pritchard, Arthur Mould, and Bob Russell. Faced as we are with the "collapse of communism," the "death of Marxism," and "the end of history," even those of us who decry the masculinist and racist politics of the socialists and labour leaders of a bygone era cannot afford to dismiss the trials they endured and lessons they learned. As Peter Beilharz points out, "if we really choose to go forward, then we must also agree to go back."[22] It is not without value to be reminded that we can reclaim, celebrate, and validate our identities for decades more, but it will not change the fact that the public and private lives of wage workers in this world continue to be determined by their relationship to the means of production. Marxists of the third way make it possible for us to look forward to the day when the theft of the product of one's labour will be seen as much a form of discrimination as the denial of black identity, religious identity, or sexual identity is seen in the last days of the twentieth century.

Winch, Pritchard, Mould, and Russell would not want us to see them as heroes or villains; they would want us to learn from their lives and then move on. They remind us that there can be no human liberation without the end of capitalism and the freedom of the working class, and that knowledge of, and desire for, socialism are not necessarily bounded by one's objective class position. They reveal to us the simple truth that in order to find struggle, one must go where struggle is. They give us themselves and the "daring, courage, imagination, and idealism" that the Francis Fukuyamas of the world see coming to an end with the end of history.[23] They allow us to once again believe with Bill Pritchard that in the union of the workers lies the peace of the world. They remind us that the capitalist system itself demands a revolutionary politics if alternative ways of organizing human society are to be found; they leave us with the faith that the workers themselves will find a way to be human.

Notes

INTRODUCTION

1 Desmond Morton, although derisive in his treatment of Marxian socialists in Canada, does acknowledge both the widespread appeal of Marxist ideas and the impact Marxists had in the trade union movement. See his *Working People*, 93.

2 I can only echo the similar conclusions drawn by Ian McKay, whose work on Colin McKay represents a long overdue appreciation of the rich intellectual history of the Canadian working class. McKay's work may actually convince a few people that if one is to understand the socialists of the past, it might be a good idea to actually read what they read, to understand what they understood, *before* moving on to condescension. See *For a Working-Class Culture in Canada: A Selection of Colin McKay's Writings on Sociology and Political Economy, 1897–1939*, 378.

3 Karl Marx and Friedrich Engels, *Collected Works*, vol. 20, 14.

4 Roger Fletcher, *Revisionism and Empire*, 14, 17.

5 Mark Pittenger, *American Socialists and Evolutionary Thought, 1870–1920*, 129–31, 158. Paul Buhle also points out that Berger and Hillquit identified socialism "with the inevitable growth of monopolies." See his *Marxism in the USA*, 95.

6 Peter Stearns, *Revolutionary Syndicalism and French Labor*, 9.

7 Nick Salvatore, *Eugene V. Debs: Citizen and Socialist*, 206–8, 211–12.

8 Marx and Engels wrote: "When people speak of ideas that revolutionize society, they do but express the fact, that within the old society, the elements of a new one have been created, and that the dissolution of the old ideas

keeps even pace with the dissolution of the old conditions of existence." Karl Marx and Friedrich Engels, *The Communist Manifesto*, 102–3.

9 John Amos (Jack) McDonald was a major contributor of articles to the Socialist Party of Canada's journal the *Western Clarion*, and a member of the Dominion Executive Committee of the SPC during the First World War. Born into a family of eight on a Prince Edward Island potato farm, he went on to become a major figure in the history of socialist thought and activism in western Canada, New Zealand, and the United States. When he was struck down by a car in Oakland, California, in 1968 at the age of 79 it was observed that he had always been proud of his association with the IWW "as a life-long radical and supporter of Marxian socialism." See *San Francisco Chronicle*, 6 July 1968; Kerry Taylor, "'Jack' McDonald: A Canadian Revolutionary in New Zealand," 261–8. For Jack Leheney, see the *OBU Bulletin*, 16 December 1926, and Nicholas Fillmore, *The Life and Times of Roscoe Fillmore*, 38–9. See also Fred Thompson and David Roediger, *Fellow Worker: The Life of Fred Thompson*, 13, 54.

10 Louis Boudin, *The Theoretical System of Karl Marx*, 273–4; Pittenger, *American Socialists and Evolutionary Thought*, 146.

11 For the history and ideas of the League see Michiel Horn, *The League for Social Reconstruction.*

12 Martin Robin, *Radical Politics and Canadian Labour, 1880–1930*, 277–8.

13 Stuart MacIntyre, *A Proletarian Science: Marxism in Britain, 1917–1933*, 238–9.

14 Stanley Pierson, *British Socialists: The Journey from Fantasy to Politics*, 94–5; M.P. Cowen and R. W. Shenton, *Doctrines of Development*, 283.

15 Richard N. Hunt, *The Political Ideas of Marx and Engels: Classical Marxism, 1850–1895*, 275.

16 See Aileen Kelly, *Mikhail Bakunin: A Study in the Psychology and Politics of Utopianism*, 233–4.

17 V.I. Lenin, *What Is to Be Done?*, 199–200; and *"Left Wing" Communism: An Infantile Disorder*, 27–9.

18 Hunt, *Classical Marxism*, 253.

19 For two notable dismissals of these Marxian socialists see Robin, *Radical Politics and Canadian Labour*, 275, and Morton, *Working People*, 93.

20 A notable exception is Ross Johnson's 1975 PhD thesis "No Compromise – No Political Trading: The Marxian Socialist Tradition in British Columbia."

21 Many more works have been done on Canadian socialists who were members of the Communist Party. They include Gregory S. Kealey, "Stanley Brehaut Ryerson: Canadian Revolutionary Intellectual," 103–31, and "Stanley Brehaut Ryerson: Marxist Historian," 133–70; Jack Scott, *A Communist Life: Jack Scott and the Canadian Workers Movement, 1927–1985*, edited by Bryan D. Palmer; George MacEachern, *George MacEachern, an Autobi-*

ography: The Story of a Cape Breton Labour Radical, edited by David Frank and Donald MacGillivray.

22 Ross Johnson's observation that the Socialist Party made "no attempt to develop Marxist ideology to suit the economic situation in British Columbia or Canada" is, for all intents and purposes, correct. See Johnson, "No Compromise – No Political Trading," 17.

23 Ibid., 2.

24 Phyllis Clarke, "Application of Marxist Thought to Canada," 4.

25 Ibid., 88.

26 It is not only in Canada that non-Communist Party Marxists have been so summarily dismissed. British Marxist groups such as the Socialist Labour Party, the Socialist Party of Great Britain, and the Trotskyists are characterized by Stuart MacIntyre as being "irrelevant" after 1920. See MacIntyre, *A Proletarian Science*, 24.

27 John Goode, "E.P. Thompson and 'the Significance of Literature,'" in Harvey J. Kaye and Keith McClelland, eds., *E.P. Thompson: Critical Perspectives*, 188–9.

28 Paul Heywood, *Marxism and the Failure of Organised Socialism in Spain, 1879–1936*, x.

29 It must be understood that there were literally dozens of Marxists of the third way, Marxian socialists, and other leftists who were as impressive, or more impressive, as theorists and writers than the individuals I am writing about in this study. Of note are D.G. McKenzie, Wilfred Gribble, Sanna Kannasto, Charles O'Brien, Bertha Merrill Burns, John Houston, Frank Woodward, Chris Stephenson, Geordie Morgan, Sarah Johnston-Knight, Charles Lestor, Moses Baritz, Adolph Kohn, John Henry Burrough, Elizabeth Morton, E.T. Kingsley, George Weaver, Rose Henderson, Jack McDonald, Frank Roberts, Colin McKay, Roscoe Fillmore, A.M. Stephen, Wallis Lefeaux, Sophie Mushkat, Jack Kavanagh, and H.M. Fitzgerald.

30 Claude Larivière, *Albert Saint-Martin: Militant D'Avant-Garde (1865–1947)*; and Marcel Fournier, *Communisme et anticommunisme au Québec (1920–1950)*, 16–22.

31 Meridel Le Sueur, "The Fetish of Being Outside," in Charlotte Nekola and Paula Rabinowitz, eds., *Writing Red: An Anthology of American Women Writers, 1930–1940*, 299.

32 In an international context, Marxism of the third way is a broad category capable of encompassing figures such as Karl Kautsky on the right to Rosa Luxemburg on the left. Other major figures in the period of study include the Dutch council communists Herman Gorter and Anton Pannekoek. On Kautsky, see Dick Geary, *Karl Kautsky*; Patrick Goode, ed., *Karl Kautsky: Selected Political Writings*; and Massimo Salvadori, *Karl Kautsky and the Socialist Revolution, 1880–1938*. On Luxemburg, see Raya Dunayevskaya, *Rosa Luxemburg, Women's Liberation, and Marx's Philosophy of*

Revolution and Mary-Alice Waters, ed., *Rosa Luxemburg Speaks*. On Gorter and Pannekoek, see D.A. Smart, ed., *Pannekoek and Gorter's Marxism*.

33 Marxists of the third way realized, if only intuitively, the enormous difficulty of the Marxist project, the creation of a society based in the concurrent realization and destruction of the capitalist system.

34 As this religious influence was a product of childhoods spent in Great Britain, it will be looked at in more detail in the individual chapters.

35 Linda Kealey suggests that "less than 10 per cent" of the Socialist Party's membership was female. Her figure, while impressionistic, is undoubtedly accurate. I also agree with her assessment that we are dealing here with an essentially male culture. See Kealey, "Socialism and the Woman Question," 83.

36 In 1903 the Polish Marxist Rosa Luxemburg argued that one of the tasks of the working class in a class system is to "safeguard bourgeois culture from the vandalism of the bourgeois reaction." See "Stagnation and Progress of Marxism," in Waters, *Rosa Luxemburg Speaks*, 110.

37 For Russell's own statement that he remained a trade unionist first and a political socialist second see Provincial Archives of Manitoba (PAM) MG 10 F2, Lionel Orlikow, Interview with Bob Russell, transcript 4, 1.

38 On the labour aristocracy in England see Eric Hobsbawm, *Workers: Worlds of Labor*; John Foster, *Class Struggle and the Industrial Revolution*; and Robert Q. Gray, *The Labour Aristocracy in Victorian England*. The Canadian literature is much less extensive, but important contributions include Bryan D. Palmer, "Most Uncommon Common Men: Craft and Culture in Historical Perspective," 5–31; Ian McKay, "Capital and Labour in the Halifax Baking and Confectionery Industry during the Last Half of the Nineteenth Century," 63–108; and Craig Heron, "The Crisis of the Craftsman: Hamilton's Metal Workers in the Early Twentieth Century," 7–48.

39 My differences with Kenneth McNaught's work notwithstanding, he was right about the influence of Christianity and the British literary tradition on Canadian socialists. See his "E.P. Thompson vs Harold Logan: Writing about Labour and the Left in the 1970s," 168n62.

40 E.P. Thompson, *William Morris: Romantic to Revolutionary*, 770, 774.

41 Ibid., 802.

42 SPCer Arthur Turner is a good example. It was Turner, a member of the Victoria Metal Trades council, who proposed to the council that Canada adopt the Soviet system of government. In the early 1930s Turner and Carl Robinson wrote a play entitled "John Ball," based on the work by William Morris. Turner apparently also wrote a play about Wat Tyler's rebellion. See Dorothy Steeves, *The Compassionate Rebel: Ernest Winch and the Growth of Socialism in Western Canada*, 73; and University of British Columbia Special Collections (UBCSC), Arthur J. Turner Papers, box 1, folder 6, Manuscripts and Dramas.

43 For Lestor, Burns, Johnston-Knight, Mushkat, and Kannasto, see Linda Kealey, *Enlisting Women for the Cause*, 100–6, 135–42, 211–13, 250–1. I have reluctantly left Helen Armstrong, one of the Socialist Party of Canada's most prominent members over three decades, off this list. Armstrong, the daughter of Ontario labour leader Alf Jury and the wife of SPCer George Armstrong, was the mother of SPCers as well. She was a Marxian socialist but an activist rather than a theoretician. Kealey, in *Enlisting Women for the Cause*, states that Armstrong was "purely an activist," but evidence to the contrary may yet be found. Her role in the Winnipeg General Strike of 1919 is chronicled in Mary Horodyski's "Women and the Winnipeg General Strike of 1919," 30, 32, 34, and Linda Kealey's "No Special Protection – No Sympathy: Women's Activism in the Canadian Labour Revolt of 1919," 137–8, 140–1, 151. As Varpu Lindstrom-Best points out, Sanna Kannasto's socialist activism was curtailed by a male partner who wanted her to remain in the home, and much of her marvellous legacy is lost to us because most of her writings have been destroyed. See Lindstrom-Best's *Defiant Sisters: A Social History of Finnish Immigrant Women in Canada*, 151–2.

44 Mari Jo Buhle, *Women and American Socialism, 1870–1920*, 8.

45 Ibid., 171.

46 Ibid., 9.

47 Pittenger, *American Socialists and Evolutionary Thought*, 186.

48 Newton, *Feminist Challenge*, 25–7.

49 Buhle, *Women and American Socialism*, 28.

50 My own research indicates that Bebel's *Woman under Socialism* failed to attract the interest or support among Canadian Marxists that it did among European and American Marxists.

51 Buhle, *Women and American Socialism*, 289.

52 Pittenger, *American Socialists and Evolutionary Thought*, 186.

53 Roscoe Fillmore himself admitted that in the late 1920s he "became something of a domestic tyrant." See Fillmore, *Maritime Radical*, 157.

54 See Alf Budden, "The Woman's Place," *Western Clarion*, 10 December 1910. Budden's legacy was carried into the 1930s and 1940s by Marxists of the third way like George Weaver. As Joan Sangster observes in *Dreams of Equality: Women on the Canadian Left, 1920–1950*, 97, "his writing represented a fairly sophisticated attempt to construct a dialectical understanding of the class and sexual oppression of women."

55 Anonymous author, "Can Socialism Destroy the Home?" *Western Clarion*, 23 March 1912; A. Percy Chew, "Woman and Labor," *Western Clarion*, 27 April 1912; George Paton, "Woman in Society," *Western Clarion*, 3 August 1912.

56 Marxists of the third way were, in my own estimation, more likely to be sexist than racist. Joseph Dietzgen, a major influence, explicity argues

that in all races religious beliefs are the product of "experience and culture," and not "inherent." Revealingly, he claims that "it is but peasants and women that are the true believers," thereby suggesting that peasants and women are predisposed to being "irrational" or "superstitious" in a way that people of colour are not. See Dietzgen, *Some of the Philosophical Essays on Socialism and Science, Religion, Ethics, Critique-of-Reason and the World-at-Large*, 114–15.

57 For Teit see Judith Judd Banks, "Comparative Biographies of Two British Columbia Anthropologists: Charles Hill-Tout and James A. Teit," and Wendy Wickwire, "Women in Ethnography: The Research of James A. Teit," and "To See Ourselves as the Other's Other: Nlaka'pamux Contact Narratives."

58 *Western Clarion*, 11 April 1908.

59 The other city in Canada in which Jewish socialists, male and female, appear to have been an integral part of the socialist movement was Montreal. See Larivière, *Albert Saint-Martin*, 106, 109–10, 119, 123–4, 133.

60 Newton, *Feminist Challenge*, 25.

61 Lionel Orlikow, Interview with Bob Russell, transcript 4, 4.

62 David Hollinger, *Morris R. Cohen and the Scientific Ideal*, 58–9.

63 I fully recognize the dangers of pushing this argument too far, given that some Jewish Marxists, including Winnipeg's Sam Blumenberg, were, at least for a time, Marxist Zionists.

64 Hollinger, *Morris R. Cohen and the Scientific Ideal*, 201.

65 McKay, *For a Working-Class Culture in Canada*, 379.

66 Ibid., 511.

67 Arthur Morrow Lewis, *Evolution Social and Organic*, 164.

68 A. Ross McCormack, Interview with Bill Pritchard, tape 3, side A.

69 Lewis, *Evolution Social and Organic*, 160.

70 John McGowan, *Postmodernism and Its Critics*, 11.

71 Labriola's influence stretched much beyond the Socialist Party of Canada. See, for example, the list of books for sale in the 9 September 1909 issue of *Cotton's Weekly*, Canada's most widely read socialist paper.

72 Antonio Labriola, *Essays on the Materialistic Conception of History*, 26–7, 179.

73 The classic argument is that Marxism fared poorly in Great Britain because it was too German, too Hegelian, too idealist, too abstract to appeal to the great majority of British workers. MacIntyre, *A Proletarian Science*, 233, argues that in the 1920s British Marxists themselves believed in a distinctive "British aversion to theory." A.W. Wright, in *G.D.H. Cole and Socialist Democracy*, 3, observes that the theorists of British socialism "have been lightly dismissed with a word about the British incapacity for high theory." This is not to deny that British socialists – and British idealists such as D.G. Ritchie who influenced them – could be very critical of Hegel, especially concerning

his writings on the state. See Sandra Den Otter, *British Idealism and Social Explanation: A Study in Late Victorian Thought*, 28–32.

74 H.M. Bartholomew, "A Philosophy of Revolt," *Western Clarion*, 27 March 1915.

75 Bartholomew, "The Meaning of 'Value,'" *Western Clarion*, 30 January 1915.

76 Chew had been expelled from the SPC on 12 January 1915 for contravening the party's position on the war (*The Voice*, 15 January 1915).

77 A. Percy Chew, "The S. P. of C. Again," *The Voice*, 11 August 1916; "A Reply to Harrington," *The Voice*, 27 October 1916. For Harrington's response, see the October, November, and December 1916 issues of the *Western Clarion*.

78 For Dietzgen's influence on working-class socialists in Great Britain, see Jonathan Ree, *Proletarian Philosophers: Problems in Socialist Culture in Britain, 1900–1940*, 23–45. For evidence of Dietzgen's influence in Canada, especially on Colin McKay, see McKay, *For a Working-Class Culture in Canada*, 113–14, 172–3. Dietzgen still shared top billing with Marx in the One Big Union's educational classes in the mid-1920s (*OBU Bulletin*, 10 December 1925).

79 Dietzgen, *Philosophical Essays*, 149.

80 *Western Clarion*, November 1916.

81 Dietzgen notes that the Hegelian idea, in its "striving for realisation," is a "materialism in disguise." See Dietzgen, *Philosophical Essays*, 89.

82 MacIntyre, *A Proletarian Science*, 109.

83 Russell Jacoby, *Dialectic of Defeat: Contours of Western Marxism*, 21.

84 Perry Anderson, *Arguments within English Marxism*, 130.

85 E.P. Thompson, *The Poverty of Theory and Other Essays*, 112–13.

86 Ibid., 578.

87 Ibid., 379.

88 W.A. Pritchard, *Address to the Jury*, 59, 64.

89 Marx and Engels, *The Communist Manifesto*, 91.

90 Gregory S. Kealey, "State Repression of Labour and the Left in Canada, 1914–20: The Impact of the First World War," 283n5.

91 I will deal with Pritchard's efforts to deny the role of ideas in 1919, and his agreement with academics who make this claim, in the Pritchard chapter. See Tom Mitchell, "'Repressive Measures': A.J. Andrews, the Committee of 1000 and the Campaign against Radicalism after the Winnipeg General Strike," 136, 154. Mitchell and James Naylor place their analysis of the labour revolt of 1919 in the context of "the battle of ideas that accompanies any moment of social crisis." See their "The Prairies: In the Eye of the Storm," in Craig Heron, ed., *The Workers' Revolt in Canada, 1917–1925*, 191.

92 Bercuson posits the existence of an "SPC-influenced western Canadian syndicalism" in 1919, while Newton argues that the SPC's wartime shift in

favour of industrial unionism is "reputed to have occurred." See Bercuson, *Fools and Wise Men: The Rise and Fall of the One Big Union*, 82–3; Newton, *Feminist Challenge*, 153.

93 One can, of course, go through the *Western Clarion* and extract from it all kinds of anti-trade union statements and attacks on rival union-based organizations such as the Industrial Workers of the World. Mark Leier, for example, builds a case against the leadership of the SPC on the basis of statements made by the party's most intemperate spokespersons, while ignoring similar statements from members of the Industrial Workers of the World. Few SPCers went as far as prominent Wobbly leader Joseph Ettor, who condemned craft unions as "capitalist institutions with a labor name." See Salvatore Salerno, *Red November Black November: Culture and Community in the Industrial Workers of the World*, 98. For Joseph Ettor and SPC attacks on the Wobblies, see Mark Leier, *Where the Fraser River Flows*, 43–4, 57–9.

94 This was true of Marxists who did not come from the British Isles as well. Abe Karme, a Finnish Marxist who was for several years on the Dominion Executive of the SPC, had been involved in trade union organizing in Finland in the 1890s before coming to Canada.

95 Marx's position on the trade unions also appeared in labour papers. See, for example, the *BC Federationist*, 9 December 1911.

96 Norman Penner, Interview with Bill Pritchard, Vancouver City College, 31 July 1973, tape 1, side B.

97 Bercuson, *Fools and Wise Men*, 258–9.

98 This remains the position of the Socialist Party of Great Britain and her sister parties around the world, including the Socialist Party of Canada, to this day.

99 Ian Angus, *Canadian Bolsheviks: The Early Years of the Communist Party of Canada*, 113.

100 Thompson and Roediger, *Fellow Worker*, 6.

101 Wallis Walter Lefeaux, *Winnipeg-London-Moscow; A study of Bolshevism*, 44–5.

102 See the report of a speech Chris Stephenson gave at the Empress Theatre in Vancouver on 13 February 1921, in which he defined dictatorship as a "self-imposed discipline," in the *Western Clarion*, 18 February 1921.

103 In this sense Canada's Marxists of the third way resembled those socialists in Great Britain, such as John MacLean, who came out of the social democratic tradition, although they were much more hostile to involvement with labour parties and nationalism than was the Scottish socialist. As Stanley Pierson points out, MacLean sought a course independent of social democracy and Bolshevism, just as his Canadian counterparts sought a third way. See his *British Socialists*, 291–4.

104 The classic formulation is Rosa Luxemburg's critique of Lenin's conception of the dictatorship of the proletariat, in which she argued that the way forward was by means of "the active, untrammeled, energetic political life

of the broadest masses of the people." See Rosa Luxemburg, *The Russian Revolution* and *Leninism or Marxism?*, 62.

105 Like Rosa Luxemburg, SPC critics of the dictatorship of the proletariat did not reject it outright but rather cautioned against it becoming more repressive than necessary to safeguard the revolution. See Luxemburg, *Marxism or Leninism*, 86.

106 Historians have spent so much time and effort condemning the "impossibilism" of the SPC that they have paid little attention to what happened to the SDP. Many SDP locals were devastated by their members going off to war, and by the late war period SDP supporters were turning to the SPC, even proposing a merger of the two parties. It was the SPCers, who understood the mood of radical labour in this period, who benefitted, and who led the radical forces in 1919.

107 There were, of course, many SPCers who did not accept the politics of the OBU, and felt that Bob Russell and other OBU leaders had essentially abandoned the SPC position. Among the critics of the OBU was Bob Russell's old ally Alex Shepherd.

108 Robin, *Radical Politics and Canadian Labour*, 176.

109 David J. Bercuson, *Confrontation at Winnipeg*, 98.

110 Houston was a much admired figure on the Canadian left. See PAM, Alex Shepherd Letters (ASL), MG 14 C86, Shepherd to David Bercuson, 10 March 1969.

111 Marx and Engels argued that in the course of the revolutionary transformation "a portion of the bourgeoisie goes over to the proletariat, and in particular, a portion of the bourgeois ideologists, who have raised themselves to the level of comprehending theoretically the historical movement as a whole." See Marx and Engels, *The Communist Manifesto*, 91.

112 Labriola, *Essays on the Materialistic Conception of History*, 210.

113 Enrico Ferri, *Socialism and Modern Science*, 137.

114 For individual members of the SPC who fit this description, and their occupations, see Mark Leier, "Workers and Intellectuals: The Theory of the New Class and Early Canadian Socialism," 95–6.

115 James Naylor, "Politics and Class: The Character of 1930s Socialism in Canada," 10–11. Leier's claim that the leaders of the pre-1919 SPC "felt compelled to defend the middle class as carriers of the socialist message" is very misleading. SPCers did not reject middle-class support, but they rarely acknowledged the existence of the middle class, let alone defended it. See Leier, "Workers and Intellectuals," 96.

116 Salvadori, *Karl Kautsky*, 319–20, 349.

117 Lenin would have described their inactivity as "slavish cringing before spontaneity." While not Leninists, pre-1919 Marxists of the third way were certainly more willing to take the revolutionary lead. See V.I. Lenin, *Collected Works*, vol. 5, 378.

118 See, for example, Charles Lestor on the theory of state capitalism in the *OBU Bulletin*, 24 January 1929; and Alex Lyon's "The Fallacy of Nationalization" in the *OBU Bulletin*, 27 February 1930.

CHAPTER ONE

1 Leier, *Where the Fraser River Flows*, 119.

2 Steeves, *Compassionate Rebel*, 7.

3 The "labour aristocracy" question has been broached in many national contexts and from many thematic directions. In terms of the 1919 labour revolt and the events leading up to it, the key consideration is the role played by skilled craftsmen from the British Isles in radicalizing less skilled workers. In Vancouver, for example, a successful sympathetic strike depended on the actions of the loggers and longshoremen, both groups which looked to British tradesmen such as Ernest Winch for leadership. See James R. Conley, "Frontier Labourers, Crafts in Crisis and the Western Labour Revolt: The Case of Vancouver, 1900–1919," 9–37, who makes an excellent case for the centrality of this relationship in explaining the 1919 labour revolt.

4 Steeves, *Compassionate Rebel*, 7.

5 Dorothy Steeves suggests that it was the "spirit of adventure" that led young Ernest to leave England, which may be true, but it does not explain why he took a job as a railway office clerk before he left and did not work with his father. Winch's later correspondence indicates that he was closer to his mother than to his father, and he may have had personal or work-related disagreements with the elder Winch. See Steeves, *Compassionate Rebel*, 8.

6 Ibid., 8–9.

7 Burnaby Village Heritage Museum (BVHM), Ernest Edward Winch Papers (EEWP), HV 978.40, EEW to Mother & Carrie, 22 January 1899; 19 February 1899.

8 Steeves, *Compassionate Rebel*, 10.

9 Ibid., 10–11.

10 Steeves says he returned to Canada in 1910, but a letter Winch sent home in November 1909 indicates that he left England the year before. See Steeves, *Compassionate Rebel*, 11; and BVHM, EEWP, file 300–6, EEW to Alf, 27 November 1909.

11 The author of *Evolution of the Japanese: Social and Psychic*, Sydney Lewis Gulick (1860–1945), was a Congregational missionary to Japan. In his book, which is a study of the Japanese "national character," Gulick rejects the "physiological theory" of racial difference, arguing instead that differences among races are "civilizational." As a result of the Japanese joining the civilized races at the turn of the century, Gulick argues, they have

become responsible for helping the western nations rule "the lawless and backward races," notably the Chinese. I am not certain why Winch chose to read this particular book, although his encounters with Japanese in Vancouver may have motivated him to learn more about the country and its people.

12 BVHM, EEWP, HV 978.40, EEW to Carrie, Alf, & Mother Winch, early March 1910.

13 *Vancouver Daily Province*, 14 February 1910. Although Winch did not sign his name to the letter, there is no doubt that it is his. Some of the same phrases which appear in the paper he uses in the letter he later sent home to his family.

14 While still in England Winch had joined the Good Templars, an organization which promoted abstention from alcohol (Steeves, *Compassionate Rebel*, 8).

15 *Vancouver Daily Province*, 14 February 1910.

16 Steeves, *Compassionate Rebel*, 18.

17 Winch has both the author and the title of the "Foster" book wrong. He is referring to Hugh Oakeley Arnold-Forster, *English Socialism of To-Day* (1908). The book is one of those searching critiques of socialism that adopts a tone of quiet reason, sets out a panoply of socialist failings, and then with an air of complete impartiality asks readers to make up their own minds. Not, one suspects, the kind of approach Winch was looking for.

18 BVHM, EEWP, HV 978.40, Letter to Carrie, Alf, & Mother Winch, 22 February–March 1910.

19 Ibid.

20 BVHM, EEWP, HV 978.40, Letters to Carrie, Alf, and Mother Winch, 9 May 1910.

21 BVHM, EEWP, HV 978.40, EEW to Alf, 25 September 1910; EEW to Mother & Carrie, 9 October 1910; EEW to Mother & Carrie, 20 October 1910.

22 BVHM, EEWP, HV 978.40, EEW to Walter and Alf, 24 May 1910.

23 BVHM, EEWP, HV 978.40, EEW to Alf, 27 November 1909.

24 UBCSC, Angus MacInnis Memorial Collection (AMMC), EEWP, box 56A, folder 13A-D.

25 Steeves, *Compassionate Rebel*, 25–6.

26 Ibid., 26.

27 For Ernest and Bertha Merrill Burns's involvement with the Socialist Party, see Newton, *Feminist Challenge*, 30–2.

28 The history of the break is long, detailed, and complicated, and cannot be gone into here. It began late in 1909 and was completed at the Ontario SPC convention in Toronto on 15–16 April 1911. At that meeting the Canadian Socialist Federation was formed, more power given to local units, the Federation voted to join the International Socialist Bureau, and economic action and work with the trade unions was endorsed. The defection represented a

severe blow to the SPC, as there were now 1,196 paid-up members in the Ontario party. See *Cotton's Weekly*, 4 May 1911, for the convention proceedings.

29 Place won in Nanaimo on an SDP ticket, aided by the endorsement of the Socialist Party's paper, the *Western Clarion*. Williams actually ran for the SPC in Newcastle, but his local had switched to the SDP prior to the election. Williams had joined the SDP but remained a member of the SPC. He was expelled from the SPC after the election for holding dual membership. See *Electoral History of British Columbia, 1871–1986*, 118–19.

30 *The Voice*, 26 January 1911.

31 Steeves, *Compassionate Rebel*, 29.

32 Kealey, "Socialism and the Woman Question," 90. Kealey points out that in January 1909 owner W.U. Cotton himself described both the manager and editor as members of the SPC. See also "Socialism and the Woman Question," 91n28.

33 *Cotton's Weekly*, 4 May 1911.

34 *The Voice*, 12 August 1910.

35 *Western Clarion*, 21 December 1912.

36 *Western Clarion*, 5 April 1913.

37 *Western Clarion*, 1 August 1914.

38 *Cotton's Weekly*, 4 June 1914.

39 Steeves, *Compassionate Rebel*, 30; BVHM, EEWP, file 300–6, and *Political Pamphlets/Broadsheets*.

40 *Cotton's Weekly*, 26 November 1914.

41 As Ian McKay and Suzanne Morton point out, even prominent Maritime members of the Socialist Party of Canada such as Fred Hyatt and Colin McKay were unable to resist the siren song of patriotism. See their "The Maritimes: Expanding the Circle of Resistance," in Heron, *The Workers' Revolt in Canada*, 53.

42 BVHM, EEWP, HV 978.40, EEW to Alf, 17 May 1913.

43 Steeves, *Compassionate Rebel*, 31–3.

44 Woodsworth also lived with the Winch family for a short period of time (ibid., 42).

45 BVHM, EEWP, HV 978.40, EEW to Alf, 10 August 1917.

46 *BC Federationist*, 20 July 1917.

47 BVHM, EEWP, HV 978.40, EEW to Alf, 10 August 1917.

48 *BC Federationist*, 6 July 1917.

49 Ibid., 7 September 1917.

50 Ibid., 18 January 1918.

51 *Victoria Daily Times*, 2 February 1918.

52 It seems reasonable to assume, but I have seen no evidence to prove, that Winch was a member of the SPC at this time.

53 *BC Federationist*, 26 July 1918.

54 Ibid., 2 August 1918.
55 UBCSC, AMMC, box 52, folder 6, Interview with Stan Lefeaux.
56 UBCSC, AMMC, box 52, folder 1, Interview with Ernest Burns.
57 Ibid.
58 UBCSC, AMMC, box 55A, folder 16, Interview with Helena Gutteridge.
59 For Ginger Goodwin and the controversy his death has generated, see Derek Hanebury, *Ginger Goodwin: Beyond the Forbidden Plateau*; Susan Mayse, *Ginger: The Life and Death of Albert Goodwin*; and Mark Leier, "Plots, Shots, and Liberal Thoughts: Conspiracy Theory and the Death of Ginger Goodwin," 214–24.
60 *Vancouver Daily Sun*, 3 August 1918.
61 *BC Federationist*, 9 August 1918.
62 Ibid., 9 August 1918.
63 For the "conspiratorial elite" argument, see Bercuson, *Fools and Wise Men*, 128; and for the "hopeless romantic" interpretation see Angus, *Canadian Bolsheviks*, 53, 56.
64 *BC Federationist*, 11 October 1918.
65 Ibid., 15 November 1918. The man who replaced Winch as secretary of the Auxiliary was also killed by influenza.
66 Like a number of other Marxian socialists, Winch neither drank nor smoked.
67 *BC Federationist*, 24 January 1919.
68 The figure of $50 comes from Gordon Hak, "British Columbia Loggers and the Lumber Workers Industrial Union, 1919–1922," 81.
69 Ibid., 69.
70 Ibid., 70–1.
71 Melvyn Dubofsky, *We Shall Be All: A History of the Industrial Workers of the World*, 406–7.
72 Hak, "British Columbia Loggers," 77–8.
73 Winch advocated the One Big Union to the Moulders' Union in a speech on 7 March 1919. See *BC Federationist*, 14 March 1919.
74 *Vancouver Daily Sun*, 10 March 1919.
75 Ibid., 15 March 1919.
76 *BC Federationist*, 21 March 1919.
77 Ibid.
78 National Archives of Canada (NA), Strikes and Lockouts Files (SLF), vol. 314, strike no. 190C, F. Horrigan, Superintendent O.C. "E" Division to R.N.W.M. Police Commissioner, Regina, 21 May 1919. Horrigan's assessment was confirmed in a 26 May letter to "E" Division by Special Agent #24.
79 NA, SLF, vol. 314, strike no. 190C, Special Agent #24 to "E" Division, 27 May 1919.
80 NA, SLF, vol. 314, strike no. 190C, Inspector A.H. Vernon to the Commissioner, 28 May 1919.

81 NA, SLF, vol. 314, strike no. 190C, *Report of Special Agents #33 and #37*, 4 June 1919.

82 Ibid., 30 June 1919.

83 Kavanagh and Lestor spoke to a meeting of the B.C. Ex-Soldiers and Sailors Council on 18 May 1919. The *Federationist* described Kavanagh as a man who "well knows and thoroughly understands the position an ex-serviceman finds himself in on his return to civil life and conditions that confront him." See *BC Federationist*, 16 May 1919. Several other SPCers spoke to the council during the summer of 1919, including Bill Pritchard, but I have no record of Winch doing so. My suspicion is that the reports by the special agents may be exaggerated versions of statements they got from Winch himself. It is also not beyond the realm of possibility that the Mountie agents could not tell Winch and Kavanagh apart.

84 Midgley's links with the Loggers' Union are somewhat obscure, although he was involved in publishing literature for loggers in languages other than English.

85 *Vancouver Province*, 30 May 1919.

86 NA, SLF, vol. 314, strike no. 190C, *Extracts from the Secret and Confidential Reports of the Royal North West Mounted Police*, 27 May to 2 June 1919.

87 The charge was likely prompted by the VTLC's refusal to make the results of the vote public. They were made public the day after the strike was over. There were 3,305 votes for and 2,499 against, a majority of 806. Twenty-two unions had supported the strike, with fifteen opposed. See *BC Federationist*, 4 July 1919.

88 It would be misleading to push this argument too far. In the spring of 1919 Winch sent a telegram to the acting prime minister charging that a parcel of Lenin pamphlets entitled "Letter to American Workingmen" was being held by postal authorities. Winch observed that attempts to censor working class literature would be met "by more effective action by organized labour" (*Camp Worker*, 2 June 1919).

89 I find problematic Irene Howard's suggestion that Winch resigned the presidency of the VTLC to become secretary of the Loggers' Union because he almost certainly held both positions for some period of time. I think it more likely that he resigned the presidency because of pressure to do so, or out of a desire to do the kind of work he did best. See Irene Howard, *The Struggle for Social Justice in British Columbia: Helena Gutteridge, the Unknown Reformer*, 128.

90 When the *BC Federationist* reported the names of the labour leaders whose homes had been broken into, Winch's name was mysteriously absent. It should also be noted that at the 3 July 1919 meeting of the VTLC J.G. Smith was nominated for president. Again there was no mention of Winch or why he was not seeking the presidency for another term. See the *BC Federationist*, 4 July 1919.

91 Steeves, *Compassionate Rebel*, 55.
92 Hak, "British Columbia Loggers," 73.
93 *Camp Worker*, 26 April 1919.
94 For the British Shop Stewards' movement see James Hinton, *The First British Shop Stewards' Movement.*
95 *Camp Worker*, 26 April 1919.
96 For evidence of Winch's respect for what the Wobblies were doing in the logging camps, see Gregory S. Kealey and Reg Whitaker, eds., *R.C.M.P. Security Bulletins: The Early Years, 1919–1929*, 256.
97 NA, SLF, vol. 317, strike no. 340, Corporal H.E. Taylor to "E" Division, Vancouver, 6 August 1919.
98 NA, SLF, vol. 317, strike no. 340, Inspector H.M. Newson to O.C. "E" Division, 8 August 1919.
99 NA, SLF, vol. 317, strike no. 340, Superintendent Commanding "E" Division to the Commissioner, 11 August 1919. The superintendent's use of the phrase "the means of production" demonstrates the extent to which the language of Marxism reached even into the upper echelons of the Mounted Police in this period of Canadian history.
100 *The Worker*, 30 October 1919.
101 *BC Federationist*, 5 December 1919.
102 See editorials in *The Worker*, 19 September, and 3, 16, and 30 October 1919.
103 *BC Federationist*, 10 June 1921.
104 Ibid., 29 October 1920.
105 Steeves, *Compassionate Rebel*, 62.
106 Ibid., 64.
107 Ibid., 68.
108 NA, J.S. Woodsworth Papers, reel C-9160, frames 686–7, Vancouver Trades and Labour Council to J.S. Woodsworth, 3 March 1926.
109 Dorothy Steeves makes no mention of Winch returning to longshoring at this time.
110 It has generally been assumed that the Socialist Party ceased to exist in 1925, but there is some evidence to suggest that small locals continued to function. Bill Pritchard later claimed that he remained a member of the party until 1927, and there appears to have been an SPC local of some sort in Calgary in the late 1920s. No doubt some B.C. locals also continued to at least hold meetings and publish pamphlets.
111 UBCSC, AMMC, box 45, folder 5, Socialist Party of Canada, *Convention of C.C.F. Affiliates Vancouver*, 27–28 July 1935.
112 Steeves, *Compassionate Rebel*, 75.
113 UBCSC, Walter D. Young Papers, box 5, folder 16, EEW to Walter Nevison, Ocean Falls B.C., 4 October 1931.
114 UBCSC, AMMC, box 45, folder 1, *Minutes of ILP Meeting*, 21 June 1931.

115 Ibid., 6 December 1931.
116 Ibid., 16 January 1932.
117 The legacy of the "Third Period," and especially of the Workers' Unity League, has been a hotly debated topic in Canadian labour history. For the prosecution see Angus, *Canadian Bolsheviks*, 277–88; and for the defence see John Manley, "Canadian Communists, Revolutionary Unionism, and the 'Third Period': The Workers' Unity League, 1929–1935," 167–91.
118 *Labor Statesman*, 10 July 1931.
119 Ibid., 17 July 1931.
120 Ibid., 23 January 1931.
121 Ibid., 23 August 1931.
122 UBCSC, AMMC, box 45, folder 4, *SPC Annual Convention President's Report*, 21–2 January 1933.
123 *Labor Statesman*, July 1932.
124 Thomas Fisher Rare Book Library (TFRBL), Woodsworth Memorial Collection (WMC #35), EEW to Bert Robinson, 9 March 1932.
125 Ibid., 23 July 1932.
126 Ibid., 15 August 1932.
127 Ibid., 17 October 1932.
128 Ibid., 25 April 1933.
129 David Lewis, *The Good Fight: Political Memoirs, 1909–1958*, 381.
130 Winch's support for sex education and nudism should caution us against making broad generalizations about the sexual attitudes of Marxists of the third way. Clearly, he questioned the Victorian values of the society in which he was raised much more strongly than Bill Pritchard or Bob Russell ever did.
131 Eugene Forsey, *A Life on the Fringe: The Memoirs of Eugene Forsey*, 56.
132 UBCSC, AMMC, EEW's Parliamentary Report to SPC for 1934.
133 UBCSC, AMMC, Speech by EEW, mid-1930s.
134 TFRBL, WMC #35, EEW to Bert Robinson, 8 September 1933.
135 UBCSC, AMMC, EEW to J.G. King, 9 June 1935.
136 *B.C. Workers' News*, 1 February 1935.
137 Ibid., 8 February 1935.
138 Ibid., 3 May 1935.
139 Ibid., 31 May 1935. In all probability J. Taylor is Jack Taylor, secretary of the Communist Party (B.C. Section).
140 Ibid., 2 August 1935.
141 Steeves, *Compassionate Rebel*, 107–8.
142 *Vancouver Sun*, 3 July 1937.
143 For the Popular Front in Canada, see Norman Penner, *Canadian Communism: The Stalin Years and Beyond*, 22–3, 150; and for the opportunities opened up for women in the Communist Party by the Popular Front, see Sangster, *Dreams of Equality*, 124–64.

144 *Vancouver Sun*, 2 March 1937.
145 Ibid., 6 July 1937.
146 On 17 March 1937, Ruby Hall had written from Coombs, British Columbia, to tell Eve Smith that at a recent meeting Stephen had declared that Marxian socialism was "an empty impossible theory, utopian" (UBCSC, Evelyn Grey Smith Papers, box 1, folder 1–3, Letters: Incoming H-K).
147 *Vancouver Sun*, 3 July 1937.
148 Steeves, *Compassionate Rebel*, 203; UBCSC, Evelyn Grey Smith Papers, box 1.
149 For an argument that the Winnipeg Declaration did not represent the rightward drift of the party, see Dan Azoulay, "The CCF's 'Winnipeg Declaration': Watershed or Grand Illusion," 110–11, 122.
150 UBCSC, AMMC, EEW to Comrade Darling, 1 October 1956.
151 UBCSC, AMMC, EEW to Lorne Ingle, 13 December 1956.

CHAPTER TWO

1 This was the golden age of the open forum, Sunday night meetings that occurred from Halifax to London, Winnipeg to Vancouver. Attended by thousands of people each week, they brought together priests, ministers, anarchists, Marxists, labourists, military officers, homemakers, feminists, teachers, and many others to debate everything from Christ to currency, Marx to margarine. Marxists of the third way in the SPC, which attacked all other political tendencies, were willing to debate anyone of any political persuasion, any time, anywhere. Pritchard points out that whenever there was an event or issue of political importance, it was often the SPC that invited Liberals, Conservatives, Wobblies, Social Democrats, and others to debate. See Bill Pritchard, Autobiography, Los Angeles (October 1974), tape 1, side A. My thanks to William Rab for providing me with copies of the Pritchard tapes.
2 By the early 1920s articles by leading SPC Marxists were replete with references to "worker" psychology and "middle class" or bourgeois psychology. See, for example, an article by W.H. Hoop entitled "Psychics of the Working Plug" in the *Western Labor News*, 30 April 1920. Rahim sought to use the study of psychology to make the Marxist perspective "more fully comprehensive." See his *The Psychology of Marxian Socialism*, 7.
3 For an excellent analysis of the SPC and the 1919 labour revolt, see Angus, *Canadian Bolsheviks*, 61–2.
4 Alan M. Wald, *The New York Intellectuals*, 268.
5 James Pritchard was a labour activist in England who organized steelworkers and women chain-makers. After emigrating to Canada, along with Samuel Mottishaw he led the drive to organize the coalminers of Extension, on Vancouver Island, into the Western Federation of Miners. See Gloria

Montero, *We Stood Together: First-Hand Accounts of Dramatic Events in Canada's Labour Past*, 2; A. Ross McCormack, *Reformers, Rebels, and Revolutionaries*, 19, 42.

6 Friedrich Engels, *The Condition of the Working Class in England*, 74.

7 The population figure is from John K. Walton, *Lancashire: A Social History, 1558–1939*, 219.

8 Robert Roberts, *The Classic Slum: Salford Life in the First Quarter of the Century*.

9 Penner, Interview with Bill Pritchard, tape 3, side B.

10 Gerald Parsons, ed., *Religion in Victorian Britain*, vol. 1, *Traditions*, 87.

11 Hugh McLeod, *Class and Religion in the Late Victorian City*, 71.

12 Penner, Interview with Bill Pritchard, tape 1, side A.

13 Ibid., NA, David Millar Collection (DMC), Interview with Bill Pritchard, transcript 2, 5. In 1931 Pritchard referred to these schools as the Royal Technical Institute in Salford and the Technical College in Manchester. See the *Municipal Review of Canada* 27, no. 10 (October 1931), 33.

14 Penner, Interview with Bill Pritchard, tape 1, side B; UBCSC FC 3803 U54, SP Series SP5.6, Interview with Bill Pritchard.

15 Penner, Interview with Bill Pritchard, tape 1, side B.

16 Walton, *Lancashire*, 274.

17 Roberts, *The Classic Slum*, 16.

18 Walton, *Lancashire*, 275.

19 Penner, Interview with Bill Pritchard, tape 1, side A.

20 Pritchard does not talk about his mother in this period in any of his interviews, and I do not know if she had accompanied her husband to Canada at the turn of the century, came to Canada with her son, or arrived at a later date.

21 Donald George McKenzie, born in India, had trapped and fished in the Great Slave Lake region and been a coal miner in the Crows Nest Pass. He joined the Socialist Party of Canada in 1904, became secretary in 1908, and was editor of the *Western Clarion* for several years. In February 1916 the *Clarion* published his introduction to the fourth edition of the SPC Manifesto. In his last years he managed a fox farm in Port Alberni, British Columbia. He died of blood poisoning on 11 January 1918 at the age of 42 (*Western Clarion*, 18, 25 January 1918; February 1918). For Kingsley, see 249n29.

22 DMC, Interview with Bill Pritchard, transcript 2, 7, transcript 8, 8; Pritchard, Autobiography, tape 1, side A.

23 See the Winch chapter, 50.

24 *Western Clarion*, 20 May 1911; February 1918. For Hawthornthwaite, see Robin, *Radical Politics and Canadian Labour*, 42–3, 98–9, 101–2.

25 A key figure in the survival of both the party and its journal was Husain Rahim, a South Asian militant who organized a South Asian local, gave the party office space, raised funds, and was on the Dominion Executive Committee for almost two years.

26 *BC Federationist*, 20 May 1912.
27 *Western Clarion*, 24 October 1914.
28 Pritchard said in his interview with David Millar that he "took over ownership" of the *Clarion*. I have not been able to either confirm or deny his claim (DMC, Interview with Bill Pritchard, transcript 3, 7).
29 Born in New York State, Eugene Thornton Kingsley was forced to abandon manual labour following a disabling industrial accident. He gained his fame as a writer and speaker for the Socialist Party of Canada, and published the *Western Clarion* in his print shop for a number of years. He died on 9 December 1929 at the age of 73. In his remembrance of Kingsley old comrade John Sidaway observed: "From Argentine to Alaska, from Florida to Australia, where migratory workers seeking the end of the rainbow have carried the reputations of the stalwarts of the struggle, news of his death will revive in those who knew him memories of earlier battles in the class conflict." See *Labor Statesman*, 13, 27 December 1929; Mark Leier, *Red Flags and Red Tape: The Making of a Labour Bureaucracy*, 145. For Kingsley's impact on the pre-1912 "first generation" of SPCers, see McCormack, *Reformers, Rebels, and Revolutionaries*, 60–1.
30 *Western Clarion*, 15 March 1913.
31 Aileen Kraditor, *The Radical Persuasion, 1890–1917*, 51, 113–53.
32 *Western Clarion*, 22 November 1913.
33 My observations here draw on John Cowley's analysis of Ernest Belfort Bax's ideas on women and the family in his *The Victorian Encounter with Marx: A Study of Ernest Belfort Bax*, 68–90.
34 *Western Clarion*, 14 February 1914.
35 For an insightful analysis of both Rosa Luxemburg's belief in the self-directed revolutionary capacity of the masses and her acceptance of the inevitable unfolding of the objective, "scientific" laws of class struggle, see Stephen Bronner, *Socialism Unbound*, 140.
36 *Western Clarion*, 15 March 1913.
37 Ibid., September 1915.
38 Ibid., November 1916. A possible source of Pritchard's argument is Enrico Ferri, who calls for the "class-conscious organization" of all workers, and the creation of a "class-conscious party." See his *Socialism and Modern Science*, 87.
39 *Western Clarion*, August 1917.
40 On 9 June 1913 Pritchard had married Eleanor Hanson in Vancouver. The marriage took place on a Monday, indicating a civil rather than religious ceremony.
41 Pritchard, Autobiography, tape 1, side B.
42 The 1917–18 period saw the creation of the Federated Labour Party in B.C., the Dominion Labour Party in Manitoba, and the Independent Labour Party in Ontario.

43 *Western Clarion*, August 1917. Pritchard's description is almost identical to the way Bob Russell would later describe the One Big Union.
44 Penner, Interview with Bill Pritchard, tape 3, side B.
45 *BC Federationist*, 5 April 1918.
46 *Western Clarion*, August 1917.
47 Ibid., October 1915.
48 Ibid., August 1917.
49 Penner, Interview with Bill Pritchard, tape 3, side B.
50 *BC Federationist*, 26 July 1918.
51 *Western Clarion*, September 1918.
52 Irving Howe makes this point about the rhetoric and actions of the American Socialist Party during the First World War and the American state's response to it. See his *Socialism and America*, 44–5.
53 Pritchard's repudiation of the syndicalist connection can be found in DMC, Interview with Bill Pritchard, transcript 6, 1–4.
54 Gregory S. Kealey, "1919: The Canadian Labour Revolt," 11–44.
55 DMC, Interview with Bill Pritchard, transcript 8, 6.
56 DMC, Interview with Bill Pritchard, transcript 8, 5–6.
57 Gerald Friesen, "'Yours in Revolt': The Socialist Party of Canada and the Western Canadian Labour Movement," 141. See also Kealey, "1919: The Canadian Labour Revolt," 36.
58 Angus, *Canadian Bolsheviks*, 53.
59 One Big Union, *The Origin of the One Big Union*, 11.
60 Ibid., 30.
61 DMC, Interview with Bill Pritchard, transcript 6, 3.
62 Angus, *Canadian Bolsheviks*, 46–7.
63 *BC Federationist*, 25 April 1919.
64 Ibid., 9 May 1919.
65 *Camp Worker*, 2 June 1919.
66 Ibid., 26 April 1919.
67 Bercuson, *Fools and Wise Men*, 127.
68 Ibid., 128.
69 Pritchard made this point in the speech he gave to the jury at the end of his trial on 24 March 1920. Commenting on a statement Kavanagh made at the Western Labour Conference, Pritchard asserted: "An economic organization of the workers cannot pretend to lay down political lines of action for these workers – that is purely within the province of those workers themselves." See William A. Pritchard, "Excerpts from W.A. Pritchard's Address to the Jury March 23–24, 1920," in Norman Penner, ed., *Winnipeg 1919: The Strikers' Own History of the Winnipeg General Strike*, 270.
70 DMC, Interview with Bill Pritchard, transcript 6, 5–8.
71 Ibid., 10–12.

72 A copy of the letter from Russell to Chris Stephenson, dated 30 January 1919, appeared in the *Red Flag*, 21 June 1919.
73 OBU *Bulletin*, 6 July 1919.
74 Ibid., 30 August 1919.
75 Ibid., 6 September 1919.
76 Pritchard later estimated that he lost some $1,300 in books in the raid. He never again attempted to rebuild this library.
77 In his 1973 interview with Norman Penner, Pritchard stated that he had given only one prepared speech in his entire life.
78 Pritchard, *Address to the Jury*, 4–5.
79 It is interesting to note, however, that Pritchard does not see himself in the tradition of Keir Hardie, H.M. Hyndman, Tom Mann, Ramsay MacDonald, or any of the other leading figures of the British left at the turn of the century.
80 Pritchard, *Address to the Jury*, 39.
81 Marx's statement to this effect was made in Amsterdam following the 1872 Hague Congress of the International Workingmen's Association. According to Hunt, *Classical Marxism*, 334, it was first published in *La Liberté*, 15 September 1872.
82 Pritchard, *Address to the Jury*, 38.
83 Marx, and Lenin and Trotsky as well, could not believe that the working class, faced with the choice, would fail to choose socialism.
84 Bob Burns, secretary of the Calgary local of the SPC, made the point in his 1969 interview with David Millar, that bloodshed is a product of the counter-revolution, not of the revolution itself. Both the French and Russian revolutions stand as clear testimony to Pritchard's and Burns's position. In all probability Pritchard had read Marx and Engels' *Revolution and Counter-Revolution*, which was being sold by the SPC prior to the First World War.
85 Pritchard, *Address to the Jury*, 13.
86 D.C. Masters, *The Winnipeg General Strike*, 133.
87 Kealey, "1919: The Canadian Labour Revolt," 11–44.
88 Angus, *Canadian Bolsheviks*, 55.
89 I can only echo the observations of Gerald Friesen, who is entirely right on this point. See "'Yours in Revolt,'" 154.
90 Montero, *We Stood Together*, 18–19; Penner, Interview with Bill Pritchard, tape 2, side A. It is revealing that Robert Roberts specifically identifies going to Gilbert and Sullivan productions as something the Salford upper class, not the working class, did (Roberts, *The Classic Slum*, 151).
91 Pritchard, Autobiography, tape 2, side B. According to Winnipeg SPCer Alex Shepherd, Kohn set up three study classes upon arrival – in history, economics, and speaking. He also engaged in five debates, one with a Professor Clark of the University of Manitoba, who "frankly admitted that Kohn knew more about economics than he did." In 1916 Kohn helped establish

what would later become the World Socialist Party of the United States and was for many years an influential Marxist critic of the Bolshevik Revolution. He died in Wales of tuberculosis on 28 December 1944. *Western Socialist*, February 1945.

92 Pritchard became ill while in prison, and his ear ran for about six months after he got out. The infection resulted in a slight loss of hearing which he suffered from for the rest of his life.

93 *OBU Bulletin*, 5 March 1921. The daily press claimed that the total number of people who filled the hall or were turned away was only six thousand (*Manitoba Free Press*, 1 March 1921).

94 *OBU Bulletin*, 5 March 1921.

95 Later in life Pritchard observed that he had looked back "on my own misguided past and discovered I was emotional more often than not" (McCormack, Interview with Bill Pritchard, tape 3, side A).

96 *OBU Bulletin*, 2 April 1921.

97 Penner, Interview with Bill Pritchard, tape 2, side A.

98 Helena Gutteridge later recalled that, while Pritchard was in prison, Winch collected money for his family (UBCSC, AMMC, M397, box 55A, folder 16, Interview with Helena Gutteridge).

99 *Vancouver World*, 31 October 1923.

100 Ibid., 7 November 1923.

101 Ibid., 14 November 1923.

102 *Vancouver Province*, 5 December 1923.

103 *Vancouver Sun*, 8 December 1923.

104 *Vancouver Province*, 28 January 1924.

105 In the mid 1930s A.M. Stephen, a member of the B.C. section of the Socialist Party of Canada, argued that a revolutionary program is something you develop, not something you adopt.

106 UBCSC, FC 3803 U54, Tape Recordings, SP Series #5.6, Interview with Bill Pritchard.

107 *Western Clarion*, 16 July 1921.

108 Two points need to be made here: The first is that even leading supporters of the Third International – notably Jack Kavanagh – had serious reservations about the formation of an underground party. The second is that new information now coming to light through the Access to Information process is revealing just how well infiltrated the Communist Party was with police agents.

109 Canadian Security Intelligence Service (CSIS), Kavanagh File, *RCMP Report*, 30 December 1921. I would like to thank David Akers for directing me to this reference.

110 Angus, *Canadian Bolsheviks*, 72–5. It should be noted that former SPCers such as Jack Kavanagh and Malcolm Bruce, who did join the Communist Party, made speaking engagements one of their major activities as well.

111 *BC Federationist*, 29 February 1924.
112 In the 1930s and '40s the CCF would use a very similar argument to great effect in discrediting the role of the Communist Party in the trade unions.
113 *Western Clarion*, 16 November 1923.
114 Ibid., 16 July 1924.
115 *Labor Statesman*, 25 April 1924.
116 Ibid., 11 July 1924.
117 Running in Comox in the 1916 provincial election, Pritchard received 246 votes, 11.57 per cent of the total. In the 1924 provincial election he ran in Nanaimo, winning a very respectable 31.14 per cent of the vote (*Electoral History of British Columbia*, 125, 152).
118 *Western Clarion*, July–August 1925.
119 UBCSC, Vertical File #284, W.A. Pritchard Typescript, 24.
120 Pritchard was thinking specifically of the right to picket peacefully during strikes.
121 *Labor Statesman*, 13 August 1926.
122 Pritchard was not alone in the emphasis on the national context. The Communist Party was firmly ensconced in a debate about the nature of Canada. The key issue was whether the country should be seen as an imperialist power or as an economic colony of Britain and the United States. In these same years the One Big Union was drifting toward a more nationalist stance, which was perhaps inevitable given its emphasis on local union control and breaking away from the American-led international unions.
123 *Labor Statesman*, 27 August 1926.
124 UBCSC, FC 3803 U54, Tape Recordings, SP Series P #5.6, Interview with Bill Pritchard.
125 *Labor Statesman*, 3 June 1927.
126 Ibid., 8 July 1927.
127 Ibid., 12 August 1927.
128 Ibid., 23 December 1927. In the 1918–19 period, police agents considered Pritchard a difficult speaker to follow. He had a rambling style, and his many allusions to Marxist theory and historical and literary figures could have been confusing, especially for anyone not schooled in the working-class culture of the time.
129 *OBU Bulletin*, 27 December 1927. On the rise of the CIO, see David Brody, *Workers in Industrial America*, 82–119.
130 Simon Fraser University Archives (SFUA), Burnaby Council Minute Book, 28 September 1927 – 13 November 1928.
131 Later in life Pritchard tried to give interviewers the impression that he had been talked into almost every political involvement of his entire career. While there may be some truth to the claim in certain instances, as in the case of running for councillor in Burnaby, in others he was being deliberately misleading. A case in point was his involvement with the CCF.

132 South Burnaby was more middle class, while North Burnaby was essentially a bedroom community for workers employed in Vancouver and New Westminster. For more details on the class composition of Burnaby, see Bettina Bradbury, "The Road to Receivership: Unemployment and Relief in Burnaby North Vancouver City and District and West Vancouver, 1929–1933."

133 PAM, MG 10 A14–2 file no. 24, OBU–CLC, Joint Executive Board Minutes, 13 June 1928.

134 Ibid., 26 June 1928.

135 SFUA, Burnaby Council Minute Book, 28 September 1927 – 13 November 1928.

136 *Burnaby Broadcast*, 2 January 1930.

137 Ibid., 23 January 1930.

138 Pritchard once described the late 1920s as "probably a period I want to forget" (UBCSC FC 3803 U 54, Tape Recordings, SP Series P #5.6, Interview with Bill Pritchard).

139 *Burnaby Broadcast*, 16 January 1930.

140 PAM, ASL, Alex Shepherd to David Bercuson, 24 September 1969.

141 *Labor Statesman*, 24 January 1930.

142 See the *Burnaby Broadcast*, 28 August 1930, for a copy of a letter Pritchard sent to the Minister of Labour, charging him with seriously underestimating the unemployment problem.

143 The Burnaby Council may have been the only one in Canada that met with the unemployed on a weekly basis.

144 *Burnaby Broadcast*, 9 and 30 March 1931.

145 NA, R.B. Bennett Papers, Reel M-1451 Frames 491885–491888, W.A. Pritchard to R.B. Bennett, 22 July 1931.

146 *Burnaby Broadcast*, 24 September 1931. Also in September 1931, Pritchard attended the 31st Annual Convention of the Union of Canadian Municipalities at Vernon, British Columbia, where he served on the Resolutions Committee and spoke in defence of working-class families whose mortgages were being foreclosed or whose homes were reverting to the municipality in tax sales. See *Municipal Review of Canada* 27, no. 12 (December 1931), 21.

147 From *Burnaby Broadcast*, 24 September 1931.

148 *Vancouver Sun*, 23 September 1931.

149 NA, SLF, F.E. Reid, manager, to all Barnet foremen, 21 September 1931.

150 *New Westminster British Columbian*, 8 October 1931.

151 *Unemployed Worker*, 10 October 1931.

152 Ibid., 24 October 1931.

153 *New Westminster British Columbian*, 10 November 1931.

154 *Vancouver Sun*, 2 December 1931.

155 *New Westminster British Columbian*, 8 December 1931.

156 *Vancouver Daily Province*, 4 January 1932.
157 *Burnaby Broadcast*, 18 February 1932.
158 Ibid., 21 April 1932.
159 Ibid., 17 December 1931.
160 Penner, Interview with Bill Pritchard, tape 3, side A. One of the highlights of the trip for Pritchard was meeting and talking to Bob Russell. The full text of his talk on unemployment can be found in the *Municipal Review of Canada* 28, no. 8 (August 1932), 14–19.
161 Burnaby *Broadcast*, 3 March 1932.
162 Ibid., 24 August 1932.
163 SFUA, Burnaby Council Minute Book, 27 December 1932.
164 *OBU Bulletin*, 11 May 1933.
165 UBCSC, AMMC, box 54A, folder 4, Robert Skinner to Angus MacInnis, 4 May 1933.
166 UBCSC, AMMC, box 54B, folder 10A, W.A. Pritchard to J.S. Woodsworth, 4 July 1934. In his letter Pritchard refers sarcastically to "our Socialist Party friends, wedded more to phrases than to facts."
167 *Commonwealth*, 31 May 1933.
168 There are many attacks in the old *Western Clarion* on the Dominion Executive Committee, but rarely were the individual members of that committee singled out.
169 UBCSC, Associated CCF Clubs, box 45, folder 8.
170 UBCSC, CCF Provincial Party, box 45 folder 9.
171 PAM, ASL, Alex Shepherd to David Bercuson, 4 April 1969.
172 *Commonwealth*, 7 June 1933.
173 Ibid., 19 July 1933. Emphasis on "feelings" is in the original.
174 *OBU Bulletin*, 10 August 1933. Note the biblical reference from the pen of a scientific socialist.
175 Ibid., 14 September 1933. Section 4 of the Regina Manifesto refers to agriculture as "the greatest Canadian industry."
176 Ibid., 28 September 1933. Morrison's letter bears witness to both the staying power of the SPC's educational efforts and the fact that those efforts had an impact even in rural Saskatchewan.
177 Ibid., 5 October 1933.
178 *Commonwealth*, 18 October 1933.
179 Ibid., 20 December 1933.
180 In fact, the evidence suggests that both Pritchard and Vic Midgley, another old SPC radical, were essentially spying on Winch and other B.C. SPCers and reporting their activities to the CCF leadership.
181 *Commonwealth*, 27 September 1933.
182 Ibid., 3 May 1934.
183 Ibid., 1 March 1934.
184 Ibid., 14 June 1935.

185 Of note is the fact that Pritchard used the occasion to call for more cultural, particularly musical, development in the socialist movement (*Commonwealth*, 12 July 1935).
186 Ibid., 2 August 1935.
187 UBCSC, AMMC, box 45, folder 10.
188 Steeves, *Compassionate Rebel*, 83.
189 *Commonwealth*, 24 January 1934.
190 Steeves, *Compassionate Rebel*, 83.
191 Ibid., 111.
192 *Commonwealth*, 28 August 1936.
193 UBCSC, AMMC, box 45, folder 12.
194 *Commonwealth*, 4 September 1936.
195 Later in life Pritchard recognized that Winch had not wanted to take the leadership of the party from Connell but had wanted it very badly for his son Harold.
196 J. M., "Social Saviors in Business," *Western Socialist*, February 1937.
197 J.N. B., "Notes from the West Coast: The B.C. Election," *Western Socialist*, June 1937.
198 J.N. B., "Notes on the B.C. Election," *Western Socialist*, July 1937.
199 *Vancouver Sun*, 24 September 1937.
200 UBCSC, AMMC, box 54A, folder 10, Dorothy Steeves to Angus MacInnis, 25 January 1938.
201 *Commonwealth*, 4 January 1935.
202 UBCSC, AMMC, box 54A, folder 10, Dorothy Steeves to Angus MacInnis, 25 January 1938.
203 Ibid., Dorothy Steeves to Angus MacInnis, 7 February 1938.
204 *Socialist Fulcrum* 11, no. 4 (1978).
205 W.A. Pritchard, "Some Thoughts on the Philosophy of History of Karl Marx," July 1970.
206 W.A. Pritchard, "Hegel – The Profound Philosopher!," 30 April 1971.
207 I would like to thank Adam Buick of the Socialist Party of Great Britain for providing me with a list of these papers and copies of some of Pritchard's theoretical articles.
208 It should be pointed out that in his later years Pritchard placed more emphasis on the education of young people and less on the education of workers than he had in his youth.
209 *Western Socialist* 42, no. 5 (1975).
210 Here one is reminded of the fact that Pritchard's article on the demise of the *Western Clarion* was entitled "The Curtain Call," a striking example of his tendency to see life as theatre.
211 W.A. Pritchard, "The State Trials Winnipeg, Manitoba, 1920: Text of a proposed address to the student body of the Winnipeg University by the only living defendant of that famous trial" (no date), 1.

212 UBCSC, AMMC, box 56A, folder 19, Bill Pritchard to Dorothy Steeves, 15 June 1959.
213 William Rab to the author, 28 September 1994.
214 W.A. Pritchard, "Materialist Conception of History," May 1972.
215 *Democrat* 22, no. 1 (December 1981/January 1982).
216 Pritchard, Autobiography, tape 2, side B.
217 Penner, Interview with Bill Pritchard, overflow tape no. 1.

CHAPTER THREE

1 A notable exception to the general decline of the IWW in Canada occurred in northern Ontario, where the Wobblies retained a vibrant political and cultural presence in the 1920s and early 1930s among Finnish bushworkers. As elsewhere, however, many Wobblies, both before and after the labour revolt of 1919, became Communists. See Ian Radforth, *Bosses and Bushworkers: Logging in Northern Ontario 1900–1980*, 111–13, 119–20, 123–4, 131–2. For key Wobbly organizers who became prominent Communists see J. Donald Wilson, "The Ethnic Voice: The Canadian Sojourn of a Finnish-American Radical" and A.T. Hill, "Historic Basis and Development of the Lumber Workers Organization and Struggles in Ontario."
2 University of Western Ontario Regional Collection (UWORC), London Labour Project (LLP), box 4982, file 26, Interview with Charles Buck, 19 January 1974. Buck, a London high school teacher and political "progressive" in the 1930s, considered Mould a Christian Socialist who was more sentimental than theoretical.
3 UWORC, Reminiscences and Papers of Arthur Mould, 1879–1961 (RPAM), Reminiscences of Arthur Mould, 16.
4 All biographical information about Arthur Mould's life in the years 1879–1919 is drawn from Reminiscences of Arthur Mould, unless otherwise noted. Page references are to Mould's own handwritten copy.
5 In the session of 1879, the year of Arthur Mould's birth, the British House of Commons passed four inclosure bills. In the 1880 session seven were passed, to be followed by three in 1881, and another three in 1882. See *Hansard's Parliamentary Debates*, vols. 249 (1879), 256 (1880), 265 (1881), 275 (1882).
6 David Howell, *British Workers and the Independent Labour Party, 1888–1906*, 181.
7 For a concise, informative definition of the "new unionism," see Hobsbawm, *Workers: Worlds of Labor*, 152.
8 Howell, *British Workers*, 181–4.
9 RPAM, Reminiscences of Arthur Mould, 13.
10 Ibid., 14.

11 Richard Price, *An Imperial War and the British Working Class: Working-Class Attitudes and Reactions to the Boer War, 1899–1902*, 46–96.
12 Ibid., 73.
13 RPAM, Reminiscences of Arthur Mould, 35.
14 Anti-British sentiment was fleeting and may have been used by English immigrants as a way of rationalizing their lack of success in finding better-paying jobs in Canada. As a baker, Mould practised a trade that was in demand and gave him an advantage over many other immigrants, anti-British sentiment notwithstanding. See A. Ross McCormack, "Cloth Caps and Jobs: The Ethnicity of English Immigrants in Canada, 1900–1914," 178–9.
15 RPAM, Reminiscences of Arthur Mould, 40.
16 Charles Davies, *Bread Men: How the Westons Built an International Empire*, 20.
17 Ibid., 39–40.
18 Ibid., 39.
19 RPAM, Reminiscences of Arthur Mould, 51.
20 James Naylor, *The New Democracy: Challenging the Social Order in Industrial Ontario, 1914–25*, 166–7.
21 UWORC, LLP, Bryan D. Palmer, "Industrialization and the Emergence of a Local Proletariat: The Case of London, Ontario" (unpublished paper, 1973), 25–6.
22 RPAM, Reminiscences of Arthur Mould, 68.
23 Bryan D. Palmer, *Working-Class Experience*, 70.
24 Gregory S. Kealey and Bryan D. Palmer, *Dreaming of What Might Be*, 62–3.
25 Bryan D. Palmer, "'Give Us the Road and We Will Run It': The Social and Cultural Matrix of an Emerging Labour Movement," 106–24.
26 Naylor, *The New Democracy*, 167.
27 Mould does not say why he did not attempt to organize one, although it is likely that he felt he could not risk losing his job when his family was young and growing.
28 Naylor, *The New Democracy*, 76.
29 In southern Ontario working-class linkages with the Conservative Party went back to the passing of the Trades Union Bill in 1872. The ties were reinforced when Conservative politicians enlisted labour support for the National Policy of 1879. They were appealed to again during the federal election of 1911, when Canadian manufacturers opposed to reciprocity with the United States told workers that a vote for the Conservatives, and against the Liberal free traders, was a vote to save their jobs. On the Trades Union Bill see Palmer, *Working-Class Experience*, 93; Morton, *Working People*, 27.
30 RPAM, Reminiscences of Arthur Mould, 56.
31 Robin, *Radical Politics and Canadian Labour*, 30.
32 Peter Campbell, Interview with Helen Mould Rawson and Jesse Mould Mihlik, 19 December 1994, tape 1, side A.

33 Their friendship apparently did not survive Mould's joining the Communist Party. See RPAM, Reminiscences of Arthur Mould, 60.
34 *London Free Press*, 3 January 1916.
35 Ibid., 20 March 1916.
36 Ibid., 3 April 1916.
37 Ibid., 28 February 1916.
38 Ibid., 29 May 1916.
39 Ibid., 8 May 1916.
40 For the organization and program of the ILP see Naylor, *The New Democracy*, 91–6.
41 Ibid., 99.
42 RPAM, Reminiscences of Arthur Mould, 68.
43 Roderick Lewis, *Centennial Edition of a History of the Electoral Districts, Legislatures and Ministries of the Province of Ontario, 1867–1968*, 203.
44 *London Advertiser*, 5 May 1919.
45 RPAM, Reminiscences of Arthur Mould, 73.
46 *London Free Press*, 16 October 1919.
47 RPAM, Reminiscences of Arthur Mould, 65.
48 The history of federal labour unions in Canada is discussed in Robert H. Babcock, *Gompers in Canada: A Study in American Continentalism before the First World War*, 39–40, 99–100, 102–3, 188–9.
49 Thomson, like Mould, was not a trade unionist.
50 UWORC, London Trades and Labour Council Minute Book, 1918–1923, Minutes, 21 May 1919.
51 RPAM, Reminiscences of Arthur Mould, 66.
52 Ibid., 83.
53 *Labour Herald*, 21 April 1921.
54 Ibid., 24 March and 21 April 1921.
55 RPAM, Reminiscences of Arthur Mould, 86.
56 Ibid., 78.
57 Ibid., 88.
58 Jack Scott, *A Communist Life: Jack Scott and the Canadian Workers Movement, 1927–1985*, 23.
59 RPAM, Reminiscences of Arthur Mould, 74, 83.
60 Near the end of his life Mould insisted that he was not seeking power and wealth, the proof being that he ended up without it (RPAM, Reminiscences of Arthur Mould, 67).
61 *Industrial Banner*, 24 January 1919.
62 *London Free Press*, 3 April 1920.
63 *Labour Herald*, 19 May 1921.
64 UWORC, LLP, box 4982, file 13, *London Labour, 1921–1930*.
65 *Labour Herald*, 17 November 1921.
66 Ibid., 19 May 1921.

67 UWORC, RPAM, Frank Burke to Frank Morrison, 6 July 1923. In his letter Burke points out that Mould "is an employer of labor and roofing contractor," while Thomson "runs a little tea and sandwich booth in the market house basement."
68 Ibid., Frank Morrison to Frank Burke, 20 July 1923.
69 RPAM, Reminiscences of Arthur Mould, 66.
70 Robin, *Radical Politics and Canadian Labour*, 248–50.
71 The situation was more contradictory than this, because right-wing candidates were also endorsed by the CLP.
72 UWORC, RPAM, *Ruling of Tom Moore.*
73 Naylor, *The New Democracy*, 236.
74 Campbell, Interview with Helen Mould Rawson and Jesse Mould Mihlik, tape 1, side A.
75 Robin, *Radical Politics and Canadian Labour*, 258.
76 Subsequent developments, especially the ousting of Communists from the LLP, would suggest that Menzies was right.
77 *The Worker*, 14 August 1926.
78 Ibid., 11 September 1926. The Labour Organization in Canada (LOC) (*Sixteenth Annual Report* (1926), 162, claims that he was expelled from the London Labour Party, but given that he was still eligible to be nominated as a candidate in the election, *The Worker* version makes more sense.
79 Ibid., 11 September 1926.
80 LOC, *Sixteenth Annual Report* (1926), 162.
81 Menzies was a member of the Canadian Brotherhood of Railway Employees.
82 *Canadian Labor World*, 29 April 1926.
83 Allen Mills, *Fool for Christ: The Political Thought of J.S. Woodsworth*, ix.
84 Ibid., 19.
85 Ibid., 255.
86 *Canada Forward*, 15 April 1927.
87 LOC, *Seventeenth Annual Report* (1927), 223–4.
88 Ibid., 224.
89 Robin, *Radical Politics and Canadian Labour*, 269.
90 Ibid., 263.
91 LOC, *Eighteenth Annual Report* (1928), 175.
92 LOC, *Twentieth Annual Report* (1930), 178–9.
93 Scott, *A Communist Life*, 23.
94 NA, RG27, vol. 3130, file no. 89, *3rd Annual Convention of the LPO*, London Labour Hall, 3–4 April 1931.
95 Gerald Caplan, *The Dilemma of Canadian Socialism: The CCF in Ontario*, 23. Caplan's claim that SPC membership "probably never reached one thousand" is low, even for Ontario. At its peak the party's national membership was closer to four thousand than to one thousand. In the spring of 1911 there were twelve hundred members in Ontario alone.

96 Caplan, *The Dilemma of Canadian Socialism*, 57.

97 TFRBL, WMC, box 9, SPC Ontario, Minutes, 1932–35, Minutes of Conference called to Consider the Formation of a Socialist Party. The conference cannot have been too far out on the fringe, as greetings from the Socialist Party of America were read.

98 Both MacDonald and Moriarty were expelled from the Communist Party of Canada in 1930, although MacDonald's expulsion did not become "official" until February 1931. A more in-depth analysis of the expulsions can be found in Angus, *Canadian Bolsheviks*, 305–13.

99 A report drawn up by the Toronto branch of the International Left Opposition in 1934 claimed that the party started out in the fall of 1932 with eight or nine members. By May 1934 the membership had grown to thirty-six or thirty-seven. There does not appear to have been a concerted effort to take over the OSP, described in the report as "a playground for Stalinites, Lovestoneites and a couple of our own people" (Public Archives of Ontario [PAO], MacDonald-Spector Collection, box 1, series 1, Toronto Branch Report, 1934.)

100 NA, CCF Files, MG28 IV 1, vol. 10, Conference–1932, Minutes of Ontario Conference – Political Labour and Socialist Groups.

101 NA, CCF Files, MG 28 IV 1, vol. 41, Ontario General Correspondence, 1932–34, Minutes of Labor Conference Held in Cumberland Hall, Toronto.

102 Naylor, "Politics and Class," 10–11.

103 Ibid., 4.

104 Ibid., 14.

105 TFRBL, WMC, box 9, SPC Ontario, Minutes, 1932–35, Secretary's Annual Report, March 1933.

106 NA, CCF Files, MG 28 IV 1, vol. 41, Ontario General Correspondence, 1932–34, Bert Robinson to J.S. Woodsworth, 16 April 1933.

107 NA, CCF Files, MG 28 IV 1, vol. 41, Ontario General Correspondence, 1932–34, Minutes of Labor Conference in Cumberland Hall, Toronto, 23 April 1933.

108 NA, CCF Files, MG 28 IV 1, vol. 41, Ontario General Correspondence, 1932–34, Arthur Mould's Address to the Labour Party of Ontario Convention, Brantford, 1933.

109 *Toronto Star*, 3 May 1933.

110 Woodsworth, in a letter to Bert Robinson, said that for years he had tried to cooperate with the Communists, and "every time was double-crossed." See NA, CCF Files, MG 28 IV 1, vol. 41, Ontario General Correspondence, 1932–34, J.S. Woodsworth to Bert Robinson, 18 April 1933.

111 NA, CCF Files, MG 28 IV 1, vol. 41, Ontario General Correspondence, 1932–34, Minutes of Labor Conference ... Resolutions.

112 TFRBL, WMC, box 9, SPC Ontario, Minutes, 1932–35, Secretary's Quarterly Report, 25 June 1933.

113 *London Free Press*, 27 June 1933.
114 Ibid., 26 June 1933.
115 Ibid., 28 June 1933.
116 Ibid., 30 June 1933.
117 Ibid., 12 July 1933.
118 Ibid., 28 August 1933.
119 TFRBL, WMC, box 8, SPC General Manuscript Material, Fred Hodgson to Bert Robinson, 21 September 1933.
120 NA, CCF Files, MG 28 IV 1, vol. 41, Ontario General Correspondence, 1932–34, Arthur Mould to J.S. Woodsworth, 10 October 1933.
121 TFRBL, WMC, box 8, SPC General Manuscript Material, Elizabeth Morton to the Annual Convention of the Ontario Association of C.C.F. Clubs, 17 November 1933.
122 *London Free Press*, 28 August 1933.
123 NA, CCF Files, MG 28 IV 1, vol. 41, Ontario General Correspondence, 1932–34, Arthur Mould to J.S. Woodsworth, 10 October 1933.
124 Campbell, Interview with Helen Mould Rawson and Jesse Mould Mihlik, tape 1, side A.
125 TFRBL, WMC, box 8, SPC General Manuscript Material, Fred Hodgson to Al Downs, January–February 1934.
126 Buck and seven other Communists had been arrested in August and convicted in November 1931 under Section 98 of the Criminal Code for belonging to an illegal organization. See Penner, *Canadian Communism*, 118–21.
127 NA, CCF Files, MG 28 IV 1, vol. 41, Ontario General Correspondence, 1932–34, Arthur Mould to J.S. Woodsworth, 23 February 1934.
128 Caplan, *The Dilemma of Canadian Socialism*, 54.
129 *Toronto Daily Star*, 12 March 1934.
130 Caplan, *The Dilemma of Canadian Socialism*, 58.
131 *London Free Press*, 12 March 1934.
132 Ibid., 19 April 1934.
133 Mould may have been involved in one final effort to give the third way an organizational home in Ontario. The report of the CCF Provincial Council Meeting held on 18 August 1934 comments that "the 6 branches of the Socialist Party of Ontario will have nothing to do with the CCF and have attempted to form still another party, somewhere to the left between the CCF and the Communist party" (Queen's University Archives, CCF/NDP Records, Coll. 1001a, Box 29, Secretary's Report for Provincial Council Meeting, 18 August 1934).
134 Naylor, "Politics and Class," 31.
135 Maurice Isserman, *If I Had a Hammer: The Death of the Old Left and the Birth of the New Left*, 13.
136 *London Free Press*, 1 May 1935.

137 Ibid., 20 January 1936.
138 *OBU Bulletin*, 21 March 1929.
139 CSIS, RCMP Report, Mould File, no. 90-A-44, 2 July 1935.
140 *London Free Press*, 23 February 1942.
141 United Church Archives (Toronto), Micro. PP, SM1 no. 1, A.E. Smith Personal Papers, National Conference for Democratic Rights Held in Convention Hall, Chateau Laurier, Ottawa, 22–23 February 1942; CSIS, RCMP Report, Mould File, 25 February 1942.
142 CSIS, RCMP Report, Mould File, 13 March 1942.
143 Ibid., 10 August 1943.
144 *Canadian Tribune*, 4 September 1943.
145 CSIS, RCMP Report, Mould File, 9 March and 30 May 1950.
146 Ibid., 6 November 1950.
147 *London Free Press*, 25 May 1951.
148 *Canadian Tribune*, 4 June 1956.
149 *National Affairs Monthly*, November 1956.
150 Penner, *Canadian Communism*, 245.
151 *National Affairs Monthly*, November 1956.
152 Penner, *Canadian Communism*, 245.
153 *National Affairs Monthly*, April 1957.
154 *Canadian Tribune*, 5 October 1959.
155 *Canadian Tribune*, 1 September 1958.
156 Campbell, Interview with Helen Mould Rawson and Jesse Mould Mihlik, tape 1, side B.
157 *Canadian Tribune*, 16 May 1960.
158 *Marxist Review*, July–August 1961.
159 *Canadian Tribune*, 18 December 1961.

CHAPTER FOUR

1 PAM, R.B. Russell Collection (RBRC), MG 10, A14–2, Biography.
2 Parsons, *Religion in Victorian Britain*, 133.
3 Ibid., 138.
4 T.C. Smout, *A Century of the Scottish People, 1830–1950*, 202. Russell, unlike many Marxists of the third way, was prone to "vice": like his hero, Robert Burns, he was known to take a drink or two, especially at New Year's.
5 Orlikow, Interview with Bob Russell, transcript 4, 1.
6 The best general analysis of labourism in Canada is Craig Heron, "Labourism and the Canadian Working Class," 45–75. For labourism in Ontario see James Naylor, "Ontario Workers and the Decline of Labourism," 278–300. On the labourist milieu that Bob Russell encountered on his arrival in Winnipeg, see McCormack, *Reformers, Rebels, and Revolutionaries*, 77–97.

7 Mary Jordan, *Survival: Labour's Trials and Tribulations in Canada*, 8. According to Jordan the materials were provided by the CPR, a company not noted for its benevolence but obviously willing to promote the "right" cause.
8 Ibid., 8. A similar split existed in the Winch household, which resulted in Linda Winch becoming a spiritualist in the 1920s.
9 Orlikow, Interview with Bob Russell, transcript 4, 1.
10 *Western Labor News*, 26 December 1919. Max Tessler says that he met Russell in the SPC in 1913 (NA, Shirley Chusick, Interview with Max Tessler, 23 July 1967).
11 Orlikow, Interview with Bob Russell, transcript 4, 1–2.
12 Ibid., transcript 4, 3.
13 Russell's attempt to divide the history of the Winnipeg SPC into "academic" and "trade union" segments clearly overlooks major "first generation" figures, such as George Armstrong of the Carpenters and W.C. (Bill) Hoop of the Letter Carriers.
14 Chusick, Interview with Max Tessler.
15 Johns, a leading member of the Socialist Party of Canada in 1919, had earlier been a member of the Social Democratic Party. See *The Voice*, 22 January 1915.
16 Orlikow, Interview with Bob Russell, transcript 4, 2.
17 Machinists' *Bulletin*, October 1914.
18 Bercuson, *Confrontation at Winnipeg*, 8.
19 Ibid., 3.
20 The war did not so much produce the construction of new factories as it saw re-tooling of existing plants to manufacture shells. The indispensability of machinists during the war contrasted sharply with the relatively non-essential nature of the building trades.
21 Bercuson, *Confrontation at Winnipeg*, 36.
22 *The Voice*, 21 February 1913.
23 Orlikow, Interview with Bob Russell, transcript 5, 6.
24 Trades and Labour Congress of Canada (TLCC), Thirty-First Annual Convention, Vancouver, Report of Proceedings, 20–25 September 1915.
25 *The Voice*, 2 June 1916.
26 Bercuson, *Confrontation at Winnipeg*, 55.
27 TLCC, Thirty-Second Annual Convention, Toronto, Report of Proceedings, 25–30 September 1916.
28 Orlikow, Interview with Bob Russell, transcript 5, 6.
29 Machinists' *Bulletin*, January 1917.
30 "Women in Railway Shops," *The Voice*, 15 December 1916.
31 "Calgary – C.P.R.," Machinists' *Bulletin*, July 1918.
32 Bercuson, *Confrontation at Winnipeg*, 33.
33 Ibid., 34.

34 The most influential work on the topic of workers' control has been David Montgomery's *Workers' Control in America*. For Canadian labour historians Montgomery's work is important because he consistently attempts to include developments in Canada.

35 Orlikow, Interview with Bob Russell, transcript 5, 12.

36 Russell's formulation may have come from *The Poverty of Philosophy*, which was being sold by the SPC prior to the First World War. It contains the clearest and simplest statement of the thesis that I am aware of, although Russell's understanding may also have come from *Capital*. See Karl Marx, *The Poverty of Philosophy*, 46–7.

37 David Bercuson is the leading exponent of the theory, although Norman Penner, in *The Canadian Left: A Critical Analysis*, 251, also identifies craft unionism with conservatism, and industrial unionism with radicalism, too categorically. As James Conley points out, portraying skilled workers as the key to labour radicalism in eastern Canada while seeing frontier labourers as the key to radicalism in western Canada is misleading. Conley argues, correctly I think, that the relationship between the two should be the focus. See Conley, "Frontier Labourers, Crafts in Crisis and the Western Labour Revolt," 9–37. His thesis may be even more applicable to Winnipeg than to Vancouver.

38 *The Voice*, 21 January 1916.

39 PAM, RBRC, MG 10 A14–2, Winnipeg Strike Trials – Court of King's Bench, *King vs Russell*.

40 Russell's advocacy of a national industrial union, Gerald Friesen points out, "should not be mistaken for nationalist sentiment on Russell's part." It was a political strategy engaged in by a committed Marxian socialist who saw himself as "a member of an international proletariat." See Friesen, "Bob Russell's Political Thought: Socialism and Industrial Unionism in Winnipeg, 1914 to 1919," in his *River Road: Essays on Manitoba and Prairie History*, 131.

41 Bercuson, *Confrontation at Winnipeg*, 57.

42 Machinists' *Bulletin*, November 1917.

43 Ibid., April 1915.

44 Ibid., November 1917.

45 Bercuson, *Fools and Wise Men*, 35–6.

46 Bernard Moss, *The Origins of the French Labor Movement, 1830–1914*, 2.

47 The best general discussion of syndicalism and industrial unionism in Canada is Larry Peterson's "The One Big Union in International Perspective: Revolutionary Industrial Unionism, 1900–1925," 41–66. I am in agreement with his basic argument, and also agree with his critiques of David Bercuson and Martin Robin. His article suffers, however, from a conscious decision to ignore the role of ideas.

48 McCormack, *Reformers, Rebels, and Revolutionaries*, 116.

49 See the following articles in the Machinists' *Bulletin*: "Revolution The Stepping-Stone of Progress," by A.M., and "Winnipeg – C.P.R.," by D.R., November 1918; "A Reply to the Real Disrupters," by R.J.J., February 1919; and "The Way Out," Winnipeg R. House, March 1919.

50 As Larry Peterson points out, railway shop workers were one group of skilled labourers in this period who "tended to see the advantage of industrial organization" (Peterson, "The One Big Union in International Perspective," 61).

51 Orlikow, Interview with Bob Russell, transcript 4, 2. While it may seem a simple point for labour to make, Russell recalled that this type of argument really threw some company negotiators. My suspicion is that Grant Hall was not the only company executive in this period who read Marx in order to meet the workers on their own turf. Without access to the files of the major Canadian companies in this period, however, it is impossible to verify the hypothesis.

52 PAM, RBRC, MG 10 A14–2, Winnipeg Strike Trials – Court of King's Bench, *King vs Russell*.

53 *The Voice*, 5 April 1918.

54 PAM, MG 10 A14–2, Winnipeg Strike Trials – Court of King's Bench, *King vs Russell*.

55 Robin, *Radical Politics and Canadian Labour*, 161.

56 See Craig Heron and Myer Siemiatycki, "The Great War, the State, and Working-Class Canada," in Heron, *The Workers' Revolt in Canada*, 32.

57 Bercuson, *Confrontation at Winnipeg*, 203–4.

58 Ibid., 204. I am not for a moment denying that the IAM itself was racist. The pledge that Russell and Johns refused to take when they joined the union was in existence until 1948. That very fact, however, indicates that members of the Socialist Party were consistently more progressive on the race question than most other unionists. On racism in the IAM see Montgomery, *The Fall of the House of Labor*, 198–201.

59 *Western Labor News*, 10 January 1919.

60 As Tom Mitchell and James Naylor observe, in Calgary one of the manifestations of labour's reaching out to non-Anglo-Saxon workers was the Federal Workers' Union, which sought to organize workers of all ethnic backgrounds, the Chinese included. See their "The Prairies: In the Eye of the Storm," 191.

61 *Western Labor News*, 4 October 1918.

62 Ibid., 20 December 1918.

63 The Socialist Party of Canada was not one of the fourteen banned organizations. The predominantly Anglo-Saxon composition of the party's leadership may have been a key factor, because the federal government and the Mounties identified Bolshevism and anarchism almost exclusively with the "foreign" element in Canadian society.

64 The rules of the SPC prevented its members from appearing on the same platform as the members of other political parties, unless it was to forthrightly denounce those parties' policies. See the *Western Labor News*, 24 January 1919.
65 There is no reason to believe, as Bercuson suggests, that the SPC may have been acting alone in calling the meeting. See Bercuson, *Confrontation at Winnipeg*, 84.
66 *Western Labor News*, 27 December 1918.
67 Ibid., 10 January 1919.
68 Ibid., 24 January 1919.
69 Ibid.
70 OBU, *The Origin of the One Big Union*, 22–3.
71 On this point I am in substantial agreement with Gerald Friesen, "Yours in Revolt," 145.
72 OBU, *The Origin of the One Big Union*, 61.
73 Ibid., 80–2.
74 Ibid., 84.
75 I am suggesting a shift in focus here, not a wholesale rejection of the party's propaganda function. Working with the active minority became an adjunct to that effort, in the way that economic action was seen as adding to, not replacing, political action.
76 PAM, MG 10 A3, OBU Correspondence, 1918–20, Bob Russell to Vic Midgley, 11 April 1919.
77 PAM, RBRC, MG 10 A14–2, Winnipeg Strike Trials – Court of King's Bench, *King vs Russell.*
78 *Western Labor News*, 16 May 1919.
79 On 20 April Dick Johns and Joe Knight had explained the OBU to some three thousand people at a meeting in the Industrial Bureau.
80 *Western Labor News*, 9 May 1919.
81 Bercuson, *Confrontation at Winnipeg*, 112.
82 *Western Labor News, Special Strike Edition* 3, 20 May 1919.
83 Rosa Luxemburg, *The Mass Strike*, 92.
84 Bercuson, *Confrontation at Winnipeg*, 113.
85 Bercuson claims there were three members elected by each union, but the *Western Labor News*, 16 May 1919, says it was two.
86 NA, MG 31 B6, DMC, Interview with Alex Shepherd, 7 August 1969.
87 Bercuson, *Confrontation at Winnipeg*, 121.
88 Quoted in Bercuson, ibid., 121.
89 Jordan, *Survival*, 175.
90 *OBU Bulletin*, 12 August 1919.
91 *Western Labor News*, 15 August 1919.
92 Ibid., 12 September 1919.
93 For Cassidy see Mitchell, "Repressive Measures," 159n89.

94 PAM, RBRC, MG 10 A14–2, Winnipeg Strike Trials – Court of King's Bench, *King vs Russell*.
95 Ibid., Winnipeg Strike Trials – Court of King's Bench, *King vs Russell* – Summation of the Prosecution.
96 Friesen, "Yours in Revolt," 154.
97 Chusick, Interview with Max Tessler.
98 *OBU Bulletin*, 3 January 1920.
99 Ibid., 1 January 1921.
100 Ibid., 25 December 1920.
101 Bercuson, *Confrontation at Winnipeg*, 215–16.
102 The key work on the IWW remains Dubofsky, *We Shall Be All*. On the IWW in British Columbia, see Leier, *Where the Fraser River Flows*.
103 Precisely this argument was presented in the *Western Labor News* in February 1923. In an article reprinted from the *Labor Leader*, the charge was made that both Bob Russell and William Z. Foster of the American Communist Party were doing the same thing. They both "picked on the best organized and best paid workers in the Dominion to try out their experiments on, in spite of the fact that there are thousands of unorganized workers waiting to be organized. But then, of course, there are no treasuries to despoil in the ranks of the non-unionists."
104 CSIS, RCMP Report, Russell File, no. 90-A-43, 10 January 1921.
105 Charles W. Gordon, *Postscript to Adventure: The Autobiography of Ralph Connor*, 361–3.
106 *Western Labor News*, 28 January 1921.
107 Ibid., 16 February 1923.
108 Scott, *A Communist Life*, 117.
109 CSIS, RCMP Report, Russell File, 30 January 1921.
110 *Edmonton Morning Bulletin*, 16 May 1921.
111 CSIS, RCMP Report, Russell File, 22 May 1921.
112 Ibid., 23 May 1921.
113 CSIS, RCMP Report – Railway Transportation Meeting, Russell File, 23 May 1921.
114 PAM, OBU-CLC, Minutes, 22 May 1921; OBU-CLC, Executive Minutes, 27 June 1921.
115 CSIS, RCMP Report, Russell File, 19 January 1921.
116 Ibid., 5 July 1921.
117 Ibid., 24 February 1922.
118 *Western Labor News*, 26 November 1920.
119 PAM, OBU-CLC, Minutes, 5 July 1921.
120 The lottery is discussed in more detail in Bercuson, *Fools and Wise Men*, 217–19.
121 *OBU Bulletin*, 5 and 12 March 1925.

122 Russell ran provincially in 1920 while still in prison. Three of his fellow prisoners – George Armstrong, John Queen, and William Ivens – were elected. Russell lost in an election carried out according to the proportional representation system of voting then in place, but only after thirty-seven counts.

123 The document, dated 15 September 1921, appeared in the *OBU Bulletin*, 17 December 1931.

124 *OBU Bulletin*, 17 December 1931.

125 I suspect his refusal had more to do with wanting to stay and organize for the OBU, and his lack of knowledge about the Profintern, than any principled opposition it.

126 Bercuson, *Fools and Wise Men*, 222–3.

127 PAM, P626, Mary Jordan file – Miscellaneous, R.B. Russell Report, 1922.

128 Communist Party members could be members of the OBU, but they were not allowed to take executive positions.

129 *OBU Bulletin*, 9 November 1922.

130 Ibid., 14 December 1922.

131 Ibid., 18 October 1923.

132 Todd McCallum, "'A Modern Weapon for Modern Man': Marxist Masculinity and the Social Practices of the One Big Union, 1919–1924," 60.

133 Ibid., 59–61.

134 *OBU Bulletin*, 15 January 1925.

135 Jordan, *Survival*, 228.

136 *OBU Bulletin*, 1 January 1925.

137 Bercuson, *Fools and Wise Men*, 228–9.

138 NA, CPC, MG 28 IV 4, vol. 8, file 5, Tim Buck to Rowland Fay, 30 April 1923.

139 The OBU in northern Ontario remains an unexplored topic. In 1927, for example, it had four organizers in northern Ontario. They included Tommy Roberts, a virtually unknown former SPCer and organizer in the B.C. metal mines, who was one of the key Canadian labour organizers in the interwar period. Roberts and other OBU organizers established important OBU bases in northern Ontario.

140 David Frank, "Class Conflict in the Coal Industry Cape Breton, 1922," in Kealey and Warrian, *Essays in Canadian Working Class History*, 169.

141 A 100 per cent strike included maintenance workers, not just miners. It produced the inconvenience of pumping out flooded mines once the strike ended, and possible damage to property.

142 Frank, "Class Conflict in the Coal Industry," 170.

143 *Halifax Citizen*, 18 August 1922; quoted in Frank, "Class Conflict in the Coal Industry," 179.

144 McKay and Morton, "The Maritimes: Expanding the Circle of Resistance," 73–4.

145 Ian McKay and Suzanne Morton observe that "Maritime support for the One Big Union was stronger and more deeply rooted than is often remembered." See ibid., 50.
146 *OBU Bulletin*, 26 July 1923.
147 Bercuson, *Fools and Wise Men*, 235–6.
148 Ibid., 236.
149 During the Lawrence strike Legere was arrested and charged with contempt of court for ignoring an injunction against picketing (*OBU Bulletin*, 31 August 1922).
150 *Workers' Weekly*, 26 September 1924.
151 *Maritime Labor Herald*, 14 June 1924.
152 The Sydney steelworkers were organized into the Amalgamated Association of Iron, Steel, and Tin Workers in 1917, but the union was broken during the 1923 strike.
153 *Maritime Labor Herald*, 23 August 1924. The history of the PWA, and a reinterpretation of its "conservative" ethos, can be found in Ian McKay's " 'By Wisdom, Wile or War': The Provincial Workmen's Association and the Struggle for Working-Class Independence in Nova Scotia, 1879–97," 13–62.
154 *Workers' Weekly*, 26 September 1924.
155 CSIS, O.B.U. – Glace Bay, Nova Scotia, Speech of Bob Russell, Russell File, 26 September 1924.
156 Bercuson, *Fools and Wise Men*, 239–40.
157 CSIS, O.B.U. – Glace Bay, Nova Scotia, Speech of Bob Russell, Russell File, 26 September 1924.
158 *OBU Bulletin*, 2 October 1924.
159 *Workers' Weekly*, 3 October 1924.
160 The gains for the OBU were tempered by the fact that UMWA locals continued to function in both Stellarton and Thorburn (Bercuson, *Fools and Wise Men*, 241).
161 Ibid.
162 *OBU Bulletin*, 18 December 1924.
163 Ibid., 15 January 1925.
164 There is a great need to deal with this issue, but it is beyond the scope of this study. The major battleground was Pictou County where in late 1924 the British Empire Steel Corporation continued to collect union dues for the UMWA from workers now affiliated with the OBU. When the protests of the OBU miners were ignored, the OBU sought and received an injunction to keep the collected dues in trust, pending a trial. In March 1926 Judge Chisholm of the Supreme Court ruled that because the individual amounts were less than $100, he could not rule on the case. Later the $23,000 was handed over to the UMWA. The OBU was caught in a trap. In cases like this they had no recourse other than the courts, which invariably ruled in favour of the companies and the established unions. See PAM, OBU-GEB

Convention Records, 1927, Minutes of Fifth Convention of the OBU, Report on Maritime Provinces, 2–5 May 1927.

165 Bercuson, *Fools and Wise Men*, 242.

166 CSIS, One Big Union Meeting at Westville – Speech of R.B. Russell, Russell File, 13 July 1925.

167 *OBU Bulletin*, 23 July 1925.

168 Ibid., 7 May 1925.

169 Ibid., 14 May 1925.

170 PAM, OBU-GEB Convention Records, 1927, Minutes of Fifth Convention of the OBU: Report on Maritime Provinces, 2–5 May 1927.

171 *OBU Bulletin*, 25 June 1925.

172 Bercuson, *Fools and Wise Men*, 244.

173 Ibid., 243–4.

174 On the role played by OBU organizers in the January 1926 strike against the Minto Coal Company see Allen Seager, "Minto, New Brunswick: A Study in Canadian Class Relations Between the Wars," 81–132.

175 PAM, OBU-GEB Convention Records, 1927, Minutes of Fifth Convention of the OBU: Report on Maritime Provinces, 2–5 May 1927.

176 Bercuson, *Fools and Wise Men*, 244.

177 For the "affair" involving Cassidy and general secretary Catherine Rose, which led to their expulsion from the OBU, see McCallum, "A Modern Weapon for Modern Man," 87–111.

178 Jordan, *Survival*, 193–4.

179 *OBU Bulletin*, 10 September 1925.

180 Ibid., 27 May 1926.

181 Bercuson, *Fools and Wise Men*, 246.

182 *OBU Bulletin*, 5 May 1927.

183 David Montgomery describes the OBU as a "dream" for its American supporters (Montgomery, *Fall of the House of Labor*, 430).

184 *OBU Bulletin*, 29 December 1927.

185 Jordan, *Survival*, 226.

186 *OBU Bulletin*, 11 August 1927.

187 Ibid., 15 September 1927.

188 Ibid., 3 November 1927.

189 Bercuson, *Fools and Wise Men*, 247.

190 *OBU Bulletin*, 4 June 1931; J.M. Milne, *History of the Socialist Party of Canada* [Winnipeg?]: Socialist Party of Canada (no date), 47.

191 PAM, ASL, MG14 C86, Alex Shepherd to David Bercuson, 20 March 1969.

192 See, for example, the 13 August 1920 issue of the *OBU Bulletin* for a report of the recent debate between Joe Knight of the OBU and long-time SPCer W.H. Hoop, who was defending the international craft unions.

193 *OBU Bulletin*, 5 March 1931.

194 Ibid., 12 March 1931.

195 Ibid., 24 September 1931.
196 Ibid., 8 October 1931.
197 Ibid., 25 February 1932.
198 Ibid., 10 and 24 March 1932.
199 Ibid., 14 April 1932.
200 Ibid., 21 April 1932.
201 Ibid., 28 April 1932.
202 Ibid., 20 October 1932.
203 Ibid., 18 May 1933.
204 PAM, RBRC, MG 10 A14–2, file no. 29 (Microfilm 365), OBU-CLC, Joint Executive Board Meeting, 28 June 1932.
205 In his on-going, one-man crusade to deny the founders of the One Big Union any and all credit for being early progenitors of the industrial union movement of the 1930s, David Bercuson continues to make the ludicrous claim that "Russell and the OBU had been arch enemies of industrial unionism." See his "Syndicalism Sidetracked: Canada's One Big Union," in Marcel van der Linden and Wayne Thorpe, eds., *Revolutionary Syndicalism: An International Perspective*, 235.
206 *OBU Bulletin*, 10 August 1933.
207 PAM, OBU-CLC, Minutes, 17 May 1932.
208 Ibid., 3 January 1933.
209 PAM, OBU-CLC, General Executive Board Minutes, 11 November 1933.
210 The appeal of social democracy had already manifested itself in the leadership of the OBU. See PAM, OBU-CLC Joint Executive Board Meeting, 28 June 1932.
211 Ibid., 20 February 1934.
212 Jordan, *Survival*, 241.
213 CSIS, RCMP Report, Russell File, 8 December 1938.
214 Bryan D. Palmer, *Working-Class Experience: Rethinking the History of Canadian Labour, 1800–1991*, 280.
215 CSIS, RCMP Report, Russell File, 8–9 October 1944. Russell's reference to the "servile state" may come from Marx, or it may indicate the influence of Hilaire Belloc's *The Servile State*.
216 *Winnipeg Tribune*, 10 March 1947.
217 CSIS, RCMP Report, Russell File, 29 October 1951. In 1957 Russell's name was still on a list entitled "Subversive Activities within the Manitoba Federation of Labour." In 1960 a Central Registry Certification Sheet listed his affiliation as being the Communist Party of Canada.
218 PAM, ASL, Alex Shepherd to David Bercuson, 20 March 1969.
219 *Winnipeg Free Press*, 28 September 1964.

CONCLUSION

1 Joseph Dietzgen, *The Positive Outcome of Philosophy*, 392.

2 Michel Foucault, *Power/Knowledge: Selected Interviews and Other Writings, 1972–1977*, 126–7.
3 McGowan, *Postmodernism and Its Critics*, 125–6.
4 Matthew Arnold, *Culture and Anarchy*, 34, 56.
5 Ellen Meiksins Wood, *Mind and Politics: An Approach to the Meaning of Liberal and Socialist Individualism*, 22.
6 Joan Wallach Scott, *Gender and the Politics of History*, 72.
7 Gay L. Gullickson, "Commentary: New Labor History from the Perspective of a Women's Historian," in Lenard R. Berlanstein, ed., *Rethinking Labor History*, 212n17.
8 This characteristic of Marxists of the third way was not confined to white working-class British immigrants to Canada. C.L.R. James, the black Trinidadian Marxist, was raised by a mother who imparted to her son the rigid moral Nonconformism of the Wesleyan Methodists, as well as a love of "middle class" British literature and thought. James would have had a great deal to discuss with Bill Pritchard or Arthur Mould, and they would have completely understood his observation that as a young man he was "as righteous as the Angel Gabriel." See C.L.R. James, *Beyond a Boundary*, 25–6, 35–6.
9 Karl Mannheim, *Ideology and Utopia*, 217.
10 Ernesto Laclau and Chantal Mouffe, *Hegemony and Socialist Strategy: Towards a Radical Democratic Politics*; Gareth Stedman Jones, *Languages of Class: Studies in English Working Class History, 1832–1982*. On the first page of his introduction Jones tells us that his English working class is decentred and discursively constructed, claiming that it "may not be possible for a historian to ask what sort of substantive reality 'the working class' as such might have possessed outside the particular historical idioms in which it has been ascribed meaning."
11 Ellen Meiksins Wood, *The Retreat from Class: A New "True" Socialism*, 17–18.
12 Ibid., 76.
13 Francis Fukuyama, "The End of History?" 4.
14 Labriola, *Essays on the Materialistic Conception of History*, 127.
15 Elaine Freedgood, "Banishing Panic: Harriet Martineau and the Popularization of Political Economy," 34, 49–50.
16 King concludes: "It is not alone a new dawn Labor and Capital may summon forth; they can create a wholly new civilization. Let Labor and Capital unite under the inspiration of a common ideal, and human society itself will become transformed. Such is the method of creative evolution." See W.L. Mackenzie King, *Industry and Humanity*, 528.
17 Bryan D. Palmer, *E.P. Thompson: Objections and Oppositions*, x.
18 The intensity of the socialist belief in the education of the workers in late nineteenth and early twentieth century Britain is nicely captured in two books by Stanley Pierson: *Marxism and the Origins of British Socialism* and *British Socialists: The Journey from Fantasy to Politics*.

19 Peter Beilharz, *Labour's Utopias: Bolshevism, Fabianism, Social Democracy*, 126.
20 Ian McKay, "Changing the Subject(s) of History of Canadian Sociology: The Missing Spencerian Marxists, 1890–1940," 22.
21 Den Otter, *British Idealism and Social Explanation*, 94.
22 Beilharz, *Labour's Utopias*, 128.
23 Fukuyama, "*The End of History?*" 18.

Bibliography

ARCHIVAL COLLECTIONS

BURNABY VILLAGE HERITAGE MUSEUM

Ernest Edward Winch Papers

CANADIAN SECURITY INTELLIGENCE SERVICE

Arthur Mould: File No. 90-A-44

Robert Boyd Russell: File No. 90-A-43

METRO TORONTO REFERENCE LIBRARY

James Simpson Papers

J.W. Buckley Collection

NATIONAL ARCHIVES OF CANADA

Communist Party of Canada Records

Co-operative Commonwealth Federation Files

David Millar Collection

Department of Labour, Record Group 27

Department of National Defence, Record Group 24

Royal Canadian/Northwest Mounted Police, Record Group 18

Robert L. Borden Papers

R.B. Bennett Papers

PROVINCIAL ARCHIVES OF MANITOBA

Alex Shepherd Letters

Lionel Orlikow Interviews

Mary Jordan File
One Big Union File
R.B. Russell Collection
William Ivens File
Winnipeg Strike Trial Records

PUBLIC ARCHIVES OF ONTARIO
MacDonald-Spector Collection
Ministry of the Attorney-General, Record Group 22

QUEEN'S UNIVERSITY ARCHIVES
Andrew Glen Papers
CCF/NDP Files

SIMON FRASER UNIVERSITY ARCHIVES
Burnaby Council Minute Book

THOMAS FISHER RARE BOOK LIBRARY
Mrs Helen Rawson (Mould) Papers
Robert J. Kenney Collection
Woodsworth Memorial Collection

UNIVERSITY OF BRITISH COLUMBIA SPECIAL COLLECTIONS
Angus MacInnis Memorial Collection
Arthur J. Turner Papers
Colleen Toppings-Bourke Collection
Dorothy Steeves Papers
Evelyn G. Smith Papers
Reynoldston Research and Studies, Oral History Programmes
Tape Recordings, SP Series
Vertical File 284, Interview with Bill Pritchard

UNITED CHURCH ARCHIVES (TORONTO)
A.E. Smith Personal Papers

UNIVERSITY OF WESTERN ONTARIO REGIONAL COLLECTION
Bricklayers and Masons Files
London Labour Project
London Trades and Labour Council Minutes
Reminiscences and Papers of Arthur Mould, 1879–1961

YORK UNIVERSITY
E.A. Beder Collection

ORAL INTERVIEWS FROM NON-ARCHIVAL SOURCES

McCormack, A. Ross. Interview with Bill Pritchard (16–18 August 1971)
Penner, Norman. Interview with Bill Pritchard (31 July–2 August 1973)
Pritchard, W.A. Autobiography (Los Angeles, 1974)

LABOUR AND SOCIALIST PAPERS

B.C. Workers' News
British Columbia Federationist
British Columbia Labor News
Camp Worker
Canada Forward
Canadian Labor World
Canadian Tribune
Canadian Unionist
The Commonwealth
Cotton's Weekly
Democrat
The Indicator
Industrial Banner
Labor News (Hamilton)
Labor Statesman
Labor World (Montreal)
Labour Herald (London, Ontario)
Machinists' *Bulletin* (Winnipeg)
Maritime Labor Herald
Marxist Review
National Affairs Monthly
One Big Union Bulletin
Red Flag
Socialist Fulcrum
Unemployed Worker
The Voice
Western Clarion
Western Labor News
Western Socialist
Western Wage Earner
The Worker
The Worker (CPC)
Workers' Weekly

NEWSPAPERS AND NON-LABOUR PUBLICATIONS

Burnaby Broadcast
Hansard's Parliamentary Debates (Great Britain)
London Advertiser
London Free Press
Manitoba/Winnipeg Free Press
Municipal Review of Canada
Toronto Star/Daily Star
Vancouver Province/Daily Province
Vancouver Sun
Vancouver World
Victoria Daily Times
Western Lumberman

SECONDARY SOURCES

Anderson, Perry. *Arguments within English Marxism*. London: Verso 1980.

Angus, Ian. *Canadian Bolsheviks: The Early Years of the Communist Party of Canada*. Montreal: Vanguard Publications 1981.

Arnold, Matthew. *Culture and Anarchy.* Indianapolis and New York: Bobbs-Merrill 1971.

Arnold-Forster, Hugh Oakeley. *English Socialism of To-Day.* London: Smith Elder 1908.

Azoulay, Dan. "The CCF's 'Winnipeg Declaration': Watershed or Grand Illusion." *Journal of History and Politics/Revue d'Histoire et de Politique* 10 (1992): 109–27.

Babcock, Robert. *Gompers in Canada: A Study in American Continentalism before the First World War.* Toronto and Buffalo: University of Toronto Press 1974.

Banks, Judith Judd. "Comparative Biographies of Two British Columbia Anthropologists: Charles Hill-Tout and James A. Teit." Master's thesis, University of British Columbia 1970.

Beilharz, Peter. *Labour's Utopias: Bolshevism, Fabianism, Social Democracy.* London and New York: Routledge 1992.

Belloc, Hilaire. *The Servile State.* London and Edinburgh: T.N. Foulis 1912.

Bercuson, David. *Confrontation at Winnipeg.* Montreal and London: McGill-Queen's University Press 1990.

– *Fools and Wise Men: The Rise and Fall of the One Big Union.* Toronto: McGraw-Hill Ryerson 1978.

Blatchford, Robert. *Merrie England.* New York and London: Monthly Review Press 1966.

Bottomore, Tom. *Critics of Society: Radical Thought in North America.* New York: Vintage Books 1969.

Bottomore, Tom, and Patrick Goode. *Austro-Marxism.* Oxford: Clarendon Press 1978.

Boudin, Louis. *The Theoretical System of Karl Marx.* Chicago: Charles H. Kerr 1907.

Bradbury, Bettina. "The Road to Receivership: Unemployment and Relief in Burnaby, North Vancouver City and District and West Vancouver, 1929–1933." Master's thesis, Simon Fraser University 1975.

Brody, David. *Workers in Industrial America.* New York and Oxford: Oxford University Press 1980.

Bronner, Stephen Eric. *Socialism Unbound.* New York and London: Routledge 1990.

Buhle, Mari Jo. *Women and American Socialism, 1870–1920.* Urbana: University of Illinois Press 1981.

Buhle, Paul. *Marxism in the USA.* London: Verso 1987.

Canada. Department of Labour. *Labour Gazette.*

– *Labour Organization in Canada.*

Caplan, Gerald. *The Dilemma of Canadian Socialism: The CCF in Ontario.* Toronto: McClelland & Stewart 1973.

Clarke, Phyllis E. "Application of Marxist Thought to Canada." PhD diss., University of Toronto 1977.

Conley, James R. "Frontier Labourers, Crafts in Crisis and the Western Labour Revolt: The Case of Vancouver, 1900–1919." *Labour/Le Travail* 23 (Spring 1989): 9–37.

Cowen, M.P., and R.W. Shenton. *Doctrines of Development*. London and New York: Routledge 1996.

Cowley, John. *The Victorian Encounter with Marx: A Study of Ernest Belfort Bax*. London and New York: British Academic Press 1992.

Davies, Charles. *Bread Men: How the Westons Built an International Empire*. Toronto: Key Porter 1987.

Den Otter, Sandra. *British Idealism and Social Explanation: A Study in Late Victorian Thought*. Oxford: Clarendon Press 1996.

Dietzgen, Joseph. *The Positive Outcome of Philosophy*. Chicago: Charles H. Kerr 1906.

– *Some of the Philosophical Essays on Socialism and Science, Religion, Ethics, Critique-of-Reason and the World-at-Large*. Chicago: Charles H. Kerr 1917.

Dubofsky, Melvyn. *We Shall Be All: A History of the Industrial Workers of the World*. New York: Quadrangle Books 1969.

Dunayevskaya, Raya. *Rosa Luxemburg, Women's Liberation, and Marx's Philosophy of Revolution*. Sussex: Harvester Press 1981.

Electoral History of British Columbia, 1871–1986. Victoria: Elections British Columbia and the Legislative Library 1988.

Engels, Friedrich.*The Condition of the Working Class in England*. Stanford: Stanford University Press 1968.

– *Socialism: Utopian and Scientific*. New York: International Publishers 1985.

Engels, Friedrich, and Karl Marx. *Germany: Revolution and Counter-Revolution*. London: Martin Lawrence 1933.

Ferri, Enrico. *Socialism and Modern Science*. Chicago: Charles H. Kerr 1909.

Fillmore, Nicholas. *Maritime Radical: The Life and Times of Roscoe Fillmore*. Toronto: Between the Lines 1992.

Fletcher, Roger. *Revisionism and Empire*. London: George Allen & Unwin 1984.

Forsey, Eugene. *A Life on the Fringe: The Memoirs of Eugene Forsey*. Toronto: Oxford University Press 1990.

Foster, John. *Class Struggle and the Industrial Revolution*. London: Methuen 1974.

Foucault, Michel. *Power/Knowledge: Selected Interviews and Other Writings, 1972–1977*. New York: Pantheon Books 1980.

Fournier, Marcel. *Communisme et anticommunisme au Québec (1920–1950)*. Laval: Les Editions Coopératives Albert Saint-Martin 1979.

Frank, David. "Class Conflict in the Coal Industry: Cape Breton 1922." In *Essays in Canadian Working Class History*, edited by Gregory S. Kealey and Peter Warrian, 161–84. Toronto: McClelland & Stewart 1976.

Frank, David, and Nolan Reilly. "The Emergence of the Socialist Movement in the Maritimes, 1899–1916." *Labour/Le Travailleur* 4 (1978): 85–113.

Freedgood, Elaine. "Banishing Panic: Harriet Martineau and the Popularization of Political Economy." *Victorian Studies* 39, no. 1 (Autumn 1995): 33–53.

Friesen, Gerald. "Bob Russell's Political Thought: Socialism and Industrial Unionism in Winnipeg, 1914 to 1919." In *River Road: Essays on Manitoba and Prairie History*, 121–46. Winnipeg: University of Manitoba Press 1996.

– "'Yours in Revolt': The Socialist Party of Canada and the Western Canadian Labour Movement." *Labour/Le Travailleur* 1 (1976): 139–57.

Fukuyama, Francis. "The End of History?" *National Interest* no. 16 (Summer 1989): 3–18.

Geary, Dick. *Karl Kautsky*. Manchester: Manchester University Press 1987.

Goode, John. "E.P. Thompson and 'The Significance of Literature.'" In *E.P Thompson: Critical Perspectives*, 183–203, edited by Harvey J. Kaye and Keith McClelland. Philadelphia: Temple University Press 1990.

Goode, Patrick, ed. *Karl Kautsky: Selected Political Writings*. London and Basingstoke: Macmillan 1983.

Gordon, Charles W. *Postscript to Adventure: The Autobiography of Ralph Connor*. New York: Farrar & Rinehart 1938.

Gray, Robert Q. *The Labour Aristocracy in Victorian Edinburgh*. Oxford: Clarendon Press 1976.

Gulick, Sydney L. *Evolution of the Japanese: Social and Psychic*. New York: Fleming H. Revell 1903.

Gullickson, Gay L. "Commentary: New Labor History from the Perspective of a Women's Historian." In *Rethinking Labor History*, edited by Lenard R. Berlanstein, 200–13. Urbana and Chicago: University of Illinois Press 1993.

Hak, Gordon. "British Columbia Loggers and the Lumber Workers Industrial Union, 1919–1922." *Labour/Le Travail* 23 (Spring 1989): 67–90.

Hanebury, Derek. *Ginger Goodwin: Beyond the Forbidden Plateau*. Vancouver: Pulp Press 1986.

Hegel, G.W.F. *Lectures on the Philosophy of World History: Introduction: Reason in History*. Cambridge: Cambridge University Press 1975.

Heron, Craig. "The Crisis of the Craftsman: Hamilton's Metal Workers in the Early Twentieth Century." *Labour/Le Travailleur* 6 (Autumn 1980): 7–48.

– "Labourism and the Canadian Working Class." *Labour/Le Travail* 13 (Spring 1984): 45–76.

– ed. *The Workers' Revolt in Canada*. Toronto: University of Toronto Press 1998.

Heywood, Paul. *Marxism and the Failure of Organised Socialism in Spain, 1879–1936*. Cambridge: Cambridge University Press 1990.

Hill, A.T. "Historic Basis and Development of the Lumber Workers Organization and Struggles in Ontario." Thunder Bay Museum, Box 980.83.27–46, File A17/1/8.

Hinton, James. *The First British Shop Stewards' Movement*. London: George Allen & Unwin 1973.

Hobsbawm, Eric. *Workers: Worlds of Labor*. New York: Pantheon Books 1984.

Hollinger, David. *Morris R. Cohen and the Scientific Ideal*. Cambridge, MA: MIT Press 1975.

Homel, Gene Howard. "Fading Beams of the Nineteenth Century: Radicalism and Early Socialism in Canada's 1890s." *Labour/Le Travailleur* 5 (Spring 1980): 7–32.

Horn, Michiel. *The League for Social Reconstruction*. Toronto: University of Toronto Press 1981.

Horodyski, Mary. "Women and the Winnipeg General Strike of 1919." *Manitoba History* no. 11 (Spring 1986): 28–37.

Howard, Irene. *The Struggle for Social Justice in British Columbia: Helena Gutteridge, the Unknown Reformer*. Vancouver: University of British Columbia Press 1992.

Howe, Irving. *Socialism and America*. San Diego: Harcourt Brace Jovanovich 1985.

Howell, David. *British Workers and the Independent Labour Party, 1888–1906*. Manchester: Manchester University Press 1983.

Hunt, Richard N. *The Political Ideas of Marx and Engels: Classical Marxism, 1850–1895*. Pittsburgh: University of Pittsburgh Press 1984.

– *The Political Ideas of Marx and Engels: Marxism and Totalitarian Democracy, 1818–1850*. Pittsburgh: University of Pittsburgh Press 1974.

Isserman, Maurice. *If I Had a Hammer: The Death of the Old Left and the Birth of the New Left*. New York: Basic Books 1987.

Jacoby, Russell. *Dialectic of Defeat: Contours of Western Marxism*. Cambridge: Cambridge University Press 1981.

James, C.L.R. *Beyond a Boundary*. London: Stanley Paul 1963.

Jay, Martin. *Marxism and Totality*. Berkeley and Los Angeles: University of California Press 1984.

Johnson, Ross Alfred. "No Compromise – No Political Trading: The Marxian Socialist Tradition in British Columbia." PhD diss., University of British Columbia 1975.

Jones, Gareth Stedman. *Languages of Class: Studies in English Working Class History, 1832–1982*. Cambridge: Cambridge University Press 1983.

Jordan, Mary. *Survival: Labour's Trials and Tribulations in Canada*. Toronto: McDonald House 1975.

Kaye, Harvey J., and Keith McClelland, eds. *E.P. Thompson: Critical Perspectives*. Philadelphia: Temple University Press 1990.

Kealey, Gregory S. "Labour and Working-Class History in Canada: Prospects in the 1980s." *Labour/Le Travailleur* 7 (Spring 1981): 67–94.

– "1919: The Canadian Labour Revolt." *Labour/Le Travail* 13 (1984): 11–44.

– "Stanley Brehaut Ryerson: Canadian Revolutionary Intellectual." *Studies in Political Economy* 9 (Fall 1982): 103–31.

– "Stanley Brehaut Ryerson: Marxist Historian." *Studies in Political Economy* 9 (Fall 1982): 133–70.

– "State Repression of Labour and the Left in Canada, 1914–20: The Impact of the First World War." *Canadian Historical Review* 73, no. 3 (September 1992): 281–314.

Kealey, Gregory S., and Bryan D. Palmer. *Dreaming of What Might Be: The Knights of Labor in Ontario, 1880–1900*. Toronto: New Hogtown Press 1987.

–, and Reg Whitaker. *R.C.M.P. Security Bulletins: The Early Years, 1919–1929*. St John's: Canadian Committee on Labour History 1994.

Kealey, Linda. *Enlisting Women for the Cause: Women, Labour, and the Left in Canada, 1890–1920*. Toronto: University of Toronto Press 1998.

– " 'No Special Protection – No Sympathy': Women's Activism in the Canadian Labour Revolt of 1919." In *Class, Community and the Labour Movement: Wales and Canada, 1850–1930*, edited by Deian R. Hopkin and Gregory S. Kealey, 134–59. Wales and Canada: Society for Welsh Labour History and the Canadian Committee on Labour History 1989.

– "Socialism and the Woman Question." *Labour/Le Travail* 13 (Spring 1984): 77–100.

Kelly, Aileen. *Mikhail Bakunin: A Study in the Psychology and Politics of Utopianism*. Oxford: Clarendon Press 1982.

King, W.L. Mackenzie. *Industry and Humanity*. Toronto: Thomas Allen 1918.

Kraditor, Aileen S. *The Radical Persuasion, 1890–1917*. Baton Rouge: Louisiana State University Press 1981.

Labriola, Antonio. *Essays on the Materialistic Conception of History*. Chicago: Charles H. Kerr 1908.

Laclau, Ernesto, and Chantal Mouffe. *Hegemony and Socialist Strategy: Towards a Radical Democratic Politics*. London: Verso 1985.

La Monte, Robert Rives. *Socialism: Positive and Negative*. Chicago: Charles H. Kerr 1914.

Lapides, Kenneth. *Marx and Engels on the Trade Unions*. New York: Praeger 1987.

Larivière, Claude. *Albert Saint-Martin: Militant d'avant-garde (1865–1947)*. Laval: Les Editions Coopératives Albert Saint-Martin 1979.

Lefeaux, W.W. *Winnipeg–London–Moscow: A Study of Bolshevism*. Winnipeg: Canadian Workers Defense League 1921.

Leier, Mark. "Plots, Shots, and Liberal Thoughts: Conspiracy Theory and the Death of Ginger Goodwin." *Labour/Le Travail* 39 (Spring 1997), 214–24.

– *Red Flags and Red Tape: The Making of a Labour Bureaucracy.* Toronto: University of Toronto Press 1995.
– *Where the Fraser River Flows.* Vancouver: New Star Books 1990.
– "Workers and Intellectuals: The Theory of the New Class and Early Canadian Socialism." *Journal of History and Politics/Revue d'Histoire et de Politique* 10 (1992): 87–108.
Lenin, V.I. *Collected Works*, vol. 5. Moscow: Foreign Languages Publishing House 1961.
– *"Left-Wing" Communism, an Infantile Disorder.* Moscow: Progress Publishers 1970.
– *The State and Revolution.* Moscow: Progress Publishers 1949.
– *What Is To Be Done?* London: Penguin 1988.
Le Sueur, Meridel. "The Fetish of Being Outside." In *Writing Red: An Anthology of American Women Writers, 1930–1940*, edited by Charlotte Nekola and Paula Rabinowitz, 299–303. New York: Feminist Press 1987.
Lewis, Arthur M. *Evolution: Social and Organic.* Chicago: Charles H. Kerr 1910.
Lewis, David. *The Good Fight: Political Memoirs, 1909–1958.* Toronto: Macmillan 1981.
Lewis, Roderick. *Centennial Edition of a History of the Electoral Districts, Legislatures and Ministries of the Province of Ontario, 1867–1968.* Toronto: Queen's Printer 1978.
Lindstrom-Best, Varpu. *Defiant Sisters: A Social History of Finnish Immigrant Women in Canada.* Toronto: Multicultural History Society of Ontario 1988.
Luxemburg, Rosa. *The Mass Strike.* London, Chicago, Melbourne: Bookmarks 1986.
– *The Russian Revolution* and *Leninism or Marxism.* Edited by Bertram D. Wolfe. Ann Arbor: University of Michigan Press 1961.
McCallum, Todd. "'A Modern Weapon for Modern Man': Marxist Masculinity and the Social Practices of the One Big Union, 1919–1924." Master's thesis, Simon Fraser University 1995.
McCormack, A. Ross. "Cloth Caps and Jobs: The Ethnicity of English Immigrants in Canada, 1900–1914." In *Interpreting Canada's Past*, vol. 2, *After Confederation*, edited by J.M. Bumsted. Toronto: University of Oxford Press 1986: 175–91.
– *Reformers, Rebels, and Revolutionaries: The Western Canadian Radical Movement, 1899–1919.* Toronto and Buffalo: University of Toronto Press 1977.
McDonald, Robert A.J. "Working Class Vancouver, 1886–1914: Urbanism and Class in British Columbia." *BC Studies* 69/70 (Spring-Summer 1986): 33–69.
MacEachern, George. *George MacEachern, an Autobiography: The Story of a Cape Breton Labour Radical.* Edited by David Frank and Donald MacGillivray. Sydney, NS: University College of Cape Breton Press 1987.

MacEwan, Paul. *Miners and Steelworkers*. Toronto: A.M. Hakkert 1976.

McGowan, John. *Postmodernism and Its Critics*. Ithaca and London: Cornell University Press 1991.

MacIntyre, Stuart. *A Proletarian Science: Marxism in Britain, 1917–1933*. Cambridge: Cambridge University Press 1980.

McKay, Ian. "'By Wisdom, Wile or War': The Provincial Workmen's Association and the Struggle for Working-Class Independence in Nova Scotia, 1879–97." *Labour/Le Travail* 18 (Fall 1986): 13–62.

– "Capital and Labour in the Halifax Baking and Confectionery Industry during the Last Half of the Nineteenth Century." *Labour/Le Travailleur* 3 (1978): 63–108.

– "'Changing the Subject(s) of History of Canadian Sociology': The Missing Spencerian Marxists, 1890–1940." Kingston: Queen's University 1995.

– *For a Working-Class Culture in Canada: A Selection of Colin McKay's Writings on Sociology and Political Economy, 1897–1939*. St John's: Canadian Committee on Labour History 1996.

McKillop, A.B. *Contours of Canadian Thought*. Toronto: University of Toronto Press 1987.

McLellan, David. *Marx: The First 100 Years*. London: Fontana 1983.

McLeod, Hugh. *Class and Religion in the Late Victorian City*. Hamden, CT: Archon Books 1974.

McNaught, Kenneth. "E.P. Thompson vs Harold Logan: Writing about Labour and the Left in the 1970s." *Canadian Historical Review* 62, no. 2 (1981): 141–68.

Manley, John. "Canadian Communists, Revolutionary Unionism, and the 'Third Period': The Workers' Unity League, 1929–1935." *Journal of the Canadian Historical Association* 5 (Calgary 1994): 167–94.

Mannheim, Karl. *Ideology and Utopia*. London: Routledge & Kegan Paul 1936.

Marx, Karl. *A Contribution to the Critique of Political Economy*. Moscow: Progress Publishers 1970.

– *Capital: A Critique of Political Economy*, vol. 1. Chicago: Charles H. Kerr 1909.

– *Critique of the Gotha Programme*. Peking: Foreign Language Press 1972.

– *The Eighteenth Brumaire of Louis Bonaparte*. New York: International Publishers 1963.

– *The Poverty of Philosophy*. London: Martin Lawrence n.d.

– *Value, Price and Profit*. New York: International Publishers 1969.

Marx, Karl, and Friedrich Engels. *Collected Works*, vol. 20. New York: International Publishers 1975.

– *The Communist Manifesto*. Harmondsworth, Middlesex: Penguin 1967.

– *The German Ideology*. Ed. C.J. Arthur. New York: International Publishers 1985.

Marx, Karl, and V.I. Lenin. *Civil War in France: The Paris Commune*. New York: International Publishers 1968.

Masters, D.C. *The Winnipeg General Strike*. Toronto: University of Toronto Press 1950.

Mayse, Susan. *Ginger: The Life and Death of Albert Goodwin*. Madeira Park, BC: Harbour Publishing 1990.

Meiksins Wood, Ellen. *Mind and Politics: An Approach to the Meaning of Liberal and Socialist Individualism*. Berkeley and Los Angeles: University of California Press 1972.

– *The Retreat from Class: A New "True" Socialism*. London: Verso 1986.

Mills, Allen. *Fool for Christ: The Political Thought of J.S. Woodsworth*. Toronto: University of Toronto Press 1991.

Milne, J.M. *History of the Socialist Party of Canada*. [Winnipeg?]: Socialist Party of Canada n.d.

Mitchell, Tom. "'Repressive Measures: A.J. Andrews, the Committee of 1000 and the Campaign against Radicalism after the Winnipeg General Strike." *left history* 3, no. 2, and 4, no. 1 (Fall 1995/Spring 1996): 133–67.

Molyneux, John. *Marxism and the Party*. London: Pluto Press 1978.

Montero, Gloria. *We Stood Together: First-Hand Accounts of Dramatic Events in Canada's Labour Past*. Toronto: James Lorimer 1979.

Montgomery, David. *The Fall of the House of Labor*. Cambridge, MT: Cambridge University Press 1987.

– *Workers' Control in America*. Cambridge, MT: Cambridge University Press 1979.

Morton, Desmond. *Working People*. Toronto: Summerhill Press 1990.

Moss, Bernard. *The Origins of the French Labor Movement, 1830–1914*. Berkeley, Los Angeles, and London: University of California Press 1976.

Naylor, James. "Ontario Workers and the Decline of Labourism." In *Patterns of the Past: Interpreting Ontario's History*, edited by Roger Hall, William Westfall, and Laurel Sefton MacDowell, 278–300. Toronto: Dundurn Press 1988.

– "Politics and Class: The Character of 1930s Socialism in Canada." Paper Presented to the Seventy-Second Annual Meeting of the Canadian Historical Association. Ottawa: Carleton University 1993.

– *The New Democracy: Challenging the Social Order in Industrial Ontario, 1914–25*. Toronto: University of Toronto Press 1991.

Newton, Janice. *The Feminist Challenge to the Canadian Left, 1900–1918*. Montreal and Kingston: McGill-Queen's University Press 1995.

One Big Union. *The Origin of the One Big Union*. Winnipeg: OBU [1919].

Palmer, Bryan D. *E.P. Thompson Objections and Oppositions*. London and New York: Verso 1994.

– "'Give Us the Road and We Will Run It': The Social and Cultural Matrix of an Emerging Labour Movement." In *Essays in Canadian Working Class History*, edited by Gregory S. Kealey and Peter Warrian, 106–24. Toronto: McClelland & Stewart 1976.

– "Industrialization and the Emergence of a Local Proletariat: The Case of London, Ontario." London, ON: University of Western Ontario 1973.
– "Listening to History Rather Than Historians: Reflections on Working Class History." *Studies in Political Economy* 20 (Summer 1986): 47–84.
– "Most Uncommon Common Men: Craft and Culture in Historical Perspective." *Labour/Le Travailleur* 1 (1976): 5–31.
– *The Making of E.P. Thompson: Marxism, Humanism, and History.* Toronto: New Hogtown Press 1981.
– *Working-Class Experience.* Toronto and Vancouver: Butterworth 1983.
– *Working-Class Experience: Rethinking the History of Canadian Labour, 1800–1991.* Toronto: McClelland & Stewart 1992.
Parsons, Gerald, ed. *Religion in Victorian Britain*, vol. 1, *Traditions.* Manchester: Manchester University Press 1988.
Penner, Norman. *Canadian Communism: The Stalin Years and Beyond.* Toronto: Methuen 1988.
– *The Canadian Left: A Critical Analysis.* Scarborough: Prentice-Hall 1977.
– ed. *Winnipeg 1919: The Strikers' Own History of the Winnipeg General Strike.* Toronto: James Lorimer 1975.
Peterson, Larry. "The One Big Union in International Perspective: Revolutionary Industrial Unionism, 1900–1925." *Labour/Le Travailleur* 7 (Spring 1981): 41–66.
Pierson, Stanley. *British Socialists: The Journey from Fantasy to Politics.* Cambridge, MT, and London, UK: Harvard University Press 1979.
– *Marxism and the Origins of British Socialism.* Ithaca and London: Cornell University Press 1973.
Pittenger, Mark. *American Socialists and Evolutionary Thought, 1870–1920.* Madison: University of Wisconsin Press 1993.
Price, Richard. *An Imperial War and the British Working Class: Working-Class Attitudes and Reactions to the Boer War, 1899–1902.* London: Routledge & Kegan Paul 1972.
Pritchard, W.A. *Address to the Jury.* Winnipeg: Wallingford Press 1920.
Radforth, Ian. *Bosses and Bushworkers: Logging in Northern Ontario 1900–1980.* Toronto: University of Toronto Press 1987.
Rahim, Husain. *The Psychology of Marxian Socialism.* Vancouver: Pacific Printers 1921.
Ree, Jonathan. *Proletarian Philosophers: Problems in Socialist Culture, 1900–1940.* Oxford: Clarendon Press 1984.
Roberts, Dorothy June. "Doctrine and Disunity in the British Columbia Section of the CCF, 1932–1956." Master's thesis, University of Victoria 1972.
Roberts, Robert. *The Classic Slum: Salford Life in the First Quarter of the Century.* Harmondsworth, Middlesex: Penguin 1973.
Robin, Martin. *Radical Politics and Canadian Labour, 1880–1930.* Kingston: Queen's University 1968.

Salerno, Salvatore. *Red November, Black November: Culture and Community in the Industrial Workers of the World*. Albany: State University of New York Press 1989.

Salvadori, Massimo. *Karl Kautsky and the Socialist Revolution, 1880–1938*. London: New Left Books 1979.

Salvatore, Nick. *Eugene V. Debs: Citizen and Socialist*. Urbana and Chicago: University of Illinois Press 1982.

Sangster, Joan. *Dreams of Equality: Women on the Canadian Left, 1920–1950*. Toronto: McClelland & Stewart 1989.

Scott, Jack. *A Communist Life: Jack Scott and the Canadian Workers Movement, 1927–1985*. Edited by Bryan D. Palmer. St John's: Committee on Canadian Labour History 1988.

Scott, Joan Wallach. *Gender and the Politics of History*. New York: Columbia University Press 1988.

Seager, Allen. "Minto, New Brunswick: A Study in Canadian Class Relations between the Wars." *Labour/Le Travailleur* 5 (Spring 1980): 81–132.

Siemiatycki, Myer. "Labour Contained: The Defeat of a Rank and File Workers' Movement in Canada, 1914–1921." PhD diss., York University 1986.

Smart, D. A. *Pannekoek and Gorter's Marxism*. London: Pluto Press 1978.

Smout, T.C. *A Century of the Scottish People, 1830–1950*. London: Fontana Press 1987.

Stearns, Peter. *Revolutionary Syndicalism and French Labor*. New Brunswick, NJ: Rutgers University Press 1971.

Steeves, Dorothy. *The Compassionate Rebel: Ernest Winch and the Growth of Socialism in Western Canada*. Vancouver: J.J. Douglas 1977.

Taylor, Kerry. "'Jack' McDonald: A Canadian Revolutionary in New Zealand." *Labour/Le Travail* 32 (Fall 1993): 261–8.

Thompson, E.P. *The Poverty of Theory and Other Essays*. New York and London: Monthly Review Press 1978.

– *William Morris: Romantic to Revolutionary*. New York: Pantheon Books 1977.

Thompson, Fred, and David Roediger. *Fellow Worker: The Life of Fred Thompson*. Chicago: Charles H. Kerr 1993.

Thwaites, James Douglas. "The International Association of Machinists in Canada: To 1919." Master's thesis, Carleton University 1966.

Trades and Labour Congress of Canada. *Report of Proceedings* (1912–18).

Troop, G.R. "Socialism in Canada." Master's thesis, McGill University 1922.

van der Linden, Marcel, and Wayne Thorpe, eds. *Revolutionary Syndicalism: An International Perspective*. Aldershot: Scolar Press 1990.

Wald, Alan. *The New York Intellectuals*. Chapel Hill: University of North Carolina Press 1987.

Walton, John K. *Lancashire: A Social History, 1558–1939*. Manchester: Manchester University Press 1987.

Waters, Mary-Alice, ed. *Rosa Luxemburg Speaks*. New York: Pathfinder Press 1970.

Wickwire, Wendy. "To See Ourselves As the Other's Other: Nlaka'pamux Contact Narratives," *Canadian Historical Review* 75, no. 1 (1994), 1–21.

– "Women in Ethnography: The Research of James A. Teit." *Ethnohistory* 40, no. 4 (Fall 1993): 539–62.

Wilson, J. Donald. "The Ethnic Voice: The Canadian Sojourn of a Finnish-American Radical." *Canadian Ethnic Studies* 16, no. 2 (1984): 102–15.

Woodsworth, J.S. *On the Waterfront*. Ottawa: Mutual Press n.d.

Wormsbecker, Kathleen O'Gorman. "The Rise and Fall of the Labour Political Movement in Manitoba, 1919–1927." Master's thesis, Queen's University 1977.

Wright, A.W. *G.D.H. Cole and Socialist Democracy*. Oxford: Clarendon Press 1979.

Index

All-Canadian Congress of Labour (ACCL), 209
Allman, Harry, 47–8, 54, 56
American Federation of Labor (AFL), 85, 202, 215; attacked by Pritchard, 96; ILA rejoins, 98; deemed antiquated by Pritchard, 103; dominates London labour movement, 133; "no politics" stance, 137; leadership challenged by Mould, 143–5; dispute with OBU in Winnipeg, 191–3; creation of the Canadian Labour Congress, 218
anarchism, 8, 87, 135–6, 172
Anderson, Perry, 22
Andrews, A.J., 189–90
Angus, Ian, 26, 89, 95, 99
Armstrong, George: helps re-establish SPC, 29, 118, 211; not at founding meeting of OBU, 91; and WGS, 168–9; attends Western Labour Conference, 184–5; defends role of "active minority," 185; conflict with OBU, 215
Armstrong, Helen, 235n43; as Marxist of the third way, 10–11; helps re-establish SPC, 29, 211; not at founding meeting of OBU, 91; and WGS, 168–9; attends Western Labour Conference, 184–5; champions women in the labour movement, 185
Arnold, Matthew, 222
Arnold-Forster, Hugh Oakeley, 35, 241n17
Asian workers, 175

Bakunin, Mikhail, 8
Baritz, Moses, 18, 136
Barnet Mills Strike, 106–7
Barnetson, A.M., 157
Barrett, Silby, 202
Bartholomew, H.M, 21
Bebel, August, 15, 235n50
Beck, Sir Adam, 138–9, 144
Beilharz, Peter, 226, 228
Bellamy, Edward, 127
Bennett, Prime Minister R.B., 106, 109
Bennett, William, 80
Bercuson, David, 23–4, 27, 89, 182, 206–7, 209–10, 272n205
Berger, Victor, 5
Blatchford, Robert, 34, 127, 129
Blumenberg, Sam, 11, 168, 236n63
Boer War, 128–9
Bolsheviks. *See* Marxism-Leninism
Borden, Prime Minister Robert, 183
Boudin, Louis, 7
Bracken, John, 212
Bradford Labour Union, 126
Bricklayers' and Masons' International Union, 34, 36
Bridge River Mines Strike, 114
British Columbia Ex Soldiers' and Sailors' Council, 49, 244n83
British Columbia Federation of Labour (BCFL), 41–2, 46, 88–9
British Columbia Federationist, 52, 54, 195

British Columbia Shipping Federation, 97
British Empire Steel and Coal Company (BESCO), 201, 203, 205, 207, 270n164
British Labour Party, 71
British radicalism, 12–13, 20, 126
British shop stewards' movement, 53, 90
Bruce, Malcolm, 25, 99, 144, 198
Bruno, Giordano, 93
Buck, Tim, 63–4, 158, 161, 163, 201, 262n126
Budden, Alf, 90, 235n54
Buhay, Becky, 198
Buhay, Michael, 198
Buhle, Mari Joe, 15
Burke, Frank, 140–1, 143–4
Burnaby Workers' Protective Association, 106
Burns, Bertha Merrill, 14, 36
Burns, Ernest, 36–7, 43, 58, 60, 102
Burns, Robert, 224
Burrough, J.H., 38, 55, 80

camp delegate system, 52–3
Campbell, Constable Dan, 44
Canadian Brotherhood of Railway Employees (CBRE), 209
Canadian Labour Defence League, 62, 66, 153, 158
Canadian Labour Party (CLP), 145; organization and role of, 42, 144; and Communist Party, 102; Mould as CLP candidate, 142; and London Trades and Labour Council, 143; radicalization of, 144; Mould challenges Communists in, 146–9; decline, 150
Canadian Pacific Railway (CPR), 97, 178–9, 264n7
Canadian Socialist Federation, 36, 241n28
Capital, 13, 73, 95, 127, 180, 199
Caplan, Gerald, 150–1, 158–9, 260n95
Carpenter, Edward, 173
Cassidy, Robert, 189–90
Cassidy, Tom, 207
Charlton, O. Lee, 57
Chew, A. Percy, 17, 21–2
Clancy, Jack, 215
Clarke, Phyllis, 9
class consciousness: and International Workingmen's Association, 4; compromised by sexism, 14–17, 213, 223; described by Antonio Labriola, 20–1; of Marxists of the third way, 23, 222; subjective and objective elements of, 61–2, 188–9; fostered by Winch, 45, 72; key to Pritchard's anti-capitalism, 82–3; as cumulative development, 84, 100; ensures proletarian revolution, 87; and industrial unionism, 90; as danger to capitalist class, 91; and 1919 labour revolt, 94–5; and rationality of the workers, 112, 226; lacking in London labour, 134; and Ontario Socialist Party, 154; basis of labour politics, 157; and OBU, 169; and WGS, 186; and working-class historical understanding, 226. *See* worker education and worker self-emancipation
Cohen, Morris, 19
cold war, 163, 218
Coldwell, M.J., 71
The Commonwealth, 67, 114–16, 215
The Communist Manifesto, 6, 13, 93–4, 153, 180, 199
Communist Party of Canada (CPC), 9, 29, 66, 75, 113–14, 150, 192, 252n108, 262n126; and Marxists of the third way, 60, 67, 71, 92, 98–9, 106–7, 115, 145–9, 154, 157–67, 195–8, 201–2, 205–9, 218–19; appeal during the Depression, 62; and CCF, 67, 157–8; and united front strategy, 67–8, 154; and Popular Front, 69, 160; conflict with SPC, 98–9; rejects Marxism of the third way, 100; and Burnaby Council, 106; and Barnet Mills strike, 106–7; and CLP, 144–9; J.S. Woodsworth on, 154; founding of LPP, 161–2; response to Khrushchev revelations, 163–5; organizes as Workers' Party, 197–8; split with OBU leadership, 197–8; conflict with OBU in Nova Scotia, 201–7
Communist Party of the Soviet Union (CPSU), 163–4
Confédération Général du Travail (CGT), 179–80
Congress of Industrial Organizations (CIO), 112, 211, 216, 218
Conley, James, 265n37
Connell, Reverend Robert, 67–8, 114–16, 118
conscription, 41, 88, 137, 178–9
Co-operative Commonwealth Federation (CCF), 219, 262n133; organization of, 62; impact on SPCBC, 62–3, 65–7, 114–15; Regina Convention and Manifesto, 64; Winch-Connell dispute in BC, 67–9; leadership's denial of Marxist roots,

71; leaders clash with Evelyn Grey Smith, 71; and Socialist Fellowship, 71; and Winnipeg Declaration, 71; supported by Pritchard, 75–6, 110–14; and *The Commonwealth*, 115–16; and class politics, 150; dispute with Labour Conference in Ontario, 151–9; transition to NDP, 165; impact on OBU, 214–15; and industrial unionism, 214
Cotterell, Ernest, 44
Cotton's Weekly, 37
craft unions, 85, 126, 186, 188; and OBU, 91, 191, 209; and federal labour unions, 139–40, 143–5; identified with conservatism, 178, 265n37; and syndicalism, 179–80; and industrial unionism, 178–82; organizing women workers, 182–3; racism and sexism in, 182. *See also* trade unions, American Federation of Labor, and Trades *and* Labour Congress of Canada
Curry, Dr W.J., 42

Darwin, Charles, 5, 15, 17, 19, 21–2
Darwinism and Politics, 227
Debs, Eugene, 5–6, 204
Devereaux, A.J., 44–5, 55, 97
Devyatkin, Boris, 196
dictatorship of the proletariat, 26, 238n102, 238n104, 239n105
Dietzgen, Joseph: on historical materialism, 21–2; advice to scientific socialists, 220; critiques religious believers, 235n56; influence in OBU, 237n78
Dominion and Nova Scotia Relief Committee, 206–7
Draper, Paddy, 181

Engels, Friedrich: on scientific socialism, 22, 224; on Salford, Lancashire, 76; his historical materialism misunderstood, 227
Essays in the Materialistic Conception of History, 20
evolution, 19, 39, 173, 189, 199
Evolution of the Japanese, 34, 240n11

Fabians, 8, 30, 104, 111, 153
fascism, 112, 160, 217
Federal Labour Union (FLU) #16523, 139–40, 143–4
Federated Labour Party (FLP), 42, 46, 58, 102
feminist socialists: marginalized in Marxist parties, 14; problems presented to by Canadian political culture, 16; contributions of, 185, 233n29, 235n43. *See also* gender relations, women
Ferri, Enrico, 28, 249n38
Fillmore, Roscoe, 11, 235n53
Finns and Finnish leftists, 18, 238n94, 257n1
First International, 4, 8
Fitzgerald, Henry M., 18
Fix, Fred, 214
Flett, John A., 143
Forsey, Eugene, 64–5
Foucault, Michel, 220
Four Ls, 88
Foxcroft, Robert, 146–7
French Revolution, 94, 136
Friesen, Gerald, 88, 190, 265n40
Fukuyama, Francis, 225, 229
Gale, Mayor Harry (Vancouver), 44, 88
Galilei, Galileo, 93
gender relations: male Marxists of the third way and their families, 16–17, 81–2, 105, 166, 207–8; and conflicts of religion and socialism, 171, 223. *See also* feminist socialists, women
general strike, 98, 179, 202; and IWW, 6; voted on in B.C., 41; Ginger Goodwin general strike, 44, 88; Vancouver sympathetic strike, 50–2; western support for a general strike, 88; and syndicalism, 89; Russell on, 189. *See also* Winnipeg General Strike
George, Henry, 35
German Social Democratic Party, 4–5, 8–9, 93
Gilbert and Sullivan, 105, 120, 224, 251n90
Goode, John, 10
Goodwin, Ginger, 42–4, 88
Gordon, Charles W., 192
Gorter, Herman, 90
Gray, Mayor (Winnipeg), 187
"Great Man" theory of history, 26, 188, 205
Gutteridge, Helena, 43, 46, 90

Hak, Gordon, 56
Hall, Grant, 180, 266n51
Hardie, Keir, 165
Harrington, J.D., 21–2, 26, 96, 99
Hawthornthwaite, J.H., 42, 79
Haywood, William, 47
Hegel, Georg, 21–3, 101, 118–19, 236n73
Henderson, Rose, 182
Heywood, Paul, 10
Hillquit, Morris, 5

historical materialism, 20–1, 223–5. *See also* scientific socialism
Hodgson, Fred, 29, 156–7
Hoop, W.H. (Bill), 194
Houston, John, 18, 27
Houston, William, 201, 203
Howe, Irving, 250n52
Hunt, Richard, 8
Hyndman, H.M, 78

Independent Labour Party (B.C.), 28, 32, 58–63, 102
Independent Labour Party (ON.), 137–40, 143–4, 149
Independent Labour Party (Socialist), 61–2
Industrial Banner, 135
industrial unions, 79–80, 133, 169, 188, 209, 265n37, 272n205; and dispute between OBU and LWIU, 55–7; and class unions, 84–5, 94; and 1918 TLCC convention, 88; and OBU, 91, 98, 214; Pritchard on, 112–13; associated with radicalism, 178; promoted by Russell and Winnipeg machinists, 178–81; and women workers, 182–3; organizational problems, 191
Industrial Workers of the World, 46, 53, 60, 124, 180, 238n93, 257n1; organization and ideas of, 6; basis in Marxism, 6–7; Marxists of the third way in, 6–7; origin of camp delegate system, 52–3; and conflict with SPCers in LWIU, 54–5; and OBU, 56–7, 191; identified with anarchism and syndicalism, 87; organizational difficulties, 191
Industry and Humanity, 225
International Association of Machinists (IAM), 174–82, 266n58
International Congress of Revolutionary Trade and Industrial Unions (Profintern), 197
International Longshoremen's Association (ILA), 58; strike of 1917, 40; and workers in ILA auxiliary, 40; and general strike, 41; influence in VTLC, 42; attack on Longshoremen's Hall, 44; impact of Spanish influenza, 45; reasons for radicalism of, 85; strike of 1923, 96–8
International Timberworkers' Union, 84–5
International Union of Fur and Leather Workers, 218
International Workingmen's Association, 4, 214
Isserman, Maurice, 160

Jacoby, Russell, 22
James, C.L.R., 273n8
Jewish National Workers' Alliance, 149
Jews and Jewish socialists, 149, 152–3, 173, 236n59; and Marxism of the third way, 18–19; in London, ON, 135–6; anti-Semitism, 138, 182; relations with non-Jews in SPC, 182, 190
Johns, Richard J., 173, 181–2, 264n15; not at founding meeting of OBU, 91; and WGS, 168–9; refuses to take IAM oath, 176; identifies with unskilled workers, 178; at Western Labour Conference, 184–5; speaks in Edmonton and Calgary, 193
Johnson, Ross, 9, 74, 233n22
Johnston-Knight, Sarah, 11, 14, 198
Joint Council of Industry, 192
Jones, Gareth Stedman, 224, 273n10
Jordan, Mary, 189, 200, 207, 215, 264n7

Kannasto, Sanna, 14, 235n43
Kant, Immanuel, 223
Kaplan, Fred, 196
Karme, Abe, 18, 238n94
Kautsky, Karl, 28, 30
Kavanagh, Jack, 40, 44, 51, 96; and lesson of WGS, 25; calls for militant action, 41; defends Winch, 48–9; as extremist on the VTLC, 49–50; and returned soldiers, 50, 244n83; on OBU-LWIU dispute, 56; at Western Labour Conference, 89, 185; and 1923 longshoremen's strike, 97–8; and Third International, 99, 252n108; at 1918 TLCC convention, 181; working against OBU, 194, 198
Kealey, Gregory S., 95, 181
Kealey, Linda, 234n35, 235n43, 242n32
Kelly, Gordon J., 42, 45
Khrushchev, Nikita, 164
King, William Lyon Mackenzie, 225, 273n16
Kingsley, Eugene Thornton, 3, 42–3, 79–80, 199, 249n29
Knight, Joseph, 197–8
Knights of Labor, 134
Kohn, Adolph, 95, 251n91
Kraditor, Eileen, 81

Labor Statesman, 58–9, 101
labour aristocracy, 12, 33, 240n3

Labour Conference, 152–9
Labour Herald, 140–1, 143
Labour Progressive Party (LPP), 161–2. *See* Communist Party of Canada
Labour Revolt of 1919, 18, 23, 237n91, 240n3; and Marxists of the third way, 9,12, 41, 75; made possible by unity of trade unionists and Marxian socialists, 24–5; impact on OBU, 51–2; historical significance, 94–5; impact on Pritchard, 120–1; and London labour, 138; and Russell's role, 181–2
Labour Temple Company, 140
labourism, 7, 135, 149
Labriola, Antonio, 20–1, 28, 224, 236n71
Laclau, Ernesto, 224
leaders and leadership: Marxists of the third way on, 14, 20, 26, 31–2, 53, 73, 85, 103, 141, 165, 169–70, 190, 202, 204–5, 213–14, 228; and labour revolt of 1919, 25, 75; Winch defends his role as labour leader, 44–5, 49; and Vancouver sympathy strike, 52; religious roots of Pritchard's position on, 76–7; Communist Party position on, 100; cult of the individual in CPSU, 163–4; Russell's and Rosa Luxemburg's ideas on, 187–8; in OBU, 199; women excluded from OBU executive, 199–200
League Against War and Fascism, 62, 68
League for Social Reconstruction (LSR), 7, 110–11, 153
Lebourdais, D.M., 158–9
Lefeaux, Stan, 43
Lefeaux, Wallis Walter, 110, 115, 152; background, 12; trip to Soviet Union, 26; in SPCBC, 61–2; and Socialist Fellowship, 71; speaks at Empress Theatre, 79; attends Ginger Goodwin's funeral, 88; and ILP (B.C.), 102
Legere, Ben, 104, 203–4, 270n149
Leheney, John (Jack), 6, 10, 18
Lenin, V.I., 8, 26, 154, 199, 208, 239n117; Winch compared to, 48; and soviets, 89–90; Marxists of the third way on, 100; on trade union consciousness, 140; Mould's admiration for, 160, 164; his tactics opposed by OBU, 191
Lerner, Max, 135–6
Lestor, Charles, 43; editor of *OBU Bulletin*, 27, 210; helps reorganize SPC, 29, 211; and returned soldiers, 50, 244n83; attacks CPC, 197; turns on SPC, 215
Lestor, Ruth, 14–15
Le Sueur, Meridel, 11
Lewis, Arthur Morrow, 19–20
Lewis, David, 63–4, 70–71
Lewis, John L., 201–5
Liebknecht, Karl, 5, 184, 220
Lindberg, E., 55
Livingstone, Dan, 201–2
Loggers' and Camp Workers' Union (LCWU), 32, 46, 53, 90
logging industry, 46–7, 50–6
London Labour Party (LLP), 146–7
London Trades and Labour Council (LTLC), 137, 139–40, 143–4
London Typographical Union, 138
Longshoremen's Strike: of 1917, 40; of 1923, 96–8
Longshoremen's Strike Bulletin, 100
Looking Backward, 127
Lumber and Agricultural Workers' Industrial Union (LAWIU), 107
Lumber Workers' Industrial Union (LWIU), 47, 52–7
Luxemburg, Rosa, 5, 93–4, 220–1, 234n36, 238n104, 249n35; praised by Russell, 184; on role of socialist leaders, 187
Lyon, Alex, 175
Lyon, Colonel H.E., 111

MacDonald, Donald C., 71, 165
MacDonald, Jack, 144, 151, 198, 261n98
Mace, Tom, 47–8
Machinists' *Bulletin*, 174, 176, 180
MacInnis, Angus, 58, 66–7, 102, 121, 158, 214
MacIntyre, Stuart, 7, 22, 233n26, 236n73
Mackenzie, Alex, 47–8, 54–5
MacLean, John, 238n103
MacLeod, A.A., 161–2
Macphail, Agnes, 66, 151, 158
Mannheim, Karl, 223
Marine Warehousemen & Freight Handlers' Union, 40
Maritime Labour Herald, 203
Marks, Joseph, 135, 137
Marsh, Leonard, 7
Marx, Karl, 20–1, 23, 25, 30, 93–4; and International Workingmen's Association, 4; and First International, 8; idea of science, 22; in defence of

trade unions, 24, 199, 214; and worker self-emancipation, 28, 84, 91, 220; impact on Pritchard, 78; theory of class struggle, 112; impact on Mould, 125; impact on Russell, 180; legacy, 222; and new true socialists, 224–5
Marxism-Leninism, 8, 26–7, 93, 98, 157
Marxism of the third way, 112, 117, 125, 139, 156, 210, 225–6, 233n29; defined, 4, 8–9, 233n32; in SPC and IWW, 6–7; characteristics of adherents, 9–14, 74–5, 213, 226–7, 247n1, 273n8; and women in the socialist movement, 14–17; and race and ethnicity, 17–18; and Jewish socialists, 18–19; theoretical underpinnings, 19–23; and labour revolt of 1919, 23–5; and Third International, 25–7; in the 1920s, 27–8; in the 1930s, 28–30; on evolution and revolution, 39, 189; and the general strike, 41–2; mistaken interpretations of, 45; confused with syndicalism, 53; contradictions of, 57, 97–8, 205, 223–4; and sexism, 81–2, 171, 176–7, 223, 235n56; and syndicalism and Marxism-Leninism, 89–90; and the OBU, 91; in Ontario, 124; and the middle class, 152–3; and the CCF, 155, 157–60; and the Communist Party, 157–60; and WGS, 168–9, 190; and Western Labour Conference, 185–6; discredited, 220; legacy of, 222, 227–9
The Mass Strike, 187
McCallum, Todd, 199–200
McClary's Manufacturing Company, 134
McDonald, John Amos (Jack), 6, 101, 232n9
McGowan, John, 221
McKay, Alex, 206–7
McKay, Colin, 11, 231n2,
McKay, Ian, 11, 19, 231n2, 270n145
McKenzie, Donald George, 18, 79, 248n21
McLachlan, J.B., 11, 201–2
McVety, J.H., 42
Meiksins Wood, Ellen, 224
Menzies, L.R., 146–7, 260n76, 260n78, 260n81
Merrie England, 34–5, 127
Methodists and Methodist Church, 126–32, 135–7, 147–8, 273n8
middle class, 28, 152–3, 160, 239n115
Midgley, Victor, 244n84; accosted by returned soldiers, 44; ordered out of Vancouver, 44; part of the extremist faction of the VTLC, 49, 51; conflict with Winch and the LWIU, 56; supports CCF leadership, 66; supports Connell faction of B.C. CCF, 68, 116; organizes for OBU, 90; at Western Labour Conference, 185–6
Miller, William, 119
Mills, Allan, 148
Milne, Jim, 29, 116–17
Mitchell, Tom, 237n91, 266n60
Montgomery, David, 189, 265n34, 271n183
Moore, Tom, 144–5
Moriarty, William, 64, 151, 159, 261n98
Morris, Leslie, 163, 166
Morris, William, 13, 23
Morrison, Frank, 143, 145
Morrison, William, 113, 255n176
Morton, Desmond, 231n1
Morton, Elizabeth, 11, 29, 155, 157, 159
Morton, Suzanne, 270n145
Mosher, A.R., 209
Mouffe, Chantal, 224
Mould, Alfred, 132, 159, 162
Mould, Alice (Pollitt): marries Arthur Mould, 129–30; arrives in Canada, 131; domestic life and duties, 129, 131, 133, 145; refuses to move to northern Ontario, 132; moves to London, Ontario, 132; family moves into new home, 134–5; family forced to leave their home, 157; injured by fall, 165–6; husband's appreciation of, 166; death, 166
Mould, Arthur: Christian-based anti-capitalism, 125; attracted by Marx's vision, 125; as Marxist of the third way, 125, 166–7; espouses Christian values, 125, 129–30, 145; birth, 125; parents, 125; religious upbringing, 126; moves to Peterborough, England, 126; moves to Bradford, 126; employed in baking trade, 125, 126–7; Christian socialism, 126–7, 136–7, 142, 156; moves to Blackburn, 127; in baking trade in Accrington, 127–8; involvement with YMCA, 128–9; pacifism, 129, 135–6; influenced by Tolstoy, 129–30; marries Alice Pollitt, 129; emigrates to Canada, 129; negative impressions of Toronto, 130–1; employed by

Weston Bakeries, 131–2; sells life insurance, 132; seeks to become a farmer, 132; employed by Phillip Carey Co., 132; moves family to London, Ontario, 132; reading, 127, 133; builds own house, 134; becomes involved in labour politics, 135; involvement with Radical Club, 135; defends Jews, 135, 138; shift to socialism, 136; joins ILP, 137; delegate to London Trades and Labour Council, 139; becomes self-employed, 137–8; joins Federal Labour Union #16523, 139; named to LTLC organization committee, 139; member of ILP executive, 140; spearheads creation of London Labour Temple, 140; president of London Labour Temple Co., 140; creates *Labour Herald*, 140; egotism, 141; attacks London labour leaders, 141; president of London local of ILP, 141; vice-president of ILP, 142; candidate in 1921 federal election, 142; speaks against women's oppression, 142; elected to CLP executive board, 144; dispute with AFL/TLCC leadership, 143–5; influence as political socialist, 145; family life, 145, 157; music, 145, 157; challenges CPC, 146; dispute with London Communists, 146–7; ideas compared to those of J.S. Woodsworth, 147–8; defines Canadian socialism, 147–8; dispute with CLP, 148–9; elected president of ILP, 149–51; supports CCF, 150–1, 153–4; chairman of Labour Conference, 152; president of OLP, 153; attacked for supporting the CCF, 154; health problems, 155–6, 162–3; defends class politics, 156; fears anti-Marxism in CCF, 156; financial problems, 157; leaves CCF, becomes Communist Party supporter, 159–60; appeal of the Popular Front, 160; speaks at the Ukrainian Labour Temple, 160; joins CPC, 161; opposes Woodsworth's pacifism, 161; meets with Louis St Laurent, 161; joins Labour Progressive Party, 161–2; addresses LPP convention, 161–2; LPP candidate in 1945 federal election, 162; death of son Alfred, 162; candidate in 1949 London municipal elections, 163; chairman of London peace council, 163; returns to England, 163; analyses his emulation of Stalin and the Soviet Union, 163–4; defends worker-directed socialism, 164; criticizes "oppositionists" in CPC, 165; poetry, 165; caring for Alice, 165–6; death, 166

Mould, Edith, 135, 145

Mould, Fanny, 125, 127

Mould, Helen (Rawson), 135, 138, 145, 157, 166

Mould, Irene, 132

Mould, Jesse (Mihlik), 135, 145, 157

Mould, John, 145

Mould, Mildred, 145

Mould, Robert, 145

Mould, Simmons, 125–6

Mould, Walter, 132

Mounted Police (RNWMP): reports on Vancouver labour leaders, 49–51; raid the Winch home, 52; on radicalism in LWIU, 53–4; recommend closing Mould's file, 161; on decline of OBU, 193; on Russell's, 216, 218

Mushkat, Sophie, 3, 11, 14

National Affairs Monthly, 164

National Conference for Democratic Rights, 161

Navis, John, 196

Naylor, James, 134, 137, 152, 160, 237n91, 266n60

Naylor, Joseph, 42, 44

New Commonwealth, 215

new true socialism, 224–5, 273n10

new unionism, 126

Newton, Janice, 18, 24

Nonconformism: and socialist thought, 20; and Plymouth Brethren, 76–7; in Mould's family, 126; and the Boer War, 128–9; and Methodism, 131–2; in Mould's thought, 136; and worker self-emancipation, 226

Norris, Premier (Manitoba), 187

Nova Scotia miners' strikes, 201–7

One Big Union: character and purpose, 24–5, 169, 188–9, 272n205; and syndicalism, 27, 179–80, 187; reinvigorated in the 1930s, 28–9; and LWIU, 47–8, 54–7; endangered by WGS, 51–2, 186, 188; organization of, 89–91, 185; and labour revolt of

1919, 94–5, 193; decline of, 96, 100, 190–1, 193–4, 214–16; SPC-CPC split in, 99; looks for new editor for *Bulletin*, 104; response to in London, 138; as conceived by Russell, 179; advocates open shop, 191–2; and *Bulletin* lottery, 195, 210–11; in conflict with CPC, 195–8; impact of Marxist thought on, 199; marginalization of women in, 199–200, 213; organizes women workers, 200–1; organizes Nova Scotia miners and steelworkers, 201–7, 270n164; Russell censored by executive, 207–8; Russell's faith in, 208; and All-Canadian Congress of Labour, 209, 253n122; still organizing in late 1920s, 209–10, 269n139; defends Sacco and Vanzetti, 210; sends greetings to Soviet Union, 210; saves working-class homes from foreclosure, 212; attempts to organize railway workers, 212–14; defends unemployed, 211–13; and CCF, 214–15; amalgamates with CLC, 218; legacy, 219

One Big Union Bulletin: looks for new editor, 104; and the lottery, 195, 210–11; as vehicle for Marxist ideas, 199; editorship of Charles Lestor, 210; ceases publication, 215

On the Waterfront, 40

Ontario Conference of Political, Labour, and Socialist Groups, 151–2

Ontario Labour Party, 149–51, 154–5

open forums, 135–7, 247n1

Palmer, Bryan, 217, 226

Pannekoek, Anton, 90

Paris Commune, 94, 99

Paton, George, 17

Penner, Jacob, 196

Penner, Norman, 85, 110, 164–5, 265n37

Peterson, Larry, 266n50

Pettipiece, R. Parmenter, 42

Philpott, Elmore, 151, 156, 159

Pierson, Stanley, 13, 238n103

Pittenger, Mark, 5, 15–16

Place, John (Jack), 37, 242n29

Plymouth Brethren, 76–7

Popovich, Matthew, 196

Presbyterians and Presbyterian Church, 171–2

Pritchard, Arthur, 123

Pritchard, Eleanor (Hanson): marries Bill Pritchard, 249n40; death of young son, 84; shaken by husband's imprisonment, 96; poor health, 104; placed in psychiatric hospital, 104–5

Pritchard, George Leslie, 84

Pritchard, Gilbert, 117

Pritchard, James, employment in Lancashire, 76; on 1908 Dominion Executive Committee of SPC, 78–9; employment on Vancouver Island, 78; as labour organizer in England and Canada, 247n5

Pritchard, Leah, 123

Pritchard, Mildred, 84, 117

Pritchard, Priscilla: influence on her son Bill, 76–8; death, 117

Pritchard, William Arthur: as worker intellectual, 73–6, 119–20; editor of *Western Clarion*, 73; view of SPC's role, 75; response to labour revolt of 1919, 75; endorses CCF, 75–6; birth, 76; religious upbringing, 76; religious roots of his Marxism, 77, 93, 112; formal education, 77; apprenticeship in building construction, 77; impact of Marx's *Capital*, 78; arrives in Vancouver, 79; meets E.T. Kingsley and D.G. McKenzie, 79; hears Wallis Lefeaux speak, 79; becomes a member of the SPC, 79; first article in *WC*, 80; attends meetings of SPC executive, 80; becomes editor of *WC*, 80; as impossibilist, 80; ridicules beliefs of workers, 80–1; attacks organized religion, 81; acceptance of Victorian attitudes toward women, 81–2; belief in worker agency, 82–3, 100; rejects economic fatalism, 83; leaves the *Clarion*, 83; "propaganda tour" of Alberta, 84; death of son George Leslie, 84; takes job as shipper in a lumber mill, 84; on trade unions, 84–5; calls for the creation of a class union, 84; attempts to organize lumber mill workers, 85; joins ILA, 85; works as checker and foreman on the docks, 85; president of ILA Auxiliary, 85; becomes delegate to VTLC, 85; attacks trade union leaders, 85; elected a trustee of the VTLC, 87; socialist revolution as long-term goal, 87; opposition to violence, 87; critic of syndicalism, 87; identifies IWW with syndicalism and anarchism,

87; on socialist revolution in Canada, 87; attends Ginger Goodwin's funeral, 88; learns about attack on Labour Temple, 88; member of the Four Ls, 88; advocates creation of industrial unions, 89; opposes sending labour delegations to legislatures, 89; on parliamentary institutions, 89–90; promotes OBU in the United States, 90; editor of the *Camp Worker*, 90; worker mobilization, 90; role in formation of OBU, 91; investigates WGS, 91–2; supports striking Winnipeg workers, 91; meeting with returned soldiers, 91–2; denies discussion of soviets, 92; speaks in Brandon and Calgary, 92; released on bail, 92; speaks at Empress Theatre, Vancouver, 92; on evolution and revolution, 92; poetry, 92, 159; trial defence, 92–4; socialist party tactics, 93; revolutionary strategy, 93–4; on counter-revolution, 94; constitutional action, 94; in prison, 95; speech at the Industrial Bureau, 95–6; attacks AFL trade union leaders, 96; returns to Vancouver following imprisonment, 96; returns to longshoring, 96; business agent of ILA, 97; refuses to support the Third International, 99; anti-communism, 99; speeches given in early 1920s, 99; defends dictatorship of the proletariat, 100; editor of *Longshoremen's Strike Bulletin*, 100; replaced as editor of *Labor Statesman*, 101; reacts to end of *WC*, 101; death of Chris Stephenson, 101–2; drifts away from Marxian socialism, 102; espouses left nationalist politics, 102; involvement with ILP (BC), 102–3; concern with educating young people, 103; questions the SPC legacy, 103, 105; defends his role in OBU, 103; critiques AFL, 103; elected councillor for North Burnaby, 103; turns down editorship of *OBU Bulletin*, 104; re-elected councillor for North Burnaby, 104; elected reeve of Burnaby, 104; dealing with Eleanor's illness, 104, 105; music, 95, 105, 122–3; praised by the press, 105–6; aids unemployed workers, 105–6; re-elected reeve of Burnaby, 106; relations with federal and provincial politicians, 106; warns R.B. Bennett, 106; meets with Gideon Robertson, 106; elected president of Union of B.C. Municipalities, 106; role in Barnet Mills strike, 106–7; attacked by CPC during Barnet Mills, strike, 107; relief for Barnet Mills strikers, 108; accused of misappropriation of funds, 108–9; named chairman of the Unemployment Committee of the Union of Canadian Municipalities, 109; attends 1932 convention of Union of Canadian Municipalities, 109; removed as Burnaby reeve, 109; critiques SPC legacy, 110; loses CCF nomination for Burnaby, 110; antagonism toward Ernest Winch, 110, 113–14; Fabian influence, 111; chairman of the Reconstruction Party, 111; launches *The Commonwealth*, 111, 115; supports CCF leadership, 111; president of the Associated CCF Clubs of B.C., 111; attends Regina conference, 111; named B.C. CCF's provincial organizer, 111; declares industrial unionism a spent force, 112; attacks "doctrinaire" Marxists, 113; defends CCF's agricultural base, 113; misplaced faith in electoral politics, 113–14; defends Soviet Union, 114; defends Marx, 114; defends striking loggers, 114; role in Bridge River mines strike, 114; speaks at opening of Jubilee Labour Hall, 114; rapprochement with Ernest Winch, 115; suspended as *Commonwealth* editor, 116; joins Social Constructives, 116; attacked by old comrades, 116–17; mother's death, 117; daughter's suicide, 117; leaves B.C. for California, 117–18; joins WSPUS, 118; effect of labour revolt of 1919, 119–20; reasons for supporting CCF, 121–2; visits William Rab, 122–3; death and burial, 123

Provincial Workmen's Association, 203

Queen, John, 172, 269n122

Rab, William, 122–3
race and racism, 218, 266n58; and SPC members, 17–18; SPCers oppose exclusion of Asian workers, 175–6; and labour revolt of 1919, 182;
Radical Club (London, ON), 135, 137
Rahim, Husain, 10–11, 152; contribution to SPC, 18, 248n25; theorist of working-class psychology, 74, 247n2
Reconstruction Party, 110
Regina Manifesto, 62, 64, 255n175
Reilly, Nolan, 181
Relief Camp Workers' Union, 66
revolutions of 1848, 94
Ritchie, D.G., 227, 236n73
Roberts, Robert, 76, 78, 251n90
Roberts, Tommy, 210, 269n139
Robertson, Gideon, 106–7
Robin, Martin, 7, 27, 87, 149, 185
Robinson, Bert, 29, 156, 157, 159; correspondence with and influence on Winch, 62–3; defends OSP, 153; supports cooperation with CPC, 154; favourable opinion of CCF, 155
Robinson, Ernest, 182
Rollo, Walter, 140
Russell, David, 172
Russell, Margaret, 172
Russell, Margaret (Hampton): marries Bob Russell and comes to Canada, 172; importance of religion, 172; impact of her husband's political activism, 207–08
Russell, Pearl, 207
Russell, Robert Boyd: promotes industrial unionism, 169, 178, 181; attitudes toward women, 170–1; efforts to organize unskilled workers, 170, 174–5; as labour organizer, 170, 181; birth, 171; influence of parents, 171; religious influences, 171; music, 172; importance of environment in his thought, 172, 204; moves to Canada, 172; joins SPC, 172; member of SDP, 172; analysis of the First World War, 173–4; joins IAM, 174; delegate to Winnipeg Trades and Labour Council, 174, 181; becomes vice-president of IAM Local #122, 174; attends 1915 TLCC convention, 175; opposes TLCC position on the war, 175; attends 1916 TLCC convention, 175; fights racism in IAM, 175–6; demands removal of women from railway shops, 176; reasons for Russell's sexism, 177; impact of Marxist ideas, 178, 180; develops "one big union" idea, 178–9, 188–9; editor of Machinists' *Bulletin*, 180; secretary-treasurer of IAM Local #122, 181; secretary of Metal Trades Council, 181, 186; attends 1918 TLCC convention, 181; challenges AFL/TLCC leadership, 181, 185; relationship with Jewish Marxists, 182; women and industrial unionism, 182–3; supports Women's Labour League, 183; defeated in WTLC elections, 183; Walker Theatre speech, 183–4; defends Russian Revolution, 184; Majestic Theatre speech, 184; attacks Dominion Labour Party, 184; attacks Canadian Reconstruction Association, 184; defends Rosa Luxemburg and Karl Liebknecht, 184; suggests general strike, 184; at the Western Labour Conference 184–5, endorses leading role of "active minority", 185; promotes OBU, 186; initial opposition to WGS, 186; speaks at Industrial Bureau, 186–7; as central figure of WGS, 187; arrested and jailed, 189; theory and practice, 189; secretary-treasurer of OBU Central Labour Council, 189; trial, 189–90; enters prison, 190; praised by Winnipeg workers, 190; release from prison, 190; reception at the Industrial Bureau, 190; general organizer for Winnipeg District of OBU, 190; forced to espouse the open shop, 191–2; failed appeal to Joint Council of Industry, 191–2; organizing tours of Western Canada, 193, 201, 207; letters of resignation, 194; despondent about state of OBU, 193–4; leaves SPC, 194; candidate in 1921 federal election, 195–6; deal with CPC members, 195–7; initial support for CPC, 197; endorses OBU affiliation with the Profintern, 197; attends founding meeting of Workers' Party, 197–8; attacked as reactionary by CPCers, 198; expulsion of Communists from

OBU executive, 198; failure to support OBU women, 200; organizes women workers, 200–1; attacks AFL and CPC, 202; protests sending government troops to Nova Scotia, 202; OBU forces hand of UMWA, 203; organizing in Nova Scotia, 203–4; on leaders, 204–5; returns to Winnipeg from Nova Scotia, 204; critiques "Great Man" theory, 205; contradictions as OBU leader, 205; attacks leadership of District #26 of UMWA, 206; neglect of his family; 207–8; censored by OBU annual convention, 207–8, death of *Western Clarion*, 208; accused of being an anarcho-syndicalist, 208; supports creation of ACCL, 209; assesses OBU strength in 1927, 209; plans a French-language *OBU Bulletin*, 210; defends Sacco and Vanzetti, 210; sends greetings to the Soviet Union, 210; estrangement from Alex Shepherd, 211; fights for unemployed Winnipeg workers, 211–13; speaks to CPR workers, 212; attacks craft union leaders, 212; meets with Manitoba premier John Bracken, 212; attempts to unite employed and unemployed, 212–13; attacks CNR officials, 212–13; appeals for working-class unity, 212–13; attacks CPC, 213–14, 215; refuses to support CCF, 214; defends trade unions, 214; no longer able to carry on as OBU leader, 215–16; employed in a Toronto munitions plant, 216; works for Unemployment Insurance Commission, 216; returns to Winnipeg and OBU, 216–17; opposes bureaucratization of labour relations, 217; advice to trade union movement, 217; appointed to Manitoba Labour Relations Board, 217; vice-president of the Winnipeg Labour Committee Against Racial Intolerance, 218; supports certification of Fur and Leather Workers' Union, 218; Mounties re-activate his file, 218; secretary of Winnipeg and District Labour Council, 218; honours late in life, 218; death, 218; legacy to the working class, 219

Russian Revolution of 1917, 198, 210; Marxists of the third way on, 26–7, 75; influence on labour revolt of 1919, 89–90, 184

Sacco and Vanzetti, 210
Saint-Martin, Albert, 11
Salsberg, J.B., 161–2, 164
Sangster, Joan, 235n54
Scarlett, Sam, 160
scientific socialism, 13, 20–1, 39, 101–2, 220; interpreted by Dietzgen, 21–2; defined by Engels, 22; and worker self-emancipation, 22–3, 112; and a distinctive Canadian socialism, 148; and the new true socialism, 224. *See also* historical materialism
Scott, Frank, 7, 70, 111
Scott, Jack, 141, 150, 192
Scott, Joan, 223
Second International, 4, 15, 82, 187
Schreiner, Olive, 17
Seneca Falls Convention, 16
Shepherd, Alex, 112, 178, 194, 211; helps re-establish SPC, 29, 118; on Pritchard's family problems, 105; organizes machinists in contract shops, 181; and accusations of prejudice, 182; on Russell's role in WGS, 187; on trade unions, 199
Shipping Federation of British Columbia, 58
Showler, Birt, 46, 90
Simpson, James, 149
Skinner, Robert, 115
sleeping-car porters, 182
Smith, A.E., 11, 146, 158, 161
Smith, Evelyn Grey, 71
Smith, Stewart, 164
Social Constructives, 68, 116–17
Social Democratic Federation, 78
Social Democratic Party of Canada (SDP), 9, 79, 172, 239n106; and racism, 17–18; organization and history of, 36–7, 183; and possible merger with SPC, 37–8; impact of First World War, 38–9; and evolution and revolution, 39
Socialism: Utopian, and Scientific, 22
socialist evolutionism, 5–8, 15, 20, 226
Socialist Fellowship, 71
Socialist Labor Party (U.S.A.), 124
Socialist Labour Party (Great Britain), 172, 233n26
Socialist Party of America (SPA), 5, 15–16, 30, 148, 250n52, 261n97

Socialist Party of Canada (SPC), 34, 79, 83, 105, 110–12, 193; relationship to IWW, 6–7, 54–5; and electoral politics, 7, 14; and worker self-emancipation, 6–7, 85, 90, 100, 112; and worker education, 14, 84, 100; and women, 17, 176–7; and race and ethnicity, 17–18, 175–6, 266n58; and Jewish socialists, 18–19; and trade unions, 24, 238n93; influence of in OBU, 27, 91, 199, 208, 215; re-established during the Depression, 29, 118, 211; loss of locals, 36, 241n28; potential merger with SDP, 37–8; opposition to war, 38; and Federated Labour Party, 42; effective collapse, 58, 245n110; as model for SPCBC, 61; characteristics of Marxists of the third way in, 74–5; Manifesto of, 93; and labour revolt of 1919, 94, 239n106; eclipsed by CPC, 98–9; and death of Chris Stephenson, 101–2; in Ontario, 124, 133, 136; and WGS, 168–9, 188–90; and conspiracy theory, 183–5; and Western Labour Conference, 184–6; Russell's drift away from, 194
Socialist Party of Canada, B.C. Section (SPCBC), 28–9, 113; organization and character of, 61–2; caught between CCF and CPC, 62, 66–7; and links with Ontario Marxists, 62–3; merges with CCF, 67, 114–15
Socialist Party of Canada, Ontario Section (OSP), 29, 124, 150; organization of, 151; and middle class support, 152–3; helps organize Labour Conference, 153; conflict with the CCF, 154–7
Socialist Party of Great Britain (SPGB), 71, 95, 233n26
Soviet Union, 29, 69, 100, 160–1, 184, 198, 210, 220
Soviets, 89–90, 92, 234n42
Soviets at Work, 92, 184, 208
Spector, Maurice, 198
Spencer, Herbert, 15, 18–19, 22, 148, 225
spiritualism, 57, 99, 172, 264n8
Stalin, Joseph, 163–4, 167, 220, 228
State of Socialism in England, 35
state repression, 86; raid on Winch's home, 52; Winnipeg Strike trials, 93–4, 189–90; Pritchard's experience of, 113; and the London Radical Club, 136; London ILP protests against, 141; banning of "alien" languages and organizations, 183; and OBU, 193
Stearns, Peter, 6
Steeves, Dorothy, 110, 118
Stephen, A.M., 66–70, 114
Stephenson, Chris, 101–2, 118
Stevenson, Dr Hugh, 138, 140
Stuart, Henry Harvey, 11
Sykes, Sam, 215
syndicalism, 52, 187; defined, 5–6; and the IWW, 6; and the OBU, 27, 169; associated with Pritchard, 87, 89; in France, 179–80

Tallon, R.J., 185
Teit, James, 18
Telford, Dr Lyle, 117
Tessler, Max, 173, 182, 190
Third International, 4, 25–6, 98–9, 198
Third Period, 60, 69, 160, 196
Thomas, George, 44
Thompson, Edward Palmer, 10, 13, 22, 189, 226
Thompson, Fred, 6, 26
Thomson, J.F., 136, 139–40, 143, 156
Thornton, Sir Henry, 213
Tillett, Ben, 126
Tolstoy, Leo, 129, 133, 136, 224
Toronto Labour Party, 152
Trades and Labour Congress of Canada (TLCC), 1915 convention, 85; 1918 convention, 88, 181–3; and women workers, 134; and organization of CLP, 144; dispute with political socialists in London, 144; and exclusion of Asian workers, 175; and OBU, 192–3
trade unions, 150; Marxists of the third way on, 24, 84–5, 89–90, 199, 217; and labour revolt of 1919, 24–5; in London, ON, 134, 137; character and role of federal labour unions, 139–40. *See also* craft unions and industrial unions
Trail Smeltermen's Union, 43
Trotsky, Leon, 48, 251n83
Trotskyism, 9, 29, 71, 76, 124, 151, 211, 233n26
Trotter, W.R., 42, 96

Underhill, Frank, 7, 111, 152
Union of British Columbia Municipalities, 106
Union of Canadian Municipalities, 109, 254n146

United Brotherhood of Carpenters and Joiners (UBCJ), 175, 191–3
United Farmers of Ontario (UFO), 139–40, 143, 152, 156–8
United Front, 60, 66–9, 154
United Mine Workers of America (UMWA), 201–7, 270n164

Value, Price, and Profit, 24
Vancouver Trades and Labour Council (VTLC), 55, 58; general strike vote of 1917, 41; 1918 executive elections, 43; and Ginger Goodwin general strike, 44–5; role of leadership in 1919 sympathy strike, 49–52, 244n87; and 1923 longshoremen's strike, 97–8

Weaver, George, 69, 235n54
welfare capitalism, 134
Wells, A.S., 42, 99
Wesley, John, 136
Western Clarion (*WC*), 73, 79, 80, 99; and proposed merger of SPC and SDP, 37–8; last issue, 58, 101, 208; in the early 1920s, 100–1
Western Labor News, 195
Western Labour Conference (1917), significance of Winch not attending it, 50–1; role of SPCers at, 88–90; impact of Winnipeg Marxists at, 184–6
Western Socialist, 118
Weston, Garfield, 131
Weston, George, 131–2
Williams, Parker, 37, 242n29
Wilshire, Gaylord, 5
Winch, Alfred, 33, 35–6, 39
Winch, Carrie, 33
Winch, Charles, 33
Winch, Eileen, 33
Winch, Ernest Edward: authoritarian tendencies, 31–2; revolutionary rhetoric, 32; birth, 33; parents, 33; religious upbringing, 33; emigrates to Canada, 33; early employment in B.C., 33; trips to Australia, 33; marries Linda Marian Hendy, 33; death of infant son, 33; son Harold, daughter Eileen born, 33; returns to Canada, 33; becomes a socialist, 34–6; and Bricklayers' Union, 34, 36; Christian beliefs, 34–6; criticizes sectarian socialism, 34; joins SDP, 36; views on revolution, 35, 39, 61, 66; defence of reforms, 35; builds a house, 35; questions his religious beliefs, 35–6; tries house-building scheme, 36; returns to England in 1912, 36; becomes secretary of B.C. SDP in 1913, 37; involved in SDP/SPC merger movement, 37–8; candidate in 1914 Burnaby, B.C., municipal election, 38; supports sex education and equal pay for equal work, 38; organizes SDP local in Mission, B.C., 40; joins Marine Warehousemen and Freight Handlers' Union, 40; delegate to VTLC, 40; supports anti-conscription drive, 40–1; does not support Vancouver general strike (1917), 41; attends BCFL convention (1917), 41; defeated in VTLC elections (Jan. 1918), 42; elected a vice-president of BCFL (Jan. 1918), 42; opposes Federated Labour Party, 42; elected VTLC president (July 1918), 43; joins SPC, 43, 45; meets with A.J. Devereaux, 44; inaugural address as president of VTLC, 44; defends labour officials, 44; physical culturist, 45; secretary-treasurer of B.C. Loggers' and Camp Workers' Union, 46–7; re-elected VTLC president (1919), 47; supports One Big Union, 47; compared to Lenin and Trotsky, 48; criticized for anti-capitalist rhetoric, 48; defends leadership role, 48; associated with returned soldiers, 49–50; position on Vancouver general strike, 50–1; as pragmatic union organizer, 51; home raided by Mounted Police, 52; during Vancouver sympathy strike, 52; commitment to rank and file democracy, 53, 56–7; supports striking Port Alberni loggers, 53; challenged by Harry Allman, 54; dispute with OBU leadership, 56; refused accreditation at OBU convention, 56; returns to longshoring, 57; leaves OBU, 57; leaves Longshoremen's Union, 57; blacklisted during longshoremen's strike of 1923, 57; family poverty, 57; job offer from Vancouver businessmen, 58; role in the ILP (B.C.), 58–9; response to Depression, 59; becomes secretary and party organizer of ILP (B.C.), 59; as opportunist, 59–60, 68–9;

commitment to working-class unity, 60; cooperation with CPC, 60; runs for Burnaby school board, 60; corresponds with Bert Robinson, 62–3; importance of Marxian economics, 63, 68, 71; critiques CCF reformism, 63, 66; secretary of CCF provincial council, 63; opposes tying CCF to constitutional action, 64; elected CCF member for Burnaby, 65; task of working-class representatives, 65–8; opposes disfranchisement of relief camp workers, 66; defended by CPC press, 67; defends the unemployed, 67; conflict with Rev. Robert Connell, 67–8; in League against War and Fascism, 68; re-elected to B.C. legislature (1937), 68; aligns himself with CCF leadership, 68–70; attacked as pro-Communist, 68; attacks A.M. Stephen, 68–9; supports aid for Spanish loyalists, 69; parliamentary career, 70; signs CPC's peace petition, 71; opposes Winnipeg Declaration, 71; decries CCF's lack of revolutionary politics, 71–2; death, 72; as Marxist of the third way, 72

Winch, Harold, 33, 57–8, 68, 116, 256n195

Winch, Linda (Hendy), 70; marries Ernest Winch, 33; moves to Canada, 33; family life, 33, 36, 57–8; her home raided, 52; and spiritualism, 57

Winning, James, 183, 192

Winnipeg Declaration, 71

Winnipeg General Strike (WGS), and Marxists of the third way, 23–4, 168–9; and OBU, 24–5; lessons for Marxists, 25; and Vancouver sympathy strike, 50–1; Pritchard's role in, 91–2; and SPC, 94; Pritchard's interpretation of, 120–1; response of London labour to, 138; Russell's role in, 186–90; meaning of, 193

Winnipeg Labour Committee Against Racial Intolerance, 218

Winnipeg Trades and Labour Council (WTLC), 181–4, 192

Woman and Labor, 17

Woman's National Committee (SPA), 16

women: distinctiveness not recognized by Marxian socialists, 15–16; Winch advocates rights of, 38; craft unions fail to organize, 134; Mould acknowledges gender oppression, 142; discrimination against in machine shops, 176–7; inclusion of women in industrial union movement, 182–3; marginalized in OBU, 199–200, 213; immigrant women organized by OBU, 200–1; contribution to Dominion and Nova Scotia Relief Committee, 206. *See also* feminist socialists, gender relations

Women's Labour League, 183, 185, 200

Woodsworth, James Shaver, 58, 96, 114, 151, 214; writes about work experience on the waterfront, 40; ideas compared to those of Arthur Mould, 147–8; opposes cooperation with CPC, 154, 261n110; role in disbanding the Labour Conference, 158–9; defended by Mould, 165

Woodward, Frank, 27, 198–9

The Worker, 54–5

worker education: importance of to the SPC, 14; declining importance of to the left, 23; ideas of Marxists of the third way on, 26, 61, 69; and the OBU, 27, 169, 199; as key to revolutionary politics, 51–2; and working-class organization, 53; importance questioned by CPC members, 198; and historical understanding, 226. *See* worker self-emancipation

worker intellectuals: marginalized in the 1920s and '30s, 7–8; Pritchard as worker intellectual, 73–6; and Hegelian influence on Marxian socialism, 101–2; as universal intellectuals, 221–2; belief in worker education, 226

worker self-emancipation: and the International Workingmen's Association, 4; and the German Social Democratic Party, 4–5; espoused by IWW, 6–7; idea of called into question, 7–8, 23, 69, 100, 214; espoused by Marxists of the third way, 8–9, 11, 25, 28, 60, 72, 75, 82–3, 119–20, 123, 199, 205, 219, 226–7; and dictatorship of the proletariat, 26; and OBU, 91, 215–16; and WGS, 121; in the thought of J.S. Woodsworth, 148; and women workers,

182–3, 213. *See also* worker education
workers' councils, 90
Workers' Unity League, 62, 211, 219
World Socialist Party of the United States (WSPUS), 76, 118, 122, 251n91

Young Communist League, 66
Young, Fred, 143–4
Young Men's Christian Association, 128–30, 137
Young People's Socialist League (ON), 151
Young, Rod, 71
Young Socialist League (B.C.), 66, 71